·B·L·U·E·P·R·I·N·T·
FRANCE

Editor
GILES ALLEN

Layout and Design
DOMINIQUE MICHELLOD

Design Leisure Routes
PHILIPPE AQUOISE

Cartography
HALLWAG AG, Bern

An abridged version of selected segments of this book is available in pocket-size format in the Berlitz Country Guide series.

Library of Congress Catalog Card No. 88-64113

Although we make every effort to ensure the accuracy of all the information in this book, changes occur incessantly. We cannot therefore take responsibility for facts, addresses and circumstances in general that are constantly subject to alteration.

BERLITZ®

·B·L·U·E·P·R·I·N·T·
FRANCE

By JACK ALTMAN
and the Staff of Berlitz Guides

Cover picture: Deauville bistrot. Photo MI-REILLE VAUTIER

Photography: pp. 7, 11, 37, 75, 76, 77, 78, 80, 85, 99, 100, 149, 169, 172, 180, 183, 187, 189, 190, 192, 193, 197, 218, 220, 222, 303, 308, 314 C. HUBER; pp. 14, 188 E. MANDELMANN; pp. 18, 262 ROGER-VIOLLET; p. 28 BERETTY/RAPHO; p. 30 SARVAL/RAPHO; pp. 35, 176, 243, 282, 283, 297, 298 D. MICHELLOD; pp. 36, 46, 151, 158, 162, 292 M. VAUTIER; pp. 37, 39, 62, 118, 134, 143, 144, 146, 188, 231, 236, 241, 254, 264, 278, 288, 291, 324 M. JACOT; p. 29 J. M. CHARLES/RAPHO; pp. 70–71, 166 MOPY/RAPHO; p. 88 HALARY/RAPHO; p. 105 BEAUNE/RAPHO; pp. 45, 108, 319 L. DEAN; p. 119 MOET/RAPHO; pp. 110, 217, 318 O. MARTEL/RAPHO; pp. 114 BIBAL/RAPHO; p. 122 CUNY/RAPHO; p. 127 GESTER/RAPHO; p. 130 S. WEISS/RAPHO; p. 136 M. CLERY/RAPHO; p. 198 L. JAHAN/RAPHO; pp. 204, 208 SCHMIED/SCHUSTER; p. 213 ARCIS/RAPHO; p. 228 ISY-SCHWARZ/IMAGE BANK; p. 228 GLOAGUEN/RAPHO; p. 234 H. SILVESTER/RAPHO; p. 246 SERRAILLIER/RAPHO; p. 256 J.-P. PIEUCHOT/IMAGE BANK; p. 260 ZUBER/RAPHO; p. 270 A. CHOISNET/IMAGE BANK; p. 271 DOISNEAU/RAPHO; pp. 311, 320 M. TULANE/RAPHO.

Acknowledgements
We would like to extend our thanks to the French National Tourist Office in Paris, Geneva and New York for cooperation and information as well as to the helpful Syndicats d'Initiative thoughout France. We are also very grateful to Anne-Karin Ratna, Alice Taucher and Caroline Filliez for their assistance in the preparation of this book.

Contents

MAPS: France 33, Bordeaux 272, Dijon 140, Lille 112, Lyon 226, Marseille 244, Nantes 179, Nice 256, Paris 66, Paris Métro 73, Strasbourg 125, Toulouse 280.

All major towns and cities have a map reference next to their relevant heading keyed into the Road Atlas Section.

FRANCE AND THE FRENCH

Something to be Arrogant About

Modest people, as Winston Churchill once said of a political opponent, often have much to be modest about—but nobody ever accused the French of modesty. Behind their carefully constructed grouchy façade, this race of perpetual malcontents clearly believes that France is the most splendid place on earth. Even their most fervent detractors have a hard time proving them wrong.

If the French do complain so much, it's perhaps because they feel they always deserve even better. In a modern world obsessed with being at the cutting edge of technology, the French still find it important to do a little polishing, too.

Not that they're duds in modern industrial achievement. Just in the field of public transport, for instance, sophisticated French subway systems are exported to major cities on every continent; Concorde, the supersonic plane they built with the British, has proved to be a great success; and their high-speed train, the TGV, is widely considered the best in the world.

The French are generally much more efficient than their international reputation. Service in hotels and restaurants is good; the road network is excellent. But Frenchmen cannot live by nuts and bolts alone. Quality of life remains their paramount preoccupation. No accident that they are best known for their food and wine, their clothes and perfumes, their dashing art and monumental architecture. French civilization is essentially an exercise in enlightened self-indulgence.

They're always looking for some way to turn the ordinary into something special. And it's all for their own pleasure and the world's admiration. Amazing the magic a French girl can perform with a comb in her hair or a simple cotton scarf around her neck. Remember what happened when good old American blue jeans were taken up by the French and turned into a thing of high fashion.

Give them a couple of eggs and they won't just boil them, fry them or make an omelette (all of which they're quite prepared to do superlatively)—they feel obliged to produce a soufflé or an hollandaise sauce that makes an egg proud to be an egg. Even hamburgers have been stretched by one fast-food chain into a more manageable long bun, apparently inspired by the traditional *baguette* sandwich.

The French just won't leave well enough alone, and occasionally overdo it. You may consider their formal, geometrically planned gardens a pompous distortion of nature, or their triumphal arches and grandiose palaces just a bit pretentious. However, this tendency to show off, frowned upon in more sober lands, and affectionately dubbed *la frime* in France, may be an irresistible desire to celebrate the riches with which nature has endowed the land.

France is blessed with an astonishing variety of landscapes. The stark, rough, dazzling expanses of naked rock and arid ruddy soil of some parts of Provence could be the setting for an American Western. But that's just as much France as the more conventional image of rolling green meadows bounded by straggling hedgerows beside an arrow-straight, shady avenue of plane trees, with a village clustering around its church on the horizon.

The country is a veritable compendium of European geography, modified with a "French touch". The plains and plateaux of Flanders and Picardy in the north and Alsace to the east are the logical conclusion of the central European steppes. The wide open spaces lend themselves to large-scale agriculture (and all-too-convenient battlefields) before ending in the gentler green fields of Normandy to the west or the vineyards of Burgundy that herald the south.

The Alps of Savoie and the Dauphiné extend the gigantic chain that rises from Austria across Germany and Switzerland

FACTS AND FIGURES

Geography:	With a land mass of 547,000 sq. km. (213,000 sq. mi.), France is by far the largest country in Western Europe, a hexagon neatly measuring 1,000 km. (620 mi.) from north to south and another 1,000 km. from east to west. It is bounded by three seas (the English Channel, the Atlantic and the Mediterranean) and three mountain ranges (the Pyrenees, the Alps and the Jura), with the Rhine river and Flanders plain to the north-east. The country's four main rivers are the Loire running west to the Atlantic from the plateau of the Massif Central, the Seine flowing north-west from Burgundy through Paris to the Channel, the Garonne which flows down from the Pyrenees, past Toulouse and Bordeaux, to unite with the Dordogne, forming the Gironde estuary, and the Rhône starting in the Swiss Alps to turn south at Lyon down to the Mediterranean. Highest mountain: Mont-Blanc (Alps) 4,807 m. (15,800 ft.).
Population:	55 million (including 4.4 million non-French, principally North African, Portuguese, Italian and Spanish).
Capital:	Paris 2.2 million (metropolitan area 8.7 million).
Major cities:	Marseille (870,000), Lyon (410,000), Toulouse (350,000), Nice (340,000), Strasbourg (250,000), Nantes (240,000), Bordeaux (210,000).
Government:	Under the Constitution of 1958, France's Fifth Republic elects a president every 7 years, exercising executive power with a prime minister and cabinet of ministers. The legislature is divided between the National Assembly, elected by universal suffrage every 5 years, and a largely subordinate Senate, chosen every 9 years by an electoral body of deputies and regional councillors. At local level, the 1982 decentralization law reorganized the country's 96 departments into 22 regional councils.
Religion:	Predominantly Catholic, 82.7%, while Muslims are estimated at 4.4%, Protestants 1.5% and Jews 1.3%.

to peter out in the rugged little *Alpilles* of Provence. The olive trees and vineyards, umbrella pines and cypresses of this Provençal countryside, and the lazy beaches of the Côte d'Azur, are a natural continuation of the classical Mediterranean landscape, until it gives way to the formidable mountain barrier of the Pyrenees at the frontier with Spain.

With mountains protecting the eastern and southern frontiers, the mild Atlantic winds penetrate deep inland, bringing all the rain and sun needed for a highly productive agriculture, while avoiding the extremes of a continental climate.

Inland from the Atlantic coast—Aquitaine, Dordogne, Périgord—the southwest is rich in farming and vineyards. It's the land of good duck and goose, of fine Bordeaux wines. A chain of extinct volcanoes runs through the plateau of Auvergne's Massif Central. At the country's western edge, Brittany's spectacular craggy shoreline has earned the region a reputation for rough weather. In fact it enjoys the mildest of climates, even in winter, and offers the surest of bets for its seaside resorts in summer.

The kings and counts and feudal lords have gone from the Loire Valley and the forests and marshes of Sologne, but the hunting and fishing country remains.

At the country's heart, slightly north of the geographical centre, Paris nestles in a basin ideal for industrial and commercial enterprise, comfortably surrounded by the forest and farmland of the Ile-de-France. And the Champagne country lies conveniently to the east to help celebrate its successes.

If the land itself is the most obvious source of a Frenchman's pride, the nation's cultural wealth is just as important. The fine arts do not intimidate the French as something to be confined to a small élite. For most people, "intellectual" is not the dirty word it seems to be in so many other countries. One of the most popular television shows devotes an hour and a half every week to talking, very entertainingly, about nothing but books.

The museums do better business than football stadiums, and crowds flock to theatre and music festivals in spring, summer and autumn all over the country. Even popular arts such as advertising, the cinema, fashion or comic strips are elevated to the level of high culture, with their own museums and festivals.

An active government cultural policy in recent years has preserved the architectural monuments of the "national patrimony" from the ravages of time, weather, war, revolution and the barbaric assaults of building speculation. The Château of Versailles has been refurbished to sparkle as in the days of Louis XIV, and the finance ministry thrown out of the Louvre, after some conservative kicking and screaming, to make way for the great museum's ambitious expansion. The simplicity of Romanesque village churches or the grandeur of Gothic cathedrals can more and more be appreciated at their best. Even the ruins, of Roman towns or medieval monasteries, have come alive again as the sites of open-air concerts or theatre.

One major boon to the visitor has been the steady replacement of most of those boring uniformed guides, who recited their facts and figures about abbeys or palaces like melancholy parrots, by bright young art historians who actually like the places they work in. Their descriptions are fresh and informative, and they'll answer questions that go beyond the brochure or guide book.

The country offers plenty of outdoor enjoyment, too: water sports and plain old sun-bathing on the beaches of Normandy and Brittany as well as the more famous resorts of the Côte d'Azur (the French would like to discourage that Italian word Riviera); first-class skiing in the Alps and the Pyrenees; hiking around the country's national parks and nature reserves. Proof that France is far from being a country of hidebound highbrows is the fact that the Walt Disney enterprise has chosen the Marne valley east of Paris for Europe's first Disneyland.

The people themselves are as varied as their landscapes, but don't let anybody tell you the cliché is a lie. The red-nosed, moustachioed fellow with a beret on his head, a crumpled cigarette drooping from his lip and a long *baguette* under his arm *does* exist. The French themselves have long acknowledged that all those who are not like that have a brother-in-law who is. But there's all the difference in the world between the prudent, close-mouthed Norman and the vociferous, easy-going Provençal, between the pious Breton and the pagan sophisticates of Paris.

For a people so fiercely proud of their identity, with all the recurrent waves of xenophobia that such nationalism encourages, the French themselves are a marvellous mixture, another compendium of the European map, this time in an ethnic sense. In the north, the Flemish influence is unmistakable. Although Alsace may celebrate Bastille Day more proudly than any other French province, its cuisine, wines and dialect are profoundly Germanic. The Côte d'Azur and Corsica have a distinctly Italian flavour, and the people north of the Pyrenees are not so very different from their Spanish cousins to the south. Then there are the Celts of Brittany, the Norsemen of Normandy, the Basques of the Pays Basque...

As the land of the Declaration of the Rights of Man, France has never for long resisted welcoming political refugees. There were Polish, German, Italian, American and British deputies in the National Assembly of the French Revolution. Russians fled to France from the Tsar and Stalin, Spaniards from Franco, Jews from Hitler, Armenians from the Turks, Lebanese from the civil war of Beirut.

However, it's in the artistic world, as a pole of attraction rather than a refuge from fear, that France has happily made a mockery of its own suspicion of foreigners. Not by accident did Van Gogh come from the Netherlands, Picasso from Spain, Max Ernst from Germany or Chagall from Russia to make their home in France. One of France's greatest poets of the 20th century, Wilhelm Kostrowitsky, better known as Guillaume Apollinaire, was born in Rome of a Polish mother and Italian father. Irishman Samuel Beckett happily writes in French. Britain's Peter Brook runs a unique avant-garde theatre in Paris. And Kenzo, Lagerfeld and Cerruti design in the international but inexorably Paris-based language of *haute couture*.

Despite occasional tensions, perhaps inevitable in times of economic uncertainty, Frenchmen increasingly recognize that immigrant workers from its former colonies—Algerians, Tunisians and Moroccans—enrich the national culture. And the cuisine.

Not least of all, they add even more flavour, colour and music to the greatest of French assets, the street scene, the sheer light and movement of life itself.

*F*rench girls are not prettier than others. They just look *prettier. Nobody knows why. Perhaps it has to do with the power of myth over reality. Unconsciously, consciously or downright self-consciously, they somehow feel obliged to live up to the myth, make the extra effort. They believe it. We believe it.*

A Quest for Liberty, Equality and Fraternity

Neanderthal man was a *homo sapiens,* literally a man who knows, but the most famous Stone Age Frenchman, Cro-Magnon, was what the anthropologists call a *homo sapiens sapiens,* a man who knows he knows. From that Stone Age caveman dug up by railway workers in the Dordogne, down to Charles de Gaulle with his "certain idea" of what France ought to be, the French have always wanted to know what it means to be a Frenchman.

Their history is a constant quest for national identity, a conflict between strong regional loyalties and the central authority of a Cardinal Richelieu, King Louis XIV, Emperor Napoleon, President de Gaulle—or his successors.

Round about 2000 B.C., Celtic tribes, probably from eastern Europe, came looking for greener pastures in Franche Comté, Alsace and Burgundy. At the same time, migrants from the Mediterranean countries were trickling into the south.

The first recorded settlement was the trading post set up by Phocaean Greeks from Asia Minor at Massalia (Marseille) around 600 B.C., followed by other ports at Hyères, Antibes and Nice. But the Greeks developed few contacts with the interior beyond a little commerce in olives and wine with the Celts of Burgundy. In a later epoch, when their position was threatened by Ligurian pirates at sea and bellicose tribes from their hinterland, the merchants of Marseille called on Rome for help. Rome's clout in the Mediterranean had been growing, and it was in a position to assist allies effectively.

From Gaul to France

In 124 B.C., the Romans came in force, conquered the "Gallic barbarians" and set up a fortress at Aquae Sextiae (Aix-en-Provence). They took advantage of this new stronghold to create Provincia (present-day Provence), stretching from the Alps to the Pyrenees, to guarantee communications between Italy and Spain.

When this province was endangered by new attacks from the north, Julius Caesar himself took charge. He had conquered practically the whole of Gaul by 50 B.C. Caesar drew Gaul's north-eastern frontier at the Rhine, thus including modern Belgium. He warned that the Germanic tribes across the river—Franks, Alamans and Saxons—would always mean trouble.

The Romanization of Gaul exiled the most energetic warriors to defend the outposts of the empire, while their families settled down to work the land, or build towns at Lyon, Orange, Arles and Nîmes—and the first great highways between them. Merchants developed a thriving trade with the rest of the empire. The pattern for the peasantry and bourgeoisie of France was thus established.

Christianity was introduced to Gaul in the 1st century A.D., but it was not really accepted until 391 when it became the empire's official religion. Large-scale conversions were led by Martin de Tours, soldier-turned-bishop—sword and cross formed a regular alliance in French history. The new religion soon cemented national solidarity in the face of more barbarian invasions, this time by the Franks.

Gallic unity collapsed with the crumbling of the empire. Clovis, leader of one of several tribes of Franks, defeated the Roman armies at Soissons in 486, and won the allegiance of most Gallo-Romans by converting to Christianity 10 years later. With Paris as his capital, he extended his rule to the Mediterranean by conquering other Frank tribes, Alamans, Visigoths and Burgundians. (He and his descendants are known today as the Merovingian dynasty, after a legendary ancestor, Merovaecus.) But the realm was divided up among his heirs and progressively fragmented by the rivalries of the dynasty that battled for power over the next 300 years.

Middle Ages

Spain's Arab rulers exploited this disunity to sweep north across Gaul, controlling Languedoc, Dordogne and a large part of Provence before being defeated at Poitiers in 732 by the army of Charles Martel. Martel, in name only a superintendent of the palace for one of Clovis's weakling royal descendants, was in fact all but king through the enormous powers he wielded over the army and finances. His son, Pepin the Short, similarly a powerful mayor of the palace, and tired of acting in the place of his do-nothing sovereign, usurped the throne to found a new line of succession, the Carolingians, named after his father.

Pepin the Short's son, Charlemagne, became the most illustrious of the princes of the Middle Ages. For 46 years he led a ferocious battle against the incursions of neighbouring peoples: the Lombards in Italy, the Saxons in Germany and the Arabs in Spain. In 800, Pope Leo III crowned him Emperor of the Romans to show his gratitude for Charlemagne's protection and generosity to the Church. By then, Charlemagne was master of almost all of the vast occidental Christian realm.

But even this mighty sovereign could not create an enduring national unity. His three grandsons split up the spoils of the empire and set about squabbling among themselves.

This time it was the Normans from Scandinavia who took advantage of the Carolingian dynasty's divided kingdom, pillaging their way inland along the Loire and Seine, plundering Paris in 845. Saracens invaded the Provençal coast from North Africa, and Magyar armies attacked Lorraine and Burgundy.

To keep the support of the nobles' armies, one king after the other had to give the nobles more and more land. The realm broke up into the fiefdoms of the feudal Middle Ages, precursors of the country's classical provinces—Provence, Burgundy, Normandy and Brittany, etc.

In 987 the last of the Carolingian kings died without issue. Nobleman Hugues Capet, whose forebears had put up a good fight against the Normans and subsequently acquired a vast realm in the central region between Normandy, the Seine and the Loire, was crowned King of France, thus establishing the new Capetian dynasty. As at the fall of the Roman Empire, it was the Christian Church that provided the essential element of national unity. Hugues was anointed at Reims with an oil said to be brought to earth by the angels. He established kingship by divine right for the French.

Cross and Sabre

Alliance with the Church was the underpinning of royal authority. In exchange for the anointment, the Church was enriched with lands and the right of taxation by tithe, a fraction of the peasants' seasonal produce.

After the more sober spirituality of the Romanesque churches, the soaring Gothic cathedrals of Chartres, Paris (Notre-Dame), Bourges and Amiens were at once monuments to the glory of God and testimony to the sheer power, spiritual and temporal, of the Catholic Church.

France, dubbed by the pope "eldest daughter of the Church", took the lead in the Crusades against the "infidels" in Palestine. Louis IX, the ideal of the Christian king for the justice he handed down to his subjects and for the Crusades he led to the Holy Land, was sainted after he died of dysentery in Tunis in 1270.

But the crusaders weren't so busy in the Orient that they neglected Europe. In their religious zeal they massacred pagan Slavs in Prussia, Saracens in Spain and smoked out Jews and heretics everywhere. A call to action by Pope Innocent III against a powerful sect known variously as the Cathari or Albigenses (it was centred around the southern French town of Albi) found great response: the ruined castles and abbeys in the south of France bear witness to the ravages inflicted.

The strength of the papacy declined after Innocent III, no longer a match for the dominant French kings. In 1309 the seat of the papacy was moved from Rome to Avignon to be under the thumb of the French king, where it remained for almost 70 years.

France's other major preoccupation was England. In 1066, as probably more British than French schoolchildren know, Duke Guillaume of Normandy crossed the English Channel and became William the Conqueror. For the next 400 years, English and French monarchs fought over the sovereignty of various pieces of France—among others, Aquitaine, Touraine, Normandy and Flanders.

It's a tiresome tale of inextricable tangles, of marital alliances or military victories more important to national morale than resolving the perennial conflict—Bouvines (1214) for the French, Crécy (1346) and Agincourt (1415) for the English. It took a teenager from Lorraine, Jeanne d'Arc, to pull the French into good enough shape to resist the English at Orléans. For her pains, the English burned her to death in Rouen in 1431, but her martyrdom stirred national pride enough, 20 years later, to boot the English out of France.

But the noble national cause was not the first concern of the ordinary Frenchman. Wars were just another hardship, taking sons away from the farm to fight, while the armies—French as much as foreign—ravaged the land or pillaged the towns.

During war or peace in this feudal age, Church and aristocracy continued to claim their respective portion of the peasant's labour, leaving barely enough for mere subsistence. But all too frequently, a cycle of drought, famine and plague would decimate the population. A Dordogne farmer rarely took time off to find out who his current monarch was.

In any case, large portions of France were independently controlled by powerful dukes whose allegiance to the king was only nominal. The unity of France was still a long way off.

Ancien Régime

Absolutism was the dominant feature of what post-Revolutionary France called the *Ancien Régime*. The monarchy began to come into its own with François I (1515–47). He strengthened the central administration and abandoned an initially tolerant policy towards the Protestants. Debonair Renaissance prince, he introduced a grand style at court.

François brought Leonardo da Vinci to work at Blois, and Rosso and Primaticcio to decorate Fontainebleau. He also commissioned paintings by Raphael and Titian, among others, for the royal collections that are now the pride of the Louvre. A new opulent architecture blossomed with the châteaux of the Loire and around Paris.

On the international scene, after François had crushed the Duke of Milan's army at Marignano, and formed a showy alliance with Henry VIII of England, his European ambitions were halted by the German Emperor Charles V. He even suffered the indignity of a year's imprisonment in Madrid following a resounding defeat at Pavia in 1525.

The bloody 16th-century conflicts between Catholics and Protestants throughout Europe centred more on political and financial intrigue than questions of theology. The French Wars of Religion pitted the Catholic forces of the regent Catherine de Médicis against the Protestant (Huguenot) camp of Henri de Navarre. They reached their climax on August 24, 1572, with the Saint Bartholomew's Day Massacre. Two thousand Protestants, in Paris for Henri's wedding with Catherine's daughter Marguerite de Valois, were killed. The general massacre of Protestants spread to the countryside, and by October, another 30,000 had lost their lives.

The conciliatory policies which painfully emerged brought the prince of Navarre to the throne as Henri IV (1589–1610), but not before he had promised to convert to Catholicism.

The enormous personal popularity of the good-natured but tough king from the Pyrenees proved vital for healing the wounds from the bitter wars. The Edict of Nantes was signed in 1598 to protect the Protestants and, five years later, the Jesuits were allowed back into France. But Henri won the hearts of the people most by finding time to pursue his calling as an incorrigible womanizer, known to posterity as the *Vert Galant*. Until he was stabbed to death by a Catholic zealot.

Too Much Starch?
Executing a king's assassin was no simple business, least of all when the king was as beloved as Henri IV. For an ordinary capital offence during those pre-Revolutionary times, hanging did the trick—the more dignified decapitation by axe being reserved for those of noble blood. But a regicide, even when he had been found guilty and sentenced to public execution, had to be tortured and, still alive, "quartered" by four horses each attached to an arm or leg. His remains were then cremated by the executioner. In the case of Henri's murderer, François Ravaillac, the frenzied crowd in front of the Paris town hall set upon his remains, and only his shirt was left over for cremation.

France floundered in intrigue under the regency of Marie de Médicis, mother of young Louis XIII, until Cardinal Richelieu took charge as prime minister in 1624.

Directing national policy until his death in 1642, he reasserted the authority of his king against both the conservative Catholics that surrounded the queen mother, and the Protestant forces who were fiercely defending the privileges granted them by the Edict of Nantes.

Ask any bunch of Frenchmen "1515?" and they'll all chorus: "Marignan!" They like to remember this famous battle in which the 20-year-old François I crushed Duke Massimiliano Sforza's redoubtable Swiss mercenaries and then had himself knighted by his great soldier, Captain Bayard. And prefer to forget his humiliating defeat and imprisonment ten years later. To spring him from jail, François had to hand over two sons and then pay 2,000,000 francs for their release. Painting by Clouet, Louvre Museum.

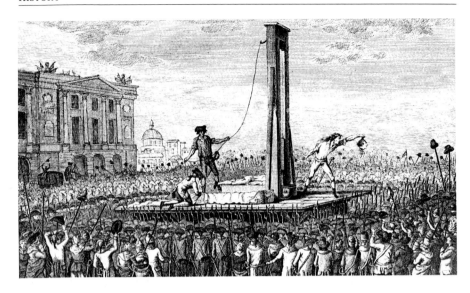

HISTORICAL LANDMARKS

Prehistory	28,000 B.C.	Cro-Magnon man in Dordogne cave.
	2000	Celts invade France from east.
Gaul	600	Phocaean Greeks found Marseille.
	218	Hannibal passes through southern France to cross Alps.
	125–121	Romans establish colony of Provincia (Provence).
	59–50	Julius Caesar conquers Gaul.
	451 A.D.	Attila the Hun defeated at Châlons.
	476	"Barbarians" end Roman control.
Middle Ages	496	Clovis, King of Franks, converts to Christianity to rule Gaul.
	732	Arabs halted by Charles Martel at Poitiers.
	768–814	Charlemagne king of Franks.
	987	Hugues Capet first king of France.
	1066	Duke Guillaume (William) of Normandy conquers England.
	1096	French lead First Crusade.
	1163	Construction of Notre-Dame begins in Paris.
	1209	Pope orders wars against Cathare "heretics" in southwest.
	1270	Crusader Louis IX dies in Tunis.
	1309–1403	Popes and anti-popes in residence at Avignon.
	1337–1453	Hundred Years' War against England.
	1431	Joan of Arc (Jeanne d'Arc) executed by English.

Ancien Régime	1515–47	François I marks ascendancy of absolutist monarchy.
	1534	Jacques Cartier goes to North America.
	1572	St. Bartholomew's Day massacre of Protestants in Wars of Religion.
	1598	Henri IV protects Protestants with Edict of Nantes.
	1624–42	Cardinal Richelieu governs for Louis XIII.
	1635	Richelieu founds French Academy.
	1642–61	Cardinal Mazarin takes over.
	1648	France seizes Alsace.
	1648–53	Paris disturbed by *Fronde* revolts.
	1661–1715	Sun King Louis XIV moves court to Versailles.
	1685	Revocation of Edict of Nantes.
Revolution and Napoleon	1763	France cedes North American territories to Britain and Spain.
	1789	Fall of Bastille (July 14); Declaration of the Rights of Man and the Citizen.
	1793	Louis XVI guillotined.
	1794	Robespierre guillotined.
	1804	Bonaparte crowns himself Emperor Napoleon.
	1805	Trafalgar lost, Austerlitz won.
	1812	Retreat from Moscow.
Kings and Emperors Depart	1815	Napoleon defeated at Waterloo, Louis XVIII restored to throne.
	1830–48	"Bourgeois monarchy" of Louis-Philippe.
	1848	Liberal Revolution overthrows monarchy.
	1852	Napoleon III proclaimed emperor.
	1852–70	Baron Haussmann undertakes gigantic town planning of Paris.
Third Republic	1870–71	Franco-Prussian War. Germans seize Alsace-Lorraine.
	1894 (Dec.)	Dreyfus jailed as German spy (rehabilitated 1906).
	1914–18	World War I. France regains Alsace-Lorraine.
	1936–37	Socialist-led Popular Front.
War and Peace	1939–45	World War II. Germany occupies France, de Gaulle leads Resistance.
	1944	Allies invade Normandy (June 6).
	1945–46	De Gaulle heads 4th Republic's first government.
	1954	Mendès France decolonizes Indochina and Tunisia.
	1958	De Gaulle president.
	1962	France gives up Algeria. 5th Republic formed.
	1968	Student rebels shake government.
	1981	Mitterrand 5th Republic's first Socialist president.
	1986	Government of right-left *"Cohabitation"*.
	1988	Mitterrand re-elected—government left of centre.

With his successful siege of the Protestant stronghold at La Rochelle, the Cardinal neutralized the threat of their military strength while guaranteeing their freedom of worship.

Richelieu's major achievement was the centralization of royal power, laying the foundations of that strong national identity that has characterized France ever since. He tightened the king's control over legislation and taxes, enraging the Vatican by daring to impose a levy on the Church. Royal stewards were sent out to diminish the autonomy of the regional *parlements*, councils with judicial rather than legislative powers, dominated by the high clergy and nobles. The Cardinal also created the *Académie française* in 1635 to ensure the purity and clarity of the French language through its *Dictionnaire* and its *Grammaire*.

Promoting overseas trade and the founding of a navy, Richelieu launched France somewhat belatedly on the road to empire with the colonization of Guadeloupe and Martinique in the Caribbean. In Europe, the Catholic Cardinal, master of political pragmatism, was not above supporting the Protestant Swedish, Danish and German forces in the Thirty Years' War against the Catholic Austrians, Italians and Spanish. All that mattered was that it serve France's interests.

Richelieu's protégé Mazarin, another cardinal, took over the job of prime minister during the minority of Louis XIV. The court and regional aristocracy were infuriated by the Italian-born churchman's intimate relationship with the king's mother, Anne of Austria. Nor did they like his astounding knack for amassing a vast personal fortune while managing, very efficiently, the affairs of state. But most of all, they despised the way he eroded the nobles' power and paved the way for an increasingly absolutist monarchy.

The *Fronde,* a series of rebellions by the nobility and the judicial bodies, attempted to check this growing power of the monarchy in general, and Mazarin in particular. The conflict broke out into war in 1649, and Mazarin, Anne and the boy-king were forced to flee from Paris. However, the royal family's triumphant return three years later, with the rebellious nobles crushed, saw the monarchy stronger than ever.

Louis XIV drew his own conclusions from Mazarin's careful coaching in the affairs of state. When he began his personal rule in 1661, at the age of 23, there was no question of a new prime minister impinging on the royal prerogative. Adopting the unequivocal symbol of the sun, Louis was to be outshone by no one. Counsellors were completely subservient. Louis never once convened the parliamentary assembly of the *Etats généraux,* even though its powers were minimal.

He moved the court to Versailles, not only to get away from the trouble-makers of Paris, but to impoverish the nobility, by forcing them to contribute to the crippling luxury of his palace, with no other function than to support the king in time of war.

Madame de Pompadour started her royal career up in a Versailles attic. She spent five years in a couple of rooms under the palace roof until Louis XV's Queen Maria Leszczyéska let it be known she was no longer interested in sex and La Pompadour could come downstairs. For 20 years, she was what the modern White House would call Chief of Staff: nobody could see the boss without her say-so. Painting by Boucher, Louvre Museum.

It's all too easy to be bedazzled by the brilliance of life at Versailles, by its architectural splendour, and most of all by the sheer hypnotic power of Louis XIV's cult of self-glorification. In his lifetime, many petty European princes tried to imitate his style with their own little Versailles, complete with court artists and sycophants. It took French historians a long time to resist the glitter for the less attractive realities of what that style cost the nation.

To enhance his glory, the Sun King turned to foreign conquest. The devastating military expedition he launched across the Rhineland and Palatinate, the series of largely fruitless wars with Spain, Holland, England and Sweden, did not endear him to the European people. Moreover, they left France's once thriving economy in ruins.

At home, his authoritarian rule required a brutal police force. Taxes soared to pay for his wars, and more and more peasants had to abandon their fields when press-ganged into his armies. Influenced in later life by the Catholic piety of Madame de Maintenon, his mistress and subsequently secret wife, Louis put an end to religious freedom for Protestants by revoking the Edict of Nantes—a move largely approved of by the people.

In the face of forced conversions, the Protestant Huguenots—many of them the most talented bankers, merchants and artisans of their generation—fled to Switzerland, Germany, the Netherlands, England and Scandinavia. Their flight underlined the dangers of this general stifling of freedoms under an absolutist monarchy.

Reaction to Louis XIV's death in 1715, a sigh of relief, was almost inevitable. Having outlived his children and sickly grandchildren, he was succeeded by his five-year-old great-grandson, Louis XV. But government was in the hands of the late king's highly cultured, libertine and atheist brother, Philippe d'Orléans.

After the morose twilight years of the Sun King—Madame de Maintenon had been a regular wet blanket at the court of Versailles—life perked up with the satiric pen of Voltaire and the ambiguous erotic fantasies of Watteau's paintings and Marivaux's comedies. The court moved back to Paris.

The generally lazy regent gave a bunch of incompetent nobles too much of a say in the running of the state. Regional *parlements* obtained the right to present remonstrances, thin end of a wedge to weaken the monarchy.

The easy-going Louis XV was called, at least in the first half of his reign, the *Bien-Aimé* (Beloved). The king seemed more interested in his mistresses than in running a tight ship of state. Despite this (or perhaps because of it) the economy recovered, the overseas empire expanded in the East and West Indies, arts and letters flourished in this age of Enlightenment as never before.

But there were some new voices posing a clear threat to the established order. Diderot's *Encyclopédie* championed reason over traditional religion, Rousseau discoursed on the origins of inequality, Voltaire shot at everything that didn't move.

Revolution and Napoleon

Louis XVI, grandson of Louis XV, faced attacks on all sides. The intransigent aristocracy and high clergy were anxious to protect ancient privileges; a burgeoning bourgeoisie longed for reforms that would give them a larger piece of the national pie; the peasantry was no longer prepared to bear the burden of feudal extortion; and a growing urban populace of artisans groaned under hardships symbolized by the fluctuating price of bread.

At the assembly of the *Etats généraux*, convened for the first time in 175 years, it was clearly the king's enduring absolutism rather than the throne itself that was under fire. For reactionary nobles, the king was guarantor of their hereditary status. Liberal reformers wanted a constitutional monarchy similar to England's, not a republic. Even grievances drawn up by peasants and townspeople insisted on continuing devotion to the king himself.

Two months later, the blindness of the king's conservative advisors and his own weakness and vacillation led to the explosion of centuries of frustration and rage—the storming of the Bastille, the régime's prison-fortress in Paris. On July 14, 1789, the king went hunting near his château at Versailles and wrote in his diary at the end of the day: *"Rien"* ("Nothing").

A National Assembly voted a charter for liberty and equality, the great Declaration of the Rights of Man and of the Citizen. The aristocracy's feudal rights were abolished, the Church's massive land-holdings confiscated and sold off.

Rather than compromise, the king fled Paris in a vain effort to join up with armed forces hostile to the Revolution. With Austrian and German armies massing on France's frontiers and the forces of counter-revolution gathering inside the country, the militant revolutionary Jacobins led by Maximilien de Robespierre saw the king's flight as the ultimate betrayal. The Republic was declared in 1792, and Louis XVI was guillotined in 1793. His son Louis XVII died in obscure circumstances under the Revolutionary government, probably in 1795.

Under pressure from the poorer classes, who did not want the Revolution appropriated for the exclusive benefit of the bourgeoisie, the Jacobin-led Revolutionary committee ordered sweeping measures of economic and social reform, but also a wave of mass executions, the Terror, aimed at moderates as well as aristocrats. Despite his attempts to quell the extremists, Robespierre was overthrown and guillotined in the counter-attack of the propertied classes.

During the rule of the *Directoire*, an executive body of five men, a new wave of executions—the White (royalist) Terror—decimated the Jacobins and their supporters. But the bourgeoisie, fearing both the royalists and their foreign backers, turned for salvation to a Corsican soldier triumphantly campaigning against the Revolution's foreign enemies—Napoleon Bonaparte.

In between his defeat of the Austrians in Italy and a less successful campaign against the British in Egypt, Bonaparte returned to Paris to crush the royalists in 1795 and, four years later, staged a coup d'état against the *Directoire*. He was 30 years old.

In the first flush of dictatorship as First Consul, he created the Banque de France, set up state-run *lycées* (secondary schools) and gave the country its first national set of laws with the *Code Napoléon*. The centralization dear to Richelieu and Louis XIV was becoming a clearer reality.

The supreme self-made man, Bonaparte became Emperor Napoleon in 1804

Royal Mistresses

Since royal marriage was an affair of state rather than of the heart, the king of France made no bones about having mistresses, too. One of them was given formal precedence as *maîtresse en titre* (titular mistress). She wasn't always a giggle, as Louis XIV discovered with the sanctimonious pillow-talk of Madame de Maintenon.

As the last person to see the king before he went to sleep, the royal mistress was ideally placed to whisper more than sweet nothings in his ear and inevitably acquired a taste for politics.

Ambitious families competed to get one of their daughters into the royal bed, and Louis XV entertained three Nesle sisters, one after the other, until the youngest, Madame de Châteauroux, got the titular job. She was succeeded by the most famous mistress of them all, Madame de Pompadour, née Jeanne Antoinette Poisson, from an important family of financiers involved in military contracts. With her famous high-flying hairdo, the extravagant Pompadour was a great patron of the arts, promoting the painting career of François Boucher and protecting Voltaire from his many court enemies.

Madame du Barry, who rose to royal favour literally from the streets, was Louis XV's last and loveliest *maîtresse en titre*, and perhaps the only one reluctant to get involved in politics. Particularly in 1793 when she was carried screaming to the guillotine.

at a coronation ceremony in which he took the crown of golden laurels from the pope and placed it on his own head.

He managed to pursue simultaneously foreign conquest in Germany and Austria, and domestic reforms—a modernized university and police force, proper supplies of drinking water for Parisians. During his disastrous campaign in Russia, he found time in Moscow to draw up a new statute for the Comédie-Française (the national theatre) that had been dissolved during the Revolution.

The nationalism that Napoleon invoked in his conquest of Europe's *Ancien Régime* turned against him in Spain, Russia and Germany. The monarchies regrouped to force him from power a first time in 1814. He made a brilliant but brief comeback the following year, when an alliance of British, Prussian, Belgian and Dutch troops inflicted final defeat at Waterloo.

Kings and Emperors Depart

More intelligent than his executed brother, Louis XVIII tried at first to reconcile the monarchy with the reforms of the Revolution and Napoleon's empire. But his nobles were intent on revenge and imposed a second, even more violent, White Terror against Jacobins and Bonapartists, including some of Napoleon's greatest generals.

Louis's reactionary successor, brother Charles X, was interested only in renewing the traditions of the *Ancien Régime*, even having himself anointed and crowned at the ancient cathedral of Reims. But the middle classes would no longer tolerate the curtailment of their freedoms and the worsening state of the economy in the hands of an incompetent aristocracy. They reasserted their rights in the insurrection of July 1830—this time the purely liberal revolution they would have preferred back in 1789—paving the way for the "bourgeois monarchy" of Louis-Philippe.

This last king of France, heir of the progressive Orléans branch of the royal

family, encouraged the country's belated exploitation of the Industrial Revolution and the complementary extension of its overseas empire in Asia and Africa (Algeria had been occupied just before the 1830 revolution). But the new factories created an urban proletariat, clamouring for improvement of its miserable working and living conditions. The response of fierce repression and other ineptitudes led to a third revolution in 1848, with the

24

*S*ince *disastrous defeat in the Battle of the Nations at Leipzig in 1813, nothing went right for Napoleon. Retreat from the British in Spain, from the Austrians in Italy; Dutch and Belgian rebellion to the north. The Grande Armée, courageous but woefully outnumbered, retrenched in France, where civil morale was at its lowest point. Ahead: abdication, short-lived comeback and Waterloo. Painting by Meissonier, Louvre Museum.*

Bonapartists, led by Napoleon's nephew, emerging triumphant.

The Second Republic ended four years later when the man whom Victor Hugo called "Napoléon le Petit" staged a coup d'état to become Emperor Napoleon III. Determined to cloak himself in the legend of his uncle's grandeur, he saw his role as champion of the people. But he used harsh anti-press laws and loyalty oaths to quell the libertarian spirit that had brought him to power.

The economy flourished with the expansion of a vigorous entrepreneurial capitalism in iron, steel, railways and overseas ventures such as the Suez Canal. Despite Napoleon's obsession with the new "Red Peril" (the 1848 Communist Manifesto of Marx and Engels was floating around Paris), he could not prevent such social reforms as the workers' right to form unions and even to strike.

With the excessive enthusiasm that characterized the age, Baron Haussmann's urban planning barrelled its way through old Parisian neighbourhoods to create a more airy and spacious capital.

Left and Right

The ideological divisions of "left" and "right", today adopted all over the world, derive from the seating arrangement of the National Assembly that legislated the French Revolution. Quite simply, supporters of the Revolution sat on the left and opponents on the right. Within the ranks of the Revolutionary left, what the British might now call the "militant tendency" sat up on the high benches, the *montagne* (mountain), while the moderates sat down in the *marais* (marshes).

Similarly, architect Viollet-le-Duc often went overboard restoring the great Gothic cathedrals and medieval châteaux in ways their original creators had never imagined.

Hugo, in exile in Guernsey because of his opposition to Napoleon III, was writing *Les Misérables* and Baudelaire

his *Fleurs du Mal*, while Offenbach was composing acid but jolly operettas like *La Belle Hélène*. Courbet was painting his vast canvases of provincial life and Manet his *Déjeuner sur l'Herbe*.

Life was generally looking up. The bourgeoisie showed off its new prosperity with extravagant furnishings, silks, satins and baubles, and in 1852 Paris opened its first department store, Au Bon Marché. In this optimistic, forward-looking society, with a necessary accompaniment of social critique and constant pressure for improvement, France was assuming its true national identity.

But Germany had an account to settle. In 1870, Prussian Chancellor Bismarck exploited an abstruse diplomatic conflict with France to bring the various German principalities and kingdoms together into one fighting force for war. And after lightning victory over the ill-prepared French armies, the German nation or Empire (Reich) was founded under Kaiser Wilhelm I in the Palace of Versailles. The confiscation of Alsace and Lorraine avenged the old but unforgotten scars left by Louis XIV's devastation of the Rhineland and Palatinate, and Napoleon's more recent invasion.

The Third Republic

Defeat shattered the Second Empire. While the new Third Republic's government under Adolphe Thiers negotiated the terms of surrender, workers' communes refused to capitulate. They took over Paris and a few provincial cities in March 1871 for ten brave but desperately disorganized weeks. They were brutally crushed by French government troops and order was restored.

France resumed its industrial progress, quickly paid off its huge war-reparations debt to Germany and expanded the overseas empire in North and West Africa and Indochina. Rediscovered national pride found its perfect expression in the great Eiffel Tower thrust up into the Paris skies for the international exhibition of 1889.

In 1874, the first exhibition of Impressionism had blown away the dust and cobwebs of the artistic establishment. Novelist Zola poured forth his diatribes against industrial exploitation. Rodin, more restrained, sculpted *Le Penseur* (The Thinker).

Leading the "republican" hostility to the Church's entrenched position in the schools, Jules Ferry enacted in 1882 the legislation that has been the basis of France's formidable state education system ever since.

On the right, nationalist forces were motivated by a desire to hit back at Germany, seeing all contact with foreigners or any form of "cosmopolitanism" as a threat to national honour and integrity.

For many, the Jews were the embodiment of this threat—Edouard Drumont's vehemently anti-semitic *La France juive* (Jewish France) was a runaway national bestseller. It appeared in 1886, eight years before Captain Alfred Dreyfus, an Alsatian Jew in the French Army, was arrested on what proved to be trumped-up charges of spying for the Germans. In a case that pitted the fragile honour of the Army against the very survival of French republican democracy, the captain had to wait 12 years for full rehabilitation.

The desire for revenge against Germany remained. Germany's own imperial ambitions grew, competition for world markets became more and more intense. Most of France went enthusiastically into World War I and came out of it victorious and bled white.

With the 1919 Treaty of Versailles, France recovered Alsace and Lorraine; but 1,350,000 men had been lost in the four years of fighting. The national economy was shattered, and political divisions were more extreme than ever.

In face of the fears aroused by the Russian Revolution of 1917, the conservative parties dominated the immediate post-war period, while a new French Communist Party, loyal to Moscow, split with the Socialists in 1920. France seemed less aware of the threat from Nazi Germany, allowing Hitler to remilitarize the Rhineland in 1936 in breach of the Versailles Treaty, a step he later said he never dreamt of getting away with.

In the 1930s, extreme right-wing groups such as *Action française* and *Croix-de-Feu* (Cross of Fire) provided a strong anti-democratic undercurrent to the political turmoil of financial scandal and parliamentary corruption. The bloody 1934 riots on Paris's Place de la Concorde offered a disturbing echo to the street fighting of Fascist Italy and Nazi Germany.

The left-wing parties responded by banding together in a Popular Front, which the Socialists led to power in 1936. In the first few weeks, Léon Blum's government nationalized the railways, and instituted a 40-hour week and the workers' first paid holidays (two weeks, today five). But Blum failed to support the Republicans in the Spanish Civil War and, in the face of financial difficulties, felt obliged to put a brake on the reforms, thereby causing the Communists to break the alliance.

No Small Affair

Over and above a judicial error, the Dreyfus Affair crystallized the passions that had burst into the open with the French Revolution, the conflicts between order and justice, conservatism and progress. It was no accident that the association formed by the *Dreyfusards* was named the *Ligue des droits de l'homme* (League of the Rights of Man), still in existence today to defend the historic Declaration of 1789.

Not least of all, the peculiar prestige that intellectuals have enjoyed in French society derived directly from their contribution to the Jewish captain's vindication, epitomized by Zola's decisive newspaper article *"J'accuse"* ("I accuse"). Coming down from their ivory tower, writers and academics demonstrated they could have a direct influence on public events. Elsewhere, "intellectual" is often an insult hurled at an overeducated troublemaker by his opponents. His French equivalent may be heard unashamedly beginning his tirades: *"Moi, intellectuel..."* ("An intellectual myself...").

War and Peace

Blum's government collapsed in 1938 and the new prime minister, Edouard Daladier, found himself negotiating the Munich agreements with Hitler, Mussolini and Neville Chamberlain. A year later, France was once again at war with Germany.

Relying too complacently on the defensive strategy of the fortified Maginot line along the north-east frontier with Germany (but not with Belgium), the French army was totally unprepared for the German invasion across the Ardennes in May 1940. With fast-moving tanks and superior air power, the Germans were in Paris 30 days later. Marshal Philippe Pétain, the old hero of World War I, capitulated on behalf of the French on June 16. Two days later, on BBC radio's French service from London, General de Gaulle issued his appeal for national resistance.

Compared with other occupied countries like Belgium, Holland or Denmark, France's collaboration with the Germans is an inglorious story. Based in the Au-

vergne spa of Vichy, the French government often proved more zealous than its masters in suppressing civil liberties and drawing up anti-Jewish legislation. It was French police who rounded up the deportees for the concentration camps, many denounced by French civilians seeking to profit from the confiscation of property.

The underground Resistance fighters were heroic but a tiny minority; a few of them conservative patriots like de Gaulle, most of them socialists and communists, and also a handful of refugees from Eastern Europe.

Deliverance came when the Allies landed on the Normandy beaches on June 6, 1944. De Gaulle, with his canny sense of history, took an important step towards rebuilding national self-confidence by insisting that French armed forces fight side by side with the Americans and British for the liberation of the country, but, above all, that the French army be the first to enter Paris itself.

After the high emotion of de Gaulle's march down the Champs-Elysées, the business of reconstruction, boosted by the generous aid of the Americans' Marshall Plan, proved more arduous. The wartime alliance of de Gaulle's conservatives and the Communist Party soon broke down. The General could not tolerate the political squabbles of the Fourth Republic and withdrew from public life.

Governments changed like musical chairs, but the French muddled through. Intellectuals dressed all in black argued whether Albert Camus was correct in writing that it was less important to be happy than to be merely conscious of what's going on. And anyway, as Jean-Paul Sartre argued at the next table, "There's nothing in heaven, neither Good nor Evil, nor anybody to give me orders."

The French empire was collapsing. After a fruitless last stand in Vietnam, Pierre Mendès France wisely negotiated an Indochinese peace settlement. He gave Tunisia its independence and handed Pondicherry over to India, but was ousted from office as hostilities broke out in Algeria.

De Gaulle returned from the wilderness in 1958, ostensibly to keep Algeria French. But he'd seen the writing on the wall, and brought the war to an end with Algerian independence in 1962. His major task was to rescue France from the chaos of the Fourth Republic. The new constitution, tailor-made to de Gaulle's authoritarian requirements, placed the president above parliament, where he could pursue his own policies outside the messy arena of party politics.

De Gaulle's visions of grandeur, independent of America's NATO and the Soviet Union's Warsaw Pact, gave France a renewed self-confidence. One of his great achievements was the close alliance with West Germany, overcoming centuries of bloodshed between the two peoples.

With self-confidence came smugness, and the French bourgeoisie was given one of its periodic frights with the massive student rebellions of 1968. The "events of May" that erupted in Paris's Latin Quarter and spread through the country disturbed de Gaulle enough for him to fly off to seek reassurance with his troops stationed in West Germany.

Georges Pompidou was an efficient manager of the business boom. His successor, Valéry Giscard d'Estaing, made some tentative changes before being swamped by inflation and unemployment. But people were reluctant to make a complete change until 1981, when the forces for reform gathered enough strength and cohesion to elect François Mitterrand, the Fifth Republic's first Socialist president.

Like the Popular Front in 1936, the new government began with a quick-fire set of reforms—a broad programme of nationalization, abolition of the death penalty, raising the minimum wage, and a fifth week of holiday-with-pay—until the world economic crisis imposed a necessary brake. Special emphasis was placed on cultural programmes, increasing subsidies for theatre, cinema, provincial museums and libraries, but also for scientific research.

Probably the most important reform was the least glamorous: the decentralization that increased regional autonomy and reversed the age-old trend of concentrating political, economic and administrative power in the national capital. By allowing the local pride of such historic regions as Provence, Normandy, Brittany or Languedoc to reassert itself, France demonstrated it was at last secure in its national identity.

The political scene took on a new and intriguing complexity in 1986 with the election of a conservative government, thrust into unprecedented right/left *"Cohabitation"* with President Mitterrand. Mitterrand moved inexorably to the centre. He was able to exploit the emergence of the neo-Fascist Front National to split the right and win a relatively easy re-election in 1988. But, like the French Revolution two centuries before, the Socialist government had a distinctly bourgeois flavour to it.

29

Travelling à la Carte

It's perhaps natural when planning a trip to France to think of it as a meal. If you're not travelling with the set menu of a package tour, but prefer to choose your destinations *à la carte,* you may at first be daunted by the sheer variety. But the key to a successful visit to France is in the artful mixture of light and rich ingredients: window-shopping as appetizer, a cathedral or museum for something more meaty, a little greenery to digest that, then a night out on the town as dessert.

We've divided the country up into just six geographic regions, themselves broken down into broad regional designations, a trifle arbitrary admittedly since areas overlap: Paris and its vicinity (known to the French as the Ile-de-France); North-East (Flanders, Picardy, Champagne, Lorraine, Alsace, Burgundy and the Jura); North-West (Normandy, Brittany and the Loire Valley); the Centre (Berry, Limousin, Auvergne, Cantal); South-East (Savoie, Dauphiné, the Rhône Valley, Provence, Côte d'Azur and Corsica); and South-West (Périgord, Atlantic coast, Poitou, the Pyrenees and Languedoc-Roussillon). If any place is hard to find, it will be in the index (p. 398).

Since we aim at a representative rather than encyclopaedic survey of the country, our selection of places within those regions is by no means exhaustive. Experienced visitors to France may feel a few of their own favourite corners of the country have been given short shrift, even though they may find others they have never heard about, but newcomers will have more than enough to choose from.*

Depending on how much time you have available, you can combine at least two or three of the regions to get a sense of that great diversity of French life: the big city and the wine country, the mountains as well as the Atlantic or Mediterranean coasts.

Any itinerary you draw up should naturally include Paris. Ideally, divide your stay in France in two: sightseeing at the beginning, before you grow lazy at a seaside resort or in some sunny village in the hills, and then shopping at the end, so that you don't have to carry your purchases around with you.

For a "green" vacation, for example, you might want to combine Paris and the Ile-de-France with Normandy and Brittany. For stark contrasts—of climate, countryside and temperament—combine the capital with Provence or Corsica.

But the mix should not just be geographic. The cultural monuments of

---

*You'll find more detailed information to specific regions in the Berlitz Travel Guides to *Paris, Brittany, Normandy, Loire Valley* and *French Riviera.*

France, its cathedrals, palaces and museums, deserve your attention, but they'll be much easier to digest and appreciate if you alternate them with lots of time at the beach or on country walks. France does not lack places where it's a simple joy to do absolutely nothing at all. And museum-going itself can be more fun if you vary the diet with some of the more offbeat collections devoted to comic-strips, toys, balloons, bread, graffiti, fire engines; you'll find plenty of suggestions between pp. 304 and 313.

Many people do not have the choice of going to France outside the major holiday periods—Easter, July and August. But if it's at all possible, think of the spring, autumn or even the winter, when the big sightseeing destinations are blessedly easier to visit. The island-abbey of Mont-Saint-Michel on the Normandy coast in the mists of December can be pure magic.

A passing tip for visiting the big museums in peak seasons: go at lunch time on a late-closing day, when at least the French feel they have something more important to do.

Not By Bread Alone

Museum opening hours vary from season to season and year to year, so check the current situation with the local tourist office. You can be sure that most museums are closed on Tuesday, a day dictated by the French need to reconcile food and culture. It enables butchers, bakers and grocers, whose day off is usually Monday, to start their week with a little fine art, while the next day, museum-guardians can get their meat, bread and potatoes.

Getting Around

Even if you're the adventurous kind of traveller who likes to improvise, don't turn your nose up at the tourist offices. In France, tourism being a major factor in the country's balance of payments, the organization for foreign visitors is very efficient. For general information, the *office de tourisme*, both in your own country and in the regional capitals throughout France, is worth a visit. They cannot usually make reservations, however.

Even the smallest towns with only one monument, vineyard or pile of prehistoric fossils to boast of have a *syndicat d'initiative*. These friendly local tourist offices offer free maps, brochures, advice about sporting and cultural events, camping facilities. The ones in the bigger towns can often provide, with advance notice, an English-language guide for local sightseeing tours.

The Berlitz-Info section at the back of the book (from p. 340) gives detailed practical guidance on the technicalities of travel through France, but here are some general thoughts to help you plan the trip. In the Berlitz Leisure Routes and Themes and Variations sections, we give ideas of groupings of interests.

First of all, *how* are you going to travel? The excellent system of roads and public transport (soon to be reinforced by the tunnel under the English Channel) makes it a good idea to use both car and train together. Take the train for long journeys, and rent a car at your destination to explore the back country. Several special rail cards include reduced rates for car rentals.

With the high-speed TGV *(Train à Grande Vitesse)* from Paris, you can be in Dijon heading for the Burgundy vineyards in an hour and a half, Lyon in two hours, and Avignon, for your Provençal adventure, in under four. A similar service is opening up to Bordeaux and ultimately north to the English Channel for the Tunnel.

The one disappointment of French trains is the relatively uninspired dining-car service. Don't despair, make up your own picnic hamper from the market before you get aboard—cold meats, salad, Camembert, grapes, *baguette* and wine add a terrific sparkle to the countryside flashing past your window.

For drivers in a hurry, the network of toll motorways (expressways) is first class if a trifle costly, linking up most of the

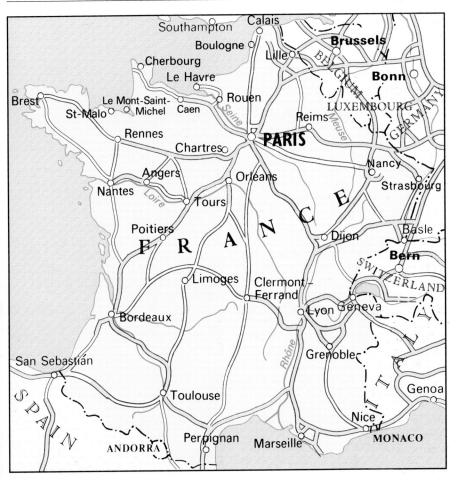

major cities and still expanding. Otherwise, it's more fun to explore the country along the good-quality secondary roads. If you're afraid of getting lost, follow the green arrows, indicating the route of *Bison futé* (Wily Buffalo—a Red Indian invented by the Ministry of Transport), which proposes alternative itineraries to avoid traffic jams.

French drivers are adventurous, even aggressive, less spectacular than, say, the Italians, but not unskilful. Defensive driving is always a good idea, but timidity will get you into an unholy mess in the Paris rush hour. In fact, try to drive as little as possible inside the cities. The métro is the fastest way around Paris, but the buses, both in the capital and other big towns, are best for taking in the sights. Unless you feel really safe in French metropolitan traffic, keep your cycling—you can rent a bike at the railway station—for the villages and country roads.

If you have plenty of time at your disposal, consider renting a sail-it-yourself barge or cabin cruiser, and coast sleepily along the Canal de Bourgogne from Dijon, the tributaries of the Loire or the Canal du Midi from Toulouse down to the sea at Sète. It's great fun helping the keepers open the locks. With a couple of bikes on board, you can always stop along the way to explore inland. Larger

33

hotel-boats for up to 20 people, plus crew, are organized for gourmet cruises from one gastronomic port of call to another.

Try to vary the kind of places you stay in. Depending of course on your budget, it's worth splashing out at least one night for the exquisite comfort and service of a great hotel, either what the French call a *palace*, which usually refers to an old-fashioned luxury hotel, or a converted château, abbey or mill house. On holiday, you owe it to yourself to be treated occasionally like a monarch and, in the right place, the French still know how to do it.

Too many modern hotels tend to be highly efficient, comfortable, well situated in the big towns, and totally characterless. It's not what you came to France for. But even if you can afford a *palace* every night, don't miss out on the great charm of a simple country inn *(auberge)*. More frugal, but with the bonus of good country cooking, are the *table d'hôte* you see periodically signposted. A converted farmhouse where the farmer's wife cooks your meal—ideal when hiking.

However and wherever you travel around France, one last piece of advice: even if you can't speak French, do try to make a tiny effort to speak just a couple of words. You've probably heard horrendous stories about how impatient the French can be with people who can't speak their language. In fact it's often been a case of the foreigner's not making the slightest attempt to say a *Bonjour, S'il vous plaît* or *Merci beaucoup* to break the ice.

It can be very disconcerting for an ordinary Frenchman to be suddenly confronted with a torrent of English (imagine someone in Houston or Huddersfield trying to cope with a Frenchman who spoke no English). Despite their reputation, the French are a very courteous people, calling each other *Madame* or *Monsieur* and always saying an appropriate *Bonjour* or *Au revoir* when entering or leaving a shop or café. It may well

LIGHT BARQUE
FAVERSHAM

be the inadvertent absence of such courtesies that raises the hackles of that touchy fellow who barks at you. But at least he doesn't bite. With the right smile, an *Excusez-moi, Monsieur* can melt the coldest Gallic heart.

Being Berlitz, we'll try to help you with some of the simplest phrases, at the back of the book. The rest is up to you and your own desire to play the French game. *Amusez-vous bien!*

34

*F*or the perfect escape-route from the stresses of
modern urban life, cruise through the French countryside in a barge.
Details on rentals for canals in Burgundy from the Auxerre reservation
office, telephone 86 52 18 99; for the Canal du Midi in Languedoc-
Roussillon, south-west France, from Montpellier tourist office,
telephone 67 60 55 42.

ON THE SHORT LIST

Even in a country with as vast and rich an array of places to see as France, there are a few "musts" you would feel very bad about missing. Occasionally, you just will not have time to see everything, so we offer you here what we think are essentials. Our Short List will point first-timers in the right direction.

Paris
Right Bank
Champs-Elysées
Montmartre
Louvre Museum
Centre Pompidou

Left Bank
Eiffel Tower
Musée d'Orsay
Saint-Germain-des-Prés

The Seine
Pont Neuf bridge
Notre-Dame cathedral
(3 days minimum or a lifetime)

Ile-de-France
Château of Versailles
Chartres cathedral
Fontainebleau forest
(3 days)

Picardy
Amiens cathedral
Arras Grande Place
(1 day)

Champagne Country
Reims cathedral
Epernay wine tour
(1 day)

Lorraine
Nancy, Place Stanislas
(1 day)

Alsace
Strasbourg cathedral
Riquewihr wine tour
Colmar Issenheim altar
(2–3 days)

Savoie
Mont-Blanc
Megève, Val d'Isère resorts
Annecy on its lake
Aix-les-Bains on Bourget lake
(2–3 days)

Burgundy
Vézelay basilica
Dijon ducal palace
Côte d'Or wine tour
(3 days)

Normandy
Rouen (Cathedral)
Deauville resort
D-Day Beaches
Mont-Saint-Michel
(3 days minimum)

Brittany
Carnac menhirs
La Baule beach resort
Saint-Malo-Dinard port and beach

(3 days)

Loire Valley Châteaux
Chambord
Chenonceaux
Azay-le-Rideau

(2 days)

Berry-Limousin
Bourges cathedral
Aubusson tapestries
Limoges porcelain

(2 days)

Auvergne
Clermont-Ferrand church of Notre-Dame-du-Port
Puy de Dôme volcano park
Orcival, Saint-Nectaire churches
Le Puy cathedral

(3 days)

Périgord
Lascaux caves
Dordogne valley
Sarlat medieval town
Padirac chasm

(3 days)

Atlantic Coast
La Rochelle port
Bordeaux wine tours

(2 days)

Rhône Valley
Lyon gastronomy
Beaujolais wine tour

(1 day)

Provence
Orange Roman theatre
Avignon papal palace
Pont du Gard Roman aqueduct
Lubéron hills, olive groves
Aix-en-Provence, Cours Mirabeau

(3 days minimum)

Côte d'Azur
Saint-Tropez port-resort
Cannes beach-resort
Saint-Paul-de-Vence art museum
Monaco casino resort

(3 days minimum)

Corsica
Bonifacio port town
Golfe de Porto red cliffs, caves

(2–3 days)

South West
Toulouse Saint-Sernin basilica
Carcassonne fortified town
Albi Toulouse-Lautrec museum

(3 days)

Pyrenees
Pau
Basque Country
Biarritz beach resort
Saint-Jean-de-Luz port town

(3 days minimum)

Going Places with Something Special in Mind

What's your pleasure? Wine cellars or monasteries, battlefields or Romanesque churches, volcanoes or three-star restaurants, hunting, fishing or music festivals? Or perhaps the landscapes that have inspired generations of painters from Watteau to Van Gogh and Cézanne? Here are some suggestions of possible circuits among a multitude of other possibilities.

Wine Tours

Touring the vineyards is a delightful way of seeing the country, while learning something about one of France's greatest gifts to mankind. From tourist offices and wine-growers' associations in Reims or Epernay for Champagne, Colmar for Alsace, Beaune for Burgundy, and Bordeaux itself, you can find out about guided tours, tasting, buying and, if you feel like it, helping with the wine-harvest.

Champagne

At the eastern edge of the Paris basin, the vineyards hug the sun-catching southern-facing slopes around the forest of the Montagne de Reims, the Marne valley and the Côte des Blancs.

1 REIMS
great Gothic cathedral of French kings; champagne distribution-centre.

2 RILLY-LA-MONTAGNE
wine-harvest scenes carved in church's 16th-century choir-stalls.

3 VERZENAY
fine view of vineyards from windmill.

4 VERZY
weird grove of ancient twisted beeches.

5 AMBONNAY
try the more fruity local champagne.

6 BOUZY
the region's red, splendid but not bubbly.

7 HAUTVILLERS
where it began, with Dom Pérignon.

8 ÉPERNAY
centre of the main champagne cellars.

9 CRAMANT
panorama of Côte des Blancs vineyards.

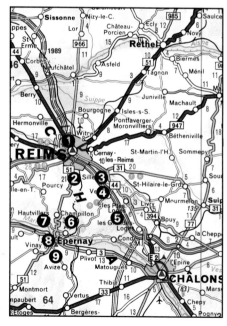

Alsace

The Alsatian white wines of the Gewürztraminer, Sylvaner and Riesling grape are cultivated among the most picturesque villages of the country's many wine routes.

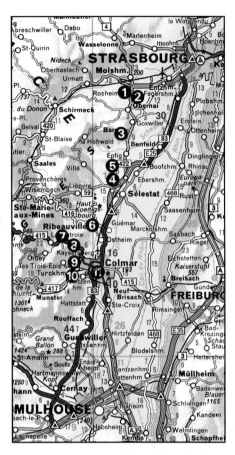

1 ROSHEIM
fortified with typical Rhineland church.

2 OTTROTT
rare Alsatian red wine; tourist railway through vineyards.

3 BARR
wine fair in 17th-century townhall

4 MITTELBERGHEIM
vineyards planted by Romans; handsome Renaissance houses.

5 DAMBACH
prosperous flower-bedecked town near shady forest.

6 RIBEAUVILLÉ
13th-century belfry, popular with storks; minstrel-show in September.

7 RIQUEWIHR
romantic Renaissance village, great Riesling wines.

8 KAYSERSBERG
Albert Schweitzer's home-town beneath ruined castle.

9 NIEDERSCHMORWIHR
oriel-windowed houses in middle of vineyards.

10 TURCKHEIM
tranquil fortified town.

11 COLMAR
home of Grünewald's Isenheim altar; wine distribution-centre.

39

Burgundy

The Côte d'Or hillsides running 60 km. (35 mi.) south of Dijon constitute France's most venerable wine region, divided into two parts, the Côte de Nuits and Côte de Beaune.

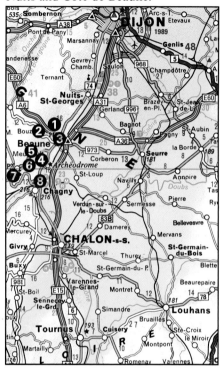

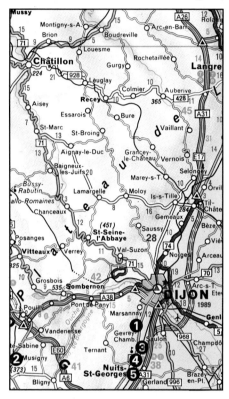

Côte de Nuits

1 GEVREY-CHAMBERTIN
aristocratic wine in medieval cellars.

2 CHAMBOLLE-MUSIGNY
most delicate and "feminine" of region's reds.

3 CLOS DE VOUGEOT
guided tour of old vats and wine presses.

4 VOSNE-ROMANÉE
seven *grands crus* (highest distinction) in 750-year-old vineyards.

5 NUITS-SAINT-GEORGES
headquarters of wine-tasting fraternity Chevaliers du Tastevin.

Côte de Beaune

1 ALOXE-CORTON
favourite wine of Voltaire and John F. Kennedy.

2 SAVIGNY-LÈS-BEAUNE
send kids to motorbike museum.

3 BEAUNE
best selection for shopping; wine museum and grand 15th-century Hôtel-Dieu.

4 POMMARD
classical château (1802) outside sleepy village.

5 VOLNAY
pride and joy of dukes of Burgundy.

6 MEURSAULT
fine white wine; townhall in remains of medieval castle.

7 PULIGNY-MONTRACHET
greatest of Burgundy whites literally worshipped by Alexandre Dumas.

8 SANTENAY
château's 500-year-old limetree planted by Henri IV; casino and spa for hangovers.

Bordeaux

The old English fief boasts the handsomest of vineyard châteaux. Visit the Médoc north-west of Bordeaux and the Saint-Emilion area to the east.

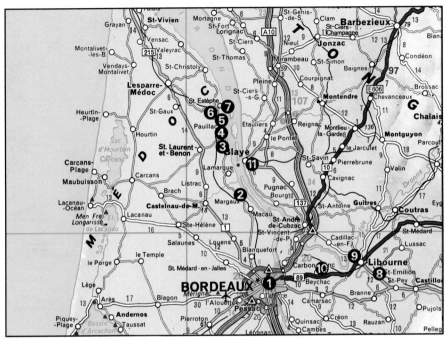

Médoc

1 BORDEAUX
visit fine arts museum before heading for vineyards.

2 MARGAUX
château-like Greek temple for most revered of Médocs.

3 BEYCHEVELLE
18th-century charterhouse with terraced gardens.

4 PAUILLAC
port on Canal du Midi, Médoc capital.

5 MOUTON-ROTHSCHILD
Tudor-style château, pretty English gardens and wine-museum.

6 LAFITE-ROTHSCHILD
prince of reds bought by Rothschilds 1868; château with cedar-shaded terrace.

7 SAINT-ESTÈPHE
biggest Médoc producer; 17th-century Château Calon-Ségur.

Saint-Emilion area

8 SAINT-EMILION
beautiful fortified town, 1000-year-old monolithic church carved out of rock.

9 POMEROL
full-bodied aromatic wine in picturesque vineyards with windmill.

10 FRONSAC
view of Dordogne valley; visit cellars at Château La Dauphine.

11 BLAYE
see Gironde estuary from citadel ramparts.

Gastronomy

As much as any cathedral or palace, the high temples of French cuisine are, as they say, worth the detour. Here, region by region, is a hint of the local fare along with a selection of the gourmet critics' choices of the country's top restaurants (with phone number for reservations).

Paris and Vicinity

Rather than drawing on regional specialities, the capital's gastronomic "monuments" combine tradition with innovations that represent the avant-garde of French cuisine.

1 5e ARR.

Tour d'Argent
(43.54.23.31)

2 8e ARR.

Lucas Carton
(42.65.22.90)

3 8e ARR.

Taillevent
(45.63.39.94)

4 16e ARR.

Jamin
(47.27.12.27)

5 VERSAILLES

Les Trois Marches
(39.50.13.21)

6 MAISONS-LAFFITTE

La Vieille Fontaine
(39.62.01.78)

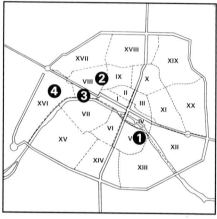

North-East

In Flanders and Picardy, look out for North Sea fish, great vegetable soups and first-class beef or pork. Alsace is renowned for its freshwater fish, wild game and *choucroute* (Sauerkraut).

LILLE	STRASBOURG	AMMERSCHWIHR
Le Flambard	Le Crocodile	Aux Armes de France
(20.51.00.06)	(88.32.13.02)	(89.47.10.12)
REIMS	ILLHAEUSERN	COLMAR
Les Crayères	L'Auberge de l'Ill	Schillinger
(26.82.80.80)	(89.71.83.23)	(89.41.43.17)

Burgundy

Wine-sauces here are of course at a premium and you'll find the best snails and most succulent beef, from White Charolais cattle.

JOIGNY
La Côte Saint-Jacques
(86.62.09.70)

SAINT-PÈRE-SOUS-VÉZELAY
L'Espérance
(86.33.20.45)

SAULIEU
La Côte d'Or
(80.64.07.66)

DIJON
Jean-Pierre Billoux
(80.30.11.00)

GÉVREY-CHAMBERTIN
Rôtisserie du Chambertin
(80.34.33.20)

CHAGNY
Lameloise
(85.87.08.85)

Loire Valley

Freshwater fish – eel, perch, trout and pike – distinguish the cooking of the château country, along with fine goat cheeses.

1 ORLÉANS
La Crémaillère
(38.53.49.17)

2 ROMORANTIN
Lion d'Or
(54.76.00.28)

3 BRACIEUX
Le Relais
(54.46.41.22)

4 BLOIS
Le Bocca d'Or
(54.78.04.74)

5 TOURS
Jean Bardet
(47.41.41.11)

6 ANGERS
Le Quéré
(41.87.64.94)

Normandy and Brittany

If Normandy cuisine is rich in butter and cream, with celebrated cheeses and great apple desserts, Brittany offers more diet-conscious menus of seafood, including the country's best oysters.

CAEN
La Bourride
(31.93.50.76)

CANCALE
Restaurant du Bricourt
(99.89.64.76)

MORLAIX
Restaurant de l'Europe
(98.62.11.99)

QUESTEMBERT
Georges Painaud
(97.26.11.12)

NANTES
Les Maraîchers
(40.47.06.51)

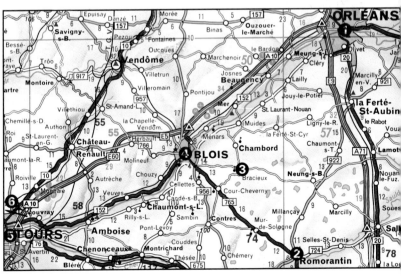

43

Rhône Valley

Within easy reach of that Charolais beef, the heartland of French gastronomy offers the best poultry, from Bresse, superb wild game and pork, and an unrivalled variety of vegetables and fruit both "northern" (apples and pears) and "southern" (peaches, apricots).

1 BOURG-EN-BRESSE
Auberge Bressane
(74.22.22.68)

2 VONNAS
Georges Blanc
(74.50.00.10)

3 MIONNAY
Alain Chapel
(78.91.82.02)

4 COLLONGES-
AU-MONT-D'OR
Paul Bocuse
(78.22.01.40)

5 LYON
Léon de Lyon
(78.28.11.33)

6 ROANNE
Troisgros
(77.71.66.97)

7 SAINT-ETIENNE
Pierre Gagnaire
(77.37.57.93)

8 VALENCE
Pic (75.44.15.32)

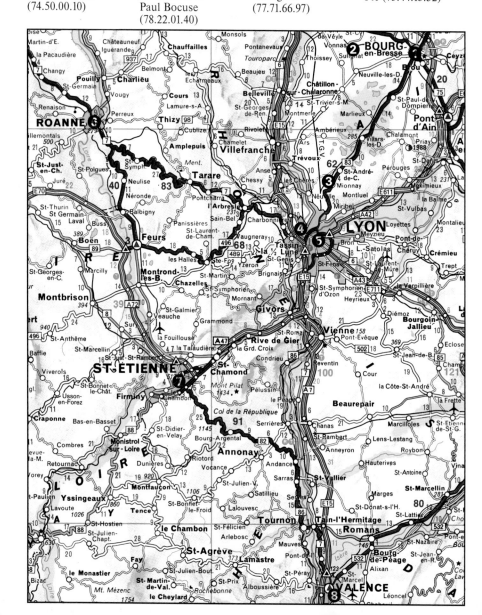

Provence and Côte d'Azur

Provençal cooking puts the accent on olives, tomatoes, garlic and fragrant herbs, while the Mediterranean resorts compete for the best seafood in an eternal contest for the supreme *bouillabaisse*.

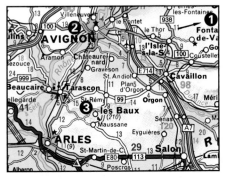

1 CHÂTEAU-ARNOUX
La Bonne Etape
(92.64.00.09)

2 AVIGNON
Hiély-Lucullus
(90.86.17.07)

3 LES-BAUX-
DE-PROVENCE
L'Oustau de
Baumanière
(90.54.33.07)

1 MOUGINS
Moulin de Mougins
(93.75.78.24)

2 CANNES
Le Royal Gray
(93.99.04.59)

3 ANTIBES
La Bonne Auberge
(93.33.36.65)

4 JUAN-LES-PINS
La Terrasse
(93.61.20.37)

5 NICE
Chantecler
(93.88.39.51)

6 MONTE-CARLO
Le Louis XV
(93.50.80.80)

South-West

This is the land of the truffle, goose, duck and, of course, *pâté de foie gras*. The Bordeaux region offers excellent seafood and lamb. Try the sheep's milk cheeses in the Pyrenees.

CHAMPAGNAC
DE BELAIR
Moulin du Roc
(53.54.80.36)

PÉRIGUEUX
L'Oison
(53.09.84.02)

LES EYZIES-DE-TAYAC
Le Centenaire
(53.06.97.18)

BORDEAUX
Le Chapon Fin
(56.79.10.10)

LAGUIOLE
Lou Mazuc
(65.44.32.24)

PUYMIROL
L'Aubergade
(53.95.31.46)

AUCH
Hôtel de France
(62.05.00.44)

TOULOUSE
Vanel (61.21.51.82)

EUGÉNIE-LES-BAINS
Michel Guérard
(58.51.19.01)

SAINT-JEAN-
PIED-DE-PORT
Les Pyrénées
(59.37.01.01)

Cheese and Apples

Sample the grand cheeses, succulent apple desserts or punchy cider (in moderation) on a trip through the dairy-farms and orchards of Normandy's Pays d'Auge, signposted *Route des Fromages* and *Route du Cidre*.

1 PONT L'EVÊQUE

savoury square cheese marketed here since 13th-century.

2 BEUVRON-EN-AUGE

beautifully preserved village of timbered houses.

3 VICTOT

16th-century chequered stone castle.

4 CAMBREMER

centre of apple-country with half-timbered houses around Romanesque church.

5 SAINT-PIERRE-SUR-DIVES

market-town, cheese museum.

6 LIVAROT

most pungent of Normandy cheeses.

7 VIMOUTIERS

Monday cheese-market day since 1030.

8 CAMEMBERT

Beaumoncel farm-house where the king of French cheeses was "invented".

World War I

The "war to end all wars" took place in large part in trenches gouged out of the bleak landscape of north-eastern France. Today, cemeteries and poignant memorials are the warfare's landmarks.

Flanders and Picardy

The region has been a battlefield since Rome's Julius Caesar and England's Henry V.

1 ARMENTIÈRES
celebrated in soldiers' song; British war cemetery.

2 NOTRE-DAME-DE-LORETTE
40,000 French buried on hill near Pétain's command post.

3 VIMY RIDGE
Canadian memorial to 1917 battle.

4 BEAUMONT-HAMEL
memorial with trenches and rusted iron recall 1916 Battle of Somme.

5 THIEPVAL
British triumphal arch, Ulster tower.

6 BELLICOURT
Cenotaph to American attack on Hindenburg Line.

7 COMPIÈGNE
in forest, replica of railway wagon in which 1918 Armistice was signed.

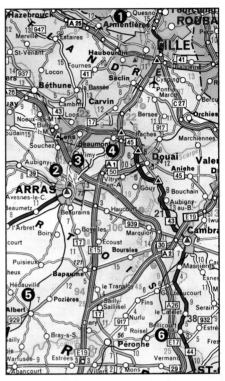

Lorraine

The arena of the war's bloodiest battle, a region inspiring in the next world war De Gaulle's emblem, the Cross of Lorraine.

1 VERDUN
citadel and museum commemorate 800,000 dead.

2 FLEURY
stone memorial marks site of village completely destroyed.

3 VAUX
guided tour of key fortress.

4 DOUAUMONT
ossuary and cemetery among trenches.

5 MONTFAUCON
U.S. monument with Statue of Liberty.

6 ROMAGNE-SOUS-MONTFAUCON
U.S. cemetery of 14,000 tombs.

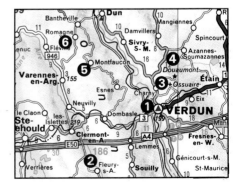

World War II –

The Normandy invasion

The 1944 D-Day landings that liberated France left their mark along the Channel beaches and across the Cotentin fields whose hedgerows nearly crippled Patton's American tanks.

1 OUISTREHAM
museum of Anglo-French Sword Beach operations.

2 HERMANVILLE
British cemetery.

3 BERNIÈRES AND COURSEULLES
Canadian memorials to taking of Juno Beach.

4 REVIERS
Canadian cemetery.

5 ARROMANCHES
transportable Mulberry harbour; museum for Gold Beach operations.

6 OMAHA BEACH
first American assault.

7 COLLEVILLE-SAINT-LAURENT
9,386 tombs in U.S. war cemetery.

8 LA CAMBE
21,160 tombs in German cemetery.

9 POINTE DU HOC
German bunkers on promontory.

10 UTAH BEACH
museum commemorates scene of stormiest beach-fighting.

11 SAINTE-MÈRE-ÉGLISE
Airborne Museum depicts town's liberation.

12 SAINT-LÔ
bombed-out town reconstructed, modern French-American hospital.

13 AVRANCHES
monument to General Patton's triumphal entry.

14 CAEN
new Memorial Museum for whole region.

15 BAYEUX
first town to be liberated, unscarred.

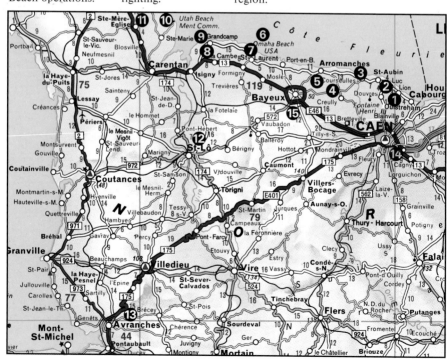

Palaces around Paris

The kings of France and their wealthiest advisors were essentially suburbanites, building homes away from the often troublesome mob and close to a hunting forest.

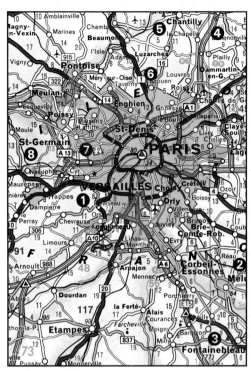

1 VERSAILLES

last and greatest of royal palaces, Louis XIV's ego in stone.

2 VAUX-LE-VICOMTE

Louis XIV jailed his financier Fouquet for building such a magnificent castle.

3 FONTAINEBLEAU

François I's "hunting lodge", now a Napoleon museum.

4 COMPIÈGNE

last home of Marie-Antoinette, houses museum of Napoleon III's opulent Second Empire.

5 CHANTILLY

residence of powerful Condé family, superb collection of European painting.

6 ECOUEN

Montmorency home now Renaissance museum.

7 RUEIL-MALMAISON

Josephine Bonaparte's palace.

8 SAINT-GERMAIN-EN LAYE

pentagonal château houses national museum of Stone Age art.

Gothic Cathedrals

In the mid-12th and 13th-centuries, the Catholic Church glorified its faith in stone with the soaring Gothic architecture of flying buttresses and elaborate rib-vaulting, nowhere more spectacular than in the cathedrals in and around Paris.

PARIS

Notre-Dame is the nation's church, dominating the Seine river.

SAINT-DENIS

grand burial place of kings in a dowdy northern suburb.

SENLIS

façade inspired Chartres and Notre-Dame, now a quiet village church.

BEAUVAIS

tallest chancel in Christendom.

ROUEN

magnificent towers, a favourite theme of Impressionist Claude Monet.

CHARTRES

supreme masterpiece, for its silhouette and the stained glass.

SENS

earliest of great cathedrals.

REIMS

appropriately majestic façade for the church of royal coronations.

LAON

distinctive stone tracery of its towers.

AMIENS

beautifully carved oak choir stalls.

Romanesque Churches

The architecture of the 11th and 12th-centuries reflected the powerful but austere qualities of feudalism. The solid square towers, round arches and simple but forceful sculpture on porches and column-capitals impose a spirit of meditation.

Auvergne

The sober Romanesque style fits admirably into the weather-beaten Auvergnat landscape. The harmoniously tiered domes of the chancel are a characteristic feature.

1 CLERMONT-FERRAND
Notre-Dame-du-Port; sculpted capitals in ambulatory.

2 ORCIVAL
superb chancel in pretty valley setting; gilded statue of enthroned Virgin and Child.

3 SAINT-SATURNIN
splendid octagonal belfry on Veyre river.

4 SAINT-NECTAIRE
fine chancel, sculpture in choir.

5 ISSOIRE
subtle geometry of chancel; imposing crypt, but garish new colours in nave.

6 BRIOUDE
abbey-basilica in rich golden stone.

7 LE PUY
Spanish-Moorish influence on cathedral's façade and cloister; 12th-century frescoes.

Burgundy

The prosperous duchy and its monasteries produced edifices that reflect the riches of this fertile region, with wine-harvest themes often depicted in the sculpture.

VÉZELAY
Sainte-Madeleine basilica still major pilgrimage; masterly tympanum over narthex entrance.

AUTUN
Saint-Lazare cathedral has fine carved capitals and tympanum over portal.

PARAY-LE-MONIAL
subtle light and shade in nave and choir of Sacré-Cœur basilica.

BERZÉ-LA-VILLE
one of many churches in Cluny orbit; frescoes in *Chapelle des Moines*.

TOURNUS
pioneering arched barrel vaults in Saint-Philibert.

DIJON
fine Romanesque crypt in Gothic Saint-Bénigne cathedral.

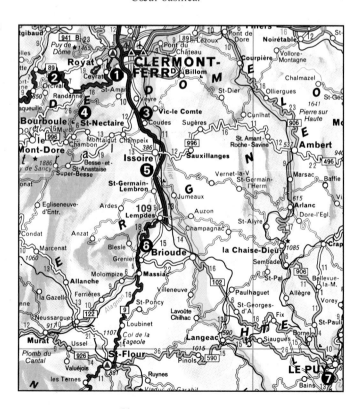

Monasteries

Right across the country, monasteries lie in more or less noble ruin, victims of 16th-century Wars of Religion, the 1789 Revolution and 19th century construction speculators. But many have been restored and are once again active.

Normandy

JUMIÈGES
consecrated by William the Conqueror, grandest of Norman ruins.

SAINT-WANDRILLE
Benedictine monks still active, Gregorian chant at Mass.

LE BEC HELLOUIN
medieval "training school" for English archbishops; monks make and sell ceramics.

MONT-SAINT-MICHEL
sublime steepled abbey set in the sea on its own island-rock.

Loire

FONTEVRAUD
once encompassed five different monastic orders; today organizes concerts and exhibitions.

Burgundy

FONTENAY
well-preserved Cistercian abbey founded by St. Bernard de Clairvaux.

CLUNY
poignant ruin of what was mightiest of all French monasteries.

Savoie

HAUTECOMBE
on Lac du Bourget, Gregorian chant at Mass.

Provence

SÉNANQUE
12th-century Cistercian abbey in valley of lavender; summer art shows and concerts.

LE THORONET
purest expression of simple Romanesque architecture in church and cloister.

Auvergne

CHAISE-DIEU
once centre of powerful monastic empire; *Dance of Death* frescoes in abbey-church.

Pyrénées

SANT-MICHEL-DE-CUXA
stages concerts of Catalan music; part of Cloisters reassembled in New York.

FONTFROIDE
yellow-pink sandstone Gothic cloister amid cypresses and flower-gardens.

Brittany's Parish Close road

The parish close *(enclos paroissial)* is quintessentially Breton, pious architectural ensemble of triumphal arch leading to church, cemetery, charnel house and intricately carved calvary. Set out from Morlaix.

1 SAINT-THÉGONNEC
supreme example of the art, Renaissance ossuary, calvary carved in 1610.

2 GUIMILIAU
200 figures on calvary, wooden baptistry in church.

3 LAMPAUL-GUIMILIAU
fine sculpted rood beam in church.

4 LA ROCHE-MAURICE
17th-century ossuary with Death declaring *Je vous tue tous* (I kill you all).

5 LA MARTYRE
fine stained-glass in church; ghoulish charnel-house.

6 SIZUN
Renaissance triumphal arch and ossuary.

7 ROC TRÉVEZEL
spectacular view over whole region.

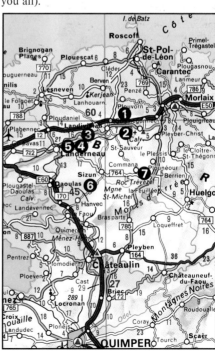

Fishing in the Jura

The mountain lakes and rivers of the Jura teem with the best of freshwater fish, exciting challenge for the wader in fast-moving streams or more contemplative from a boat on a placid lake.

Doubs and Loue Valleys

1 PONTARLIER
gateway-town to both rivers.

2 MALBUISSON AND LAC DE SAINT-POINT
resort for boat-rentals, equipment and fishing permit (details at tourist office). Lake formed by Doubs, good trout, perch, pike and tench.

3 LAC DE CHAILLEXON
3.5 km. (2 mi.) long, 200 m. (180 yards) wide, tench, pike and small fry.

4 SAUT DU DOUBS
spectacular water-fall.

5 SOURCE OF THE LOUE
picturesque cliff site.

6 MOUTHIERS-HAUTE-PIERRE
resort base for trout-fishing and great local kirsch after the meal.

7 LODS
as in "sweet and…"; delightful old village.

8 VUILLAFANS
lazybones fish off the bridge.

9 ORNANS
tranquil hometown of painter Courbet.

10 MAISIÈRES
where artist caught (and painted) giant trout near ruined castle, Châtel-Saint-Denis.

Ain Valley

1 NANTUA
famous for its cray-fish sauce, town's pretty lake also has good trout, pike and perch.

2 ALLEMENT
dam (barrage) teems with trout, pike.

3 COISELET
fat trout at confluence of Ain and Bienne rivers.

4 VOUGLANS
country's third-biggest reservoir, good boating and bathing.

5 MAISOD
charming little resort over the river.

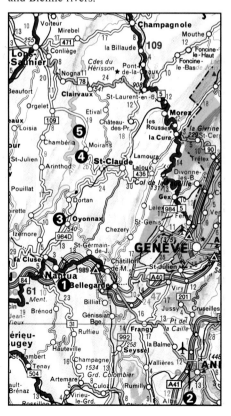

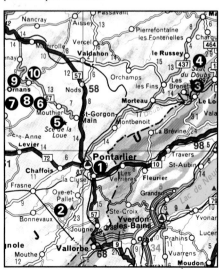

Son et Lumière

The dramatically staged "sound and light" shows (in English and French) recapture the fairytale atmosphere of the Loire Valley Châteaux far better than any tired old uniformed tour-guide.

These are the best:

1 CHAMBORD
rooftop royal flirts among the turrets.

2 BLOIS
where Henri III had 20 men stab to death his arch-enemy, the Duc de Guise.

3 CHEVERNY
comfortable Italian Renaissance residence, works by Titian and pupils of Raphael.

4 VALENÇAY
wily diplomat Talleyrand's pied-à-terre; car museum in grounds.

5 CHENONCEAU
castle bridging Cher river, confiscated from Diane de Poitiers by Catherine de Médicis.

6 AMBOISE
Mary, future Queen of Scots, watched Protestant nobles hung, drawn and quartered.

7 AZAY-LE-RIDEAU
exquisite castle where Charles VII had 350 soldiers executed for insulting him.

8 CHINON
ramparts dominate ruins of fortress in which Joan of Arc confronted Charles VII.

9 LE LUDE
most brilliant illuminations and fireworks for Renaissance costumed show.

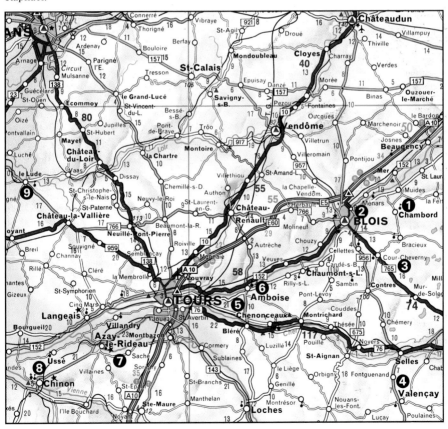

53

Hunting in the Loire

More than anything else, it was the abundant wild game that persuaded France's kings to build Châteaux in the Loire Valley. The forests and ponds are still well stocked. Tourist offices advise about permits.

ORLÉANS
wild boar in forest north-east of town.

CHAMBORD
plenty of deer and boar in Château's historic park.

ROMORANTIN
good base for Sologne's duck, snipe, pheasants and hare, in and around Bruadan forest.

VALENÇAY
stags in the castle-park; open-air zoo.

LOCHES
roe deer in Loches and Verneuil forests.

AMBOISE
wild boar in forest south of Château, look for Duke of Choiseul's 18th-century pagoda.

CHÂTEAU-LA-VALLIÈRE
stags and roe deer in dense pine and oak forest.

BAUGÉ
good stag-hunting in Chandelais forest.

Horse-riding in Camargue

In this regional nature reserve, horses and bulls roam free among ponds, marshes and meadows between two arms of the Rhône delta.

1 ARLES
bullfights in Roman arena; inquire at tourist office about horses for hire.

2 MAS DU PONT DE ROUSTY
museum of Camargue fauna and flora.

3 ALBARON
medieval fortress.

4 MÉJAMES
horse-stables and bullfight arena.

5 GINÈS
information centre and bird-sanctuary.

6 SAINTES-MARIES-DE-LA-MER
seaside resort and pilgrimage town.

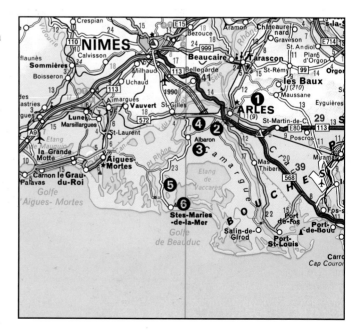

Festivals in the South of France

Summer arts festivals are a nationwide phenomenon, but many of the best are concentrated in Provence and along the Côte d'Azur. The Roman arenas, monasteries and even a papal palace offer magnificent open-air settings (practically all in July).

Provence

1 VAISON-LA-ROMAINE
opera and choral music in Roman amphitheatre.

2 ORANGE
Chorégies opera cycle in amphitheatre.

3 CARPENTRAS
ballet and opera.

4 SÉNANQUE
folk and choral music in the monastery.

5 ROUSSILLON
chamber music.

6 AVIGNON
biggest of all, in Palais des Papes: theatre, dance, classical, jazz and folk music.

7 ARLES
international photography; ballet, theatre and classical music in arena and Roman theatre.

8 SALON-DE-PROVENCE
jazz and rock music.

9 AIX-EN-PROVENCE
opera in archbishop's palace.

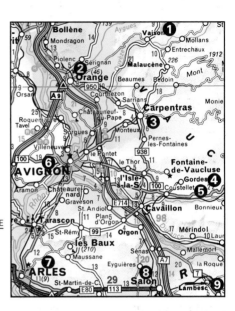

Côte d'Azur

1 CANNES
chamber music in old Le Suquet.

2 CAGNES
international painting.

3 ANTIBES
modern jazz.

4 JUAN-LES-PINS
modern jazz.

5 SAINT-PAUL-DE-VENCE
modern classical music at Fondation Maeght.

6 NICE
modern jazz.

7 MENTON
(in August) chamber music.

Route Napoléon

Napoleonic history buffs can follow the historic route the Emperor took (now signposted) when he escaped from Elba in March, 1815, to return to power in Paris. Before Waterloo.

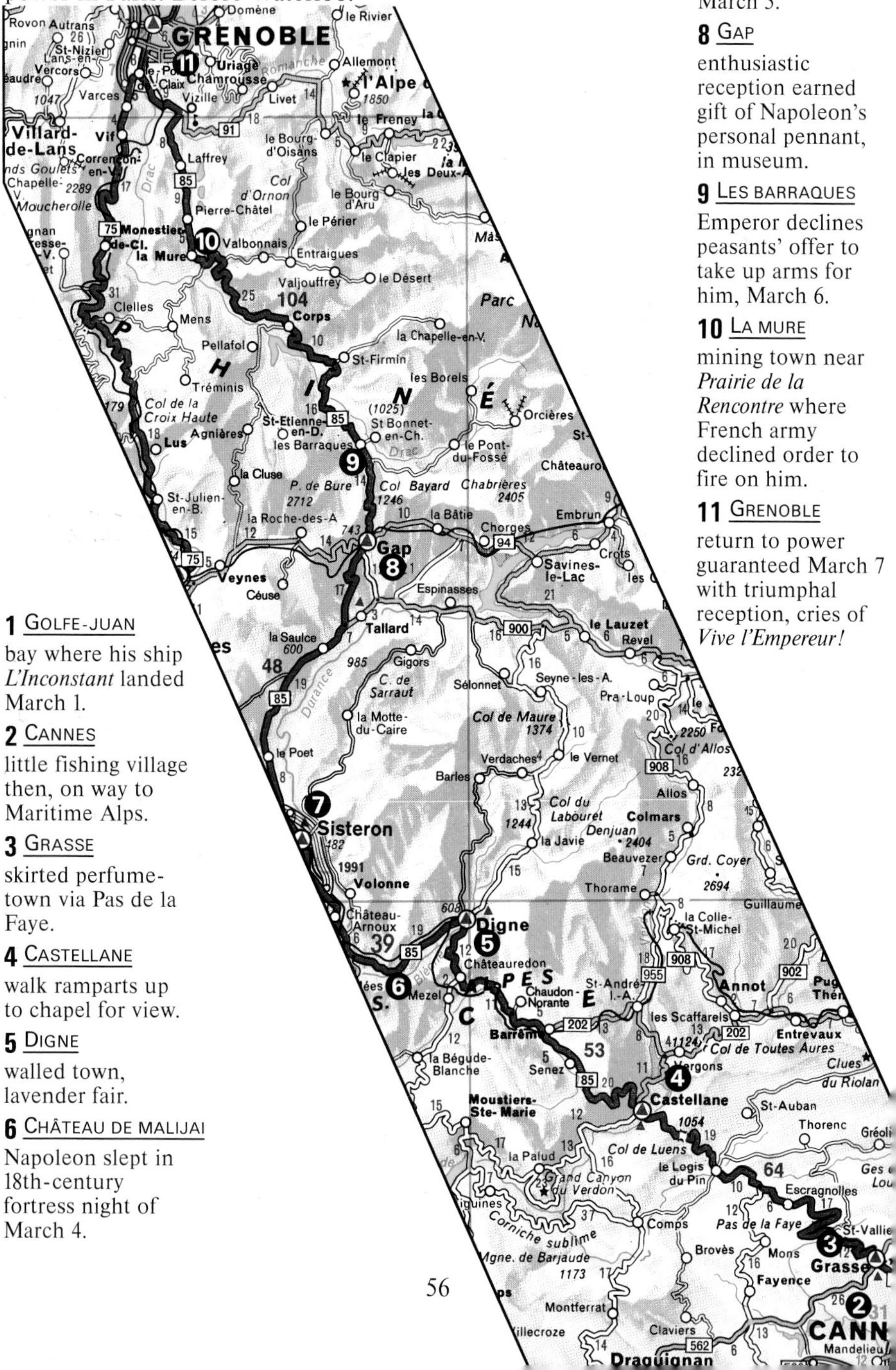

1 GOLFE-JUAN

bay where his ship *L'Inconstant* landed March 1.

2 CANNES

little fishing village then, on way to Maritime Alps.

3 GRASSE

skirted perfume-town via Pas de la Faye.

4 CASTELLANE

walk ramparts up to chapel for view.

5 DIGNE

walled town, lavender fair.

6 CHÂTEAU DE MALIJAI

Napoleon slept in 18th-century fortress night of March 4.

7 SISTERON

townspeople showed first signs of sympathy for Emperor as he lunched here March 5.

8 GAP

enthusiastic reception earned gift of Napoleon's personal pennant, in museum.

9 LES BARRAQUES

Emperor declines peasants' offer to take up arms for him, March 6.

10 LA MURE

mining town near *Prairie de la Rencontre* where French army declined order to fire on him.

11 GRENOBLE

return to power guaranteed March 7 with triumphal reception, cries of *Vive l'Empereur!*

Winter Sports in the Alps

New construction for the 1992 Winter Olympics at Albertville gives the French Alps the most up-to-date facilities in an already well-established ski-resort area.

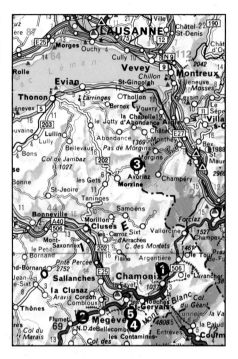

Haute-Savoie

1 CHAMONIX

traditional resort on slopes of Mont Blanc, with long history of skiing and mountaineering; good for intermediates.

2 MEGÈVE

sophisticated traditional village attracting film stars and royalty; good for beginners and intermediates.

3 AVORIAZ

futuristic purpose-built resort, centre of giant Portes du Soleil region on Franco-Swiss border; good for all standards.

4 LES CONTAMINES

mix of traditional old village and modern purpose-built resort; good for intermediate and advanced skiers.

5 ST-GERVAIS

old spa town with modern development; good for intermediates.

Savoie

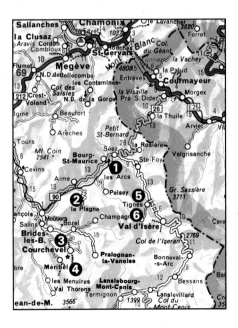

1 LES ARCS

purpose-built resort, pioneer of *ski évolutif* method of learning to ski; good for all standards.

2 LA PLAGNE

vast area comprising modern altitude centres and valley villages; intermediates' paradise.

3 COURCHEVEL

fashionable modern resort in 3 Vallées complex; good for all standards.

4 MÉRIBEL

attractive and popular village in 3 Vallées complex, with modern high-rise offshoot; good for intermediates.

5 TIGNES

high-rise concrete resort; brilliant and extensive for keen skiers of all standards.

6 VAL D'ISÈRE

traditional old village with tasteful modern development.

Volcanoes in Auvergne

The region's chain of 200 extinct volcanoes, the last of which stopped erupting some 3,500 years ago, is organized in a 120-km. (75 mi.) – long nature park that is backbone of Auvergne countryside.

Dômes and Dore Ranges

1 PUY DE DÔME
at 1,465 m. (4,310 ft.), superb introductory panorama of other volcanoes.

2 ORCIVAL
fine Romanesque church in foothills of Monts Dore range.

3 MONT-DORE
spa resort for

hiking in summer, skiing in winter.

4 PUY DE SANCY
highest peak in central France, 1,885 m. (5,673 ft.), view clear across to Alps.

5 PUY DE MONTCHAL
dramatic crater, 1,411 m. (4,287 ft.), south of Lac Pavin teeming with huge trout and char.

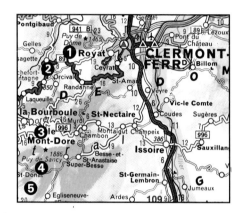

Cantal Mountains

1 MURAT
head for lookout on *Rocher de Bonnevie*.

2 LE LIORAN
winter sports resort; take cable-car to peak of Plomb du Cantal.

3 THIÉZAC
pretty summer resort in Cère valley.

4 VIC-SUR-CÈRE
family resort, former residence of princes of Monaco.

5 CHÂTEAU DE PESTEILS
medieval fortress, fine tapestries.

6 AURILLAC
volcano museum, distribution-centre for best Cantal cheeses.

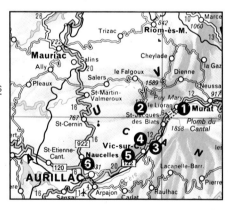

TGV (Train à Grande Vitesse)

The stations on the high-speed TGV train's south from Paris are all gateways to interesting sightseeing possibilities. Get off anywhere you like and there's an adventure.

PARIS, GARE DE LYON

before you go, have a drink in the bar of the *Train Bleu,* superb 1900 décor.

Geneva-Lausanne Route

MONTBARD

visit Fontenay abbey; Alesia, battlefield of last Gallic stand against Julius Caesar.

DIJON

palace of dukes of Burgundy, gateway to the vineyards.

DOLE

Louis Pasteur's birthplace; visit Ledoux's 18th-century urban experiment at Arc et Senans.

BESANÇON

museum's French and Italian paintings; gateway to Jura mountains.

South of France Route

LE CREUSOT

metal industry town, but close to Autun's great Romanesque cathedral.

MACON

wine-centre, close to Beaujolais country and Cluny monastery.

LYON

nation's gastronomic capital; marionette theatre for kids and their parents.

VALENCE

first olive trees of Mediterranean region; Hubert Robert drawings in museum.

MONTELIMAR

nougat, hard and soft.

AVIGNON

Palais des Papes and "le pont", gateway to Provence.

NÎMES

Roman amphitheatre; Van Gogh country on roads to Tarascon and Arles.

MONTPELLIER

lively university town; gateway to Pyrenees.

MARSEILLE

tough connection, bustling around the port, hustling on the Canebière.

NICE

sun and sea on the Côte d'Azur.

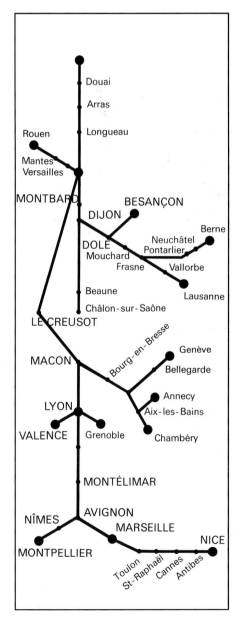

59

For the Love of the Landscape

Some leisure routes are conceived with no more (nor less) important interest in mind than the sheer beauty of the French landscape in all its infinite variety. There are hundreds imaginable; here we propose just three.

Pays Basque

Few vistas inspire greater serenity and repose than the Basque country's rolling green foothills rising into the Pyrenees. You may also want to hike over those mountains to the Spanish border.

1 SAINT-JEAN-DE-LUZ
charming fishing village where Louis XIV got married.

2 ASCAIN
handsome 17th-century houses.

3 LA RHUNE
mountaintop view of ocean and Pyrenees.

4 SARE
grand Baroque altar in church.

5 AÏNHOA
village full of character, each whitewashed house a different size and shape.

6 SAINT-JEAN-PIED-DE-PORT
important pilgrimage town on route to Santiago de Compostela.

7 COL D'OSGUICH
hike and picnic on mountain pass.

8 OLORON-SAINTE-MARIE
finely sculpted marble porch on Romanesque church.

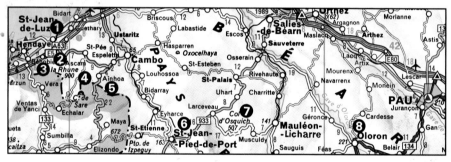

Lubéron

The very essence of the Provençal landscape: rough white or buff stone farmhouses amid olive and almond trees, vineyards, fields of lavender and other herbal fragrances.

1 CAVAILLON
home of the country's best melons.

2 OPPÈDE-LE-VIEUX
haven for artists and writers.

3 MÉNERBES
medieval fortress.

4 BONNIEUX
terrace view across russet-hued hills.

5 LOURMARIN
Renaissance castle overlooking valley.

6 APT
regional capital, market-town with antiques fair in July.

7 SAIGNON
pretty village with Romanesque church.

8 MOURRE NÈGRE
highest point in Lubéron, 1,115 m., view to Cézanne's Mont Sainte-Victoire.

9 ROUSSILLON
ochre-washed houses, arcaded streets.

10 GORDES
craftware boutiques and art galleries with 16th-century castle at top of its hill.

11 SÉNANQUE
monastery amid lavender fields.

Poitou Marshes

The *Marais poitevin* north of La Rochelle offers a wistful panorama, at once mellow and melancholy, of silent waterways bordered by poplars and weeping willows. Fishermen and peasants (with their cattle) ply the canals in long flat-bottomed punts.

1 NIORT
flowery town, with Richard the Lionheart's castle.

2 LA GARETTE
boatmen's hamlet.

3 COULON
rent your punt here.

4 MAILLEZAIS
ruins of 11th-century monastery; punt-rentals.

5 NIEULZ-SUR-L'AUTIE
fine Romanesque cloister.

6 MARANS
port connected to ocean by canal; handmade pottery.

7 ESNANDES
mussel-fishermen's whitewashed houses, fortress church.

8 SAINT-MICHEL-EN-L'HERM
hilltop Benedictine abbey, Gothic chapter-room and refectory.

9 AIGUILLON
dyke built by Dutch engineers.

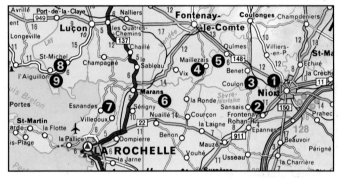

Jewish Life in France

The Jews arrived in France with the Romans, setting up trading houses across Provence. After centuries of persecution and deportation, the community is the fourth in the world, after Israel, the United States and the Soviet Union.

Paris

1 RUE DES ROSIERS
old *shtetl* (ghetto) with Eastern European delicatessen and North African falafel.

2 RUE PAVÉE
Métro-designer Hector Guimard's Art Nouveau synagogue (1913).

3 RUE GEOFFROY-L'ASNIER
Memorial to Unknown Jewish Martyr, crypt for victims of Nazism.

4 RUE DE LA VICTOIRE
main synagogue, Neo-Gothic.

5 MUSÉE D'ART JUIF
42, Rue des Saules, 18e arrondissement. Jewish art to be moved soon to 71, Rue du Temple.

Normandy

ROUEN
12th-century synagogue excavated in courtyard of Palais de Justice, on site of ghetto.

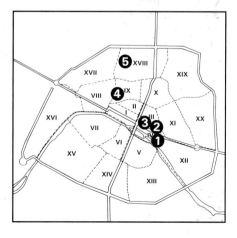

Alsace-Lorraine

NANCY

Lorraine Historical
Museum, 64,
Grande Rue, art of
important eastern
French community.

STRASBOURG

Alsatian Museum,
23, Quai Saint-
Nicolas, instru-
ments of worship
and ritual.

STRUTHOF

concentration-
camp where 10,000
died, (after building
road and camp-
barracks).

RIQUEWIHR

old ghetto in
wooden-galleried
Cour des Juifs.

Provence

1 CARPENTRAS

18th-century syna-
gogue and bakery;
cathedral's Porte
Juive for Jewish
converts.

2 AVIGNON

site of ghetto Place
de Jérusalem, 19th-
century synagogue.

3 CAVAILLON

fine Louis XV inte-
rior in 18th-century
synagogue,
Rue Hébraïque,
museum in bakery.

Basque Country

BAYONNE

Basque Museum's
reconstituted
private synagogue
of Sephardic Jews
from Portugal.

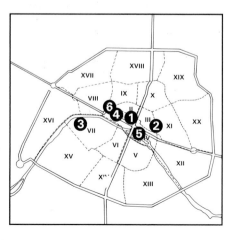

The French Revolution

More than most moments in France's turbulent history, the Revolution of 1789 was dominated by events in Paris. Each site marks an act in the great drama.

1 PALAIS ROYAL

revolutionaries met
to hear the call to
arms of journalist
Camille Desmoulins.

2 BASTILLE

square marking the
site of the infamous
prison stormed on
July 14, 1789.

3 CHAMP-DE-MARS

American Revolu-
tion's hero Lafayette
fired on angry
Parisians July 17,
1791.

4 TUILERIES

site of palace from
which Louis XVI
was taken prisoner
August 10, 1792.

5 CONCIERGERIE

jail for Louis XVI
and Marie-
Antoinette.

6 PLACE
DE LA CONCORDE

as "Place de la
Révolution", site
of the king's
beheading January
21, 1793.

62

Flowered Villages Circuit

75 km. (46 mi.) in the Rhône Valley take you to a selection of the prettiest villages you can imagine, with flowers of all sorts under clement skies. It can be easily done on cycle or foot.

1 CHARBONNIÈRES-LES-BAINS

thermal baths for aching muscles.

2 SAINT-PIERRE-LA-PALUD

Mine Museum in former copper mining region.

3 SAVIGNY

Benedictine monks from Cluny founded abbey; interesting vestiges in the Musée Coquard.

4 ANCY, SAINT-FORGEUX, SAINT-LOUP

all obtained prizes for their flowers.

5 LE BOIS D'OINGT

one of four "rose villages" created in France.

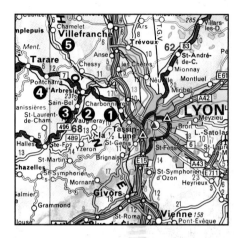

Route Jacques-Cœur

To get familiar with this immensely powerful, influential and wealthy man, follow his traces in the deepest heart of France. Appointed keeper of the Mint by Charles VII, Jacques Cœur became a fantastically successful medieval merchant adventurer.

1 GIEN

first château of the Loire, built in 1484.

2 BLANCAFORT

château contains beautiful furniture and tapestries.

3 AUBIGNY-SUR-NÈRE

city of the Stuarts with half-timbered façades.

4 CHÂTEAU DE MENETOU-SALON

ancient property of Jacques Cœur.

5 BOURGES

interesting medieval city. Visit the Gothic Palais Jacques-Cœur and the outstanding cathedral.

6 JUSSY-CHAMPAGNE

beautiful residence of Louis XII period in brick and stone.

7 MEILLANT

sumptuously furnished. Louis XII stayed here.

8 NOIRLAC

Cistercian abbey founded in 1150 by St. Bernard. One of the best examples of medieval monastic architecture.

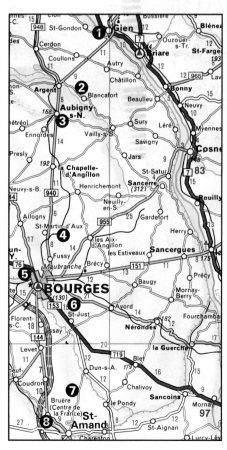

The Country's Heartbeat

Paris, more than most national capitals, dictates the country's tastes and style of life. All ambitious French people "go up" to Paris to make their fortune, and so people from every region—with every local cuisine to feed them—are represented there. The Parisian's traditional contempt for the "provinces" is matched only by his fierce loyalty to the distant home of his ancestors, most often just one generation removed.

Before it was the national capital, Paris was the home of the medieval dukes of the region still known as the Ile-de-France, which, gradually asserting itself over other duchies like Burgundy or Normandy, imposed its name on the whole country.

The Paris basin is a treasury of national monuments. Roughly bounded by four rivers—the Seine, Oise, Aisne and Marne—the Ile-de-France was the birthplace of the first great Gothic cathedrals, such as Saint-Denis, Senlis, Chartres and Beauvais. It was the cradle of the French monarchy; its surrounding greenery and dense forests also provided good sites for later kings and nobles to build their palaces away from the troublesome mob of Paris, at Fontainebleau, Chantilly and, of course, Versailles.

All the interesting sights around the capital are an easy day trip by car or local train, so that you can keep your Paris hotel if you wish (but you'd probably find the local country inns a lot cheaper). Traffic in Paris is certainly no fun in daytime, and only fractionally more at night and weekends outside rush hours. August, thank heaven, usually provides some respite, but best not count on it.

Paris   10,BC1-2

The city and the people of Paris share a boundless self-confidence that exudes from every stone in its monuments and museums, bistros and boutiques, from every chestnut tree along its avenues and boulevards, from every street-urchin, mannequin, butcher and baker, from every irate motorist and every charming maître d'hôtel.

You readily forgive the bombast of some of the monumental architecture when you see what makes this the City of Light. Stand on the Pont Royal in late afternoon and look down the Seine to the glass-panelled Grand Palais, bathed in the pink and blue glow of the river. That unique light brings a phosphorescence to the most commonplace little square or side street. In case the message isn't clear, Paris offers golden night-time illumination of its major historical buildings. To celebrate Bastille Day (July 14) or the

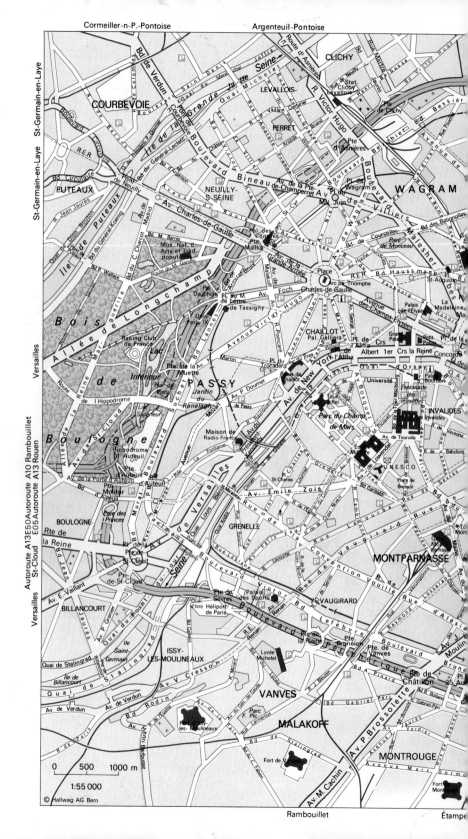

E15 Autoroute A1 Aéroport Ch-de Gaulle-Lille
E19 Autoroute A1-A2 Cambrai
Aéroport du Bourget Soissons

Reims, Chalons-s. Marne

Autoroute A3 Rosny-sous-Bois

Lagny

Nancy E50 Metz

Troyes E15 Dijon

PARIS

1944 Liberation (August 25), blue, white and red laser beams are bounced off the Eiffel Tower, Arc de Triomphe and Town Hall.

Despite the inevitable erosions of social change and urban renovation, the jargon of Paris's topography still evokes not just a place but a state of mind. The Right Bank conjures up an image of bourgeois respectability. Historically the stronghold of merchants and royalty, it remains today the home of commerce and government. Faubourg Saint-Honoré offers the luxury of jewellery shops and *haute couture*, and the more imperial than republican authority of the president's palace, while the Champs-Elysées claims the film and airline companies and car showrooms.

The Left Bank, on the other hand, has always had a bohemian and intellectual image, dating back to the founding of the university and monasteries. Today, the Sorbonne, the *Académie française*, the publishing houses and myriad bookshops continue to exercise an intellectual magnetism.

But a constant flow and interchange of citizenry from one bank to the other takes place across the bridges of the Seine, a narrower and so much more "manageable" river than, say, London's Thames or New York's Hudson.

Paris is one of the world's most densely populated capitals. Its non-stop street scene derives from the fact that nearly every one of its 20 *arrondissements*, or districts, has shops, offices and apartments side by side and on top of each other. There's always someone out there moving around. Join them.

The Seine

The river is by far the best place to begin to take the measure of Paris. Its mixture of grandeur and intimacy is the very essence of the city.

From Bog to Beaubourg

The fishing village of the Celtic Parisii on an island in the Seine (today's Ile de la Cité) was conquered in 52 B.C. by the Romans, who called it Lutetia (Marshland). In the early Middle Ages, the town expanded to the left bank with the monastery of Saint-Germain-des-Prés, the right bank being unmanageably boggy.

Although Hugues Capet, first king of France (see p.14), made it his capital in 987, Paris did not become the permanent seat of royal government for another 600 years. Crusader Philippe Auguste took time off to build the Louvre as a fortress in 1190. Fifty years later, the Sorbonne was founded as a theological college.

It was Henri IV who made Paris a truly royal capital. He built the splendid Place des Vosges and Place Dauphine, beautified the river banks and completed the grand Pont-Neuf. "Fashionable" Paris evolved in the 17th century with the first elegant houses of the Faubourg Saint-Honoré and the Cours-la-Reine built for Marie de Médicis as precursor to the Champs-Elysées. Cardinal Richelieu enhanced its intellectual standing by creating the *Académie française*, while bequeathing his magnificent home, the Palais-Royal.

After the humiliations of the *Fronde* revolts (see p. 20), Louis XIV abandoned Paris for Versailles, but the town's cultural life reasserted itself under his successors. Cafés sprang up around the Palais-Royal as centres of the intellectual ferment preceding the Revolution. Place de la Concorde became Place de la Révolution for the time of the guillotine. The Louvre became a national museum.

To celebrate his battles, Napoleon built the Arc de Triomphe and Place Vendôme, but he himself felt his most important achievements were those of a mayor rather than a conqueror—water purification, food markets (les Halles), slaughterhouses (la Villette), a new police force and streamlined municipal administration. Under his nephew, Napoleon III, troublesome working-class neighbourhoods were razed by Baron Haussmann to make way for wide boulevards and avenues, giving Paris its modern airy look—and a clear line of fire for the artillery in case of revolt.

If the Eiffel Tower was a fetish of the triumphant 19th century, the Centre Pompidou, better known as Beaubourg, is the brash symbol of today's modernism—both celebrating Paris's eternal gall.

Again and again the Seine provides a spectacular vantage point for the city's great landmarks. The Eiffel Tower, the Palais de Chaillot and Trocadéro Gardens, the Grand and Petit Palais, the Palais Bourbon, the Louvre and Notre-Dame all take on a more enchanting, dreamlike quality if you see them first when floating by in a boat. The **guided boat trip** is well worthwhile.

But this is also a river to be walked along, despite the traffic on rapid *voies express* along the banks. You can take delightful strolls between the Pont Sully, at the eastern end of the Ile Saint-Louis, and the Pont de la Concorde. Stop to rest occasionally on a bench beneath the poplar and plane trees along the Seine, ideally early morning or late afternoon, when that pink Paris light is at its best.

The river's bridges are a major attraction, four of them especially worthy of your attention. The **Pont-Neuf** (*neuf* means "new") is in fact Paris's oldest standing bridge, completed by Henri IV in 1606. It was a favourite of street-singers, charlatans, amateur dentists, professional ladies, pickpockets and above all for *bouquinistes* selling their old books and pamphlets out of boxes. Established booksellers on the Ile de la Cité were enraged and drove them off to the banks of the Seine, where they've been ever since.

The centrally situated **Pont Royal**, built for Louis XIV in 1685, commands some splendid panoramas: the Tuileries Gardens and the Louvre immediately over on the Right Bank, the Musée d'Orsay on the Left, the Grand and Petit Palais downriver and the Palais de l'Institut de France, home of the *Académie française*, up.

The **Pont de la Concorde**, truly the bridge of the French Revolution, went up between 1787 and 1790. Its support structure used stone from the demolished Bastille prison—galling for Royalists, since it had originally been named Pont Louis XVI.

On moonlit nights, lovers head for

the **Pont Alexandre III**, undoubtedly the most kitschily romantic of all with its Belle Epoque lanterns and melodramatic statues of Fame and Pegasus. They really don't care to know it once honoured the tsar for some obscure military treaty.

Right Bank

Etoile–Concorde–Les Halles

Start at the **Place de l'Etoile** (officially Place Charles-de-Gaulle, but nobody calls it that), preferably on top of the **Arc de Triomphe.** One reason for climbing up Napoleon's gigantic triumphal arch— 50 metres (164 feet) high, 45 metres (148 feet) wide—is to get a good view of the 12-pointed star, formed by 12 avenues radiating from the arch in a tour-de-force of geometric planning. The vast sloping mound of the *place* cannot be taken in properly at ground level.

Over the years the Arc de Triomphe has taken on a mythic quality as succeeding régimes have invested it with the spirit of the nation. Napoleon himself saw only a life-size wooden and canvas model. Louis-Philippe inaugurated the final version in 1836, complete with bas-reliefs and statuary celebrating victories of the Revolution and Napoleonic Empire. The Etoile's monumental ensemble was completed for Napoleon III by Baron Haussmann.

Victor Hugo was given a positively pharaonic tribute at the Arc de Triomphe after his death in 1885. The Unknown

Soldier of World War I was buried here in 1920, and three years later the Eternal Flame was lit.

When Hitler came to Paris as conqueror in 1940, this was the first place he wanted to see. But General de Gaulle gained his revenge by starting his march of Liberation here in 1944.

Avenue Foch, leading away from the Etoile to the Bois de Boulogne, is the grandest of the city's residential avenues, somewhat democratized these days by the *boules* players on its gravelled side paths.

The **Champs-Elysées** remains the town's, perhaps the world's, most glamorous avenue. It stretches in an absolutely straight line from the Arc de Triomphe to the Place de la Concorde, lined with chestnut trees all the way. The first two-thirds, as you walk down, are devoted to cinemas, shops and café terraces. You'll find the best vantage points for people-watching between Avenue George-V and Rue Lincoln on the "shady" side and at the Rue du Colisée on the "sunny" side. An interesting theory about the special appeal of the Champs-Elysées is that people look more relaxed and attractive when walking downhill—so ignore the ones going up.

After the Rond-Point, a pleasant park (stamp-collectors' market every Thursday) takes you down to the **Place de la Concorde.**

The gigantic square has had a hard time earning its name. More than 1,000 people were guillotined here during the Revolution and the counter-revolutionary White Terror that followed. In 1934 it was the scene of bloody Fascist rioting against the government and, ten years later, the Germans' last hold in Paris. Today, with floodlit fountains and elegant lamps, it is a night-time romance and a daytime adventure, both for the pedestrian pausing to enjoy the vast opening of the Paris sky and for the driver daring to make his way around it.

Smack in the centre you'll see Paris's oldest monument, the 23-metre (75-foot) pink granite Obelisk of Luxor from the temple of Ramses II, dating back to 1300 B.C., erected here in 1836. For a change, it's not something Napoleon plundered on his campaigns but a gift from Mohammed Ali, viceroy of Egypt.

After the bustle of the Champs-Elysées and Place de la Concorde, take refuge in the cool shade of the chestnut trees in the **Jardin des Tuileries**. Fragments of the royal palace destroyed in the 1871 Commune are still standing by the Jeu de Paume museum in the north-west corner. The gardens are now a favourite with children watching marionette shows, riding donkeys or sailing and sinking their boats on the circular ponds.

At the eastern end of the Tuileries stands the pink **Arc de Triomphe du Carrousel**, roughly contemporary with its bigger brother at the Etoile, visible in a straight line beyond the Obelisk. This imposing effect was originally planned for Napoleon to see from his bedroom in the Louvre. Today, the vista is somewhat spoiled by the modern skyscrapers of La Défense looming on the horizon.

Leaving the Louvre museum for a separate visit (see p. 92), cross the Rue de Rivoli to the **Palais-Royal**, built as Cardinal Richelieu's residence in 1639 (and originally named the Palais-Cardinal). This serene arcaded palace with its garden of limes and beeches and a pond where the young Louis XIV nearly drowned has always been a colourful centre of more or less respectable activity.

In the days of Philippe d'Orléans, Regent of France during Louis XV's minority, it was the scene of notorious orgies. To meet the family's extravagant debts, ground-floor rooms were turned into boutiques (today still selling coins, medals, engravings and antiques) and cafés that attracted a fashionable society. And some shady hangers-on: artists, charlatans, prostitutes, pickpockets—and intellectuals. On July 13, 1789, a young firebrand orator, Camille Desmoulins, stood on a table at the Palais-Royal's Café de Foy to make the call to arms that set off the French Revolution the next

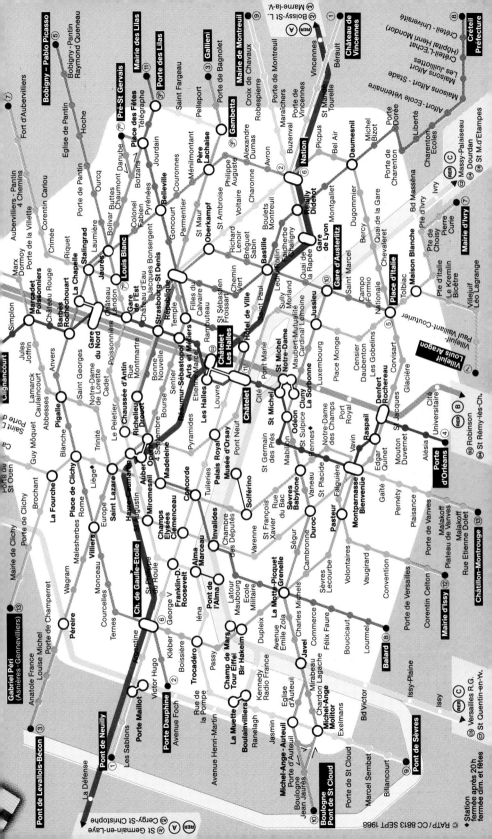

day. After Waterloo, Prussian General Blücher arrived to blow 1,500,000 francs in one night at one of the many rambunctious gambling dens.

East of the Palais-Royal, the old food markets of Les Halles (moved to the more hygienic, inevitably less colourful suburb of Rungis) have been replaced by gardens, new apartment buildings and the **Forum des Halles**, a rather garish shopping centre. Around it, the lively neighbourhood of cafés, boutiques and art galleries linking up with the Centre Pompidou (Beaubourg, see p. 97) is very popular with the young crowd. The liveliest meeting-place is around the handsome Renaissance **Fontaine des Innocents** (once part of a cemetery).

On the north side of Les Halles, another monument of the Renaissance period, but decidedly Gothic in silhouette, is the church of **Saint-Eustache**, remarkable for its stained-glass windows over the choir, crafted according to medieval traditions.

Vendôme–Opéra–Madeleine

The airy octagonal **Place Vendôme** still exudes the opulence of its original conception under Louis XIV, when only his financiers could afford the rents. Three centuries later, little has changed—a score of international banks have their offices here, along with celebrated jewellers, the Ministry of Justice and the Ritz.

The spiral of bronze bas-reliefs on the Vendôme column, commemorating Napoleon's victories and topped by a statue of the emperor himself, was cast from 1,250 cannons captured from the Austrians at Austerlitz.

Window-shop your way past the goldsmiths and furriers of the Rue de la Paix to the **Opéra**, massive monument to the gorgeous pretensions of Napoleon III's Second Empire. Started at the height of his power in 1862 (by architect Charles Garnier), when Paris claimed to be Europe's most glamorous capital, the Opéra was not completed until 1875. Its neo-Baroque style is less of an aesthetic joy than a splendid act of conspicuous consumption proclaiming the triumph of the French bourgeoisie. It is claimed to be the world's largest theatre though seating only 2,000 people.

The Boulevard des Capucines and the Boulevard des Italiens, known as the **grands boulevards**, meet at the Place de l'Opéra. They are perhaps less fashionable now than in their heyday at the end of the 19th century, but you can still recapture some of the atmosphere. On the Boulevard des Capucines, you retrace the footsteps of Renoir, Manet and Pissarro taking their paintings to the house of photographer Nadar, at number 35, for the historic 1874 exhibition of Impressionism. Today the boulevards house some of the town's most popular cinemas—appropriately, because here, at the Hôtel Scribe, the Lumière brothers staged the first public moving-picture show in 1895.

Paris by Boat

The river cruises are accompanied by multilingual commentaries on all the landmarks. Times vary, but they usually go from around 10 a.m. to 10.30 p.m. If you love boats, take a daytime trip at the beginning of your stay and a romantic night-time cruise at the end to enjoy the illuminations.

Bateaux-Mouches have open-air or covered seating according to the weather. The year-round standard 75-minute tour starts from the Quai de la Conférence, goes west to the Pont Mirabeau, then turns back upriver as far as the Pont Sully at the end of the Ile Saint-Louis. The special lunch (1 p.m.) and dinner cruises (8.30 p.m., jacket and tie for men, no anoraks or blue jeans) last 150 minutes. Telephone 42.25.22.55.

The cheaper *vedette* or motorboat tours take 60 minutes. *Vedettes Paris-Tour Eiffel* (Easter to autumn) start by the Pont d'Iéna (Left Bank) and the Quai de Montebello, going west to the Pont de Bir-Hakeim and east to the Pont Sully and back. Telephone 45.51.33.08.

Vedettes du Pont-Neuf leave from the Pont-Neuf, Square du Vert-Galant, to the Eiffel Tower and back around the islands. Telephone 46.33.98.38.

A LA MODE

**STYLE
AS A
WAY OF
LIFE**

The world leadership that
France still seems to enjoy in
fashion dates back to the glorious 17th century of Louis XIV,
but the coquetry of its women
and frequently even greater
vanity of its men began long
before.

If constant warring in the
so-called Dark Ages of the Mero-
vingians left princes and courtiers little time to change an all-
purpose military uniform for
more elegant civilian costume,
they compensated with a taste
for ostentatious gold and
jewellery.

With Church influence
reinforced by the Crusades,
short tunics and breeches were
replaced in the 12th century
by long robes for both men and
women. Crusaders brought back
Oriental-style pointed slippers,
while the French fashion of rich
silk dresses with long trains
was enthusiastically adopted by
women in Syria. Back home, the
dresses had detachable sleeves
so that the ladies could throw
them to their champions during
the tournament.

In the 15th century, the fast
and flashy dukes and duchesses
of Burgundy set wild fashions for
the whole aristocracy of Europe.
Ladies wore tight belts high
under their breasts with a deep
décolleté, and extravagant hats
like the cornet-shaped *hennin*,
up to 60 centimetres (24 inches)
long with a veil hanging from
it clear to the ground. Franciscan
friars refused to hear confes-
sion of ladies wearing too long
a train. Men's doublets had a
left and right side of different
colours, with one wide sleeve
and one narrow. Their pointed
shoes, reinforced by wire, were
sometimes three times longer
than their feet. When Duke
Philippe le Bon lost his hair in
1461, he ordered all his nobles
to shave their heads accordingly,
but their vanity soon overcame
his, and long hair came back
into style.

If Italy imposed its tastes in
the 16th-century Renaissance,
the French court enthusiastically
elaborated on the bare-bosomed
look which Catherine de Médicis
brought from Florence. And
what they didn't have, they
faked: men tucked a padded
panse d'oie (goose-belly) into
their doublet and hose to affect

an allegedly impressive-looking paunch, while women did the same thing for their posteriors. From the stiff and starchy Spanish court, the French gave the outrageously wide-hooped *vertugadin* petticoat (precursor to the crinoline) a more amusing bell-, barrel- or drum-shape. Spanish ladies welcomed the change. The homosexual *mignons* (cuties) of Henri III's court ran amok with earrings, jewels, make-up and perfume, outlandish ruffs and predictably overstuffed codpieces.

Fashion in the Versailles of Louis XIV was very much subject to the moods of the king. He imposed strict regulations on

Lanvin model, 1913

the use of gold and silver braid. A much-coveted blue jerkin with gold and silver embroidered red lining could only be worn by royal patent. The court happily indulged his taste for luxury in the 1660s, women favouring extravagant combinations of satin, velvet, brocade and moiré (watered silk), men wearing gigantic wigs, feathered hats, coats covered in fringes and ribbons. But the froufrou vanished when the king got religious at the end of his reign.

Extravagance came back in the last fling of the *Ancien Régime*, with Louis XV's mistresses, Pompadour and du Barry, and Louis XVI's Marie Antoinette—crazy hairdos, exotic Oriental, Russian, Polish or Turkish costumes, turbans, feathers and tigerskins, impossibly tight corsets. The first fashion magazines appeared:

Journal du Goût and *Cabinet des Modes*. Marie Antoinette reacted against the over-sophistication with another artifice, dressing the court up as shepherds and shepherdesses. Parasols were big.

But the Revolution guillotined all that. The National Assembly wore black, and the Jacobins decreed that courtly breeches were counter-revolutionary. The true patriot *sans culotte* (literally "without breeches") had clogs, trousers with braces, a short jacket with a cotton scarf and a red bonnet with a blue, white and red rosette. Women bore a shawl *à la Charlotte Corday*, fashionable after she murdered Marat in his bathtub.

In the respite between the Revolution and Napoleon's Empire, the Directoire dandies known as the *Incroyables* (incredibles) adopted the crippled look: humpbacked coats, breeches tied at the knee to seem knock-kneed, huge cravate muffling the mouth, lorgnette, *two* watches, and charms and chains all over the place. Empire women adopted military fashions, lots of braid, epaulettes and plumed cylindri-cal shako helmets. The corset came back with the monarchy, with a metal framework and system of pulleys to permit lacing up without a chambermaid.

France's first great modern designer was an Englishman, Lincolnshire-born Charles Frederick Worth. With Napoleon III's Empress Eugénie as his most prestigious client, he set up shop on the Rue de la Paix in 1858. He was the first to use live mannequins and abandoned the crinoline. Industrial technology enabled him to create new fashions every year.

The 20th century changed as fast as a kaleidoscope. Paul Poiret liberated women from corsets in 1910 and championed a more democratic, natural look. In the 1920s two great women designers appeared, Jeanne Lanvin with a taste for an elegant frivolity of frills and flounces, and Coco Chanel emphasizing comfort and simplicity, using modest but exquisite fabrics like jersey. French fashion-consciousness continued under the wartime German occupation almost as a patriotic gesture, with women improvising shoes with wooden soles and heels, concocting fancy hats from a piece of tulle and ribbon, and painting "stockings" on their bare legs, seams and all.

After the war, Christian Dior arrived with his New Look, longer skirts with pinched waists, infuriating women who couldn't afford them. Courrèges in the 60s drew inspiration from the astronauts for his geometric, metallic styles. Cardin went plastic, Yves Saint-Laurent transparent. The Japanese arrived in the 70s and 80s — Kenzo, Hanae Mori, Issey Miyake, Yamamoto — and Germany's Karl Lagerfeld. Even for non-French designers, Paris remained the central focus. Increasingly, *prêt-à-porter* (ready-to-wear) in Left Bank boutiques replaced the prohibitively expensive *haute couture* of the Avenue Montaigne and Rue du Faubourg-Saint-Honoré as the trend-setter. A whole new French generation emerged — Castelbajac, Gaultier, Montana, Sitbon and Christian Lacroix, both elegant and rebellious — and there's no king any more to tell you how long to wear your hair.

Variously conceived as a stock exchange, the Bank of France or a theatre, the **Madeleine** doesn't look like a church, but that's what it is. Napoleon wanted to turn it into a *Temple de la Gloire* for his Great Army, but his architect persuaded him to build the Arc de Triomphe instead. The restored monarchy opted for a church, as originally planned under Louis XV. The huge Greco-Roman edifice, consecrated only in 1842, was left without transept, aisles, bell-tower or even a cross on the roof. Parisians like it most for the flower market at its base and the grand **view** from the steps down Rue Royale to Place de la Concorde.

Down on the right is Maxim's restaurant, which began as an ice-cream parlour and is now a monument more venerable than the Madeleine. Cutting across the Rue Royale, the **Rue du Faubourg-Saint-Honoré** is the city's most luxurious shopping street. At number 55, peek through the heavily guarded gates of the French president's Elysée Palace.

·Montmartre

Long famous as the home of artists and bohemian crazies, who call it "la Butte" ("the Mound"), Montmartre is an essential piece of Paris mythology. It claims a fabled past as Mons Martyrum where, after being decapitated, the town's first bishop, Saint Denis, picked up his head and walked away. Scholars insist it was really named Mons Mercurii, site of a pagan Roman temple. Difficult to decide in a neighbourhood that includes the Sacré-Cœur and Pigalle.

Topographically, Montmartre is still the little country village of 400 years ago—narrow, winding, hilly streets and dead-ends. Leave the car behind and take the métro, Porte de la Chapelle line from Concorde to Abbesses. Do *not* get off at Pigalle; however attractive you may find its lurid glitter at night, by day it might depress you into not visiting the rest of Montmartre.

From the Place des Abbesses, take Rue Ravignan to 13, place Emile-Goudeau.

This was the site of the **Bateau-Lavoir** studio, an unprepossessing glass-roofed loft reconstructed since a 1970 fire. Here, if in any one place, modern art was born: Picasso, Braque and Juan Gris developed Cubism, while Modigliani painted his own mysteries, and Apollinaire wrote his first surrealistic verses. Nearby, the illustrious predecessors of these "upstarts"—Renoir, Van Gogh, Gauguin—lived and worked in the Rue Cortot, Rue de l'Abreuvoir, Rue Saint-Rustique (site of the restaurant A la Bonne Franquette where Van Gogh painted his famous *La Guinguette*).

In artistic terms, you move from the sublime to the ludicrous at the old **Place du Tertre.** Too rich a spot to be spoiled by the daubers, this is the very centre of Montmartre's village life, where marriages were announced, militiamen enlisted and criminals hanged. Try and visit in the early morning.

On the Rue Saint-Vincent at the corner of the Rue des Saules, look out for Paris's own vineyard, the Clos de Montmartre, whose wine reputedly "makes you jump like a goat".

At the other end of the Rue Saint-Vincent, you come around the back of the **Sacré-Cœur** basilica. You have probably spotted it a hundred times during the day, so its back view will make a welcome change. This weird Romano-Byzantine church has a dubious reputation. Aesthetes scorn its over-ornate exterior and extravagant interior mosaics; working-class people of the neighbourhood resent the way it was put up as a symbol of penitence for the insurrection of the 1871 Commune and defeat in the war against the Prussians. The miraculously white façade derives from its special Château-Landon stone that whitens and hardens with age. For many, the most attractive feature is the **view** of the city you get from the dome, covering a radius of 30 miles on a clear day, or from the terrace below.

Just down the hill from the Sacré-Cœur is **Saint-Pierre-de-Montmartre,**

*P*arisians love getting upset about their artistic
monuments—Eiffel Tower, Beaubourg and, in 1986, Daniel Buren's
columns. They were commissioned for the Palais Royal by culture
minister Jack Lang, delayed by mayor Jacques Chirac and reluctantly
authorized by Lang's successor, who hated looking at them from
his ministry window. Today, public protest has died away. Children
have invented a game tossing coins from one column onto another.
Dogs like them, too.

Marais

The Marais district, north of the two river islands, has bravely withstood the onslaught of modern construction to provide a remarkably authentic record of the development of Paris from Henri IV at the end of the 16th century to the Revolution. Built on land reclaimed from the marshes, as the name suggests, some of Europe's most elegant Renaissance houses *(hôtels)* now serve as museums and libraries. It has recently become fashionable again and trendy boutiques spring up seemingly every day.

Take the métro to Rambuteau and start at the corner of Rue des Archives and **Rue des Francs-Bourgeois,** named after the poor people allowed to live there tax-free in the 14th century. The National Archives are kept here in an 18th-century mansion, **Hôtel de Soubise.** Across a vast horseshoe-shaped courtyard you rediscover the exquisite rococo of Louis XV's times in the apartments of the Prince and Princess of Soubise. Up on the first floor is the Musée de l'Histoire de France with the only known portrait of Jeanne d'Arc painted in her lifetime and the diary of Louis XVI noting for July 14, 1789: *"Rien"* ("Nothing").

A garden (not always open to the public) connects the Hôtel de Soubise with its twin, the **Hôtel de Rohan** on Rue Vieille-du-Temple. Look out for Robert le Lorrain's fine sculpted horses of Apollo over the old stables in the second courtyard.

Two other noteworthy mansions on the Rue des Francs-Bourgeois are the **Hôtel Lamoignon** at the corner of Rue Pavée and the **Hôtel Carnavalet,** home of the illustrious 17th-century lady of letters Madame de Sévigné, now the Musée Historique de la Ville de Paris.

With a fine dramatic sense, the Rue des Francs-Bourgeois ends at what many consider to be the city's most handsome residential square, **Place des Vosges.** Henri IV had it built in 1605 on the site of a horse-market. The square achieves a classical harmony with subtle diversity of

one of Paris's oldest churches. Consecrated in 1147, 16 years before the church of Saint-Germain-des-Prés (see p. 89), it represents a significant work of early Gothic art, belied by its 18th-century façade. The Sacré-Cœur's architect, Paul Abadie, wanted to demolish Saint-Pierre, but he was overruled, and a determined group of artists succeeded in having it restored, "as a worthy riposte to the Sacré-Cœur".

detail in the gables, windows and archways of its stone and red brick façades. The gardens of the square, once a favourite spot for the aristocratic duel, and, after Louis XIII's wedding festivities here, the town's most fashionable promenade, are now a pleasant children's playground. Strangely enough, the best time to see the square as a whole is in winter, when the lovely chestnut trees are bare and don't obscure the façades. In pre-Revolutionary days, the square used to be known as the Place Royale. It received its current name for the prosaic reason that the *département* of the Vosges was the first to pay up all its taxes to the Revolutionary government. Victor Hugo used to live at number 6, now a **museum** of his manuscripts, artefacts and drawings.

Finish your visit to the Marais with a walk around the old **Jewish quarter** (or *shtetl*, as Paris Jews call it) around the Rue des Rosiers. Jews have lived there continuously, apart from recurrent persecutions, since 1230, and Rue Ferdinand-Duval was known as Rue des Juifs (Jews' Street) until 1900. The other main street of the *shtetl*, Rue des Ecouffes (a medieval slang word for moneylender), completes the lively shopping district. Jews from North Africa are gradually replacing the Ashkenazi of Eastern Europe, who themselves took over from the original Sephardim. Delicatessens and *falafel* shops keep the district nicely "ecumenical".

Cimetière du Père-Lachaise

Such is the city's perpetual homage to the great of its past that cemeteries enjoy a special, not at all lugubrious place in Paris life. In a haven of calm, the grounds are beautifully kept, the avenues of tombs a fascinating walk through history. Largest of Paris's "cities of the dead", Père-Lachaise has a population estimated at 1,350,000 buried here since its foundation in 1804.

Named after Louis XIV's confessor, a member of the Jesuits who previously owned the land, the cemetery has long been renowned as the resting place for the heroes of the country's revolutions. It even served as a battleground on May 28, 1871, for the last stand of the Communards, and a "Mur des Fédérés" at the south-east corner marks the place where they were executed by firing-squads. Napoleon's emancipation of the Jews meant that they could have their own section, and Napoleon III's deference to the Turkish ambassador for his Eastern foreign policy led to an area for Muslims. Presidents of the Third Republic like Adolphe Thiers and Félix Faure lie just a stone's throw from the radicals they bitterly opposed. Père-Lachaise remains a unique site of national unity and reconciliation. A little map available at the entrance will help you locate the famous tombs. In this pantheon of the city's artistic heritage, you will find writers Colette and Alfred de Musset and Italian composer Rossini at lot No. 4, Chopin (11), philosopher Auguste Comte (17), painters Ingres (23), Corot and Daumier (24), La Fontaine and Molière (25), Sarah Bernhardt (44), Balzac (48), Delacroix (49), Bizet (68), Proust (85), Apollinaire (86), Isadora Duncan (87), Oscar Wilde (89)—with a fine monument by sculptor Jacob Epstein) and Gertrude Stein (94).

The Islands
Ile de la Cité

Shaped like a boat, the Square du Vert-Galant as its prow, the Ile de la Cité is the veritable cradle of the city of Paris, the original dwelling place of the fishermen and bargees of early Lutetia. In the middle of the 19th century, it fell victim to the over-ambitious urban planning of Baron Haussmann. The much praised but often insensitive prefect of Paris swept away most of the medieval and 17th-century structures, leaving only the Place Dauphine and Rue Chanoinesse as testimony to the island's once rich residential life.

The baron was also thinking of replacing the triangular **Place Dauphine's** gracious gabled and arcaded red brick architecture with neo-Grecian colonnades; fortunately he was forced out of office for juggling his books before the wreckers could move in. The *place* was built in 1607 by Henri IV in honour of his son the *dauphin*, later Louis XIII. (Henri's equestrian statue can be seen on the nearby Pont-Neuf.) Sadly, only the houses at number 14 and 26 are still in their original state since 18th-century property developers found it more profitable to remodel the premises.

Today, its sidewalk cafés shaded by plane trees enjoy an intimacy worlds away from the big city.

The massive **Palais de Justice**, housing the law courts of modern Paris, holds echoes of the nation's earliest kings, who dwelt here, and of the aristocrats and Revolutionary leaders who in turn were imprisoned here before execution.

It also conceals a Gothic masterpiece, the **Sainte-Chapelle**. The delicate walls of 13th-century stained glass (Paris's oldest) and harmonious proportions confer an ethereal quality upon the chapel, in startling contrast to the ponderous palace surrounding it. It was completed in 1248 by the sainted King Louis IX to house relics such as Christ's crown of thorns. There are in fact two chapels, the lower for retainers and the upper for the king and his retinue. The 15 **stained-glass windows** depict 1,134 scenes from the Bible; 720 of them are 13th-century originals.

Between 1789 and 1815, the chapel served variously as a flour warehouse, a clubhouse for high-ranking dandies and finally as an archive for Bonaparte's Consulate. That saved the chapel from projected destruction, because the bureaucrats didn't know where else to put their mountains of paperwork. These days they find space in the endless corridors of offices around the courtrooms of the Palais and the "Maigret country" of the *police judiciaire*. The great Salle des Pas Perdus is worth a visit for a glimpse of the lawyers, plaintiffs, witnesses, court reporters and hangers-on waiting nervously for the wheels of French justice to grind into action.

But their anxiety is nothing in comparison to that of those condemned to bide their time in the prison of the **Conciergerie** during the Revolutionary Terror (1793–94). Named after the royally appointed *concierge* in charge of common-law criminals, this "antechamber of the guillotine" welcomed Marie-Antoinette and Robespierre, Madame du Barry and Saint-Just, Danton and 2,500 others who all spent their last nights in these grim dungeons after the Revolutionary tribunals had pronounced sentence. Take the guided tour of the Galerie des Prisonniers. The Salle des Girondins displays a guillotine blade, the crucifix to which Marie-Antoinette prayed before execution and the lock of Robespierre's cell. Look out on the Cour des Femmes, where husbands, lovers, wives and mistresses were allowed one last tryst before the tumbrels came.

The site of the cathedral of **Notre-Dame de Paris** has had a religious sig-

Lucrative Sacrilege

After 1789, the Sainte-Chapelle remained intact, unlike many other churches. The destruction it narrowly avoided would not have been, as is too often believed, at the hands of violent, God-hating Revolutionaries. It would have been undertaken by peace-loving, profit-minded entrepreneurs who made a fortune during and long after the Revolution by dismantling churches and monasteries to build factories and houses from their masonry. Such, for instance, was the fate of the great abbeys of Jumièges in Normandy (see p. 154) and Cluny in southern Burgundy (p. 142).

Undeniably, Revolutionary crowds did plunder the church's treasury, venting their spleen on a Church that had for centuries taxed and exploited them, more for the clerics' personal benefit than for the spiritual welfare of their flock. The aesthetic considerations of later generations did not count for much during a revolution, either for the have-nots or for the haves.

nificance for at least 2,000 years. In Roman times a temple to Jupiter stood here, followed in the 4th century by the first Christian church, Saint-Etienne. A second church, dedicated to Our Lady, joined it 200 years later. Both were left derelict by Norman invaders until the bishop Maurice de Sully authorized construction of the cathedral to replace them in 1163. The main part of Notre-Dame took 167 years to complete and, in its transition from Romanesque to Gothic, it has been called a perfect expression of medieval architecture.

One dissenting voice was that of St. Bernard, who protested that the godly virtue of poverty would be insulted by the erection of such a sumptuous structure. And some architectural purists today find Notre-Dame a bit "too much". But it was built to inspire awe.

Old Baron Haussmann comes in for criticism again, because he greatly enlarged the *parvis,* or square, in front of the cathedral, thereby diminishing, it is said, the grandiose impact of the western façade. Others argue this brought back the animated street-life of the square, recapturing some of the gaiety of the Middle Ages when the *parvis* was used for public executions and the populace was invited to throw old fruit and rotten eggs provided by the authorities.

The cathedral remains an impressive monument, truly the nation's parish church. It has witnessed, in 1239, Louis IX walking barefoot with his holy treasure, Christ's crown of thorns (before the Sainte-Chapelle was built); in 1430, the humiliation of having Henry VI of England crowned King of France; in 1594, Henri IV attending the mass which sealed his conversion to Catholicism and reinforced his hold on the French throne; in 1804, Napoleon's coronation as emperor, attended by the pope but climaxed by Napoleon crowning himself; and in more recent times, the state funerals of military heroes such as Foch, Joffre, Leclerc and de Gaulle.

Despite its gigantic size, the cathedral achieves a great balance in its proportions and harmony in its façade. The superb central **rose window**, encircling a statue of the Madonna and Child, depicts the Redemption after the Fall. Look for the **Galerie des Rois** across the top of the three doorways. The 28 statues representing the kings of Judah and Israel have been remodelled after the drawings of the great restorer-architect Eugène Viollet-le-Duc; the originals were pulled down during the Revolution because they were thought to be the kings of France. (The 21 heads discovered in 1977 are displayed in the Musée de Cluny, see p. 98.)

Inside, the marvellous lighting is due in part to two more outsize rose windows dominating the transept. On the right of the entrance to the choir is a lovely statue of the **Virgin and Child**.

As with many Gothic masterpieces, the first architect is anonymous, but the renowned Pierre de Montreuil is credited with much of the 13th-century work. In the 18th century, more damage was done

Habitués of the Métro offer tips for tired feet: avoid if possible major stations like Montparnasse, Etoile or Châtelet, where you end up walking further than you ride. For Montmartre, avoid Pigalle station, where frequent elevator breakdowns impose a climb of hundreds of stairs. Station-names offer some amusing games. Revolutionary Bastille going north-east takes you via Stalingrad (of course, say reactionaries) to the enlightened terminus of Bobigny Pablo Picasso. Next stop after Kremlin-Bicêtre is Maison Blanche (White House).

by the "improvements" of redecorators of the *Ancien Régime* than by Revolutionary iconoclasts. For the present structure, we must be grateful to Viollet-le-Duc, who worked centimetre-by-centimetre over the whole edifice from 1845 to 1863. He was working in response to the public outcry started by Victor Hugo's novel, *Notre-Dame de Paris*.

The only original bell left is the South Tower's *bourdon*, whose much admired purity of tone was achieved by melting down its bronze to mix it with gold and silver donated by Louis XIV's aristocracy. Today, the bells are operated not by a hunchback but by an electric system installed in 1953.

For greatest effect, visit alone by rising at crack of dawn when the cleaning ladies open up.

Ile Saint-Louis

Very much a world apart, the Ile Saint-Louis is an enchanted self-contained island of gracious living, long popular with the affluent gentry of Paris. President Georges Pompidou lived here (on the Quai de Béthune), much preferring it to the Elysée Palace. In the magnificent 17th-century **Hôtel Lambert**, on the corner of Rue Saint-Louis-en-l'Ile, Voltaire carried on a tempestuous affair with the lady of the house, the Marquise du Châtelet.

The island's church, **Saint-Louis-en-l'Ile**, is as elegant as the mansions, bright and airy with a golden light illuminating a marvellous collection of Dutch, Flemish and Italian 16th- and 17th-century art and some superb tapestries from the 12th century.

One of the most notable mansions is the **Hôtel Lauzun** (17, quai d'Anjou), built in the 1650s by the great architect of Versailles, Louis Le Vau. Its highly ornamental interiors provided a perfect setting for the fantasies of the Club des Haschischins founded by the poets Charles Baudelaire and Théophile Gautier.

Today, they've been replaced by a veritable club of ice-cream eaters, for whom the island's greatest attraction is to buy a cone from the local merchant and stroll along the poplar-shaded streets to the western end of Quai d'Orléans. There, you have the most wonderful **view** of the apse of Notre-Dame, much more romantic than the cathedral's "front".

Left Bank

Latin Quarter

Perfectly simple: from the 13th century, when the city's first university moved from the cloisters of Notre-Dame to the Left Bank, the young came to the *quartier* to learn Latin.

In those days *l'université* meant merely a collection of people—students who met on a street corner, in a public square or courtyard to hear a teacher lecture them from a bench, an upstairs window or balcony. Today there are classrooms—overcrowded, but the tradition of open-air discussion continues, often over an endlessly nursed coffee or glass of wine on a sidewalk café on the Boulevard Saint-Michel, in the streets around the faculty buildings or in the ever-present cinema queues.

Begin at the **Place Saint-Michel**, where Paris students come to buy their textbooks and stationery, and the young of other countries come to sniff the Latin Quarter's mystique (and other more heady stuff), around the bombastic Second Empire fountain. Plunge into the narrow streets of the Saint-Séverin quarter—to the east, Rue de la Huchette, Rue de la Harpe and Rue Saint-Séverin—into a medieval world updated by the varied exotica of Turkish pastry shops, smoky Greek barbecues and stuffy little cinemas. A moment's meditation in the exquisite 13th–15th-century Flamboyant Gothic church of Saint-Séverin, where Dante is said to have prayed, and you are ready to confront the Latin Quarter's citadel, the **Sorbonne**.

Founded in 1253 as a college for poor theological students by Robert de Sorbon, Louis IX's chaplain, it took shape as an embodiment of the university under the tutelage of Cardinal Richelieu. In the Grand amphithéâtre, which seats 2,700, you can see the Cardinal's statue along with those of Descartes, Pascal and Lavoisier, the great chemist.

As you look at Puvis de Chavannes' monumental painting on the back wall, allegorizing Poetry, Philosophy, History, Geology and the other disciplines, try to imagine 4,000 students packed into that hall in May 1968, arguing whether to have the whole thing plastered over. The student revolt against overcrowding, antiquated teaching and bureaucracy as the symbols of a dehumanized social system made the Sorbonne a focal point of the movement. When police invaded its precincts—which for centuries had guaranteed student immunity—the rebellion erupted into the streets.

Around the corner, as a kind of didactic inspiration for the students on what hard work can achieve, stands the gigantic neo-Classic **Panthéon**, resting place of the nation's military, political and literary heroes. Originally designed as the church of Sainte-Geneviève for Louis XV (1755), it was secularized during the Revolution as a vast mausoleum with the inscription "To our great men, the Fatherland's gratitude". But the Revolutionaries had a hard time deciding who merited the honour. Mirabeau and then Marat were interred and subsequently expelled. Napoleon ended the controversy by turning the Panthéon back into a church. Throughout the 19th century it went back and forth between secular and consecrated status, according to the regime's political colour. Finally Victor Hugo's funeral in 1885, the biggest the capital had seen, settled the Panthéon's status as a secular mausoleum. Hugo was buried there, followed (retroactively) by Voltaire and Rousseau, and then by prime minister Léon Gambetta, socialist leader Jean Jaurès, Emile Zola, inventor of the blind alphabet Louis Braille, President Raymond Poincaré and many others. The most recent

hero to be so honoured was the World War II Resistance fighter, Jean Moulin.

Time for a break in the **Jardin du Luxembourg**. If you want to picnic in the park (sorry, not on the grass), make a detour first to the old street market behind the Panthéon on the **Rue Mouffetard**, by the tiny Place de la Contrescarpe, old hunting-ground of Rabelais and Rabelaisians ever since. Despite their 17th-century origins, the Luxembourg Gardens avoid the rigid geometry of the Tuileries and Versailles. The horse chestnuts, beeches and plane trees, the orangery and ornamental pond were a major inspiration for the bucolic paintings of Watteau.

Montparnasse

In the twenties, Montparnasse took over from Montmartre as the stomping ground of the capital's artistic colony, or at least of its avant-garde. American expatriates such as Hemingway, Fitzgerald, Gertrude Stein, John Dos Passos and Theodore Dreiser also contributed to the free-living mystique.

Other quarters are known for their palaces and churches; Montparnasse (named after a 17th-century gravel mound since removed) has cafés and bars

Right Moves
The neighbourhoods of the Left Bank trace from east to west the inexorable career of a successful Parisian intellectual—heart on the left, wallet on the right. The forces of protest and outright revolt have traditionally been nurtured in the *Quartier latin*, before subsiding into the lifelong scepticism voiced in the cafés of Saint-Germain-des-Prés. The rebels graduate from the university and move, if they prosper, west to the more genteel Faubourg Saint-Germain, closer to their publishers. If they hit the jackpot—a bestseller, their own law practice, even a ministry—they can move on to the more spacious apartments around the Champ-de-Mars, with a view of the Eiffel Tower for the kids. Without crossing the river to the notoriously snobbish 16th *arrondissement*, they can enjoy the same comforts and claim that they're still on the Left Bank.

for landmarks, most of them along **Boulevard du Montparnasse**. The Closerie des Lilas, a centre for French Symbolist poets at the turn of the century, served as a meeting-place for Lenin and Trotsky before World War I and for Hemingway and his pals after the war; the Select, first all-night bar to open in Montparnasse, in 1925, quickly became a Henry Miller hang-out and continues resolutely to resist efforts to spruce it up; after renovation, La Coupole, more living theatre than restaurant, hopes to recapture its old glory when it was a favourite of Sartre and Simone de Beauvoir; breakfast was taken at the Dôme, for a change of air; and the Rotonde, favoured by Picasso, Vlaminck and Modigliani, is back as a restaurant after a spell as a cinema. Around the corner, on Boulevard Raspail, is a splendid Rodin bronze of Balzac.

The Latin Quarter, with the church of Saint-Séverin here at the centre of the entertainment district, has always offered hospitality to genius and thuggery, poets and pickpockets. Its patron sinner, François Villon, who hung out here in the 15th century, combined all these qualities and escaped the gallows thanks only to the intercession of Louis IX himself.

Habitués just pretend not to see the monstrous 58-floor Tour Maine-Montparnasse office block by the railway station.

Saint-Germain-des-Prés

Saint-Germain-des-Prés is the literary quarter par excellence, home of the major publishing houses, the *Académie française,* bookshops and literary cafés. But it's also a charming neighbourhood for day-long people-watching, antique-hunting and gallery-hopping.

The cafés around the **Place Saint-Germain-des-Prés** are the "village centre". On the north side is the Café Bonaparte, on the west the famous les Deux Magots (funny Chinese statues). Both provide ringside seats for the street theatre of mimes and musicians, who pass around the hat, and for the neighbourhood eccentrics, who do it for free.

The Café de Flore up the boulevard has more intellectual aspirations, with a rather confusing ideological history. During the Dreyfus Affair it was headquarters for the extreme right-wing *Action française*; in 1914 the home of Surrealists Apollinaire and André Salmon, who liked provoking brawls; and, in the fifties, Sartre's more peaceful left-wing existentialists, who never got enough sleep to find the energy to fight.

The **church** of Saint-Germain-des-Prés is an attractive mixture of Romanesque and Gothic, with an 11th-century clocktower.

North of the church, the Rue Bonaparte takes you to the prestigious **Ecole des Beaux-Arts**. Incorporated in its structure are fragments of medieval and Renaissance architecture and sculpture. On the Rue des Beaux-Arts is the hotel (now simply but expensively called l'Hôtel) where Oscar Wilde died in 1900. He complained about the "horrible magenta flowers" of his room's wallpaper, saying "one of us has to go". Now both have.

The august and handsome **Institut de France**, home of the *Académie française,* is on the Quai Conti by the Pont des Arts. It was built by Louis Le Vau in 1668 to harmonize with the Louvre across the river. The *Académie* was founded by Richelieu to be the supreme arbiter of the French language. Periodically decried as a bunch of prestigious old fuddy-duddies, the 40 lifetime members are chosen in hotly contested elections to update the Academy's French dictionary, but are distinguished mostly for their acceptance speeches and obituaries. Guides to the Institut like to point out the east pavilion, site of the 14th-century Tour de Nesle. They say Queen Jeanne de Bourgogne used to watch from there for likely young lovers whom she summoned for the night and then had thrown into the Seine.

The **Palais-Bourbon**, seat of the National Assembly, provides a rather formidable riverside façade for the Left Bank's most stately district—the elegant 7th *arrondissement* with its 18th-century foreign embassies, ministries and noble residences *(hôtels particuliers)*. The Grecian columns facing the Pont de la Concorde were added under Napoleon and belie the more graceful character of the Palais-Bourbon as seen from its real entrance on the south side. Designed as a residence for a daughter of Louix XIV in 1722, this government building can be visited only on written request or as the guest of a deputy. If you do get in, look for the Delacroix paintings on the history of civilization in the library.

The Foreign Ministry next to the *palais,* better known as the **Quai d'Orsay,** is more distinguished for its diplomatic language than its architecture (nondescript Louis-Philippe).

If you are more interested in gracious living than supreme power, you will probably agree with those who feel it's better to be prime minister and live at the **Hôtel Matignon** than be president at the Elysée Palace (in fact, President Mitterrand prefers to sleep in his Latin Quarter apartment in the Rue de Bièvre). The prime minister's magnificent residence at 57 Rue de Varenne is just a short walk from the Palais-Bourbon. Its huge private park has a delightful music pavilion much favoured for secret strategy sessions. The same tranquil street, a veritable museum of 18th-century elegance, contains the Italian Embassy, known as the **Hôtel de La Rochefoucauld-Doudeauville** (No. 47), and the Rodin Museum (see p. 98) in the **Hôtel Biron** (No. 77), which served as the home of Rodin, of poet Rainer Maria Rilke and dancer Isadora Duncan.

Invalides–Eiffel Tower

The massively monumental **Hôtel des Invalides** was founded by Louis XIV as the first national hospital for soldiers. Housing today the Musée de l'Armée, it is also the supreme celebration of Napoleon, since his body was brought here in 1840 from the island of Saint Helena. Awesomely elaborate, **Napoleon's**

tomb is set in the crypt directly under the Invalides' golden dome. His body, dressed in the green uniform of the Chasseurs de la Garde, is encased in *six* coffins, one inside the other Chinese-box-fashion. The first is of iron, the second mahogany, then two of lead, one of ebony and the outer one of oak. The monument of red porphyry from Finland rests on a green granite pedestal, encircled by 12 colossal Victory pillars sculpted by Pradier.

Also in the crypt are the remains of the Emperor's son, brought to France from Vienna in 1940 by Adolf Hitler.

The military complex continues with the Ecole militaire and the spacious gardens of the **Champ-de-Mars**, once the site of military exercises and parades and more recently the series of world's fairs held between 1867 and 1937.

There are monuments and there is the **Eiffel Tower**. Some celebrate heroes, commemorate victories, honour kings and saints. The *Tour Eiffel* is a monument for its own sake, a proud gesture to the world, a witty structure that makes aesthetics irrelevant. Its construction for the World's Fair of 1889 was an astounding engineering achievement— 15,000 pieces of metal joined together by 2,500,000 rivets, soaring 300 metres (984 feet) into the air on a base covering only 130 square metres (1,400 square feet).

Like many other World's Fair exhibits, the tower was slated for destruction, but nobody had the heart to go through with it. Though many intellectuals hated it. Guy de Maupassant signed a manifesto against "this vertiginously ridiculous tower". The poet Verlaine rerouted his journey around Paris to avoid seeing it (difficult now, almost impossible then).

Today, everyone seems to love it. It has a splendid inner illumination at night, a popular *brasserie* on the first platform, elegant gourmet restaurant on the second, and a **view** from the top stretching over 60 kilometres (40 miles) on a pollution-free day.

Bois de Boulogne

These 900 hectares (2,224 acres) of parkland on the western edge of the city constitute one of the happier achievements of Baron Haussmann. He transformed the old Rouvray forest, left completely wild until 1852, into the closest thing Paris has to a London-style park: roads and paths for cycling and rambles, horse-trails, boating lakes, restaurants and cafés with open-air dancing, plus the grand racecourse at Longchamp.

One of the main attractions is the **Parc de Bagatelle**, a walled garden with the city's most beautiful display of flowers. For the children, the **Jardin d'acclimatation** offers a miniature railway, Punch and Judy show, house of distorting mirrors, pony-rides and a miniature farm of pigs, goats and chickens.

Romance

A bewitching conspiracy that began with the 15th-century poet François Villon and continued with Maurice Chevalier, Gene Kelly and Edith Piaf has made Paris the supreme city of romance. This is the town, they say, where broken hearts come to mend, where faltering marriages perk up and casual friendships grow brighter with the city's enchanted light. There are places ideally suited for a kiss, a poem, an engagement ring, or whatever other madness this town may drive you to.

Ideal places for whispered tenderness include the Rue Berton, a country lane behind Balzac's house that seems a million miles away from its 16th *arrondissement*. No kiss ever failed here. The Jardin du Vert-Galant, at the tip of the Ile de la Cité, is imbued with the lusty spirit of Henri IV. On a moonlit night, the view of the Seine from this tree-enclosed triangle is the stuff dreams are made of. A few steps from the bustle of Place Saint-Germain-des-Prés is Rue de Furstemberg's tiny square. Let the gentle lamplight, softened by the shadows of exotic paulownia trees, work its magic.

How can you miss in a city that is love's open and unashamed accomplice?

Museums

The Louvre

The Louvre museum is so huge that people are sometimes frightened to go in at all. But you do not have to be an art fanatic to realize that to come to Paris without setting foot inside this great and truly beautiful palace would be a crime. No other museum in the world has such a comprehensive collection of painting and sculpture. If you do it right, it can be an exhilarating pleasure.

First of all, get up very early on a sunny day and walk across the gardens of the Place du Carrousel. Admire Maillol's nubile statues and then sit on a bench to take in the sheer immensity of this home of France's kings and monumental showcase of a world's treasures.

At the east end is the Cour Carrée, covering the original fortress built by Philippe Auguste in 1190 to protect Paris from river attack while he was away on a crusade. Stretching out from the Cour Carrée (of which you should see Perrault's marvellous colonnade on the east façade) are the additions of François I, Henri IV, Catherine de Médicis, Louis XIV, Napoleon, Napoleon III and of François Mitterrand, who completed eight centuries of construction with the great glass pyramid in the Cour Napoléon.

The latest addition, designed by American architect I.M. Pei, provides a spectacular modern entrance, together with underground bookshops and cafés, at the centre of corridors leading to the various wings of the museum, further expanded by the removal of the Finance Ministry from the north wing on Rue de Rivoli.

François I, the Louvre's first major art collector, acquired four Raphaels, three Leonardo da Vincis and one Titian (portrait of the king himself). By 1793, when the leaders of the Revolution declared the palace a national museum, there were 650 works of art in the collection; at the most recent inventory, there were 250,000.

So don't be depressed if you don't see everything.

If you're planning several visits, you might like to concentrate on just one section at a time—the Italians, the French, the Spanish, the Flemish and Dutch, but also the ancient Egyptians, the Greeks and Romans.

For an overall view of the collections, we've attempted a first selection:

Egyptians: lion-headed goddess *Sekhmet* (1400 B.C.) and the colossal *Amenophis IV* (1370 B.C.).

Greeks: the winged *Victory of Samothrace* and the beautifully proportioned *Venus de Milo*.

Italians: the sculpture of *Two Slaves* by Michelangelo; Leonardo da Vinci's fabled *Mona Lisa (La Joconde)*, but also his sublime *Virgin of the Rocks*; Titian's voluptuous *Woman at Her Toilet* and sombre *Entombment of Christ*; the poignant *Old Man and His Grandson* of Ghirlandaio.

French: Poussin's bittersweet *Arcadian Shepherds*; Watteau's hypnotically melancholy *Gilles* and graceful *Embarkation for Cythera*; Delacroix's *Liberty Guiding the People* and Courbet's piercing study of provincial bourgeoisie, *Funeral at Ornans*.

Dutch and Flemish: Rembrandt's cheerful *Self-Portrait with a Toque*, his beloved *Hendrickje Stoffels*, also portrayed nude in *Bathsheba Bathing*; Van Dyck's gracious, dignified *Charles I* of England; among the scores of "official" Rubens, his tenderly personal *Helena Fourment*; Jordaens' *Four Evangelists* as diligent Dutchmen.

Germans: a gripping *Self-Portrait* by Dürer; Holbein's *Erasmus*.

Spanish: the uncompromising Velázquez portrait of ugly *Queen Marianna of Austria*; El Greco's powerfully mystic *Christ on the Cross*; Ribera's gruesomely good-humoured *The Club Foot*.

English: Gainsborough's exquisite *Conversation in a Park*; Turner's *Landscape with River and Bay*; and **American** art is represented by Whistler's *Mother*.

French Painting

LOUIS LE NAIN
Repas de paysans
Peasants' Meal

GEORGES DE LA TOUR
Le vielleur
Hurdy-Gurdy Player

The first really forceful painters to emerge on the French scene were the three brothers **Le Nain,** Antoine (1588–1648), Louis (c. 1593–1648) and Mathieu (c. 1607–77). Resisting prevailing Italian and Flemish influences, they marked their 17th century with deeply felt scenes of simple, very French peasant life, light years away from Baroque opulence.

In following Caravaggio's dramatic use of light and shadow, Georges de **La Tour** (1593–1652) was less robust but added a certain Gallic style and elegance for his religious subjects and genre scenes of musicians, card players and fortune-tellers. Two other 17th-century French artists, Nicolas **Poussin** (1594–1665) and Claude **Gelée** (1600–82; known in France as Le Lorrain) went to work in Rome. With impeccable technical mastery but little emotion, Poussin was still fascinated by the classical Greek mythological scenes that Italian Renaissance painters had exhausted a hundred years earlier. For Claude Gelée, classical figures and temples, often painted almost invisibly tiny, were just pretexts for his major preoccupation, romantically lit landscapes beneath majestic skies.

On closer inspection, Antoine **Watteau's** (1684–1721) disturbing paintings of 18th-century life at court reveal something melancholy, almost sinister about all that frivolity. The worm is in the apple. François **Boucher** (1703–70) has no such worries in his jolly pink eroticism. Jean-Honoré **Fragonard** (1732–1806)

WATTEAU
Gilles

DELACROIX
Liberté guidant le peuple
Liberty guiding the people

takes his lovers more seriously. J.B. **Chardin's** (1699–1779) preoccupations are more down-to-earth, a hard-working laundress, a peasant-woman drawing water from the well, lovingly treated still-lifes of a loaf of bread or bottle of wine.

During and after the Revolution, Jacques-Louis **David's** (1748–1825) noble neo-Classic paintings extolled the heroic virtues of ancient Rome as an example for the challenges of modern life. Jean-Auguste-Dominique **Ingres** (1780–1867) was his faithful student and superior draughtsman, but occasionally escaped solemn classicism to paint vigorous and grippingly realistic portraits of his patrons.

Eugène **Delacroix** (1798–1863) cared about formal craftsmanship, too, but his romantic temperament accentuated intense emotion with bold colour and sweeping brush-strokes in his vivid portrayals of plague, insurrection and war.

CÉZANNE
Self-portrait

Meanwhile, a quiet little revolution was taking place just south of Paris, in Barbizon, where a school of artists gathered to do the unheard-of thing of painting landscapes on the spot, rather than back in the studio from sketchbooks. Camille **Corot** (1796–1875) painted his lyrical meadows and

The Impressionists burst on the scene in 1874 with their defiant exhibition of anti-academic depictions of real vibrant light, a hint of mist, shimmering colour, as it caught the attention at one particular moment. People were upset because Camille **Pissarro** (1830–1903), Claude **Monet** (1840–1926),

GAUGUIN
Femmes de Tahiti
Women of Tahiti

woodland with subdued greens and silvery greys, characteristically highlighted by the tiny red or blue bonnet of a passing peasant. Jean-François **Millet's** (1814–75) anthems to the nobility of toil placed his peasants squarely in the foreground.

Gustave **Courbet's** (1819–77) subjects were also most often the common people, but painted with such uncompromising directness, as in his famous *Funeral at Ornans*, that he was immediately branded as a dangerous socialist. In his landscapes, you could positively smell the damp earth and other things. Most unseemly.

Alfred **Sisley** (1839–99) and Edgar **Degas** (1834–1917) no longer seemed interested in eternity, whether in a landscape, a shop or a railway station. Cézanne said of Monet what he might have said of all Impressionists: "Monet is only an eye. But what an eye!"

Georges **Seurat** (1859–91) and, even more, Paul **Cézanne** (1839–1906) moved beyond the instant to treat their themes, whether landscapes or still-lifes, as a composition of form and light in which the objects themselves almost disappear. Cézanne's apples are all but abstract; Paul **Gauguin's** (1848–1903) are only slightly less.

Pablo **Picasso** (1881–1973) and Georges **Braque** (1882–1963) made the abstract leap, the Spaniard being an eternal adventurer, exploring and innovating in every corner of modern art, while Braque, his Cubist companion, pursued his art with more restraint and subtle elegance. Most inventive and daring of 20th-century artists, Henri **Matisse** (1869–1954) alternated his expressionistic use of colour, drawing on rich Oriental themes, with a sober simplified graphic style.

Beaubourg

The official name of Europe's most spectacular cultural centre is Centre d'art et de culture Georges-Pompidou, shortened to Centre Pompidou (after the French president whose pet project it was). But somehow Parisians have an aversion to naming their major monuments after their political leaders, and so this bright and dynamic monster will probably always be known quite simply as Beaubourg, after the 13th-century neighbourhood surrounding it.

The combination of public library, modern art museum, children's workshop, *cinémathèque*, industrial design centre, experimental music laboratory and open-air circus on the front plaza is the most popular show in town, a permanent hive of activity.

After an initial reaction similar to the delight and rage originally provoked by the Eiffel Tower, people have grown accustomed to the construction's resemblance to a multicoloured oil refinery. The comparison is readily accepted by its architects, Italians Renzo Piano and Gianfranco Franchi and Englishman Richard Rogers, who deliberately left the building's service system visible and colour-coded: red for the transportation (elevators and escalators), green for the water pipes, blue for the air-conditioning ducts and yellow for the electrical system.

One of Beaubourg's simplest pleasures is just going up the escalators in the long glass tubes that run diagonally from the bottom-left to the top-right-hand corner. Watch Paris unfold in front of your eyes with a stunning **view** of the city's rooftops—best on the *fourth*, not the fifth floor.

Other Major Museums

Though physically part of the Louvre, the **Musée des Arts décoratifs** is a separate museum with its own entrance at 107, rue de Rivoli. The rich permanent collection includes tapestries, furniture and porcelain, but look out for the fascinating temporary exhibitions featuring great styles and eras of design history such as Jugendstil, Bauhaus and the American fifties. Next door is the **Musée national des Arts de la mode**, devoted to the decorative art of which Paris is still the world capital, high fashion.

Right across the river, the 19th-century Orsay railway station has been transformed into the **Musée d'Orsay**. This exciting museum embraces France's tremendous creativity from 1848 to 1914 in the domains of painting, sculpture, architecture and industrial design, advertising, newspapers, book publishing, photography and the early years of the cinema. It also displays the famous collection of Impressionists and their followers transferred from the Jeu de Paume museum.

On the river side of the Tuileries, the **Orangerie** is best known for its ground-floor rooms decorated with Monet's beautiful *Nymphéas* murals, offering a moment of repose after a hard day's sightseeing. But you should also take a look upstairs at the excellent Walter-Guillaume collection of Cézanne, Renoir, Utrillo, Douanier Rousseau and Picasso.

From the private collections of Picasso's heirs, the **Musée Picasso** (5, rue de Thorigny in the Marais, métro Saint-Paul) has over 200 paintings and 158 sculptures, in addition to hundreds of drawings, engravings, ceramics and models for theatre décors and costumes. It also exhibits the artist's personal collection of masterworks by fellow painters Braque, Matisse, Miró, Degas, Renoir and Rousseau.

Housed in the beautifully restored 17th-century mansion, Hôtel Salé, the museum offers a moving portrait of the man, his family, his mistresses and friends, with letters, manuscripts, photo albums, notebooks, his French Communist Party membership card, bullfight tickets and holiday postcards.

La Villette (on the north-east corner of town, métro Porte de la Villette) has been converted from the world's biggest slaughterhouse to a striking futuristic complex of cultural and scientific activities. Refusing to call itself a museum, La Villette's **Cité des Sciences et de l'Industrie** puts the accent on public participation in all phases of space technology, computers, astronomy and marine biology. The unabashed functionalism of its architecture carries the Beaubourg principle to a logical conclusion. Its most attractive symbol is the shining stainless steel **Géode** sphere housing a revolutionary cinema with a hemispheric screen 36 metres (118 feet) in diameter. There's also a giant rock-concert hall, **Le Zénith**, alongside the avant-garde musical counterpart to the scientific museum, sorry, city: **Cité de la Musique**.

In the Palais de Chaillot (Trocadéro): **Musée de l'Homme**, devoted to man's prehistory, and the fascinating **Musée du Cinéma**, with reconstructed sets and studios, historic posters, original scripts, costumes of Greta Garbo and Catherine Deneuve, John Wayne's hat and Rudolf Valentino's jellaba.

And: **Musée de Cluny** (6, place Paul-Painlevé, métro Maubert-Mutualité), for the great *Lady with the Unicorn* tapestry, but also sculpture of Paris's Roman and Gothic past; **Musée Guimet** (6, place d'Iéna), a superb collection of Indian, Japanese and Chinese art; **Musée de l'Affiche** (18, rue de Paradis), advertising posters of the past and present.

Many museums are devoted to the work and life of just one artist, the best of these being **Rodin** (77, rue de Varenne), with its lovely sculpture garden; but look, too, for the home of **Balzac** (47, rue Raynouard) and **Delacroix's** studio (6, Rue de Furstemberg). For other similar museums outside Paris, see p. 306.

Sèvres

On the fringes of Paris, perhaps, but very much a "Paris" museum is the national **Ceramics Museum** *(Musée national de céramique)*, Place de la Manufacture at Sèvres. Don't be put off by the gloomy 19th-century building; its magnificent collections trace the history of ceramics from ancient Egypt, Greece and pre-Columbian America to the modern day. Naturally enough, Sèvres' own production figures prominently, notably a spectacular Etruscan-style vase of 1813, portraying the arrival at the Louvre of art-works pillaged by Napoleon in Italy. But other nations are not slighted: Italian Faënza, German Meissen, Dutch Delft and superb examples from Islamic Spain, Korea and China. You can buy Sèvres china and fine replicas of museum pieces at the museum-shop.

Immediately north of the museum is the delightful **park of Saint-Cloud**, perfect for picnics and bicycling along forest paths (rentals inside the park).

*I*nside, the Géode's Omnimax 180° projection system plunges you into a film-world of natural and man-made miracles. Outside, the surface of the steel dome seems to absorb the whole universe, fitting symbol for the surrounding City of Science and Industry.

Ile-de-France

There's a wide range of varied day trips from Paris within easy reach and well served by rail or coach.

If you had just one excursion to choose, it would really have to be Versailles, *gloire oblige,* which is where we begin, before moving gradually "outwards".

ⱳ Versailles *10,B2*

This most popular of excursions from Paris is an easy day trip, just 21 kilometres (13 miles) from the capital, but to do it justice, calculate a full day, with a very early start.

Organized bus tours start at the Tuileries Gardens on the Rue de Rivoli side. However, the palace and gardens are so enormous that you may prefer to do them at your own pace, leaving out what your head and feet can't take.

With a little planning, an otherwise tiring day can be a delightful treat. Try the following agenda: early start at a Paris street market to buy a picnic (better than the Versailles tourist traps); morning tour of the palace; stroll through the palace gardens to lunch beside the Grand Canal; siesta and tea in the gardens of the Petit Trianon; wander back across the palace gardens for a last sunset view of the great château.

The Palace

If you don't already have a clear idea of what kind of man Louis XIV was, take a long, hard look at his palace. Never did a piece of architecture more exactly express the personality of its builder than the Château de Versailles—extravagant, pompous, dazzling, formidable, glorious, vainglorious.

Louis XIII had hoped to turn his favourite hunting ground into a modest retirement home. For his son, Versailles became the centre of a universe, proclaiming his own grandeur in a sprawling edifice of stone and brick, marble, gilt and crystal.

The palace has been splendidly restored since World War I with private contributions, most notably of that transatlantic Sun King, J. D. Rockefeller. Wherever the original furnishings and decoration are missing, superb appropriate equivalents have been installed.

As you make your way through the gilded gates and cross the vast Cour des Ministres where the state secretaries worked, past the imperious statue of Himself to the main entrance on the right of the Cour Royale, you realize it wasn't Mussolini who invented the Long Walk to intimidate his underlings seeking an audience.

Inside, the self-guided tour is instantly more reassuring. You begin at the intimate little **Royal Chapel**, a gem of High

---

*O*n your way out to the palaces and cathedrals of the Ile-de-France, take a look at some of the more adventurous new suburbs that have sprung up around Paris in recent years. This one, Cergy-Pontoise, was designed by architect Roland Castro, a leading figure in the 1968 student revolution given the opportunity to put into practice some of his ideas for humanizing modern architecture. The results need the patina of time to confirm his promise.

Baroque, a harmonious décor of white marble with gilded altar and balustrades. You get the king's-eye-view looking down into the nave where the courtiers worshipped.

In the rooms of the **Grands Appartements,** named after the gods and goddesses whom Louis felt to be his appropriate companions, the king entertained his courtiers three times a week: Monday, Wednesday and Thursday. The **Salon de Diane** was a billiard room—not many people could beat Fast Louis. The table's gone, but Bernini has left a superb bust of the champion at 27. The ceiling painting of the Sun King in his chariot and pictorial references to Alexander the Great and Augustus Caesar make it clear the **Salon d'Apollon** was Louis XIV's throne room.

But the most astonishing of these royal apartments is the glittering **Galerie des Glaces,** 73 metres (240 feet) long, built to catch every ray of the setting sun in the 17 tall arched panels of mirrors. This

---

Statistics of Grandeur
Not just a whim of megalomania, building Versailles was Louis XIV's cold political decision to force his hitherto obstreperous nobles into submission by impoverishing them with permanent attendance at his court. To house the 3,000 courtiers and servants, the palace took 50 years to build, spanning the whole of his long reign and still incomplete at his death.

Louis Le Vau and Jules Hardouin-Mansart were the architects, Charles Le Brun directed the interior design and monumental sculpture, while André Le Nôtre laid out the gardens. Of the 36,000-strong work force (plus 6,000 horses), 227 men died on the job.

The 115 hectares (280 acres) of gardens and parkland are only a tenth of what had to be tended for the Sun King—including 150,000 flower plants that were changed 15 times a year.

And it all cost 65 million *livres* (French pounds). Exorbitant, says any self-respecting anti-royalist, but, to put it into perspective, it's been calculated as the equivalent of what republican France spends on just one aircraft carrier and was in any case a spit in the ocean compared with the 3,000 million that Louis XIV spent on his wars.

---

was the palace's grandest reception hall, where the king gave his wildest parties and received his most important foreign envoys. Le Brun's paintings depict Louis XIV's wars in Holland and his more peaceful achievements at home.

In the **Queen's Bedroom,** 19 royal children were born, many of them—as was the custom—with members of the public looking on.

On a separate guided tour, you can visit the marvellous **Royal Opera** of Louis XV, and the king's private apartments. The **King's Bedroom,** with two fine portraits by Van Dyck, is set at the exact centre of the sun's path from east to west. The court was encouraged to come every day to witness the monarch's rising from bed and moment of retirement. Louis XIV died here in 1715 of gangrene of the leg.

The Gardens
If English and Japanese gardens attempt, in their different ways, to enhance nature by "tidying it up" while imitating a "natural" landscape, the French garden, of which Versailles is the supreme expression, quite deliberately imposes a formal pattern.

Resuming a tradition of classical Rome, André Le Nôtre used the paths and avenues of trees and statuary to divide flowerbeds, ponds and fountain basins into intricate geometric patterns. Pause at the palace's western terrace along the Galerie des Glaces for a first view of his harmonious, subtly asymmetrical arrangement of the grounds.

As you make your way through the gardens, look back occasionally at the changing perspectives of the palace. Directly beyond the western terrace is the Axe du Soleil (Path of the Sun) leading down to the **Bassin d'Apollon** (Louis XIV's solar obsession is unavoidable). Adorned with classical sculptures of Greek mythology, this and the great **Bassin de Neptune** and **Bassin du Dragon** in the north-east corner were centrepieces of the royal garden parties.

Beyond the Bassin d'Apollon is the **Grand Canal**, on which the King kept his Venetian gondolas. Today, small boats are available for you to row yourself.

North-west of the château, the **Grand Trianon** palace, surrounded by pleasantly unpompous gardens, was the home of Louis XIV's mistress, Madame de Maintenon, where the aging king increasingly took refuge.

The **Petit Trianon**, where Marie-Antoinette tried to hide from that nasty Revolution, has the allure of a doll's house in comparison with the rest of Versailles. Its gardens, with ponds, mounds and shady woods, are English in style; a relaxing change from the formality of the château. The childlike playfulness of the doomed queen's hideaway is reinforced by her **Hameau**, a hamlet of thatched cottages where she and her retinue pretended to be milkmaids and farmboys.

Saint-Denis

When decapitated, Denis, first bishop of Paris, walked off with his head tucked underneath his arm, and this is where he went (now a northern suburb at the end of métro line 13). A sanctuary and then a Benedictine abbey were built around his tomb. In the 12th century, Abbot Suger began what was to become the model for the great Gothic cathedrals of the Ile-de-France. The **cathedral** lost its north tower after some unfortunate 19th-century restorations, and its main interest today is as the repository for monumental **royal tombs** from King Dagobert (died 639) to Louis XVIII (1824). The bodies were ditched during the Revolution, but 79 *gisants* (recumbent monuments) have been preserved, among them a mosaic for Clovis brought from the church of Saint-Germain-des-Prés and a double monument for François I and his wife. In the north transept, you can see two versions of Catherine de Médicis, dead and asleep. Louis XVI and Marie-Antoinette share the Bourbon family vault down in the **crypt**.

Ecouen *10,B1*

North of Saint-Denis on the N16 (20 kilometres/12½ miles from Paris), the 16th-century palace of the powerful Montmorency family has been transformed into a **Museum of the Renaissance**. Itself a handsome example of French Renaissance architecture, the Château d'Ecouen displays the superb craftsmanship of the era's gold and silverware, ceramics, glazed majolica, crystal and Limoges enamelware, as well as some fascinating precision instruments. Among the castle's remarkable monumental **fireplaces**, notice the Guard Room's depicting the Queen of Sheba and Solomon. Another highlight is the **Flemish tapestry** of David and Bathsheba stretching 70 metres/229 feet in ten pieces from the Gallery of Psyche to the King's Bedroom.

Rueil-Malmaison *10,B1*

This otherwise unprepossessing Paris suburb, 15 kilometres/9½ miles to the west, deserves a visit for its 17th-century **Château de Malmaison**. To the extent that Napoleon had any private life at all, this is where you will catch a glimpse of it. In 1799, it became the home of his wife Josephine and a favourite retreat of his in those rare moments away from the battlefield, providing what the French call a *repos du guerrier*. He saw less of the château once he became emperor in 1804, but paid one last nostalgic visit after Waterloo. It's now a splendid museum of the lavish, overly lavish décor of glittering bric-à-brac and furniture known as "Empire". Look out for **Josephine's boudoir**, her harp, her loom and her backgammon board. In **Napoleon's apartments**, you can see an original version (there were several) of the famous David painting of the great man on horseback, crossing the St. Bernard Pass.

For devotees of the Napoleon cult, the museum of the neighbouring **Château de Bois Préau** includes relics from his exile on St. Helena, notably his uniform, sword, deathbed and the clock stopped at the time of his death—5.49 p.m., May 5, 1821.

Saint-Germain-en-Laye   *10,B1*

The town on the edge of the capital, 20 kilometres/12 miles west, makes a popular excursion for Parisians combining a meal at one of the many good restaurants along the Seine river with a walk in the ancient royal **forest**. Hunting lodges are still half-hidden among the fine old oaks, birches, beeches and pines. The forest provided sport for the court of the pentagonal **château** in which Louis XIV grew up and experimented with his architects before setting them to work on Versailles. The **gardens**, especially the Grande Terrasse north-east of the palace, represent a summit of André Le Nôtre's landscaping genius. Today, the palace houses the great **Musée des Antiquités nationales**, devoted to Stone Age art and the country's earliest history. With the 20,000-year-old **Brassempouy head**, the museum boasts the oldest known representation of a human face. Look out, too, for two marvellously expressive prehistoric horses, one leaping, the other whinnying, and a whole pantheon of Gallic, Celtic and Roman gods.

Vaux-le-Vicomte   *10,C2*

State financier Nicolas Fouquet's grandiose 17th-century **château**, 51 kilometres/32 miles south-east of Paris, offers a pleasant day trip out of Paris, along with an exquisite object-lesson in the humiliation of the high and mighty. Following in the footsteps of Richelieu and Mazarin, Fouquet amassed a huge fortune from his job with the motto *Quo non ascendem?* ("What heights can I not scale?"). Louis XIV showed him. When the king was invited for dinner in 1661, he threw a temper tantrum at the extravagance of the reception and opulence of the place, tossed Fouquet in jail and appropriated his architect Louis Le Vau, painter-decorator Charles Le Brun and landscape-

*F*ouquet's Vaux-le-Vicomte is the château that
drove the jealous Louis XIV to make his Versailles the mammoth
palace of his megalomaniac dreams. These gardens were too grand,
the interior décors too splendid for a merely mortal (and imprisonable)
financier. The stars around a Sun King must never shine too
brightly.

architect André Le Nôtre to go off and build Versailles. As you can see by the unfinished splendour of the rotunda's **Grand Salon**, Le Brun had to leave in a hurry. But in Le Nôtre's **gardens**, you can still appreciate the wonderful perspectives and surprise effects of the pools and canals. On summer weekends, there are illuminated water displays in the gardens and night-time candlelit tours of the castle.

Chantilly   10,B1

Sixty kilometres (37 miles) north of Paris, Chantilly is celebrated for its château, its elegant racecourse and stables, and its *crème chantilly* (whipped cream), served at the château gates on hot waffles.

The **château**, which belonged to the powerful Condé dynasty in the 17th century, joins a not ugly but somewhat bastard reconstruction of the great edifice destroyed in the Revolution to the charming, authentic Renaissance building known as the Petit Château.

The main body of the château houses the **Musée Condé**, a superb collection of Italian, French and Dutch masters, including Raphael, Veronese and Fra Angelico, Poussin, Watteau, exquisite portraits by Clouet, Van Dyck and Teniers. You'll recognize the famous *Book of Hours* of the Duc de Berry, a fascinating picture of the times. One of the charms of the collection is that the paintings are hung, not in any classical order by school, but according to the personal whim of their last owner, the Duke of Aumale.

The palace grounds make a pleasant walk, especially the English Garden behind the Petit Château. Louis XIV was very jealous of the Grand Canal, ponds and waterfalls designed by André Le Nôtre and insisted the master gardener do even better in Versailles. You may prefer the more intimate scale of Chantilly.

In June, the Hippodrome west of the château is host to the prestigious Prix du Jockey Club horse race. But all year round, you can visit the monumental 18th-century **Grandes-Ecuries** (stables), now a horse museum, with live horses munching hay next to wooden statues.

At the western edge of Chantilly forest is the **Abbey of Royaumont**, since the Revolution an elegant ruin in which concerts and conferences are now held. The vine-covered cloister and Gothic refectory are well worth a visit for a sense of the old monastic tranquillity.

Senlis   10,C1

For your first taste of unspoiled village life just a quick 50-kilometre (30-mile) drive north from Paris, try the charming little town of Senlis, with its imposing Gothic **cathedral** and handsome 15th- and 16th-century houses, still partly encircled by Gallo-Roman ramparts. The finely sculpted porch on the western façade inspired the design for Chartres Cathedral and Paris's Notre-Dame.

Chartres   10,A2

One of the most moving experiences on a journey across France is to drive through the wheat fields of the fertile Beauce plain, and see, looming suddenly on the horizon, the silhouette of Chartres **Cathedral** 85 kilometres (53 miles) southwest of Paris.

This unquestionable masterpiece of French civilization marks the transition in the 12th century from the solid, sober Romanesque style of the Church's beginnings to the more airy, assertive Gothic of its ascendancy. Apart from a few decapitated statues, it came miraculously unscathed through the Wars of Religion and the Revolution. As you face the harmoniously asymmetrical western façade, the southern tower, **Clocher Vieux**, is a supreme expression of Romanesque simplicity, while the taller northern tower, **Clocher Neuf**, is already lighter, with its slender, more ornate steeple.

On the central porch, **Portail Royal**,

note the stately, deliberately elongated sculptures of Old Testament figures, compared with the freer, more vigorous statues round on the northern and southern porches.

Inside, the glory of the church is its 173 **stained-glass windows**; that unique "Chartres blue" and deep red bringing an ethereal light into the nave, especially from a late afternoon sun through the western rose window, depicting the Last Judgment. Among the oldest and most famous of the windows, on the southern side of the choir, is an enthroned Mary with Jesus on her lap, **Notre-Dame de la Belle Verrière**. The church is dedicated to Mary, representing her 175 times in the various sculptures and windows.

In the paving of the nave's centre aisle, you'll notice a large circular **labyrinth**; medieval worshippers traced its path from the circumference to the centre as part of a mystic spiritual exercise.

Back outside, from the Episcopal Garden *(Jardin de l'Evêché)* at the rear of the cathedral, a stairway takes you down to the **old town**. Its attractive 16th- and 17th-century houses along the Eure river afford a pretty view of the cathedral.

Fontainebleau   *10,C2*

The great forest 70 kilometres (44 miles) south of Paris was popular hunting country for François I and Henri IV; their **palace** is an elegant monument to their Renaissance tastes. Napoleon cherished it as a place for reflection, and it was there that he abdicated in 1814 to go into a first exile on the Isle of Elba.

Allegorical paintings in the **Galerie de François Ier** bear testimony to the king's preoccupation with war and death, and also to the sanctity of kingship. **Napoleon's apartments** are still decorated with the furnishings of his empire. A Napoleonic museum has been installed in the Louis XV wing.

But save most of your time for the majestic **Forest of Fontainebleau**, 25,000 hectares (over 60,000 acres) of oak, beech, silver birch, pine, chestnut and hornbeam *(charme)*. Apart from the lovely walks and indeed lengthy hikes over well-marked paths, a great attraction is the miniature "mountain range" of sheer rocks and cliffs, much appreciated by apprentice climbers for trying out their equipment and technique before tackling the Alps. The most popular are the rugged Gorges de Franchard, due west of the Palace. The Gorges d'Apremont, near the little town of Barbizon famous for its 19th-century landscape painters (p. 95), are less crowded.

Compiègne   *4,C3*

Some 80 kilometres (50 miles) up the autoroute du Nord, Compiègne is another classical Ile-de-France royal hunting forest and palace. Besides being the last home of Marie-Antoinette, the **palace** was a favourite of Napoleon III and his wife Eugénie, whose extravagant memorabilia constitute the **Musée du Second-Empire**.

Also in the palace is a fascinating **Musée de la Voiture**. It displays all kinds of vehicles, from the coach that carried Napoleon to and from Moscow in 1812 to a splendid 1900 4-horsepower Renault and other turn-of-the-century classics.

The **Forest of Compiègne** offers plenty of good walks; or you can hire a horse at the village of Saint-Jean-aux-Bois. The forest is famous for its **Clairière de l'Armistice**, where the Germans signed the Armistice of their defeat in 1918

Skewered
One day in April, 1671, Louis XIV visited Chantilly with 5,000, yes, 5,000 friends for a three-day stay. The Condé family's brilliant but highly sensitive master chef, Vatel, went berserk earning his title of *Contrôleur général de la Bouche de Monsieur le Prince* (General Supervisor of the Prince's Mouth). Bad enough on the first night when three tables had to go without their roast. When the fresh fish failed to arrive the next day, Vatel went up to his room and ran himself through with his sword.

in Marshal Foch's private train coach. Twenty-two years later, Hitler obliged the French to sign their capitulation in the same place.

At the eastern edge of the forest, **Pierre-fonds** is a popular dream-castle fashioned by 19th-century restorer Viollet-le-Duc from the massive ruins of the medieval original.

Beauvais   *10,B1*

Lying 76 kilometres (48 miles) north of Paris, Beauvais suffered horribly from the devastating bombardments of 1940 that totally destroyed the town's centuries-old tapestry industry, but left its most glorious monument, the 13th-century Gothic **Cathédrale Saint-Pierre**, intact. If its lack of a nave or steeples makes it look somewhat truncated anyway, that is due only to the over-reaching ambitions of its builders. The local clergy and architects wanted a church bigger than Paris's Notre-Dame. The magnificent flying-buttressed **choir** alone is 68 metres (223 feet) high, just one metre less than Notre-Dame, towers and all. After repeated replacements of too audaciously lofty pillars, the grandiose interior vaults remain the tallest in Christendom—48 metres (157 feet) to the keystone. Too eager then to erect the country's mightiest tower before building a nave to provide supportive counterthrust, the churchmen saw their 153-metre- (502-foot-) steeple over the middle of the transept collapse

in 1573. Then the money ran out, but even the unfinished edifice is a masterpiece of architectural daring.

Enter at the transept's Flamboyant Gothic southern portal. The best surviving **stained glass** (16th-century) is in the rose window in this southern arm of the transept—there are a few older pieces in the chapels leading off the ambulatory. There is a baffling and extremely ugly 19th-century astronomic clock north of the choir.

Sens   *11,C2*

On the edge of Burgundy, but only 113 kilometres (70 miles) from Paris, Sens wielded enormous ecclesiastic influence in its heyday; until Paris became an archbishopric in 1627, Sens lorded over all the major bishoprics in the area including Chartres. The sheer majesty of the **Cathédrale Saint-Etienne** testifies to this might. First Gothic cathedral in France, begun in 1140, its impressive façade is only slightly impaired by the fact that one of the towers collapsed at the end of the 13th century and was rebuilt with a campanile over the next centuries. The vast interior proportions of the nave and the lovely **stained-glass windows** are outstanding, but many prefer the church **treasures,** some of the best examples in the whole of France. The cathedral lies plumb in the heart of a genuinely delightful old town, surrounded by boulevards where once were ramparts.

*I*n the collective national consciousness of the French, the silhouette of Chartres Cathedral on the horizon of the wheat fields of the Beauce plain is an essential image. For Proust, who lived nearby, the church was almost as powerful a childhood memory of times past as the piece of madeleine cake that little Marcel's Aunt Léonie offered him dipped in a spoonful of tea.

From Battlefields to Vineyards

The invaders pouring over the northern and eastern frontiers these days tend to be peaceful—tourists from Britain, the Netherlands, Belgium and Germany. But the plains and plateaux of Flanders and Picardy, Alsace and Lorraine have historically been the arenas of bloody war.

In the Hundred Years' War, England knew its days of glory on the Picardy fields of Crécy and Azincourt (Agincourt). For Louis XIV's wars against the Netherlands, the great military architect Vauban built a line of fortifications in the frontier towns, at Calais, Dunkirk, Douai, Valenciennes and, still visible today, the great citadel at Lille. More recently, Flanders and the river valleys of the Somme and Marne were the major battlefields of World War I. Alsace and Lorraine suffered humiliating conquest at Wissembourg and Metz in 1870 and again in 1940, but witnessed the resurrection of the French Army at the Liberation.

The windswept countryside is dotted with poignant memorials and military cemeteries. The villages have a hardy charm, and the larger towns, Arras and Amiens to the north, Nancy and Strasbourg to the east, exude great civic pride. Linking north and east, the fields of Champagne and its royal city of Reims have also known their wars, but today prefer, for our greater joy, to bask in bubbly.

Deep in the interior, Burgundy is a more solidly implanted heartland. Most famous today for its vineyards, it was historically the stronghold of the dukes of Dijon, alongside the ecclesiastical empires of the Cluny and Cistercian monasteries and their great Romanesque churches. To the east, the Jura mountains of Franche-Comté offer visitors invigorating hikes through dense forests and along the rivers of the valley landscapes celebrated by the paintings of Gustave Courbet.

Flanders   4,C2

France's extension of the Low Countries' *plat pays*—flatlands—in fact ends the great continental sweep of the Russian steppes. Dominated by the industrial megalopolis of Lille, Roubaix and Tourcoing and broken only by an occasional sandy hillock, the plain of Flanders comes to rest in the dunes around Dunkirk.

Lille   4,C2
The building of the Channel Tunnel reinforces the regional capital's key crossroads position on northern Europe's route to the south. Stop off for a meal of mussels and beer (or white wine) and a stroll around the historic centre with its

rich architectural mixture of the French and Flemish traditions following Louis XIV's acquisition of the town in 1667. If its many redbrick buildings may also recall industrial Britain of the 19th century, the town hall's soaring belfry (a 1920s reconstruction) is unmistakably Flemish. But start out at the fine 15th-century Gothic **Palais Rihour**, with its octagonal turret and mullioned windows, now housing the tourist office. The **Rue Esquermoise** boasts many handsome 17th-century houses, but the town's grandest edifice is undoubtedly the **Ancienne Bourse** (Old Stock Exchange, 1652) on the Place du Général-de-Gaulle. Notice the remarkable sculptures of the lofty arcaded courtyard.

The splendid European collections of the **Musée des Beaux-Arts** (Fine Arts Museum) are housed in a dreary building on the Place de la République (fortunately, it is being renovated, but the collections will continue to be open to the public, at least till 1991). Spare time for the Flemish works of Dierick Bouts, Rubens and Van Dyck; the Italians Veronese, Tintoretto and a Donatello bas-relief of *Herod's Feast;* the Spanish El Greco, Ribera and Goya; and the French, Delacroix, Courbet, Monet and Sisley.

De Gaulle's birthplace (his grandfather's little lace-factory at 9, Rue Princesse) is now a museum. It displays such incongruous items as his baptism robe—the future nation-saver was born November 22, 1890—and the car in which he was nearly assassinated at Petit-Clamart in 1962.

Subject in its history to no less than 11 sieges, Lille boasts the country's biggest and best preserved military **citadel**. Encircled by the Deûle Canal, it is part of the great system of 28 such northern defences constructed for Louis XIV by Sébastien de Prestre de Vauban. Its mas-

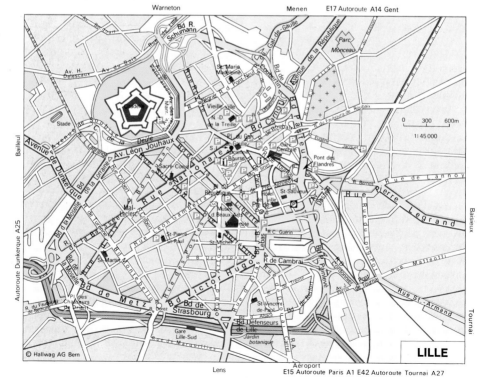

LILLE

© Hallwag AG Bern

sive bastions and ramparts enclosed a veritable city of bakers, brewers, tailors and cobblers.

Besides being at the hub of the new TGV train route from Paris to London, the town has emphasized its vital role in modern communications and transport with **Val**, the completely computerized *driverless* subway going out to the eastern suburb of Villeneuve d'Asque. Try it.

Bergues   4,B1

Surrounded by canals, this serene little medieval walled town of attractive ochre brick was bolstered by Vauban's 17th-century **fortifications** (see p. 127). It took sustained aerial bombardment for the Germans to breach the ramparts in 1940. Take a walk around the Canal du Roy—and a swim in summer—for a close-up of Vauban's masterwork, the crown-shaped **Couronne d'Hondschoote.**

The municipal **museum** has one of Georges de La Tour's greatest paintings, the *Joueur de Vielle* (Hurdy-Gurdy Player), as well as notable works by Brueghel and Van Dyck.

Saint-Omer   4,B1

Prosperous from the textile industry since the Middle Ages, the town emerged from bombardment in two world wars with a gentle serenity unusual for the austere north.

Formerly a cathedral, the 13th-century **Basilique Notre-Dame** dominates the town with an imposing grandeur. Note the fine stone sculptures of the *Virgin* and a *Last Judgment* over the south porch. Inside, the marble and alabaster treasures evoke the wealth of the diocese in the 16th and 17th centuries, particularly the elaborate chapel screens and, in the north arm of the transept, an intricate astronomical clock. Nearby, the 13th-century sculpted figures of the *Grand Dieu de Thérouanne* are strangely foreshortened because they were originally seen from below (on another church).

The **Hôtel Sandelin** museum is well worth a visit, both for the splendid 18th-

century mansion, with its Louis XV furnishings, and for its rich collections of porcelain from all over the world. The Saint-Omer decorative glazed earthenware *(faïence)* is a major feature, and the magnificent Delft collection is outstanding, not only for its celebrated blue ware but also for some exquisite polychrome pieces. Tobacco fanatics and non-smokers alike will love the display of over 2,000 beautifully modelled terra-cotta pipes. The enamelled bowls depict demons and dogs, Napoleon and Jesus and quite a few naughty scatological and erotic scenes.

Some 15 kilometres (9 miles) northwest of Saint-Omer is the monstrous **Eperlèques blockhouse** which the Germans built as a launching-pad for their V-2 rockets aimed at London in World War II. Still massively there, 22 metres/ 72 feet high with walls 5 metres/16 feet thick, it was built by Russian, Polish, French, Belgian and Dutch prisoners and then knocked out of action by a bombardment of 187 British Flying Fortresses in 1943.

Cassel, a little town full of charm halfway between Lille and the coast, has another claim to fame; the "Grand Old" Duke of York famous to all English schoolchildren (and a few others) marched his troops (10,000 of them) up to the top of its hill in 1793.

Le Touquet   4,B2

Perhaps to attract a clientele from the capital, this breezy seaside resort added the name Paris-Plage. It might more aptly have called itself Knightsbridge-Plage, being a pure creation of London's smart set at the end of the 19th century, when swimming and silly beach games became all the rage.

Today, it's something of a nicely faded museum piece, but the sailing and windsurfing are good, the riding, golf and tennis simply splendid.

In the lovely **forest** of sea pines and poplars, you'll find elegant Tudor-style timbered villas that it's more diplomatic to call "Anglo-Norman".

Picardy
4-5,BC2

If you're coming into France from the English Channel or across the Belgian border, don't just rush straight down the *autoroute* to Paris. Picardy has plenty of interesting stops and even some worthwhile short detours for a more leisurely journey.

Côte d'Opale

The region takes its name from the coast's milky white "opaline" seafoam and offers a pleasant excursion along the chalk cliffs and sand dunes between Boulogne and Calais. In the largely modern port of **Boulogne**, take a look at the medieval ramparts and perhaps the 11th-century crypt in the Basilique Notre-Dame before heading north along the D940 coast road. Just outside of town, the **Colonne de la Grande Armée** is an imposing marble monument to Napoleon's armies, for it was here that he planned his abortive invasion of England. **Wimereux** is an agreeable family seaside resort with sand and pebble beaches. The Channel and North Sea meet at **Cap Gris-Nez**, closest point to England (less than 30 km./20 mi.) affording a good view of Dover's white cliffs. It was from the sheltered sandy beaches of **Wissant** that Julius Caesar sailed to England in 55 B.C. **Sangatte** is the French side of the more peaceful crossing planned for the new Channel Tunnel. In **Calais**, take a look, in front of the town-hall, at Rodin's famous monument to the six *Bourgeois de Calais* pleading for the lives of their fellow citizens in the Hundred Years' War.

Arras
4,C2

This is the place celebrated among the British for the tapestry through which Hamlet stabbed poor old Polonius. The town, just off the *autoroute* from Calais, has two of the most beautiful city squares in France—or anywhere. The classical Flemish style of the 17th- and 18th-century arcades and gabled façades on the **Grande Place** and **Place des Héros** invites comparison with the great squares of Brussels and Bruges. Both are positively breathtaking. Try to be there on Saturday for market day.

Amiens
4,B2

The majestic **cathedral** of Picardy's capital is without doubt an authentic masterpiece of French Gothic architecture. It was almost completed in just 44 years in the middle of the 13th century, and thus preserved a homogeneous style, a noble silhouette miraculously unharmed by the heavy air raids of World War II.

Its glory is the oak carving of the 110 **choir stalls**, the work of 16th-century cabinet-makers whose names—Jean Turpin, Alexandre de Heudebourg, Arnould Boulin—deserve mention alongside their more celebrated contemporaries of the Italian Renaissance. Dramatically depicting over 400 scenes from the Old and New Testaments, 3,650 figures present a magnificent pageant of the customs and costume of the people of François I. Among the panels of Cain and Abel, Abraham and Isaac, Jesus and Mary, all very Flemish figures, are carvings of a Picardy baker, dairymaid, fruitmonger and laundress. The nearby Tour Perret, 26 storeys high, dwarfs the cathedral.

*F*rance's industrial revolution still parades down the streets of its northern towns: Roubaix, Tourcoing, Douai, Lille, heartland of the country's factory-workers—stronghold of socialism, but also the birthplace of General de Gaulle. It was perhaps the strong attachment to this region that made him more interested in social progress than some of the conservatives who have claimed his heritage.

Picardy has ever been a choice arena for Anglo-French rivalry. A trip south of Calais takes you back through history, starting at Guînes, site of the famous **Field of Cloth of Gold** *(Le camp du Drap d'Or)* where Henry VIII met François I in 1520. This extravagant summit meeting in which each monarch sought to outshine the other in sheer opulence destroyed all chances of an alliance when François beat Henry at wrestling. This did little to wipe out the memory of Henry V's devastating victory at **Azincourt** (Agincourt to the English) in 1415 when those whom Shakespeare immortalized as "we few, we happy few, we band of brothers" left 10,000 French dead on the battlefield. The site, commemorated now with a calvary 16 kilometres (10 miles) north-east of Hesdin, was cursed until 1763 with the nickname of *Carogne* (carrion). The other momentous battle was at **Crécy**, just north of Abbeville, where Edward III's 20,000 soldiers crushed a French army of 60,000 at the beginning of the Hundred Years' War. A mound marks the millhouse from which the English king watched his archers fell the cumbersomely armoured French with their revolutionary longbows.

The **Musée de Picardie** (48, Rue de la République) has a good collection of paintings, most notably a couple of Van Goyen landscapes, El Greco's *Portrait of a Man*, a witty self-portrait of Quentin de La Tour, and Boucher's erotic nymphs.

Landmarks of World War I   4,C2

Any tour of Flanders and Picardy inevitably passes by the battlefields and poignant memorials of one of the greatest collective catastrophes in the history of mankind—World War I (see p. 47). Whole towns were wiped out. Some were completely rebuilt, others replaced only by a lonely stone monument or a vast cemetery of the thousands who fell in combat—French, British, Canadians, Australians, Americans or Germans.

A few minutes north-west of Lille on D933 is **Armentières**, southern edge of the British battle salient around Ypres across the Belgian border, more famous to British and American troops as the home of the Mademoiselle to whom they sang "hinky dinky, parlez-vous?". The British war cemetery is on the east side of town.

North of Arras off the A26 *autoroute*, **Vimy** is grimly celebrated by Canadians as the site of their fiery baptism in overseas combat, losing thousands of men in defence of the strategic ridge. Amid bleak coal-mining country, the **Canadian memorial** stands above shell scars and mine craters still visible around the network of Canadian and German trenches on the southern hillside. Look west to the great French memorial of **Notre-Dame de Lorette** and its cemetery of 20,000 named graves and another 20,000 unidentified. The Germans are buried at nearby La Targette.

About 30 kilometres (19 miles) south of Arras, marking the bloody 1916 Battle of the Somme, are the Allied memorials—British, Australian and Canadian—in and around **Beaumont-Hamel** and **Thiepval**, the latter with a triumphal arch bearing 73,000 British names.

Laon   11,D1

Birthplace of St. Rémi who gave his name to the nearby city of Reims, this charming hilltop town looks out from behind its medieval ramparts over the plain of southern Picardy. The oldest part of town, the *Cité,* is grouped around the **cathedral** to the east. The 12th-century Gothic edifice is admired for its airy openwork towers with their high arched bays in the upper storeys flanked by slender turrets. Look out for the statues of oxen resting at the top, immortalized after heaving masonry up the hill for repairs. There is some fine 13th-century **stained glass** in the nave and in the chancel's rose windows.

On the south side of town, walk along the old **city walls**, with their lookouts and pepperpot towers, from the Rempart du Midi to the Porte d'Ardon looking down on the old **lavoir** (public laundry). The **Rue Vinchon** has some elegant medieval and Renaissance houses.

Champagne   *11,DE1-2*

In the great French lexicon of good living, no word is more loaded with magic than Champagne. Magic, in the miraculous conjunction of geology, topography and climate that have produced the world's most celebrated wine. In this northernmost of France's wine-producing regions, with a bright mellow summer and mild winter, the Champagne country around Reims and Epernay has ideal south-facing slopes to exploit every last ray of sun, together with just the right chalky soil to store and release the requisite heat and humidity among the vines. Add the ingenuity of the cellar masters who concoct the magic potion, and you have the makings of a very good party.

The great manufacturers will be glad to give you a glimpse of how they do it. Visits usually last 45 minutes and include cellar, vineyards... and tastings.

Reims   *11,D1*

If Champagne is the wine of kings, Reims is the town that consecrated the divine right of kingship. It was here, at the end of the 5th century, that St. Rémi is believed to have baptized the pagan Clovis and here again that Hugues Capet was anointed and crowned first King of France in 987. It was a major achievement of Joan of Arc to have Charles VII crowned at Reims Cathedral in 1429. Charles X, last of the Bourbons, sought the same divine legitimacy in 1825 with a Reims coronation.

Joy from Trouble with Bubbles

Ever since Roman times, the wine growers of Champagne knew they had a good product—in the Middle Ages they got into violent fights over it with rivals in neighbouring Burgundy. But until the end of the 17th century, they had a "problem" with bubbles, which they had the devil of a time getting rid of. Then a monk named Dom Pérignon, cellar master at the abbey of Hautvillers, decided he liked this bubbly stuff and found a way of stabilizing it by blending it with other wines and adding an exact dose of sugar. This is roughly what today's Champagne producers do, prior to the vital second fermentation.

Mere technique, the *méthode champenoise* of getting the bubbles into the wine is not enough to make real Champagne. To connoisseurs, Californian or Australian "champagne" is as sacrilegious as Japanese "scotch".

There are only 23,000 hectares (57,000 acres) of true Champagne vineyards—1.5% of the national total—and their grapes alone, black and white, are authorized to go into a Champagne bottle. The white *chardonnay* grapes growing south of Epernay on the Côte des blancs bring the light, fresh note; the black *pinot noir* on the Montagne de Reims add body; and *pinot meunier* west of Epernay add a dash of fruitiness. You'll find these grapes all over the wine-growing world, but only the Champagne region has that special chalky soil, not only for the vineyards, but also for the vaults of the gallery cellars, maintaining a constant temperature of 10.5 °C (51 °F) during the months that turn wine into Champagne.

The wine growers harvest their grapes in October and bring them to the underground galleries of the major producers for pressing and a first fermentation that turns the sugar into alcohol. By the New Year, a clear wine, usually 75% black and 25% white grapes, is ready for the all-important *cuvée,* the cellar master's secret blend with up to 30 other wines that gives each "label" its distinctive taste. Natural yeasts and a small amount of cane sugar are added prior to bottling and a second, slower fermentation, which lasts about three months. The wine is then left to age. Every day the bottles are turned alternately one-eighth to the left or to the right, to remove the deposits that attach to the sides. This takes at least a year—or three for a vintage, *millésime,* after an outstanding harvest when older wines are not needed for the *cuvée.* From time to time the bottles are carefully shaken to bring the deposit up to the top. This is removed by freezing, and the wine is topped up with a *liqueur de dosage*: a mixture of cane sugar in vintage Champagne, which determines whether the Champagne is *demi-sec, extra sec* or *brut.*

Topped with a fresh new cork, wire muzzle and shiny little seal, that, at last, ladies and gentlemen, is Champagne. Cheers!

*B*urrowed away beneath the vineyards, the Champagne cellars benefit from the region's unique chalky soil maintaining a constant temperature of 10.5 °C (51 °F) during the months that turn mere wine into the magic potion. In the hierarchy of bottles, everybody knows a Magnum (1.6 litres) is the equivalent of 2 bottles, but did you know a Jeroboam bottle is 4, Rehoboam 6, Methusalah 8, Salmanazar 12, Balthazar 16 and Nebuchadnezzar 20 bottles?

The magnificently proportioned 13th-century **cathedral** was badly damaged by fire in World War I, but it has been well restored and remains one of the country's great Gothic edifices. Try to see its lovely buff stone façade in the late afternoon sun, with a pair of binoculars to study the rich sculpture of the Gallery of Kings high above the windows.

In the interior, the most noteworthy of the surviving 13th-century **stained-glass windows** are the rose window above the western entrance, illustrating the life of the Virgin Mary, and one devoted to the Creation in the north arm of the transept. Directly beyond the altar is the **Chagall chapel** in which the Russian artist connects his Jewish origins to the Christian religion with a window depicting Abraham and Jesus.

The originals of the cathedral's major sculptures are on display next door in the museum of the archbishop's residence, the **Palais du Tau**. The most famous pieces are the Smiling Angel, symbol of Reims hospitality, and the allegorical figure of the Synagogue, blindfolded because it was felt the Jews were too stubborn to behold the truth of Christianity.

For an hour's tour of the city's **Champagne cellars**, you can get details at the Office de tourisme, 1, Rue Jadart, 51100 Reims, telephone: 26.47.25.69. The cellars are in fact 250 kilometres (155 miles) of galleries quarried out of the city's chalk foundations back in the days of Roman Gaul. Practically all the major Champagne "labels" offer tours. Piper-Heidsieck has a little train; Ruinart, the oldest, is organized on three levels; Taittinger is partly installed in the crypt of a demolished abbey.

Epernay   *11,D1*

The town's advantage over Reims is that you can combine a visit of its cellars— Moët & Chandon or Mercier—with a drive south along the great **Côte des blancs** vineyards that produce the white *chardonnay* grapes. The prettiest view of the vines and the Marne valley is just 10 kilo-metres (6 miles) down the D10 at **Cramant**.

You can see a reconstitution of Dom Pérignon's famous 17th-century cellar and laboratory in the abbey museum of **Hautvillers**, just 6 kilometres (4 miles) north of Epernay.

Troyes   *11,D2*

Sandwiched between Burgundy and Champagne, **Troyes** became an important artistic centre during the Renaissance, with its sculptors and glass workers; see their work in the 13th–16th-century **Cathédrale Saint-Pierre-et-Saint-Paul** with its panorama of stained glass from the fairly simple but charming 13th-century work in the choir to the explosion of technical mastery with Linard Gontier's 1625 window in the fourth chapel on the left. More superb glass is to be seen at the **Eglise Sainte-Marie,** oldest church in Troyes, that also claims a magnificent **rood screen.** The town's medieval core is a burrow of narrow streets bordered by timbered, turreted and corbelled houses (particularly Rue des Chats, Rue Champeaux and Rue de la Trinité).

Housed in the imposing Hôtel de Valuisant is the **Musée Historique de Troyes,** with remarkable sculptures and a wing devoted to Troyes' chief industry, hosiery. The **Musée d'Art moderne** (Place Saint-Pierre) is strong in the works of the Fauves and Cubists, while the **Musée des Beaux-Arts** (1, Rue Chrestien-de-Troyes) is proud of its Van Dyke, Watteau and local sculptor François Girardon.

Those that like outdoor life will not want to miss a sidetrip out to the **Lac et Forêt d'Orient** to visit the bird sanctuary.

Colombey-les-Deux-Eglises, a tiny village to the east, has become a place of pilgrimage for admirers of General de Gaulle, whose country house La Boisserie has been turned into a little museum. Occasionally, you'll see the odd Gaullist up for re-election bowing in prayer before the huge red granite Cross of Lorraine up on a hill over the village.

Lorraine *12-13,BCD1-2*

A region of strategic importance guarding the eastern approaches to Paris, Lorraine has long been a pawn in France's perennial conflicts with Germany. Amid the resulting devastations of war and the more recent depression of the region's declining coal, iron and steel industries, the historical town of Nancy stands out as a gleaming survivor. Its golden 18th-century architecture makes it a rewarding stopover on any journey between Paris and Alsace.

Nancy *13,C2*

Head straight for the **Place Stanislas**. Surrounded by elegant Classical mansions and gilded wrought-iron grilles with ornamental gateways framing the marble fountains of Neptune and Amphitrite, the square is one of the most harmonious urban spaces in Europe.

Visit the **Hôtel de Ville** (town hall), in the largest of the mansions, for its fine staircase, designed by the same Jean Lamour who created the wrought-iron grilles, but above all for the marvellous view of the square. In the centre stands a statue of the man responsible, King Stanislas Leszczyński of Poland.

Deposed by the Russians in 1736, he had the good fortune to be Louis XV's father-in-law and was given the Duchy of Lorraine as compensation. He expressed his gratitude by devoting the rest of his life to refurbishing a town devastated by the Thirty Years' War of the previous century.

The square's grand, spacious effect is completed to the north by an **Arc de Triomphe** (dedicated to Louis XV) at the entrance to the long **Place de la Carrière**, also graced by 18th-century mansions and Jean Lamour's iron grilles.

In the old ducal palace, the **Musée Historique lorrain** offers a fascinating glimpse of Nancy before Stanislas. Jacques Callot's horrifying engravings of the Thirty Years' War have their anti-dotes in the more serene paintings of Georges de La Tour.

Stroll back to Place Stanislas through the **Pépinière** gardens. In the north-west corner is Rodin's statue of the painter whom the French know by his pseudonym, Claude Lorrain, and the British as Claude Gelée.

The **Musée des Beaux-Arts** at 3, Place Stanislas has a good collection of European art, notably Tintoretto, Ruysdael and Rubens, with the French represented by Delacroix, Courbet and Manet.

Wearing the Pants
Born on January 6, 1412, and raised in Lorraine where she heard "the voices", most of Joan's "active" life was spent elsewhere, pulling, or trying to pull, the French together.

Joan of Arc was tried as "schismatic, apostate, liar, witch, heretic and blasphemer" —charges drawn up by professors of the University of Paris. The established order felt threatened by her highly personal religious experience of hearing, without Church help, the saints' voices exhorting her to lead the French against the English. Jobs were at stake.

To the English, she was a meddling morale-booster who seemed to be giving the hitherto feeble French army just enough backbone to boot them out of France. So, when she finally fell into English hands in 1430 after being captured at Compiègne, they had to find a means of getting rid of her.

Pierre Cauchon, Bishop of Beauvais hoping to get the vacant archbishopric of Rouen, was her chief judge and inquisitor. With the threat of burning her at the stake, he got Joan to give up her sinful men's clothing and sign a document denying the saints' voices and vowing submission to the Church.

But the English wanted her out of the way, so she was thrown back into prison where, to protect herself from her jailers, she had to don men's clothing again. She further proved she was an incorrigible heretic by retracting her denial of the voices. On May 30, 1431, she was burned at the stake on Rouen's Place du Vieux-Marché.

Happy endings: Joan's martyrdom inspired the French to boot the English out anyway, Cauchon didn't become archbishop, and Joan became, in 1920, a saint.

Verdun
12,B1

This synonym for total war—800,000 men killed in battle raging on and off for 20 months from February, 1916, to October, 1917—has become a town of patriotic pilgrimage. French and German leaders regularly meet here in symbolic acts of peace and reconciliation. The underground galleries of the **citadel**, where soldiers recuperated from shell-shock, have been converted into a **war museum** *(Musée de la Guerre)*.

Exhibits include battle documents, flags, weapons and ammunition. A not-too-tasteful waxworks scene recreates the choice made here in 1920, from among eight coffins, of the Unknown Soldier to lie beneath the Arc de Triomphe in Paris.

Complete your visit with a tour of the surrounding villages embroiled in the slaughter. Of **Fleury**, just north of Verdun, nothing is left but a stone memorial. **Douaumont** is now just a chapel and ossuary for 130,000 unidentified soldiers. **Louvemont** remains in eloquent ruin.

Lunéville
13,D2

An unconditional admirer of Louis XIV, the Duke of Lorraine had this miniature Versailles built between 1702 and 1714 by a pupil of Mansard. He entertained the local nobility in much the same way—if a little less lavishly—with concerts, theatre performances, fêtes, dancing and hunting. Since 1946, the château has been restored and the park has recovered some of its former glory, when Voltaire and Diderot were frequent visitors.

Domrémy
12,C2

An annual pilgrimage in May maintains the cult of Joan of Arc in the town where she spent the first 16 years of her life. The **church** has been considerably altered over the centuries, but Joan could have seen one or two of the objects including the baptismal font. In her **birthplace** reigns the atmosphere of a relatively successful peasant family home; beside it a little **museum** contains objects and documents pertaining to the life of the erstwhile *pasionaria* of French nationhood.

The unique gilded iron grilles wrought by master craftsman Jean Lamour gird Nancy's Place Stanislas like a golden necklace. For the Duke of Lorraine, Stanislas Leszczyński, they formed the centrepiece in his untiring efforts to make Nancy a vivid urban embodiment of the Age of Enlightenment. After the statue of his son-in-law Louis XV was destroyed in the Revolution, it was an act of poetic justice to put that of the Polish prince in its place.

Alsace
13,DE1-2

One of the reasons the Germans and French have always fought for the possession of this province is very simply that it's such a good place to live. Rich farmland, vineyards and dense forest, with the solidly protective Vosges mountain range on one side and the great Rhine river on the other, make it a nicely self-contained region.

The turmoils of history have left a dialect and an architecture of unmistakably Germanic origin, a political tradition indelibly marked by the French Revolution, and a cuisine that subtly mixes the two. The people seem to feel neither more German nor more French, just Alsatian —the best of both worlds.

Very appropriate for a region which houses the European Parliament in its capital, Strasbourg. Make your base there or in Colmar for excursions into the surrounding wine country and its spotless medieval villages.

Strasbourg
13,E2

The city has emerged handsome, if not unscathed, from its troubled past. Gothic and Renaissance buildings have been lovingly restored. The *Winstuben* (wine bars) of its old neighbourhoods are hospitable gathering places for university students whose predecessors include Goethe, Bonaparte and Metternich.

It's a good town for walking the narrow streets, or for taking a **boat cruise** on the river Ill, that divides into two branches to loop the historic centre. Launches start from the Pont Sainte-Madeleine.

The celebrated asymmetrical silhouette of the Gothic **cathedral**, with its single tower and steeple rising on the north side of its façade, gives your visit an inspiring start.

Alsace or Elsass?

In the perennial tug-of-war between French and Germans, the Alsatians themselves have often been more concerned with their own livelihood than espousing one cause over the other.

The French base their historical claim on the lands of their Gallic ancestors for whom, with Julius Caesar's blessing, Germany began on the other side of the Rhine. The Germans claim the territory as an inheritance of the German-controlled Holy Roman Empire after the death of Charlemagne.

Nominally under the Germans throughout the Middle Ages, Alsace was submerged among hundreds of petty German principalities until it became a vital buffer zone in the Franco-German rivalry.

After the butchery of the Thirty Years' War had halved its population, Alsace was more than happy to accept French protection—consecrated by Louis XIV's formal acquisition of Strasbourg in 1681. The Revolution of 1789 was decisive in injecting the French language and customs into Alsatian life. The *Marseillaise* was composed in Strasbourg in 1792 for the French Army of the Rhine; later it was adopted by the volunteers of Marseille. Alsace provided some of Napoleon's most distinguished generals— Kléber, Kellermann and Rapp.

When the Germans seized Alsace (and Lorraine) in the war of 1870, thousands of Alsatians preferred exile in Algeria, or elsewhere in France. But the province of Elsass prospered under Kaiser Wilhelm, and not everybody was delighted in 1918 by the welcome back to France's chaotic Third Republic.

The Third Reich helped most of them change their mind. Under the Nazis, the French language was outlawed. Names had to be changed from Charles to Karl, Jean to Hans, French-style wreaths were forbidden in cemeteries, along with a ban on *baguettes* and berets—"this ridiculous headgear, totally un-Germanic". Alsace was supposed to disappear as a distinct cultural entity and become part of an administrative district of "Oberrheingau".

This time, there was no reason to regret the return to French rule, and today no province waves the French flag more fervently than Alsace. But Alsatian workers don't hesitate to commute across the border into Germany for the higher salaries; and the great two- and three-star restaurants of Ammerschwihr, Strasbourg and Illhaeusern are overflowing with Germans.

When Goethe arrived in Strasbourg, he just dropped his bag at his hostel, Zum Geist, and rushed off to the cathedral. The stout-limbed can follow his example, and start by climbing the 300-odd stairs to the platform just below the steeple for a fine **view** over the city.

Combining the architectural style of Ile-de-France Gothic with Rhenish German sculpture, the church is an apt symbol of Alsatian culture. The original designer, Erwin von Steinbach, began the magnificent pink Vosges sandstone façade in 1277 but only got as far as the splendid **Gallery of Apostles** over the central rose window.

Ulrich von Ensingen, master builder of the great cathedral of Ulm, set about construction of the octagon of the north tower in 1399. The graceful openwork spire was added in the 15th century by Johannes Höltz of Cologne. The French Revolutionaries threatened to tear the steeple down, as it offended their principle of equality, but were reassured when a local townsman coiffed it with a patriotic blue-white-and-red bonnet. All traces of an ugly 19th-century attempt to "balance" it with a second tower have been removed.

The Revolutionaries did destroy most of the cathedral's statues, but 67 were saved (many of the originals now housed in the Musée de l'Œuvre Notre-Dame next door). The central porch is still intact, depicting Jesus' entry into Jerusalem, the Crucifixion and other scenes from the New and Old Testaments.

Inside, there's a formidable Flamboyant Gothic **pulpit**, built for preacher Geiler von Kaysersberg to match his terrifying fulminations against the Protestant Reformation. Among the admirable 12th–14th-century **stained-glass windows** in the nave and northern aisle are portraits of medieval German emperors.

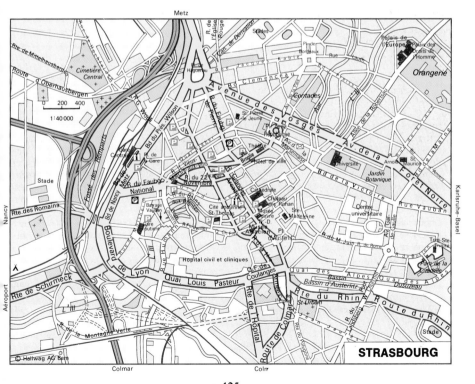

The "popular attraction" of the south arm of the transept, approached through the Portail de l'Horloge, is the 19th-century **astronomical clock** in which Death and all kinds of other jolly little figures parade around the dial to announce 12 noon. For some reason, this happens at 12.30 p.m., but in the summer, get there at noon anyway or you won't see a thing. Then after everyone's gone, stay on to see in peace the marvellous 13th-century sculpted **Angel's Pillar** *(Pilier des Anges)*.

A sound and light show *(Son et Lumière)* is held at the cathedral in summertime, one in German, one in French, recounting 2,000 years of history.

On the Place de la Cathédrale, at the beginning of the Rue Mercière, stands the 13th-century **Pharmacie du Cerf** (Stag Pharmacy), older than the cathedral and reputedly the oldest pharmacy in France.

Neuf-Brisach, south of Strasbourg, was the last of 160 such fortified citadels around France's frontiers built for Louis XIV by the indefatigable Sébastien le Prestre de Vauban (1633–1707). A man of all-round talent, Vauban also built ports, canals and aqueducts and perfected military assault techniques, especially the art of siege craft. In his spare time, he wrote treatises on piracy and pig-farming, a courageous pamphlet advocating the recall of the banished Huguenots and another, awfully unpopular in Versailles, proposing a national income tax.

The other venerable house of the square, now a restaurant, is the **Maison Kammerzell**. The ground floor dates from 1467; the beautifully sculpted wooden façade of the superstructure from 1589.

Guardian of the city's medieval and Renaissance treasures, the **Musée de l'Œuvre Notre-Dame** is itself made up of a superb group of 14th-, 16th- and 17th-century houses around a secluded Gothic garden on the Place du Château south of the Cathedral. Besides sheltering the most vulnerable of the Cathedral's statuary and some stained-glass windows from the earlier 12th-century Romanesque building, the museum has a fine collection of Alsatian Renaissance painting by Konrad Witz, Martin Schongauer and Hans Baldung Grien.

In the middle of the predominantly Germanic old city centre, the **Château des Rohan,** the classical 18th-century residence of Strasbourg's princes and cardinals, makes an emphatically French statement.

The furniture collection of the château's **Musée des Arts décoratifs** offers interesting comparisons between Parisian and Alsatian aristocratic and bourgeois tastes of the 17th and 18th centuries. But the museum's pride and joy is its great ceramics collection, displaying beside Europe's finest porcelain and faïence the astonishing Rococo craftsmanship of the Strasbourg Hannong family, most remarkably a huge tureen in the form of a turkey. If you didn't get enough of the astronomical clock in the cathedral, you'll get a close-up view here of figures from the original 14th-century model.

The château also houses the **Musée des Beaux-Arts,** noteworthy for a Giotto *Crucifixion,* Raphael's *La Fornarina,* and the unusual sombre realism of Watteau's *L'Ecureuse de cuivre.*

Behind the château, cross the Pont Sainte-Madeleine over the Ill and stroll along the Quai des Bateliers, past the remnants of old Strasbourg, to the bizarre 14th-century **Place du Corbeau** near the bridge of the same name. Continue along the Quai Saint-Nicolas to the **Musée alsacien** at number 23, a group of 16th- and 17th-century houses appropriate to the colourful collections of Alsatian folklore. Children love the ancient toys and dolls. Instruments of worship and ritual illustrate the life of the province's important Jewish community.

Make your way west to the Pont Saint-Martin for a first view of the city's most enchanting quarter, the old tannery district known as **La Petite France.** At a point where the Ill divides into four canals, the tanners shared the waterways with millers and fishermen. Their sturdy gabled houses line the Rue des Dentelles and Rue du Bain-aux-Plantes. The timbered façades and immaculate balconies festooned with geraniums are the most delightful part of Strasbourg's German past. On an uncrowded day, splash out on an expensive meal at one of the waterside restaurants.

The **Barrage Vauban,** remains of the fortifications Vauban built for Louis XIV, spans the Ill to the west. Its roof affords a splendid panoramic view across the canals and La Petite France to that soaring silhouette of the cathedral. At sunset, it makes the perfect finish to a day's walk. But many like to start out from here with an early morning view of the ensemble and then reverse the order of the walk we have proposed, reserving the Cathedral for a triumphant climax.

Route du Vin   13,E2

Sheltered from the cold, damp, northwest winds by the Vosges mountains, the vineyards of Alsace enjoy a microclimate ideal for a majestic white wine that confidently holds its own against the more internationally renowned wines of Burgundy and Bordeaux.

The vineyards hug the gentle slopes between the Vosges and the Rhine valley along one narrow 120-kilometre (75-mile) strip, stretching from Marlenheim, just west of Strasbourg, down to Thann, outside Mulhouse. The winding "wine route" is well signposted; its charming medieval and 16th-century villages and ruined castles (Haut-Koenigsbourg, Kaysersberg) make it the prettiest vineyard tour in the country, best of all during the October wine harvest.

Tasting and purchases are possible at many of the properties. Inquire at the local *syndicat d'initiative* or Colmar's Maison du vin d'Alsace about specific vineyard tours organized from Obernai and Turckheim, among others.

A walk around the lovely lime-shaded ramparts of **Obernai** will convince you of the perennial prosperity of its wine growers and farmers. Among the elegant, spotless timbered houses of the 16th-century Place du Marché, note the fine **Halle aux blés** (Corn Market) and **Hôtel-de-Ville**, as well as the handsome Renaissance **Puits aux six seaux** (Six Pails Well) between the town hall and the parish church.

As famous for its Riesling wines as for its Renaissance houses, **Riquewihr** is almost too "picturesque" to be believed and so too often overcrowded. Cars must be left at the southern end of town. If you can get there on a quiet day, have a good look at the stately **Maison Liebrich** (1535) and **Maison Preiss-Zimmer** (1686) on the main street, Rue du Général-de-Gaulle. Just before you reach the main gate and town symbol, the 13th-century **Dolder**, turn off to the right to take a peep at the little **ghetto** in the wooden-galleried Cour des Juifs. For people who like instruments of torture, there is also a medieval chamber of horrors in the **Tour des Voleurs** (Thieves' Tower).

Nestling at the foot of its ruined castle, the pretty medieval town of **Kaysersberg** is famous as the birthplace of the Nobel Peace Prizewinner Dr. Albert Schweitzer (1875–1965). His parents' house has become the **Centre culturel Schweitzer** (124, Rue du Général-de-Gaulle) devoted to the life of the humanitarian, who was also a great performer of Bach's organ works. The parish church, **Eglise Sainte-Croix**, is worth a visit for its splendid 16th-century **altarpiece** by Jean Bongartz of Colmar. It is a polychrome sculpted wooden triptych of 18 panels portraying in moving detail the last days of Jesus. A 10-minute walk up the wooded hill to the **castle tower** gives you a delightful view of the town and valley of the Weiss river.

To flee the madding crowds, seek out the unspoiled little town of **Turckheim**, epitome of the shiny bright Alsatian village. Its 16th- and 17th-century charm is preserved within a triangular rampart.

Colmar *13,E2*

Some people make a pilgrimage to this town just to visit the great Musée d'Unterlinden. But the town itself, with a miraculously preserved old city centre, has much else to offer and makes a quieter alternative to Strasbourg as a base for your vineyard excursion.

Converted from a 13th-century convent of Dominican nuns, the **Musée d'Unterlinden** provides the perfect setting for one of the world's undisputed masterpieces of religious art, Matthias Grünewald's awe-inspiring **Isenheim Altarpiece,** displayed in the chapel. Created for the Isenheim convent of Saint Antony between 1512 and 1516, the altarpiece originally folded out in three panels which are now mounted for exhibition in separate sections.

To appreciate the climactic impact of the whole work, view it in the reverse order, starting at the far end with the stately sculpted polychrome wooden panel of Saints Augustine, Antony and Jerome, carved by Niklaus Hagenauer. The first of Grünewald's painted panels depicts on one side the conversion and temptation of Antony and, on the other, the birth of Jesus and a chorus of angels. The second panel is devoted to the Annunciation and Resurrection and, on the reverse side, what is perhaps the most pain-filled and exalted Crucifixion ever realized. Grünewald's illuminated colour and uncompromising realism achieve an almost terrifying emotional intensity.

When you've recovered your composure, be sure to see the superb altarpiece of Martin Schongauer, Hans Holbein's portrait of a woman and, a proud new acquisition, Lucas Cranach's exquisite *Mélancolie*. The fine modern collection of Braque, Bonnard and Picasso offers an interesting counterpoint.

The old town centre is closed to traffic. Keep an eye open for the many handsome gabled houses of the Renaissance period: the **Ancienne Douane** (Old Customs House, Grand-Rue), **Maison des Arcades** (Grand-Rue), **Maison Pfister** (Rue des

Marchands) and **Maison des Têtes** (Rue des Têtes).

As soon as a town has a couple of canals with quaint bridges across them, likely as not the neighbourhood will be called Little Venice. Colmar is no exception. Its **Petite Venise** is south of the old town. From the Saint-Pierre bridge, you have a lovely view of its flowery banks, weeping willows and timbered houses, with the tower of Saint Martin's church in the distance, none of it remotely Venetian but still very pretty. The district on the opposite bank of the river was once a fortified enclave, inhabited mainly by market gardeners who used to sell their wares from barges on the river. It holds on to its original, colourful name of **Krutenau** (Vegetable Waterway).

Because it was recently vandalized, the **Eglise des Dominicains** is open only in the summer months, when it exhibits its great treasure (stolen and recently recovered), Martin Schongauer's altar painting *Vierge au buisson de roses* (Madonna in the Rose Bower). Take a look, too, at the remarkable 14th- and 15th-century **stained-glass windows**.

Americans may be pleased to note that Colmar is the birthplace of Auguste Bartholdi, designer of the Statue of Liberty. His 17th-century house (30, Rue des Marchands) is now the **Musée Bartholdi**, displaying his models and drawings. His statue of Napoleon's general Jean Rapp, another local boy, can be seen on the Place Rapp.

Haut-Koenigsbourg 13,E2

At a height of 755 metres (2,477 feet), it dominates the plain of Alsace. Perched like a Grimm Brothers fairy-tale castle on an isolated peak near Sélestat, visible for miles around, the history of the castle of Haut-Koenigsbourg goes back into the mists of the Middle Ages, until it was burnt to the ground by the Swedes in 1633. For centuries it stayed as a ruin, until the town of Sélestat, short of cash to restore it, presented it to Kaiser Wilhelm II in 1899 (Alsace was, don't forget, German at that moment) who had it rebuilt as it was in the 15th century—or as he thought it was. But the effect is not unappealing, and the two rings of walls with the drawbridge have a good, solid medieval flavour. Inside, the rooms are much as Wilhelm left them, with in the Salle des Fêtes a blood-curdling inscription he apposed in the course of his last visit in April 1918 when World War I was going badly for him: *"Das habe ich nicht gewollt"* ("I never wanted *this*").

*I*f the good people of Barr have a problem for their mayor to settle, they are more likely to find him out in his vineyard than sitting behind a desk in his handsome 17th-century town hall. This is grassroots politics at its best. And the stuff for electoral victory parties is strictly home-grown.

Burgundy
17,E2;18,AB1-2

Burgundy has a marvellous variety of attractions: the wines, of course, and the fine gastronomy that goes with them, lazy days on the Canal de Bourgogne drifting past green meadows, the grand ducal palace of Dijon, its museums and its mustard.

While the Ile-de-France is the cradle of the great Gothic cathedrals, the major jewels of French Romanesque architecture are to be found in Burgundy, from Vézelay to Autun and south to the noble ruins of Cluny. The special joys of Burgundy are in the tiny villages, some of which we'll tell you about, but more that you'll be delighted to discover for yourself. Their manor farms and millhouses, exquisite parish churches and open-air stone laundries down by the stream are the rural soul of France.

If you're driving down from Paris, you'll get the best out of Burgundy by leaving the *autoroute* at the Courtenay or Auxerre exit and touring the rest of the way on the perfectly good, but above all beautiful secondary roads. The TGV goes through to Montbard, Dijon and Beaune (see p. 59). Auxerre makes a good stop for your first excursions into the Burgundy interior, particularly if you want to stock up for a picnic or pick up some bottles of the famous Chablis white wines; you may prefer, however, to drive out to the vineyards in delightful undulating country east of the *autoroute* for your picnic, precisely.

The Good, the Bad and the Ugly

From 1363 to 1477, the Dukes of Burgundy amassed wealth and power that were the envy of most of the kings of Europe, but what they really liked was fancy nicknames.

Philippe le Hardi (the Bold) won his when, at the age of 14, he slapped an English soldier in the face for insulting the King of France, Philippe's father. He was equally slap-happy with the enormous dowry he got from his wife Marguerite de Flandres, bringing the greatest Flemish artists to his court, covering himself in gold, silver, jewels and ostrich feathers and, 20 years before his death, ordering the most magnificent tomb in France. He died broke and his sons had to hock the family silver to pay for the funeral.

Jean sans Peur, notoriously ugly but Fearless, earned his name by slaughtering Turks, but it's more difficult to explain what, from a French point of view, was so Good about Philippe le Bon, who sold Joan of Arc to the English for 10,000 pieces of gold.

The last of the four great dukes got the name he deserved. He sought to consolidate the veritable empire that the family estates had become by invading Lorraine to link up Burgundy and Franche-Comté with possessions in Luxemburg, Picardy, Flanders and Holland. Proclaiming himself a latterday Alexander the Great, he lost everything at the Siege of Nancy and went down in history as Charles le Téméraire—the Foolhardy.

Auxerre
17,DE2

The old town centre with its cobbled streets climbing up a hill from the Yonne river is delightful looked at from below or wandered around in on top.

Down on the Paul-Bert bridge, you have a fine **view** of a skyline dominated by the handsome apses of the town's churches.

The Flamboyant Gothic **Cathédrale Saint-Etienne**, with its single unsteepled tower, is not at all typical of Burgundian architecture, but still very attractive. Inside, you'll find some fine 13th-century **stained-glass windows** in the ambulatory beyond the choir.

East of Auxerre and Tonnerre, the elegant little Renaissance **Château de Tanlay**, with its bizarre bulbous towers surrounded by a watered moat and park, has a dozy, dreamlike quality to it. Don't worry too much about the unexceptional interiors, though they have plenty of history: Huguenot leader Gaspard de Coligny's friends, the Protestant conspirators, plotted in the "loft" room, for instance. Just peek in at the main courtyard and then stroll around the lovely tree-shaded grounds, ideal for shaking off travel-aches. The stables house a **modern art museum** with first-class temporary exhibitions.

Châtillon-sur-Seine   *18,B1*

The Seine is little more than a modest stream here, fed by the Douix which has its **source** beside a pleasant rocky promenade on the eastern edge of town. Almost completely bombed out in 1940, the modern city's claim to fame is the **Celtic princess's treasure** housed in the **Archaeological Museum** *(Musée archéologique du Châtillonnais)*, Rue du Bourg. The fabulous 2,500-year-old *Trésor de Vix* was excavated from the nearby *oppidum* (community) of Vix at the foot of Mount Lassois. The princess's golden diadem, gold and silver goblets and jewels are displayed with the four-wheeled ceremonial chariot (which contained the remains of her body) and an astounding, huge 208-kilo (458-pound) bronze **vase** believed to come from a Greek colony in southern Italy.

Vallée du Serein   *17,E2*

This is just one of a score of lazy back-road excursions you can make through northern Burgundy's meandering green valleys. Either cutting across from Tonnerre or starting out from the village of Chablis, follow the little Serein river, tributary of the Yonne, towards Avallon.

Notice as you go the massive farm-houses, veritable fortresses, characteristically roofed with *laves*, flat volcanic-stone tiles, that add to the landscape a marvellous patina of colour and texture. The finely arched front doors are often at the top of a sturdy staircase over the street-level cellar. If you look carefully, you can spot, set in the stone walls, little sculpted heads of angels or demons, floral motifs or the scallop shell *(coquille Saint-Jacques)* marking the route of medieval pilgrims.

Noyers is a fortified medieval village with 16 towers in its ramparts. Many of its timbered and gabled houses date back to the 14th and 15th centuries, particularly on the Place de l'Hôtel-de-Ville and the Rue du Poids-du-Roy. From the little Renaissance church, there's a pretty view over the winding river.

At **L'Isle-sur-Serein**, the river divides momentarily to encircle the tranquil little town and the ruins of its 15th-century château.

Leave the river briefly to loop east around Talcy and its Romanesque church and the 13th-century château of Thizy, before ending the excursion at **Montréal**. This medieval town boasts a fine Gothic church with a remarkable Renaissance interior, notably the carved oak choir stalls and a Nottingham alabaster altarpiece.

Abbaye de Fontenay   *18,A1*

This venerable Cistercian abbey, 6 kilometres (4 miles) east of TGV-station Montbard, turns its back on the world, standing behind high walls in a lovely valley at the edge of a forest. The abbey has been rescued from its humiliating 19th-century conversion into a paper-mill, and the cloisters present once more the calm and simplicity that were the ideals of its 12th-century founder, Saint Bernard de Clairvaux.

As you go through the gate decorated with the arms of the Cistercian order, you'll notice a niche for a guard dog below the staircase. On the right is an austere hostel and chapel for the few pilgrims that passed this way, and beyond it is the forge of the hard-working Cistercians. Left of the entrance is the monks' bakery and an imposing pigeon loft.

Paid for by Bishop Everard of Norwich, for whom Fontenay was a refuge from the hostility of Henry II of England, the **abbey-church** has a sober unadorned beauty—no bell-tower, as there were no distant faithful to be called to worship, but harmonious proportions in the interior, and fine acoustics because Saint Bernard was a great lover of music. A serene statue of the Virgin Mary (13th century) stands in the north arm of the transept.

Château de Bussy-Rabutin   *18,B1*

A sharp tongue under Louis XIV could be a great advantage—or a severe hand-

*O*ne *of the largest nature reserves in the country,
the Morvan regional park covers some 175,000 hectares. The mountain
plateau's vast woodlands and half a dozen lakes made it a welcome
refuge from the turbulence of national politics for its most famous
citizen, François Mitterrand. Before becoming president, he was for
22 years mayor of the regional capital, Château-Chinon, and
always returned to his old headquarters there, "Au Vieux Morvan",
to await electoral results.*

neatly proportioned house is particularly fascinating for its jewel of a garden, for its various **portrait galleries,** including one, the so-called Chambre Sévigné, with 26 women; Bussy-Rabutin's second wife is sandwiched in a triptych between Mme. de Sévigné, the famous letterwriter, and her daughter. Equally impressive is the circular room in the west tower, simply covered with portraits taken from mythology or the nobility of the time— accompanied in many cases by mischievous quatrains, some of which doubtless have arcane meanings, lost on us today.

Nearby, above the little village of **Alésia,** took place one of the decisive battles in "French" history when Caesar (but only just, and then thanks to Ger-

Keep It Simple, Brother

Son of an aristocratic family near Dijon, Bernard de Clairvaux was determined to counter the pomp and opulence displayed by the powerful Cluny monastery with a return to the austerity of the earliest Benedictine monks.

"Why," he wrote to a fellow abbot, "all this excessive height in the churches, disproportionate length and superfluous width, why the sumptuous ornament and curious painting to catch the eye, distract the spirit and disturb meditation?"

While Cluny's preoccupation with worship left no time for manual or intellectual labour, Bernard's Cistercian monks led a rigorous life of scholarship, hard work and frugal diet. Today, the monastery at Clairvaux at the northern edge of Burgundy, of which Bernard was abbot, observes another form of frugality—it has been converted into a prison.

icap. Count Roger de Bussy-Rabutin learnt to his cost just what trouble it could bring, when he found himself exiled—twice—from Versailles to his château for writing songs or—worse—satires of court life that offended the king. Luckily his **château,** beautifully situated, not far from the Abbaye de Fontenay, was lovely and he wasted no time in further improving it. Set in beautiful formal gardens by the famous Le Nôtre, the

man reinforcements) beat Vercingetorix, the Gaul, thereby ending all resistance to Roman occupation of France. Caesar, ungallantly, had him tortured and executed—along with most of his troops.

Vézelay   17,E2

An exquisite centre of spirituality in a beautiful rustic setting, home of one of the major churches on the pilgrims' route from Germany and the Netherlands to

Santiago de Compostela in Spain, Vézelay is today the target of new pilgrims —tourists in search of quintessential Burgundy.

If you're travelling at high season, this is one of those places where you should make a really early start to get in ahead of the crowd.

To recapture something of the experience of the medieval pilgrim, park your car (or get out of the bus) down at the Place du Champ-de-Foire. Pass through the turreted Porte Neuve and follow the **Promenade des Fossés** along the ancient ramparts lined with walnut trees. At the Porte Sainte-Croix, you have a fine view over the Cure river valley and the path which leads to the place where, in 1146, Saint Bernard exhorted King Louis VII to lead the French on the Second Crusade. It was also the starting point of the Third Crusade in 1190, when England's Richard the Lion-Heart joined forces with Philippe Auguste.

The **Basilique Sainte-Madeleine**, originally under the obedience of Cluny and repository of the relics of Mary Magdalene, remains a masterly achievement of French Romanesque architecture, despite suffering from natural disasters, wars and revolution. The restorations of Viollet-le-Duc have maintained its majestic harmony—one of the best achievements of this 19th-century monument-restorer.

The narthex, or entrance hall to the nave, is crowned by a magnificent sculpted **tympanum** of Jesus enthroned after the Resurrection, preaching his message to the Apostles. On the central supporting pillar is a statue of John the Baptist, beheaded not by Herod but by Huguenot vandals.

The nave is a wonder of light and lofty proportions, enhanced by the luminous beige stone and splendid ribbed vaulting. In contrast to the exalted quality of the tympanum's sculpture, the robust carvings of the **capitals** in the nave are lively and down-to-earth, making a clearly popular appeal to the church's pilgrims. The themes are from the Bible and the legends of the saints. Beside David and Goliath, Daniel in the Lion's Den, the building of Noah's Ark, Lazarus and the death of the Rich Man, one curious sculpture shows St. Eugenia, tonsured and disguised as a monk, opening her robe to convince a sceptical friar that she's a woman. Although the church is dedicated to Mary Magdalene, she is surprisingly absent from the sculpture.

On the tree-shaded **terrace** beyond the church, relax on one of the benches and enjoy the view over the forested plateau of the Morvan. Then explore the old houses, wells and courtyards in the town's narrow lanes leading back down to the Place du Champ-de-Foire.

*C*rowning *a hill above the Cure river in eastern Burgundy, Vézelay's glorious Basilique Sainte-Madeleine holds pride of place among the Cluny abbots' many grandiose achievements in Romanesque architecture. But, imbued with its serenity, you can easily forget the pilgrimage church was once the focal point for Saint Bernard's call to arms in the bloody Second Crusade of 1146. An added warlike touch, it is also the last resting place of Vauban, the great military engineer.*

Autun 18,A2

To the south-east of the Morvan, Autun's 12th-century **Cathédrale Saint-Lazare** makes a natural point of comparison with Vézelay's Basilique Sainte-Madeleine.

While the Autun **tympanum** may lack the elevated spiritual impact of its counterpart at Vézelay, its rich carving of Jesus presiding at the Last Judgment is full of vitality. On the left, you see the happy few being welcomed by Peter. Immediately to the right of Jesus is the weighing of the souls, with Saint Michael trying to stop Satan cheating. On the far right, a cauldron is boiling a few of the unlucky ones.

Below Jesus' feet is a Latin inscription suggesting the tympanum to be the work of one man, Gislebertus (Gilbert). It says: "Gilbert did this. May such terror terrify those in thrall to earthly error, for the horror of these images tells what awaits them."

Gilbert is also believed to have carved the superb **capitals** on the pillars of the nave and aisles. Some of the more fragile pieces are exhibited in an upstairs **chapter room**, worth a visit for a close-up view of his magnificent workmanship. The sculpture places a graphic emphasis on the ugliness of sin (hanging of Judas, devil tempting Jesus) and the simple beauty of virtue (flight to Egypt or Mary Magdalen).

The nearby **Musée Rolin** shows a fine collection of Burgundian and Flemish sculpture and painting. The museum is partly housed in the elegant 15th-century mansion of Nicolas Rolin, a wealthy dignitary and benefactor of the famous Hôtel-Dieu at Beaune (see p. 141).

Le Morvan 18,A1-2

Here's another chance to get off the beaten track into some of the most beautiful unspoiled countryside in Burgundy—a favourite stomping ground of François Mitterrand. The rocky hills and dense forests of birch, oak and beech south of **Avallon** (good hotels and restaurants) give you plenty of opportunity for exercise: hiking and horseback riding along well-marked paths, canoeing in the fast-moving rivers or, for the more contemplative, fishing in the ponds.

Down the D10 road, **Quarré-les-Tombes** is so named for the scores of stone sarcophagi you'll see lying around the church—just how they got there or why still baffles the scholars. The **Saut de Gouloux** waterfall is a refreshing sight after a long (or short) walk. The pretty reservoir of the **Lac des Settons** with its little islands of pines and larches is a favourite both for fishing in summer and duck-shooting in the autumn.

The most spectacular panorama in the Morvan is up on the **Mont Beuvray** (821 metres/2,694 feet) high—drive or hike to the top. From the summit you have a rare bird's-eye view of the town of Autun and, with luck, a glimpse of the Alps and Mont Blanc. Mont Beuvray has a certain symbolic significance in the long march towards French national unity, for it was here, at the Gallic citadel of Bibracte, that the Gallic warrior Vercingetorix brought his rival chiefs together for a council of war before their courageous but vain last effort against Julius Caesar in 52 B.C. (see also p. 135).

Paray-le-Monial 18,A2

At the edge of the Charolais country where France rears its best beef, Paray-le-Monial cherishes one of Burgundy's finest Romanesque churches, the basilica of the **Sacré-Cœur**. It stands on the bank of the quiet little Bourbince river and is best seen when the pale golden towers of its façade are bathed by a late afternoon sun. Built under the direction of Abbot Hugues of Cluny, the church exemplifies at its best the brilliant architecture of that powerful monastic empire (see p. 142). Brilliant most of all for the interior's stunning contrast between the light flooding the nave and the contemplative shadow of the great choir and the chapels off the ambulatory. After the elaborate Arab-style carving on the arches and columns of the transept's north and south portals, the sculpted ornament inside the church is minimal, just a few half-finished figures on the capitals and a checkered pattern in the ambulatory.

Walk into the town centre to see the faintly tipsy-looking but still elegant Renaissance **Hôtel de Ville**, decorated on its façade with the emblems of the kings of France.

Bourg-en-Bresse   18,B2

Some people come here for the chickens, the *poulets de Bresse* celebrated for the whiteness of their flesh—often enhanced by a milk-bath before being sent to market. Others are drawn by the amazing 16th-century **mausoleum-church of Brou** erected by Marguerite of Austria for her dead husband, Count Philibert le Beau. In either case, a succulent treat is guaranteed.

Built by Flemish architect Loys Van Boghem, the church (deconsecrated) offers a profusion of Flamboyant Gothic and Renaissance ornament. A sophisticated tone is set in the sculpture of the **porch** with Marguerite and Philibert kneeling on either side of an equally elegant Jesus. This soon veers to opulence in the stone tracery of the triple-arched **choir screen** *(jubé)* and the elaborate carving of the **choir stalls**. It all culminates in sheer extravagance with the three **monumental tombs** of the noble couple and Philibert's mother, sculpted in Carrara marble white as a Bresse chicken. Notice how the husband and wife are portrayed alive on top of their tombs and dead below—smaller and barefooted.

The **cloisters** house a modern sculpture garden and a fine regional museum, the **Musée de l'Ain**. It recreates a typical rural house with its furniture, costumes, ornaments, household utensils and farm implements. The art collection includes Bernard Van Orley's masterly portraits of Marguerite of Austria and Habsburg Emperor Charles V, and a room devoted, perhaps inevitably, to *La Volaille dans l'Art*—"Poultry in Art".

Dijon   18,B1

Dijon is Burgundy's stately capital. It's the ideal gateway for the vineyards to the south and a drive around the pretty Val-Suzon to the north. It's also a starting point for barge cruises on the Canal de Bourgogne.

Not the least of the town's attractions is the shopping centre around the Place Darcy and Rue de la Liberté where you can hunt for such regional delicacies as the famous mustards, *pain d'épices* (gingerbread) and *cassis*, the blackcurrant liqueur that turns an ordinary white wine into a refreshing *kir*. For wines other than your immediate picnic needs, you're better off waiting for your tour of the vineyards or the wider selection available at Beaune.

To evoke the town's past glories, you must head for the semi-circular Place de la Libération (formerly Place Royale), designed by Jules Hardouin-Mansart, architect of the Château de Versailles. The elegant 17th- and 18th-century façades of the **Palais des Ducs** conceal the Renaissance structures of the dukes' heyday, but many of their treasures remain to be seen in the interior, as part of the **Musée des Beaux-Arts**.

You get a notion of the magnificence of Burgundian court life by starting your visit at the **ducal kitchens**, built in 1435. Imagine the banquets prepared in the six huge walk-in cooking hearths, blackened now by a couple of centuries of barbecue smoke, arching over in a soaring Gothic vault to the central ventilation.

The ground-floor rooms of the museum have a model of the old palace and a collection of Burgundian sculpture from the 15th century to the present day. In the upstairs painting galleries, the dukes' close links with the Flemish masters of their day are illustrated by the fine *Nativité* of the anonymous Maître de Flémalle and Dierick Bouts' *Tête de Christ*. The collection also includes important works by Peter Paul Rubens, Frans Hals, Veronese, Konrad Witz and Martin Schongauer.

But the museum's greatest treasures are the dukes' tombs in the **Salle des gardes** (brought there from the Charterhouse of Champmol, destroyed in the Revolution). It took the artists Jean de Marville, Claus Sluter and Claus de Werve 26 years (1385 to 1411) to complete the intricate marble and alabaster sculpture for the **mausoleum** of Philippe le Hardi. On the sides of the tomb bearing the recumbent statue of the duke are carved 41 marvellously expressive figures of mourners cloaked in monastic capes, variously praying, meditating, lamenting. The double tomb of Jean sans Peur and wife Marguerite de Bavière is also lavishly sculpted, but more stylized.

Near the tombs is Rogier van der Weyden's portrait of the third great duke, Philippe le Bon with the Golden Fleece, symbol of the chivalrous order he founded in 1429.

North of the palace, along the Rue de la Chouette and Rue Verrerie, you'll find some attractive late Gothic and Renaissance houses with picturesque inner courtyards, transformed into antique shops. In the Rue des Forges, note the **Hôtel Chambellan** at number 34 and the **Hôtel Aubriot** at number 40, home of the Provost of Paris who built the accursed Bastille prison.

Côte d'Or 18,B1

The kingdom of wine, the power of legend. For some people, this destination is *the* reason for coming to France.

Delightful as the Burgundy vineyards may be, the landscape and villages of some other *routes des vins* may be considered prettier—Alsace, for instance. And other wine growers, such as those around Bordeaux, may have more handsome châteaux. But none can compose a true connoisseur's poem like this, just by citing a few names on the map.

First verse, strictly red wine, *Côte de Nuits*: Gevrey-Chambertin, Cham-

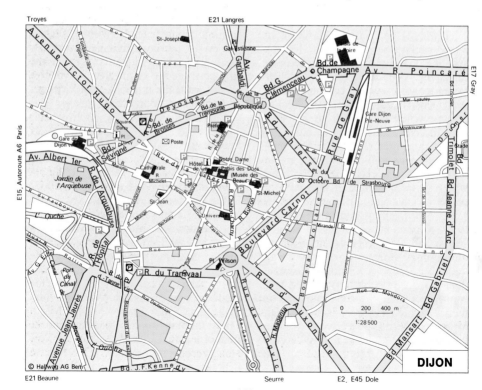

bolle-Musigny, Vougeot, Vosne-Roma-née, Nuits-Saint-Georges. Second verse, where the whites follow the reds, *Côte de Beaune*: Aloxe-Corton, Beaune, Pommard, Volnay, Meursault, Puligny-Montrachet, Chassagne-Montrachet, Santenay. The two together make up the *Côte d'Or*, the most expensive and delicious poem in the world.

From Dijon down to Santenay, the Côte d'Or is just 60 kilometres (37 miles) long. Nothing to do with "coast", *côte* here means the hillside. As you drive south from Dijon, be sure to get off the main road, N74, on to the parallel D122, signposted as *Route des grands crus* (Route of the great vintages), rejoining the N74 at Vougeot.

You may notice a sign at the edge of the vineyards: *"Grappillage interdit"*, which means just what it says—don't pinch the grapes (referring more particularly to those you might think were free for all, left hanging at the end of the harvest). Don't even try: Burgundians are ardent hunters.

Many of the famous vineyards are open to visitors, but tasting is strictly for serious customers with the clear intention of buying. The village of **Gevrey-Chambertin** makes a good first stop. The medieval château shelters the wine harvest in its great cellars. But the best cellars open to the public are in the château at **Clos de Vougeot**, owned by the Cistercian monks until the Revolution, now the property of the Chevaliers du Tastevin (fraternity of wine tasters). The grand old vats and wine-presses are worth the visit, and the guides will tell you more than you ever wanted to know about wine.

For the beginner (and most others, too), **Beaune** is the place to buy. It's the centre of the industry, and practically all the great wines are represented here. You won't get a better bargain at the vineyard unless you know the owner. A little **Musée du Vin** (Rue d'Enfer) tells the history of wine-making, with all its paraphernalia, from Roman times to the present day.

Of more artistic interest, the **Hôtel-Dieu** is a beautifully preserved 15th-century hospital (only recently converted to an old folks' home) founded by Chancellor Nicolas Rolin. Be sure to see the masterpiece of Flemish art commissioned by Rolin for the hospital chapel, Rogier van der Weyden's **altarpiece** of the Last Judgment, now on display in the museum, along with tapestries that adorned the walls of the unheated hospital wards to keep the patients warm. Just to see a hospital of centuries ago, however *"avant-garde"* in its time, sends shivers down one's back.

Mâcon   18,B2

Mâcon's site beside the Saône is not without charm, but it is chiefly as a wine-capital that the town provides a convenient stopping point, surrounded by the great vineyards of Pouilly, Fuissé and Vinzelles. The Rock of **Solutré**, a few miles south, contrasts strangely with the "civilized" Mâconnais. In 1866, an excavation uncovered a huge mass grave of horses, dating from between 15,000 to 12,000 B.C., bringing new light on a little known period of prehistory. From the top of the rock, at nearly 500 metres (1,640 feet), the inspiring view helps get the world into perspective.

Tournus   18,B2

It took monks fleeing the Norman invasions in the Dark Ages some thirty years to cross France and to transfer the remains of St. Philibert from Noirmoutier island off the Atlantic coast to a safer home in Tournus. His rather ghoulish remains are still to be seen in a golden casket after a fairly tumultuous career.

Burgundian to the core, the magnificent **abbey church's** towers are reflected in the peaceable Saône. The **Eglise Saint-Philibert** is one of the prides of Burgundy; its 14th-century façade has a faintly military aspect. Inside, the huge unadorned nave leads down towards five small rectangular chapels. Don't leave without a visit to the **Greuze Museum** given over to the local artist Jean-Baptiste Greuze (1725–1805) or a look at the regional folklore in the **Musée Perrin-de-Puycousin**. Even those not interested in chemistry will enjoy the **pharmacy** in the Hôtel-Dieu, the hospital.

Cluny *18,B2*

The **abbey** that today stands in ruin at the southern tip of Burgundy ruled its medieval world the way Louis XIV's Versailles dominated 17th-century France. Imagine the Sun King's palace reduced to rubble, with a few isolated but noble structures left standing to bear the weight of the vanished splendour, and you can appreciate something of the exquisite melancholy that rises from the stones of Cluny.

The 12th-century **Abbatiale Saint-Pierre-et-Saint-Paul** was the biggest

Not With a Bang, But a Whimper
Founded in 910, Cluny organized the first Crusades and masterminded the pilgrimages to Santiago de Compostela. Its abbots were emperors. At the beginning of the 12th century, it ruled over 1,450 monastic institutions with 10,000 monks, beyond French borders to Spain, Italy, Germany and Britain.

Its destruction began in 1798, when a merchant from nearby Mâcon bought the abbey for 2,000,000 francs. He systematically dismantled it over a period of 25 years. To build a set of national riding stables.

church in Christendom until the completion of Saint Peter's in Rome in the 17th century. Only the right arm of one of the two transepts and the octagonal bell-tower, the **Clocher de l'Eau-Bénite**, remain. But even this truncated edifice imposes its grandeur, and Cluny's excellent young guides (English-speaking in summer) help us conceive the rest. There had been five naves, two transepts, five bell-towers, 225 choir stalls.

The elegant classical 18th-century **cloisters** make a poignant contrast with the Romanesque church.

The 13th-century **granary**, beside an even older flour mill, has been turned into an admirable **museum** for the abbey's sculpted capitals displayed on reconstructed pillars.

To see some of Cluny's impact on the surrounding countryside, visit a few of the villages whose Romanesque churches were built by Cluny craftsmen, among them, Saint-Vincent-des-Prés, Taizé, Berzé-la-Ville and Malay, each a little gem.

*O*ne of the city of Dijon's most appreciated gifts
to world civilization is the kir. *Ideally one-third blackcurrant liqueur
(Dijon* cassis*) and two-thirds light white* aligoté *wine, it has been a
traditional Burgundy apéritif for centuries, probably first served in the
kitchens of the ducal palace. But it didn't achieve world renown until
championed in the 1960s by Félix Kir, a wily Catholic canon, energetic
mayor of the city and master of public relations.*

Jura

19,CD1-2

The Jura mountains, a northern extension of the Alps, cover several eastern departments making up the region of Franche-Comté. Proudly independent of France until finally "tamed" by Louis XIV in 1678, the area relies on the geography of its rampart-like mountains and dense pine forests to stay remote and blessedly unspoiled for nature-lovers.

Besançon

19,C1

A useful base for your excursions, the capital of Franche-Comté has an attractive town centre around the pedestrian zone of the **Grande-Rue**.

The **Musée des Beaux-Arts** (Place de la Révolution) claims to be the oldest in France (1694), but can in any case be proud of its fascinatingly remodelled interior, displaying the paintings on a progressive series of ramps. Of the Italians, Bellini's *L'Ivresse de Noé* (Drunkenness of Noah) and Giordano's *Philosophe cynique* are outstanding. Look, too, for Cranach's *Lucrèce* and *Le Repos de Diane* and fine French works by Ingres, Courbet and Bonnard.

Vallée de la Loue

19,C1

A favourite excursion is to trace the Loue river and its tributary, the Lison, back to their cascading **sources** through landscapes that inspired the paintings of Gustave Courbet.

His home town was **Ornans**, 26 kilometres (16 miles) south-east of Besançon. Stand on the Grand Pont for the celebrated view of the town's strange old timbered houses reflected in the calm waters of the river (a view known as the *Miroir de la Loue*). Close by the bridge is the **Musée Courbet** in the artist's house, where the exhibits include his palette and the old walking stick depicted in his celebrated *Bonjour, Monsieur Courbet*.

Dole

18,C1

Besançon took over from Dole as capital of the Franche-Comté under Richelieu, so the two have something of a common feel. The Doubs river meanders below the town, with its pleasant old centre and rust-red roofs on the hilltop, capped by the lofty Eglise **Notre-Dame**. From the top of the tower, at 74 metres (243 feet), the watchman would shout out the start of any fires (he did this till 1925). Inside the church, the organ (1750) is particularly noteworthy.

Squatting below the church, the old roads slope down beside the lovely well-concealed houses of the bourgeoisie, in particular Rue du Collège de l'Arc and Rue Mont-Roland with the **Hôtel Froissard**.

Arc-et-Senans

19,C1

The 18th-century **Saline Royale** (saltworks), now abandoned, is surely one of the most elegant factories in the world, in fact the nucleus of a Utopian city conceived by Claude-Nicolas Ledoux. He had the outlandish idea of making working conditions for the salt labourers pleasant. In green surroundings, the build-

*T*he Loue river of Gustave Courbet's childhood was—and still is—much more tranquil than the life led by the great painter of 19th century realism. His fellow townspeople of Ornans raged at him for depicting them with uncompromising fidelity, warts and all, in such works as L'Enterrement and L'Après-dîner. Ardent participant in the Paris Commune of 1871, he was condemned to 6 months jail for allegedly instigating the toppling of the victory column on the Place Vendôme—and ruined financially by having to pay for its restoration.

ings of the saltworks are set in a semi-circle around administrative offices, each with easy access to the other and all in simple classical style.

A **museum** is devoted to Ledoux's plans, models and avant-garde theories, and seminars are held on urban and industrial planning for the future.

The salt mines at **Salins-les-Bains,** 23 kilometres (14 miles) south-east, provided the salt water needed for the salt that was "ferried" via a system of wooden pipes to Arc-et-Senans—if it wasn't waylaid or the pipes didn't split or freeze. Visit the interesting museum in working order, too.

Arbois   18,C2
Arbois wine has a faint taste of fir-resin, for the town, at the foot of the Jura, stands at the crossroads of the coniferous Jura uplands and wine-growing Bur-

gundy. Wine is the main industry of this well-preserved medieval *bourgade,* home for most of his youth of Louis Pasteur, who arrived aged 5 in 1827. A visit to **Pasteur's house** brings to life the career of one of France's greatest scientists.

Les Reculées   *18,C2*
These horseshoe-shaped valleys nestle like narrow amphitheatres against abrupt rocky cliffs.

One of the best is the **Cirque de Baume,** between Lons-le-Saunier and Baume-les-Messieurs (visit the cowering abbey in the lovely village while you're at it). South-east of Arbois, the **Reculée des Planches** takes you to the fairytale waterfalls of the Cuisance and ends at the dramatic **Cirque du Fer à Cheval.** By then you'll be ready to sample some heady Arbois wine; try the *vin jaune* with a chunk of Comté cheese.

Orchards, Oyster-Beds and Royal Châteaux

The dominating influence on Normandy, Brittany and the Loire Valley has always been the sea. Normandy's history was launched by the Scandinavians in their longships, and its freedom retrieved by the American, British and Canadian Allied forces in their more cumbersome landing craft.

Brittany has ever been a seafaring province, largely untouched by the Roman invasions, and then populated by Celts fleeing from the Angles and Saxons across the English Channel. The Loire Valley was also subject to Norman invasions, penetrating as far as Angers and Tours. It owed much of its subsequent prosperity to the exotic Eastern trade coming upriver from the Atlantic, until the river succumbed to the competition of the railways in the 19th century.

Today, Normandy offers a patchwork landscape of rich green hedgerowed farmland, and a rich dairy cuisine to go with it; lazy days at the elegant old seaside resorts; the timeless wonder of Mont-Saint-Michel; the monumental reminders of medieval Norman warriors at Bayeux and the latterday liberators on the D-Day beaches.

Brittany's is a wilder, less civilized countryside, with a rugged coastline to match. Its oysters and mussels are as fresh as the sea breezes, its people as weather-beaten as their granite houses. But nestling in the hollows of the windswept heaths are havens of pious calm among the parish closes, and you'll find plenty of peaceful sandy beaches in sheltered coves along the buffeted coastline.

From its aristocratic past, the Loire Valley has preserved not only its countless châteaux. The good life is there in abundance for anyone with the leisure to enjoy it. Its wines are more than respectable accompaniments for the game from the forests of Sologne and the freshwater fish of the Loire's tributaries.

Normandy   8-9,AE1-2

The region divides into an eastern half, Haute-Normandie, along the Seine valley, similar in scenery to the Ile-de-France; and the more rugged Basse-Normandie to the west, more akin to neighbouring Brittany. Vast expanses are cultivated for agribusiness; the more traditional orchards and lush meadowland cattle pastures produce strong cider and pungent cheeses.

The settled, tranquil existence of the solid bourgeoisie of Rouen or Caen and the even more solid farmers surrounding them makes you wonder whether the tumultuous history of their murdering, raping, pillaging ancestors isn't all a jolly myth. Normandy is rural France at its most civilized; the soil's fertility tamed all conquerors.

Dieppe
9,D1

France's oldest seaside resort and the closest beach to Paris is a popular and active gateway to Normandy for those crossing the English Channel from Newhaven.

The **harbour** conjures up, in miniature, something of the bustle of the grand ocean ports in the heyday of transatlantic liners and sea-trade with exotic lands. Holiday-makers at the Avant-Port (ferryport) do without baggage-porters or chauffeur their own cars off the boat. Across the **Pont Colbert** drawbridge, almost a horizontal version of its contemporary, the Eiffel Tower (1889), is the **Bassin Duquesne** fishing-port. The nearby **fish-market** for scallops, sole, turbot and sea-bass, early in the morning, is about as lively as the phlegmatic Dieppois fishermen ever get. At the **Bassin de Paris**, in place of the old freighters from Guinea that brought elephant-tusks and whales' teeth for Dieppe's time-honoured ivory-carvers, you'll find colourful banana-boats from Morocco.

The bracing pebble **beach** is more popular these days for stretching your legs than bathing, with a good **view** west to the Ailly lighthouse.

The 15th-century **Château de Dieppe**, built to defend the port against the English after driving them out in the Hundred Years' War, is now a **museum** (Rue de Chastes) devoted to the town's venerable sea-faring traditions. Among its collection of model sailing ships is the *Dauphine* with which Giovanni da Verrazzano sailed from Dieppe in the 1520s to discover the bay of what he proposed calling Land of Angoulême but is now known as New York. Pride of place goes to the intricate scrimshaw carving in ivory—compass-boxes, sewing caskets and bottled ships dating from the 18th century, but also fine 19th-century work by Pierre Graillon who raised the craft to the art of sculpture. Look, too, for the comprehensive collection of engravings by Cubist Georges Braque.

The courageous but abortive Anglo-

Canadian raid on Dieppe in World War II is commemorated in the **Musée de la Guerre et du raid du 19 août 1942** (2 kilometres [1¼ miles] west of town on the D75). Built at the radar station that was one of the raid's main targets, the museum also exhibits Allied and German tanks and the deadly V-1 pilotless aircraft loaded with explosives that were catapulted across the Channel from German air bases in Normandy in 1944.

At quiet moments like this, it is hard to believe
that the Channel coast has been an almost permanent launching pad
for invasion and war. Julius Caesar and William the Conqueror
going one way, Henry V, Eisenhower and Montgomery coming in
the other direction while, in between, Napoleon and Hitler tried
but never made it.

Just west of Dieppe, on a grassy hedgerowed plateau overlooking the sea, the tranquil, rustic resort of **Varengeville-sur-Mer** offers bracing cliff-top rambles as alternatives to the sea-bathing at nearby Pourville and Quiberville.

The **Parc des Moustiers** is a year-round delight, famous for its giant rhododendrons and azaleas blooming in May and June, for roses and hydrangeas in July and August, and for the autumn foliage of its exotic trees from China, Japan and the Americas. In the middle of the park is a fine 19th-century **mansion** designed in the style of the English Arts and Crafts movement by Edwin Lutyens, architect of Imperial New Delhi. Take a

---

Getting the Ants Out of their Pants

It took a long time to stop the Normans (Norsemen, or Northmen) moving around. The Scandinavian seamen made their first isolated incursions into France while exploring the northern Atlantic in the 2nd and 3rd centuries. But they found nothing to hold their attention until prosperous Christians along the Seine valley began building monasteries and churches with a treasure of gold, silver and jewels.

In 820, the Norsemen staged their first major invasion in their dragon-headed longships, subsequently plundering their way up the river to Paris. Masters of guerrilla warfare and ambush, they had horses aboard for lightning raids into the interior. Chartres was one of their prime targets. To cut his losses, the French king Charles le Simple had the simple idea in 911 of giving these madcaps some land to settle down on: the duchy of Normandy.

Duke Rollo and his men made their capital at Rouen. They converted to Christianity and happily set about organizing towns and farms and trade, just like any other civilized people. And those who couldn't take to the sedentary life went off on Crusades to the Holy Land, to devote their bloodthirsty pillaging and pirating to a Good Cause.

Within a few decades, thanks, it's said, to the extraordinary wives that Frenchwomen were, the Normans were as French as the other "French". And William the Conqueror had long since forgotten any "Norseman" connection when he set out to conquer England in 1066.

While their cousins stayed home to watch the skin set on the cheese.

---

peek inside at the fine furniture and Pre-Raphaelite décor that includes a Burne-Jones tapestry.

A house of another age is the **Manoir d'Ango** (south of town, off the D75). The grand 16th-century residence was built for Dieppe's greatest shipping magnate, Jean Ango, by Italian Renaissance architects and sculptors. The spacious arcaded courtyard is dominated by the ornate dovecote of the main lodge subtly combining brick, flint-and sandstone. Ango made his fortune by rounding up pirates in the Mediterranean and sharing their spoils with King François I, a guest of this manor.

In the village **church** is a stained-glass window by Georges Braque, who spent his last days at Varengeville and is buried in the church cemetery.

Rouen 9,D2

The Norman capital's historic civic pride breathes from every stone, every timber frame lovingly restored or reconstructed after the crippling bomb damage of 1944. After all, this is the ancient centre of Normandy's thriving textile industry, and the place of Joan of Arc's martyrdom—a symbol of national resistance to tyranny.

Hugging a loop in the Seine, the town did draw at least one advantage from the war—the factories on the left bank were destroyed, leaving room for a modern residential area. The industries were rebuilt on the outskirts. On the right bank, the charming medieval and Renaissance centre around the cathedral has been renovated and reserved for pedestrians.

Start your walk, not at the cathedral, but at the western end of the historic district, on the **Place du Vieux-Marché**. Old and new Rouen come together around the bright and airy market halls (marvellous selection of cheese and fruit) and the attractive modern **Eglise Sainte-Jeanne-d'Arc**. Nearby is a monument to mark the spot where Joan was burned at the stake in 1431. Some stones have been excavated from the rostrum of her judges. The years have passed but Joan of Arc remains a touchy subject. While probably only a few Frenchmen still bear a real grudge against the British (notably when it comes to negotiating agricultural prices for the European Community), ironic remarks should be avoided—the French take their Freedom Fighters seriously. Inside the church are some fine 16th-century **stained-glass windows** salvaged from an older church bombed in 1944.

Leading south-east from the market is Rouen's most celebrated street, the **Rue du Gros-Horloge**, now as always the city's bustling commercial centre. Its timber-framed houses of the 15th, 16th and 17th centuries are splendid examples of sturdy Norman architecture, achieving a very pleasing irregularity in the way the plaster is set in oblique forms between the solid oak posts and collar beams supporting the balconies. The elegant Renaissance arched clock-tower of the **Gros-Horloge** is the town's emblem, its Eiffel Tower. The ornamental gilded clock face has only one hand, for the hours.

Beside the clock is a 14th-century belfry which still rings its bell at 9 p.m., time of the old curfew. Take the spiral staircase to the roof for a fine **view** of the city and its circle of hills around the Seine valley.

East of the Gros-Horloge stands the great **cathedral**, made famous in the modern age by Claude Monet's many Impressionist studies of its façade. The asymmetry of the two towers embracing the delicate tracery of the slender steeples creates a highly original silhouette among France's best-loved cathedrals.

The façade offers a remarkably harmonious anthology of Gothic architecture. The north tower, **Tour Saint-Romain**, has the sober simplicity of the cathedral's early Gothic beginnings in the 12th century, while the taller, more elaborate south tower, **Tour de Beurre**, is Flamboyant Gothic of the 15th century. According to local belief, this "Butter Tower" was paid for by Catholic burghers in exchange for the privilege of eating good Normandy butter during Lent. The

austerely sculpted porches flanking the main entrance are from the early period, and the more ornamental elongated central porch and the gabled upper windows were added in the 15th and 16th centuries. The main steeple is neo-Gothic of the 19th century.

The rather severe interior contrasts with the elaborate exterior, but the impact of the double-storeyed nave is lightened by the tall arches of the choir. In the Chapelle de la Vierge beyond the choir is the monumental Renaissance **tomb** of the Cardinals of Amboise, with superbly sculpted allegories of the cardinal virtues. On the south side of the choir is the more modest tomb of the most heroic of medieval English kings, portrayed recumbent above the inscription in Latin: "Here is buried the heart of King Richard of England, known as the Lion-Heart."

Behind the cathedral, cross over the Rue de la République to the 15th-century **Eglise Saint-Maclou**, the richest example of Flamboyant Gothic in the country. Note the masterful Renaissance carving of the oak doors on the central and north portals. In the interior, the same exuberant artistry can be admired in the sculpted wood organ frame and the stone tracery of the spiral staircase.

Turn north on **Rue Damiette**, graced by some of the town's handsomest old houses. The street leads to the elegant 14th-century Gothic abbey church, **Abbatiale Saint-Ouen**, with its splendid flying buttresses best observed from the little park east of the chancel.

The last great monument of the old town, in the Rue aux Juifs, is the grand **Palais de Justice**, a jewel of Renaissance and Flamboyant Gothic architecture built on the site of the medieval ghetto. Recent excavations uncovered a 12th-century **synagogue** (visits by arrangement with the Office de Tourisme, Place de la Cathédrale).

The prosperous town has a well-endowed **Musée des Beaux-Arts** (Square Verdrel), with important works by Velázquez, Caravaggio, Perugino, Veronese and Rubens. French artists include François Clouet, Delacroix and Rouen-born Théodore Géricault who is represented by a series of dramatic paintings of horses.

Jumièges *9,D2*

The D982 leading west from Rouen is the beginning of the **Route des Abbayes** that winds through woodland and meadows around the medieval Norman abbeys—most of them enjoying their heyday under William the Conqueror—at Saint-Martin-de-Boscherville, Jumièges, Saint-Wandrille, Le Bec-Hellouin and Caen, culminating in their masterpiece, Mont-Saint-Michel.

Among them, the grandiose ruins of the **abbey of Jumièges** occupy a special, inevitably romantic place. The white granite shells of its two churches, the Romanesque Notre-Dame and smaller Gothic Saint-Pierre, with trees and grass growing in and around the nave and chancel, survive their troubled end with moving dignity.

Duke William returned from his conquest of England to attend the consecration of Notre-Dame in 1067. Seven centuries later, the Benedictine monastery was disbanded by the Revolution, and the buildings were blown up with explosives by a local wood merchant who had bought them cut-price in an auction. But the sturdy edifices resisted total destruction and are still dominated by Notre-Dame's two soaring square towers (minus their original spires).

Honfleur *9,C2*

On the Seine estuary, this pretty little port has witnessed the beginning of nearly all of Normandy's great seafaring adventures—and is still a mecca for sailing enthusiasts. Towering over the sheltered yachting harbour of the **Vieux Bassin**, the tall slate- and timber-façaded houses gleam in the sun or, even more striking, glisten in a thunderstorm. Explore the old ship-builders' quarter along the **Rue Haute** running north-west from the Lieutenance, 16th-century remains of the royal governor's house at the harbour mouth.

Normandy isn't just cheese and apples. This fisherman is sorting tourteau crabs in the harbour of Saint-Vaast-la-Hougue, an increasingly important centre for oysters, too. During the Hundred Years' War, the English launched an offensive here that culminated in their famous victory over the French at Crécy in 1346.

Fécamp 9,C1

To appreciate the panorama across the cliffs to the harbour with the old abbey-church dominating the town behind it, leave the main highway to approach the town along the D79 coast-road via Senneville. The best **view** is from beside the small roadside chapel of Notre-Dame-du-Salut.

Liveliest time at the **harbour** is when the fishing catch comes in at high tide to be sold on the Quai Bérigny. Details of boat-cruises from the *syndicat d'initiative.*

The considerable Renaissance and Baroque reconstruction from the 16th to the 18th century and the iconoclasm of the Revolution have not overwhelmed the massive Gothic structure of the 13th-century **Eglise de la Trinité**. Since 1748, a classical façade replaces two towers at the church's western end, and the handsome remaining bell-tower now has a pyramidal roof in place of its spire, but the overall effect is still powerful. The most rewarding of its additions is the chancel's 15th-century Flamboyant Gothic **Chapelle de la Vierge** at the south-east corner—the main entrance.

But it's the interior that is most impressive. Take in the magnificently vaulted nave 127 metres (417 feet) long (just 3 metres or 9½ feet shorter than Paris's Notre-Dame) from the rostrum at its west end. The Gothic sculptural group immediately facing the entrance is the 15th-century **Dormition de la Vierge**, the Sleeping Virgin surrounded by the Apostles. The classical 18th-century **choir** culminates in a grandiose late Baroque gilded high-altar, and beyond it, the more subdued white marble Renaissance altar of Italian sculptor Girolamo Viscardo. In the north arm of the transept are some superb fragments of the 15th-century **choir-screen**, late Gothic sculptures of the Apostles at prayer.

In an almost hilariously ugly neo-Renaissance-cum-neo-Gothic building, the **Musée de la Bénédictine** (110, Rue Alexandre-le-Grand) is devoted to the dis-

Strong Medicine

In 1510, Brother Vincelli went gathering wild hyssop, melissa and angelica (also known as goutweed) on the Fécamp cliffs and distilled them with a few exotic Oriental spices to produce a miraculous health elixir. The recipe was lost when the monastery was disbanded in the Revolution. In 1863, an enterprising entrepreneur rediscovered it among some old family papers, added Cognac and Armagnac to pep it up, called it Bénédictine and made it a popular tipple for maiden aunts and their beaux, who convince each other it's good for their health.

tillery of the famous liqueur and some art-works salvaged from Fécamp's Benedictine monastery. Note the fascinating collection of fakes.

Etretat 9,C2

This quiet little resort has long been famous for the spectacular forms of the cliffs that frame its **beach**—on which the white marble-like pebbles are for once smooth enough to fall asleep on. (Local confectioners make sweets *(galets)* in imitation of the pebbles.)

The beautiful effects of erosion on its cliffs have attracted to Etretat some of France's most illustrious artists and writers. Monet was fascinated by the delicate play of light on the sea and rocks, as were Courbet and Boudin before him, and later, Dufy, Matisse and Braque. Maupassant spent his childhood here and featured it in his novels and stories, and it was equally prominent in the adventures of that most sophisticated rascal of the Belle Epoque, gentleman-burglar Arsène Lupin, created by Maurice Leblanc.

For a close-up of the **Falaise d'Aval** (Downstream Cliff) take the enjoyable cliff-top walk, 60 minutes there and back, from a stairway at the south end of the beach-promenade. There are three formations: the slender "Gothic" arch of the **Porte d'Aval** jutting out from the cliff; offshore, the sharply pointed 70-metre (230 feet) high **Aiguille** (Needle) which the Germans painted black during World War II; and, further south, the massive, more Romanesque arch of the 90-metre (295-foot)-high **Manneporte** (Magna Porta or Great Gate).

The **Falaise d'Amont** (Upstream Cliff), at the north end of town, is also worth a trip for the cliff-top walk and **view** back over Etretat from the Chapel of Notre-Dame-de-la-Garde (drive to the Avenue Damilaville, then 45 minutes' walk there and back).

Pays de Bray   *10,AB1*

This cheerful country of woods and meadows, with an excursion-circuit clearly signposted *Promenade dans le Pays de Bray*, constitutes Normandy's historic frontier with the Paris basin (Ile-de-France).

Guarding the southern approaches, **Gisors** has made a lovely park out of the massive ramparts and towers of the **Château fort** (fortress) built by William Rufus, son of the Conqueror, and expanded by Philippe Auguste. This strategically vital stronghold was a perennial bone of contention between the dukes of Normandy and the King of France till the end of the Hundred Years' War. The remarkable Gothic and Renaissance church, **Eglise Saint-Gervais-et-Saint-Protais**, has been restored to its former glory and is well worth a visit. Note the town's pretty *lavoir* (open-air laundry) using the clear waters of the Aunette river beside the Rue des Argillières.

Itchy Feet

Conquest and exploration, often amazingly far from home, were always a useful safety valve for the Normans' natural aggressive energies: England and Sicily in the 11th century, Sierra Leone in 1364, Brazil in 1503, Canada in 1506, Florida in 1563. Chicagoans to this day honour the passage of a great Rouen sailor who set out from Honfleur: the financial district of the Middle West's "Wall Street" bears the name of La Salle, who passed that way on his exploration of Lake Michigan and the Mississippi River in 1682.

The ancient wars are long forgotten in the charming villages of **Saint-Germer-de-Fly**, with its 12th-century abbey church, and fortified **Gerberoy**, notable for its old houses of timbered red and yellow brick and their exquisite little gardens.

The heights of **Les Andelys** command a wonderful view of the Seine river and valley from the fortress of **Château Gaillard**, built by Richard the Lion-Heart in 1197 to stop his old ally Philippe Auguste from approaching Rouen. It was Philippe's conquest of this fortress by siege (and a final assault up through the latrines) that ended the duchy's independence from the French crown. The chalk cliffs that you see to the north-west were once interspersed with slopes of vineyards, before wine was gradually edged out by cider.

Giverny is famous as the home of Claude Monet. His home has been lavishly restored with brand-new furnishings, artefacts from his studio and the collection of Japanese prints that provided some of his inspiration. His paintings are presented only in ingeniously deceptive photographic reproduction. The main attraction is the beautiful garden, complete with the Japanese bridge, water lilies and rose bowers that were among the Impressionist master's favourite subjects.

In attractive hilly surroundings south of the Seine's tributary, the Eure, the proud old cathedral city of **Evreux** was bombed first by the Germans in 1940, then by the Allies in 1944, but has made an impressive revival. Look first at the miraculously preserved **Tour de l'Horloge**, an imposing 15th-century clock tower opposite the town hall, and take the **lover's promenade** by the Iton river.

The treasure of the old abbey church of **Saint-Taurin** is the exquisite 13th-century **reliquary**, designed like a miniature cathedral of gold, silver and enamel with rubies and other precious stones, its delicate statuary depicting the legendary life of Saint Taurin, first Bishop of Evreux.

Deauville 8,C2

Cleverly blending old-fashioned elegance with modern comforts, the most prosperous of Normandy's seaside resorts is also the most expensive. But even if your budget doesn't extend to one of those seafront *palaces*, as the French call their luxury hotels, stop off on the wooden promenade of the celebrated **planches** for some of the most amusing people-watching in France. This is where a company director takes his secretary for weekend business conferences and runs into his wife with the chairman of the board. The white sandy **beach** with its colourful canvas sun shelters is a delight and the swimming perfectly good, but amazingly few people turn away from the spectacle on the *planches* long enough to go into the water.

Horse-lovers come for the summer racing, flat and steeple, and the prestigious

The strange rock formations eroded in Etretat's cliffs that attracted painters from Delacroix and Courbet to Braque and Matisse were only the "picturesque" pretext. They found more essential inspiration in the dramatic effects of light and the sea itself. Guy de Maupassant describes a visit to Courbet's seaside cottage-studio when waves were splashing against the windows and streaming down the walls as the artist painted between gulps of a heady cider.

159

yearling sale. What they win on the racing, they lose at the casino. The tennis and golf are first class; yachtsmen should bear in mind a Deauville proverb: if you can see the port of Le Havre, it will rain in the afternoon, and if you can't, it's already raining.

Côte Fleurie   8,BC2

Between the estuaries of the Touques and Dives rivers, 20 kilometres (12 miles) of sandy beaches, handsome villas and beautifully weather-beaten old hotels have great appeal for nostalgics of Napoleon III's Second Empire and the Belle Epoque of the 1900s.

The oldest of this coast's resorts, **Trouville** (where the gentry used to send their domestics) is now a slightly down-market Deauville but just as lively, with an excellent beach where people seem less frightened of swimming, and the bistros on the port serve much better seafood. It's only just across the river from Deauville, too.

The charm of **Houlgate** is in the trees and flowers of its gardens and the fine sands of its beach. Take the beautiful long walk at low tide east to the cliffs of the **Vaches Noires** (Black Cows).

Cabourg is the most stately of the old resorts. Take tea at least at its splendid **Grand Hôtel**, a true national shrine in which Marcel Proust wrote part of his *A la recherche du temps perdu*. It is the custom to fall asleep over a leather-bound copy in your deckchair.

Across the river is the little town of **Dives-sur-Mer** where, as they like to remind English visitors, William embarked in 1066. To rub it in, there's a Rue d'Hastings and a list of the Conqueror's companions on a wall of the parish church.

Pays d'Auge   8-9,C2

A delightful excursion inland from either end of the Côte Fleurie takes you to the very essence of the world's image of Normandy, its orchards, rolling green valleys and massive timbered manor houses, the land where the apples become cider and Calvados and the dairies churn out the pungent, creamy Camembert, Livarot and Pont-l'Evêque cheeses (see p.318).

You can buy the best Camembert, for instance, (labelled VCN, *Véritable Camembert de Normandie*) at the Monday-morning market in **Vimoutiers**, 55 kilometres (34 miles) south of Deauville. But local tourist offices will guide you to farms where you can sample and buy the regional cheeses on the spot—more fun than in the unexceptional towns of Camembert, Pont-l'Evêque and Livarot themselves. Drivers should be wary of the cider—in longer draughts, it can pack as much punch as the Calvados.

Industrial and commercial capital of the Pays d'Auge, and badly bombed in World War II, **Lisieux** has become an immensely popular pilgrimage town since the 1925 canonization of Sainte-Thérèse. A huge modern **basilica** has been built in her honour to receive the thousands of faithful.

The 12th-century Gothic **Cathédrale Saint-Pierre** has a lofty simplicity appropriate to the town of Thérèse. The Flamboyant Gothic chapel added beyond the choir is the burial place of Pierre Cauchon, judge of Joan of Arc and, denied the Archbishopric of Rouen he coveted, Bishop of Lisieux.

Not signposted as such, but meriting your attention as you follow the cheese and cider routes (see p. 46), is an itinerary south of Lisieux around the great **manoirs** (manor houses) reigning in solitary splendour over the countryside of the Pays d'Auge. Enjoying their heyday from the 16th to the 18th century, they range from handsome but modest timbered farmhouses to veritable châteaux that add to the timber framework subtle and colourful combinations of stone, brick and slate, with all the turrets and fortifications needed in their troubled times. One of the grandest is the 16th-century **Saint-Germain-de-Livet,** built in Italian Renaissance style beside a tributary of the Touques river. Its turreted walls have a checkered pattern of sandstone and green-varnished bricks around a courtyard with arcaded gallery. The 17th-century **Grandchamp** is another elegant combination of a brick and stone château joined on to a traditional timbered farmhouse. Other fine examples are the moated **Coupesarte**, still part of an active farm, **Bellou** amid its apple orchards, and **Chiffretot**, with an imposing octagonal tower.

In a region where the horse is still treated with particular reverence, the once royal stud farm of the **Haras du Pin** clings to three centuries of tradition with some 80 of the finest stallions in the country. They include Thoroughbreds, Arabs, Anglo-Arabs, French trotters and saddle-horses, sturdy Norman cobs and a dwindling stock of magnificent Percherons.

The Haras du Pin was completed under Louis XV and is justifiably known as the "Horse's Versailles" *(le Versailles du cheval)*. Drawing on their experience with the Palace of Versailles, Mansart designed the stud farm director's classical residence and red-brick stables—laid out in the shape of a stirrup—and Le Nôtre drew up the plans for the grounds, with characteristic geometrical avenues through the lawns and forest.

From February to July, the horses are farmed out to breed in the surrounding region. The rest of the year, you see them all here in their splendid stables, but even during those breeding months, a few are kept on the premises for special treatment and grooming. The best of the Thoroughbreds appear at the yearling sales in Deauville at the end of August.

Apart from the stable tour, there's a Thursday-afternoon parade of the horses, with coaches and all the traditional trappings of horsemanship. Show-jumping and *dressage* competitions are held in the spring and summer. To see some of the offspring of these prize stallions grazing in the meadows, drive south-east of the Haras du Pin around the stud farms of the Merlereault region.

South-west of the Haras du Pin, the **Château d'O** is a fine mixture of Renaissance styles with Flamboyant Gothic details, a flourish of gabled roofs reflected in its pond. Take a quiet walk around the woods in the château's park.

After admiring in **Sées** the 13th-century stained-glass windows of the cathedral, visit the town's *syndicat d'initiative* for its excellent maps of the marked hiking paths in the nearby **Forêt d'Ecouves**.

Caen
8,BC2

Little remains of Caen's historic centre, but its good hotels and excellent seafood restaurants make it, with Bayeux, a useful starting-point for visits to the D-Day beaches.

Caen was the first major objective of the D-Day landings. It took two months to capture and was devastated by Allied bombs and the shells of the Germans as they retreated.

Luckily, the noble silhouette of the **Abbaye aux Hommes** has survived (best seen from the Place Louis-Guillouard). Its church, **Eglise Saint-Etienne**, harmo-

---

The Way of All Flesh

Handsomest of all workhorses, aging from black to grey to gleaming white, the Percheron has been a steady victim of man's evolving technology.

Once, he was the favoured warhorse of the Crusader. In addition to the great strength that enabled him to carry the enormous weight of a knight in steel armour—the Percheron himself might weigh a ton—he had just the touch of Arab blood to make him fast enough to get his master out of trouble. With the advent of gunpowder and Napoleon's demands for ever speedier cavalry charges, just a humiliated few were needed for dragging artillery uphill. The rest went back to the farm.

Today, tractors and tanks have made him redundant, but still he is lovingly groomed at the Haras du Pin, three times a day, even though everybody knows his only destiny is horsemeat.

The Pays d'Auge counts over 100 manor houses like this splendid example at Victot (on the Cider Route), built in the 16th century with additions in the 18th. Victot's stables continue to enjoy a national renown established as a supplier of horses for the cavalry of Napoleon's Grande Armée.

des Beaux-Arts. Highlights include Poussin's *La Mort d'Adonis*, Perugino's *Le Mariage de la Vierge*, Tiepolo's *Ecce Homo*, Veronese's *La Tentation de Saint Antoine* and Rubens' *Abraham et Melchisédech*. The nearby **Musée de Normandie** makes a handsome introduction to regional folklore. Latest addition to the museum is the futuristic **Museum of the Battle of Normandy** where Peace, not War, is celebrated and the roots of the World War II conflict are studied in a modern, brilliantly conceived setting.

Bayeux   8,B2

Proudly the first French town to be liberated in World War II, the day after D-Day, Bayeux was blessedly preserved from destruction. Its fine Gothic cathedral dominates a charming **old town** *(vieille ville)* of medieval and Renaissance houses on the Rue Saint-Martin, Rue Saint-Malo and Rue Bourbesneur.

But the town's most cherished treasure is the magnificent **Bayeux Tapestry** (or more correctly *embroidery*) created for Bayeux Cathedral in 1077 to tell the story of Duke William's conquest of England. It is lovingly mounted in the Centre Guillaume-le-Conquérant (Rue de Nesmond) and accompanied by a fascinating film (in an English and French version) explaining the work's historic background. It's worth taking the commentated walking tour in English to follow the episodes.

No dry piece of obscure medieval decoration, the beautifully coloured tapestry gives a vivid and often humorous picture of life at William's court, with insights into medieval cooking, lovemaking and the careful preparations for war. These and the climactic Battle of Hastings are depicted with all the exciting action and violence of a modern adventure film, with a cast of 626 characters, 202 horses, 55 dogs and 505 other animals.

Adding insult to injury, it was a group of defeated Anglo-Saxon artisans who had to do the wool-on-linen embroidery, 70 metres (230 feet) long and 50 cen-

niously combining Romanesque towers and nave with Gothic steeples, choir and chancel, was begun in the momentous year of 1066, and William the Conqueror made its first abbot his archbishop of Canterbury. The elegant 18th-century monastery buildings have now become the town hall.

The remains of William's 11th-century castle house an excellent collection of European painting in the town's **Musée**

timetres (20 inches) high, under the supervision of William's half-brother, Odon de Conteville, Bishop of Bayeux.

D-Day Beaches   8,BC2

Until June 6, 1944, the peaceful stretch of coast west of Cabourg, from Ouistreham to the Cotentin peninsula, was known simply as the Côte du Calvados, a flat, undramatic shoreline broken by a few unspectacular chalk cliffs and sand dunes. Then, at 6.30 a.m. came the first of a fleet of 4,266 vessels to turn the beaches into beachheads with their now illustrious code names of Sword, Juno, Gold, Omaha and Utah Beach.

Today, with the flames and dust of battle long gone, the coast has retrieved its calm. At a site so charged with the emotion of death and war, the atmosphere of rather bleak serenity is in itself as evocative as the few remaining hulks of the Allies' rusty tanks and boats, the Germans' concrete bunkers and blockhouses, some simple monuments on the sites of the action and the miles of crosses at the military cemeteries.

To see where the British and Canadians, with the support of the Free French forces, attacked on the eastern half of the beaches, start out at the port town of **Ouistreham-Riva-Bella**. A museum (Place Alfred-Thomas, opposite

---

Getting it in the Eye

The story told in the tapestry from the Norman point of view may come as a bit of a shock to the average patriotic British schoolchild. English King Harold is shown as a treacherous weakling who cheated noble, generous William out of the throne promised him by King Edward the Confessor.

Some scenes to watch out for: a unique view of Mont-Saint-Michel without, of course, its later Gothic additions (panel 17); Halley's Comet (April 1066) flies over the newly crowned Harold: a bad omen (panels 32–33); Battle of Hastings, William raises his visor to reassure his men that he's still alive (panels 53–55); *Harold Rex Interfectus Est*—Harold gets it in the eye (panel 57).

---

the casino) details the combined Anglo-French operation to capture this stretch of Sword Beach, with uniforms and weapons used during the action, including a "pocket" submarine and Goliath tank.

Drive west along the D514 to **Bernières** and **Courseulles**, where the Canadians staged their Juno Beach landings, marked by monuments on the beaches, and the Canadians' cemetery 4 kilometres (2½ miles) to the south at Reviers.

At **Arromanches**, you can see the most fascinating monument to British ingenuity in the Allied landings—the remains of the artificial **Mulberry harbour**. The floating steel and concrete jetties and pontoons, hauled across the English Channel, were the only way of unloading tanks and heavy artillery on a coastline (Gold Beach) without natural harbours. The **Musée du Débarquement** on the seafront includes an exciting film explaining the whole heroic action.

The Americans' **Omaha** and **Utah beaches,** from Colleville to La Madeleine, are now official map references, a cartographer's tribute to the theatre of the fiercest fighting in the D-Day landings. The still desolate coastline frequently recalls the stormy conditions that prevented the Americans from setting up their own Mulberry harbour to land their equipment. More eloquent than any museum are the 9,386 white marble crosses of the **American military cemetery** on a cliff overlooking Omaha Beach at Colleville-Saint-Laurent.

There are 21,160 tombs in the **German military cemetery** at La Cambe on the N13, 7 kilometres (4 miles) inland from Grandcamp-les-Bains. The Utah Beach museum and monument are 5 kilometres (3 miles) inland from La Madeleine, near Sainte-Marie-du-Mont. Caen, Bayeux and local tourist offices can direct you to the 27 Allied and German military cemeteries in the region.

For a change of mood, don't overlook **Port-en-Bessin,** a delightfully genuine and active fishing town, light years from the high drama of the landings yet tucked away just around a corner from Omaha Beach.

Mont-Saint-Michel 8,A3

No way of getting round the claim of its most fervent admirers, the island sanctuary at the border between Normandy and Brittany is indeed a *Merveille de l'Occident*—a "Wonder of the Western World". That first glimpse of the steepled abbey rising on its rock from the sea is a moment invested with ineffable mystery. Whatever your faith or lack of it, sooner or later, a visit to this formidable and exquisite fortress of the Christian Church is imperative.

Sooner or later, because you must choose your moment carefully. If you want to recapture something of the atmosphere of the medieval pilgrimages, when thousands of the faithful swarmed across the island, loading up with souvenirs and fake relics and fighting their brethren for a meal or a bed, join the new secular pilgrims in the summer months, arriving by the busload rather than mule. But if your mood is more contemplative, go in the early spring, autumn or even winter, when you can wander around the abbey and its village like a monk.

A detailed visit of Mont-Saint-Michel is certainly worthwhile, but it's that perspective from a distance that's the most moving. Those coming from Caen should stop in Avranches (p. 167) for a panorama of the bay from the Jardin des Plantes or drive out to the coast road (D911) between Saint-Jean-Le-Thomas and Carolles. Best of all, if you're prepared to splash out and get high above the madding crowd, fly over the abbey on the special excursions organized from Avranches airport. But if you have no time for any of these, do at least get off the main highway, N176, when approaching the mount to take the D43 coastroad via Courtils for that all-important first view.

The bay around the mount's granite outcrop has been steadily silting up in

Whose Abbey?

It is understandable that Brittany and Normandy should fight over the paternity and ownership of such a prestigious monument as the island-abbey of the Mont-Saint-Michel, at the frontier between the two provinces. The Bretons claim seniority. The Romans did lump the Cotentin peninsula together with Brittany as "Armorica" and, geographically, the rugged region is certainly part of the Armorican plateau, completely different from the greener, hedge-rowed meadows of the Normandy *bocage* to the east. Under the Franks, as part of the Avranches diocese in the *comté* (county) of Cotentin, it was handed over to Brittany in 867 by King Charles the Bald. But the Cotentin was ceded 70 years later to the newly founded Duchy of Normandy and has remained part of Normandy ever since. To make things worse—for the Bretons—the river that had provided a sort of frontier from the Normans changed course in the 14th century and placed the mount firmly in Normandy.

recent years, so that it's an island only during the moon tides. These are most dramatic during the spring and autumn equinox, when the sea comes in at a rate of nearly 50 metres (164 feet) a minute over a distance of 15 kilometres (9 miles). This proved highly dangerous to the pilgrims who approached the abbey across the sands (the causeway joining the island to the mainland was not built until 1874).

On what was once a Celtic burial ground (originally named Mont-Tombe), the bishop of nearby Avranches began by building an oratory in the 8th century, at the prompting, he said, of the Archangel Michael. In 1017, Benedictine monks started on the flat-roofed abbey that you can see in the Bayeux Tapestry, propped up on a platform with blocks of brown granite brought from the Channel islands of Chausey, 40 kilometres (25 miles) away.

By the 14th century, the abbey was surrounded by a fortified village of hotels and shops. The pilgrims flocked there throughout the Hundred Years' War, paying tolls to the English who controlled

the surrounding territory but could never break through the mount's defences. After a steady decline, the monastery was dismantled even before the Revolution, but was saved from total destruction only to end ignominiously as a state prison.

Beginning on the upper terrace with a splendid **view** of the bay, the hour's guided tour (English, French and German) takes you through three levels of abbey buildings: the church, cloister and refectory at the top; the Salle des Chevaliers (Knights' Hall) and Salle des Hôtes (Guests' Hall) in the middle; and the store room and almonry underneath.

The **abbey-church** combines a sturdy Romanesque nave with a lighter, more airy Flamboyant Gothic chancel. The choir and chancel stand not on the island's granite core but on a platform formed by three crypts, with the massive columns of the **Crypte des Gros Piliers** doing most of the work. In a magic space looking out to sea, the beautifully sculpted columns of the **cloister** create a perfect framework of grace and delicacy for a moment's meditation.

With the cloister, the etherially lit **refectory**, grand **Knights' Hall** and elegant **Guests' Hall** together make up the masterpiece of 13th-century Gothic architecture which earned the abbey its name of *la Merveille*.

Avranches 8,A3

Situated at the mouth of the Sée river on the Baie du Mont-Saint-Michel, the Avranches diocese that supervised the building of the first sanctuary preserves in its **Musée de l'Avranchin** (Place de Saint-Jean-Avit) an exquisite collection of the abbey's illuminated manuscripts. Documents trace the life of the abbey from the 8th to the 15th century.

Villedieu-les-Poêles 8,B2

Why has this pretty little town attached "frying pans" to its name? Because, as you'll see when you drive down the main street, that's its age-old glory: gleaming hand-made copperware. Over the centuries, the town converted from bells—for cathedrals from Normandy to Quebec—to frying pans, saucepans and kettles, nowadays coated inside with stainless steel or aluminium.

Visit the **museum** (Rue du Général-Huard) to see the fascinating range of copperware made here since the 13th century.

The ruins of the great Romanesque-Gothic Benedictine **Abbaye de Hambye,** built in the 12th and 13th centuries, enjoy a magnificent setting in the wooded valley of the Sienne river. Besides the shell of the church, the surviving monastery buildings include a cider press, kitchen, stable and pigsty.

*I*f the legends are to be believed, Archangel Michael had his work cut out getting his Mont-Saint-Michel. He had to pay three visits to Bishop Aubert of Avranches before the good man would start building the sanctuary—the bishop's skull preserved in Avranches' church of Saint-Gervais has a dent resulting, they say, from the Archangel's prodding with his staff. Later, when construction was held up by a couple of huge rocks that wouldn't budge, Michael persuaded a villager to go out to the island with his 12 sons to bulldoze them out of the way.

Brittany

6-7;14-15

This province, as its natives never tire of telling you, is a country apart, proud of its regional culture, its robust separateness. The people are remote on their Armorican peninsula, the Far West of Europe, suspicious of the vacationing Parisian but unostentatiously hospitable to the foreign visitor.

Only a separate holiday can do the region complete justice, but for a first visit as part of a larger French tour, you get at least a sense of Brittany's craggy coasts on the Côte d'Emeraude (Emerald Coast) from Cancale to Cap Fréhel. Relax a while at the gentler seaside resorts of Dinard on the north coast or La Baule on the south, and explore the prehistoric Menhir country around Carnac. In the interior, capture the essence of Breton piety in the calvaries of the parish closes *(enclos paroissiaux)* at Saint-Thégonnec and Guimiliau, and perhaps hike around the forests and rocky landscapes between Huelgoat and Roc Trévezel. And for warm, varied beach holidays try the Gulf of Morbihan for size.

Côte d'Emeraude

7-8,CD2-3

After Mont-Saint-Michel, the Emerald Coast's 70 kilometres (43 miles) of rugged cliffs and caves alternating with quiet beach resorts offer a delightful confrontation with nature and sunny self-indulgence.

Start out at the little port town of **Cancale**, a major centre of oyster breeding since earliest Celtic times. Modern techniques now make the oysters good to eat all year round and not, as of old, just in the months with an "r" (see p. 322). Look out over the oyster beds from the port's jetty, **Jetée de la Fenêtre**.

Take the coast road D201 to **Pointe du Grouin**, a cliff 40 metres (130 feet) high, with a spectacular view of the Chausey Islands to the north and itself a good example of Brittany's coastal wilderness.

Look east across the Bay of Mont-Saint-Michel for a last glimpse of the abbey before heading west to **Saint-Malo**. This town is steeped in seafaring history; its sailors left their name on the Malouines, claimed by the British as the Falklands. It remains an important fishing port for cod and, more romantically, an attractive yacht harbour.

In World War II Saint-Malo was badly bombed as a last bastion of the Germans, but the old town, surrounded on three sides by the sea, has been tastefully restored. Its **ramparts**, built and rebuilt from the 12th to the 18th century, make a bracing walk, with the stretch between Saint-Philippe bastion and the Tour Bidouane opening up a vista along the whole Emerald Coast. At low tide you can walk or wade out to the little island of Grand Bé, with its simple, unadorned tomb of the locally born Romantic writer François-René de Chateaubriand.

The fancy headdress—coiffes—of the ladies of Bigouden are the pride and joy of Brittany. These lacy concoctions used to be short and neat little caps until as late as the 1930s when they were stretched to skyscraper proportions, reminiscent of the courtly ladies' high, cone-shaped hennin of the 15th century.

In the **Musée d'Histoire de la Ville**, just across the lively Place Chateaubriand, the town's naval history is told through the lives of its great navigators and pirates and all the colourful paraphernalia of sailing.

Like many French seaside resorts, **Dinard** is a "discovery" of the British in the 19th century, long before French city slickers even dreamed of dipping a toe in the sea or lying on that gritty stuff called sand. The British, soon followed by Americans, appreciated the broad, sheltered beach, the particularly mild microclimate —palms, fig trees, tamarisk and camellias all flourish here—and easy access across the Channel.

In a still faintly Victorian atmosphere, Dinard has preserved all the assets of a good resort: luxury villas, long paved promenades, plush hotels, elegant boutiques, casino, discothèques, parks and gardens and a public Olympic-size swimming pool.

The spectacle at **Cap Fréhel** is one of the most thrilling in Brittany. From cliffs 70 metres (230 feet) above the tumultuous sea, you look out across a wild defenceless promontory, a chaos of ruddy sandstone and slabs of black schist, huge waves breaking across the rocks of the Grande and Petite Fauconnière bird sanctuaries, scattered with colonies of cormorants and black and white guillemots. On a clear day, the **light-house** (145 stairs), gives you a view of over 100 kilometres (60 miles).

Dinan 7,D3

Behind its stone ramparts, the old centre of town breathes the essence of medieval Brittany, vibrant and very much alive in the maze of tiny cobblestoned streets. The sagging, cantilevered timbered dwellings lean tipsily against each other, housing butchers, bakers and pharmacies. The town commands a vital strategic site at the head of the Rance Estuary, on a rocky spur towering above the river. By the time William the Conqueror besieged Dinan in 1065, the original Roman fort had become a fortified city with a castle. That's what you see in the Bayeux Tapestry (see p. 163).

The **castle** standing today is largely 14th-century and houses in its Tour de Cöetquen a **museum** devoted to Breton traditional life as seen through its furniture and costumes. But it also boasts a fine collection of recumbent tomb-statues (no rubbings allowed). The tourist office occupies the **Hôtel Kératry**, a proud Renaissance mansion on the Rue de l'Horloge, next to the imposing **Tour de l'Horloge**, a 15th-century quadrangular belltower. Local historians like to point out that the beloved Duchess Anne de Bretagne, who became France's queen in 1491, donated one of the tower's four bronze bells.

For a feel of the town's medieval charm, wander around the **Place des Merciers** and **Place des Cordeliers**. The artisans' houses have been beautifully restored along the **Rue du Jerzual** and **Rue du Petit-Fort**, meandering down to the **port**.

Côte de Granit Rose 6,B2

The violet-pink hue of the rock formations gives the Côte de Granit Rose its name. This scenic stretch of beach begins at l'Arcouest beside Paimpol and continues west as far as Trébeurden. Rock formations call to mind weird and wonderful animals of myth—a phenomenon that gets more and more marked as you continue along this wild coast. But first comes delightful **Tréguier**, situated on a hill 5 kilometres (3 miles) inland, at the confluence of the Guindy and Jaudy rivers.

No cathedral of Brittany's nine is quite as beloved as its **Cathédrale Saint-Tugdual.** The church, built mostly between 1339 and 1468, is a masterpiece of delicacy. Three towers rise above the transept: the square 12th-century Tour Hastings (all that remains of an earlier edifice), the Gothic centrepiece, the Tour du Sanctuaire, and an openwork spire of 1787. Each pair of pillars has a different design and colour of stone, corresponding to various different periods of construction. Richly decorated chapels flank the aisle, particularly the vast **Chapelle Saint-Yves,** which contains the saint's tomb, built in 1420 and reconstructed in 1890. Elegant granite arcades propped by buttresses surround the **cloister,** a haven of hydrangeas—and peace.

Inland hub of the Côte de Granit Rose, **Lannion** symbolizes the new dynamism of Brittany. The market bustles round the quayside and sprawls up the side streets to the main square, **Place du Général-Leclerc,** with some superb medieval houses. The **Eglise de Brélévenez,** a Templars' church, stands at the top of a beautiful 142-step stairway.

Perros-Guirec, some 12 kilometres (7½ miles) north of Lannion, has not only managed to keep its Breton character but to develop its coastline harmoniously. The centre of town lies uphill, spilling out into a commercial district that reaches down again to the beaches of Trestignel and **Trestraou.** The clean, pure sand sweeps round in front of the congress hall and thalasso-therapy centre.

The coast road, the Corniche Bretonne (or, more prosaically, D788), carries on to **Trégastel.** Mounds of huge rocks, in infernal disorder, lie everywhere, stacked crazily upon each other, dubbed "Napoleon's Hat", "The Palette", "The Dice"—and more scabrous.

Finally **Trébeurden,** end-station of the Côte de Granit Rose, has all the trappings of a good beach resort.

Rennes   7,D3

Provincial capital and arch-rival of Nantes, Rennes is a bustling university town prospering from its electronic and printing industries. While Nantes served as capital of the old Duchy of Brittany —now transferred administratively to the Loire region—the dukes were crowned at Rennes. After union with France, Rennes became in 1561 the seat of Brittany's parliament.

Fire in 1720 and World War II bombardments destroyed much of the medieval centre, but there's still an easy and pleasant day's stroll to be had around the few surviving dwellings of the 16th century—wood-beamed, paunchy and cock-eyed. They cluster around the **Rue des Dames,** behind the cathedral (19th-century but worth a peep inside for the late-Gothic gilded wooden **altarpiece** in the south aisle). The medieval jousting square of **Place des Lices** has given way to a lively meat market.

But the more handsome part of town is the district restructured in the 18th century around the classical **Palais de Justice** (Law Courts) after the devastating fire. The grid street plan should be familiar to Americans, whose first cities were being laid out at roughly the same time. The same geometric principles apply in the elegant gardens in front of the Law Courts, an austere yet noble edifice with a richly decorated interior. Guided tours visit the **Grand'Chambre,** the Breton parliament's coffer-ceilinged debating chamber, decorated with modern Gobelins tapestries, and the vast barrel-vaulted **Salle des Pas Perdus,** where clients and lawyers meet before their day in court— the impressive wood-panelled **Salle des Assises.**

The city's pride, indeed one of the best regional museums in the country, is the **Musée de Bretagne,** at 20, Quai Emile-Zola. The whole history of Brittany is traced by a skilful combination of traditional exhibits of archaeological remains, reconstitution of prehistoric habitats, the costumes and implements of everyday life and the most up-to-date audio-visual aids devoted to 20th-century techniques.

Upstairs in the same building is the **Musée des Beaux-Arts,** covering European art from the 15th to the 20th century. Look out for important paintings by Veronese, Georges de La Tour, Rubens, Van Loo, Chardin and Gauguin. The rich collection of drawings includes works by Botticelli, Dürer, Rubens, Rembrandt and Watteau.

Parish Close Road   6,AB3

The *enclos paroissial* epitomizes the pious life of rural Brittany. This architectural ensemble encompasses church, cemetery, charnel house and calvary, grouped in a square and entered via a triumphal arch. In a morning's tour from Morlaix, 160 kilometres (100 miles) west of Dinard, you can take in three of the most important on a route signposted as the *"Circuit des Trois Enclos"*.

Saint-Thégonnec represents the ultimate flowering of the art, its triumphal arch setting the tone for the majestic **calvary** of 1610. Among the 40-odd expressively sculpted figures dressed in the costume of Henri IV's time, notice the roped hands of the blindfolded Jesus and the angels collecting his blood; his tormentor, in breeches, is thought to be Henri IV himself, never forgiven in these parts for his Protestant inclinations. The

*R*ural Brittany is alive with the spirits of pious ages past. Within the Parish Close, the stone figures of the calvary gather at nightfall to consider the tragedy of Christ's crucifixion. By the light of day, you will see that any of the villagers might have served as their models.

ossuary, now a chapel, is late Renaissance in the very elaborate Breton manner—Corinthian columns, lanterns, niches and caryatids. The **church** has an even more elaborate Baroque pulpit.

At **Guimiliau**, over 200 Old and New Testament figures are sculpted on its **calvary**. The elegant Renaissance style lends an unusual sophistication to the nightmarish superstitions of medieval Brittany also incorporated in the sculpture. Look for the servant girl hurtled into hell for flirting with the devil. The **church** has fine granite statues of Jesus and the Apostles on its porch. Inside, eight spiral columns support the mighty canopy of the 17th-century carved oak **baptistry.**

A lightning bolt toppled the church tower of **Lampaul-Guimiliau** in 1809; the interior of the **church** remains impressive. The 16th-century polychrome rood beam spanning the nave is decorated with 12 prophetesses (chancel side) and scenes from the Passion. In the Flagellation, the artist seems quite carried away with the sadistic brutes wielding whip and cudgel on Jesus, tied to a tree. The triumphal arch and mini-calvary are relatively unimpressive, but the ossuary has some interesting sculpture.

Other remarkable examples of parish closes are scattered round Brittany, either virtually complete as at **Pleyben** or as simple calvaries.

Facing Brest, for instance, within its roadstead, is the Presqu'île de Plougastel. Little strawberry bushes cover the length and breadth of the peninsula. But art-lovers head straight for the calvary at **Plougastel-Daoulas,** standing alone in the great square. It was built between 1602 and 1604 to commemorate the end of the plague: some 150 figures heave, sigh, grovel and gesticulate, seized in motion almost as at Pompeii.

In perhaps the most intensely Breton area of all, at Pointe de Penmarc'h, huddles the chapel of **Notre-Dame-de-Tronoën,** a few hundred yards from the sea. Here, isolated amid the dunes, stands a calvary, the oldest (1450)—and for some—the most moving of all Breton calvaries. It relates incidents in the life of Jesus in a simple, naïve way. Time, wind and weather have battered the lower two levels of statues, erasing some faces, but many of the 100-odd personages retain their fresh, frank expressions. Unable for the most part to read, the rustic community could find instruction in these sculptures as in a comic strip.

Quimper 6,A3

This treasurehouse of the Bretons' values and traditions is the capital of Cornouaille, a district named by nostalgic Celts after their native Cornwall in England. Here lies its true core, its soul, where the language and customs are faithfully upheld. The Romans set up camp here at the point where the Steir and Odet rivers meet. The town's architectural pride is the Gothic **Cathédrale Saint-Corentin,** dedicated to the first bishop and patron saint of Quimper. Begun in 1240, work continued for 600 years. The delicate stone tracery of the steeples, already as weatherbeaten as the much older upper façade, is in fact the most recent part (1856). Inside, probably due to a construction error, the nave makes an unusual curve at the beginning of the choir. Notice the very fine late Gothic **stained-glass windows.**

The cathedral is flanked by two museums. The **Musée Breton** occupies the former Bishopric, a graceful Renaissance building incorporated into the city walls. A highlight of its collection of church art is some fine 15th-century wooden sculpture, while the miniature garden displays delicately carved stone fragments salvaged from local cloisters. The collection of European painting at the **Musée des Beaux-Arts,** 40, Place Saint-Corentin, includes works by the school of Siena, Guido Reni and Rubens, but the most noteworthy are French: Corot, Eugène Boudin and the Pont-Aven School, for once without Gauguin.

Explore the town's old quarters along **Rue Kéréon**, with its grand half-timbered houses, to **Place Terre-au-Duc,** literally the Duke's Land, i.e., the part that the Duke of Brittany claimed beyond the original medieval walled town owned by the Bishop of Cornouaille. Frighten the kids with the leering, jeering wooden grotesques carved on some of the houses' façades.

Pointe du Raz   *6,A3*

This is where it all ends. Not counting a couple of God-forsaken storm-lashed islands like the Isle of Sein or Ouessant (Ushant)—both the bane of shipwrecked fishermen—the Pointe du Raz is the westernmost point of the Sizun peninsula, of Brittany, of continental France itself. The Atlantic is at its most savage here, thundering onto the rocks with an impact that can be felt, they say, vibrating all the way to Quimper, 30 kilometres (18 miles) inland.

From the pretty port of **Audierne,** where crayfish, lobster and tunny fish boats bob in the harbour, the D784 takes you through the peninsula's wild, windswept grasslands to Plogoff, the last real village before the Pointe du Raz. Hereafter, the vegetation gets sparser, the terrain eerie, bleak and barren enough to persuade the ancients that this was the end of the world. In high season, the traffic jams, tour-buses and souvenir-sellers may convince you they were right. But at quieter times, the hour-long guided tours of the cape (with an accredited guide) make an exhilarating adventure as you clamber down into the hissing "hell" of the **Enfer de Plogoff.**

Head north across the peninsula to the **Cap-Sizun Bird Reserve** *(Réserve ornithologique),* open from March to the end of August. Expert guides will point out choughs, razorbills, fulmers and petrels, but you can probably recognize the puffins by yourself. Take binoculars.

Concarneau   *6,B3*

Concarneau is one of the best preserved, most picturesque walled towns in Brittany if somewhat over-commercialized.

From the quayside, Place Jean-Jaurès faces the old city's solid walls, shaped like an inverted comma and approached by a small bridge, the only entrance. First walk along the 14th-century **ramparts,** enclosing three-quarters of the Ville Close. At the start of the busy **Rue Vauban,** backbone of the town, is the fascinating **Musée de la Pêche,** devoted to the history of the town and its fishing activity. Displays include tanks of fish of all shapes and colours, models of the different craft and fishing techniques.

Take advantage of the chance to watch Concarneau's traditional *criée* (fish auction), held at the Quai Carnot from about 6.30 to 11 a.m.

A small Breton town gave its name to one of the great art movements of the 19th century, the School of Pont-Aven. If the painter Paul Gauguin chose **Pont-Aven** in 1886, he had his reasons. On an overcrowded summer day it's not always obvious what precisely they were. Still you'll agree that the kernel of the village, where the stream hurtling down over the rocks meets the mill and the inn of Moulin de Rosmadec, is infinitely charming.

If you want to pursue Gauguin's tracks, follow the signs at the top of the village up through the Bois d'Amour to the 16th-century **Chapelle de Trémalo.** (Gauguin used the Christ inside as a model for his *Yellow Christ.*) At Nizon stands an unusual, weather-worn **calvary** that Gauguin transformed into his *Green Christ.*

Huelgoat   *6,B3*

This pretty little town is mainly attractive as a base for excursions and hikes into the nature reserve of forests, rivers and lakes in the **Parc Régional d'Armorique.**

You can fish for perch and carp in the lake or trout in the Rivière d'Argent (Silver River); or just glide around the lake among the swans. At the top end of the lake, you wander into dense forest through a fantastic chaos of rocks and grottos variously inhabited by the Devil, some more or less innocent virgin, and King Arthur himself.

*T*he town of Le Palais, Belle-Ile, saw the birth
of that great gourmet delicacy, pommes frites, which Americans duly
acknowledge as slim, elegant, crispy French fries, while the British
settle for fat and greasy chips. It all began in the 1760s, when a couple
of hundred French Canadian refugees settled in this charming island,
now a popular resort, after Britain had turned their Acadia into
Nova Scotia. They brought with them the potato, till then practically
unknown in France. The rest is culinary history.

Scholars timidly suggest the alignments are associated with cults of the sun or moon, and the cromlechs may be astronomical arrangements for predicting such phenomena as eclipses.

The alignments occupy three main fields a short walk north of town along the D196. **Le Ménec,** the biggest, has 1,099 menhirs in 12 rows (plus 70 menhirs in a cromlech around part of the hamlet of Le Ménec). The field of **Kermario** has a dolmen (chamber built of flat slabs) and 1,029 menhirs in 10 rows. Among them is the Giant of Manio, a menhir over 6 metres (20 feet) high, shaped like a clenched fist. Most impressive is the **Kerlescan** alignment, 594 menhirs that form what local legend calls a frozen army. Once a year, the stones rise up in the middle of night and march around.

The best time to see them is early morning, looming out of the mist, or at sunset, throwing dramatic shadows.

If the Carnac area enjoys a gentle climate and calm shores, it's thanks to the **Quiberon Peninsula**, a narrow tapering strip of land bravely lunging out into the Atlantic. If beaches on the protected east are pleasantly sandy, the ocean-battered **Côte Sauvage** of jagged rock on the west offers some of the most spectacular seascapes in Brittany. A coast road hugs the shoreline for some 12 kilometres (7½ miles) from Portivy, but you should also explore the footpaths past some of the tiny uninhabited bays. Frequent notices warn of the dangers of the deceptively calm-looking creeks—and commemorate those who gave their lives for the careless.

Quiberon town is a high-class resort devoted to thalassotherapy, and the seafront **promenade** attracts a fashionable crowd all day long. From Port-Maria, take the hour-long boat ride out to **Belle-Ile,** beautiful as its name, with some lovely beaches on the sheltered east coast near Port-Donnant and Le Palais and a dramatic shoreline facing the ocean. You'll recognize some famous Monet land- and seascapes and see actress Sarah Bernhardt's holiday home.

Carnac

14,A2

Like the wild countryside of the interior, the megalithic monuments of Brittany's **Menhir Country** on the south coast take you back into the legends and the mists of time.

Carnac is surrounded by fields full of thousands of gigantic stones (menhirs) in mysterious alignments and circles (cromlechs) set up some time between 5500 and 3500 B.C., at the rate of one stone a year.

La Baule   *14,B2*

Best beach in Europe, say its regulars. Five kilometres (3 miles) of fine sand from Pornichet to Le Pouliguen stretch in a perfect half-moon, past chic sailing and beach clubs, along an **esplanade** of luxury hotels with a casino at the centre. If you tire of the easy life on the beach front, take an excursion west around the wilder coast of the peninsula past Batz-sur-Mer (pronounced *Bah*) to the pretty little fishing port of Le Croisic.

Vannes and the Golfe du Morbihan   *14,B2*

Capital of the Morbihan *département,* **Vannes** is a provincial town in the best sense of the word with ramparts still enclosing one side of the old centre (beautifully illuminated at night).

The **cathedral,** a hodge-podge of styles from the 13th to the 19th centuries, is notable for its **Chapelle du Saint-Sacrement,** decorated outside with scallop shells, pure Italian Renaissance and a rare sight in Brittany.

Just beside the cathedral is the **Cohue,** a medieval covered market where artisans in a bubble of activity sell their crafts and wares. Explore the Place Henri IV and the cock-eyed timber houses of its charming little side-streets, Rue Noë in particular, site of the **Musée archéologique** housed in the 15th-century Château-Gaillard. This museum contains important prehistoric items from Carnac, Locmariaquer and the Rhuys Peninsula.

The Bono and Auray rivers empty into the broad **Gulf of Morbihan,** best visited by boat. Some 50 islands (more or less, depending on the tides) lie scattered through a gulf 20 kilometres (12 miles) across, with an opening half a mile wide between Locmariaquer and Port-Navalo. Only 40 islands are actually inhabited but all are blessed by the clement climate, lush Mediterranean vegetation, subtle effects of light, and sudden changes at high and low tide. The long mud flats, oyster beds, fishermen, thatched or stone houses create a fascinating world apart.

Regular launches *(vedettes vertes)* leave from Quai de la Rabine (several kilometres outside Vannes proper). The complete round-trip takes two hours, but a day's not too much to spend if you stop en route.

The little **Ile d'Arz** lives mostly from oyster culture, sheep farming and agriculture. The **Ile-aux-Moines** is not only the biggest island, it's also the most picturesque, especially around the flower-bedecked whitewashed houses of Locmiquel.

The minute island of Gavrinis has a fascinating megalithic cairn 8 metres (26 feet) high and 100 metres (328 feet) in circumference.

Marais Salants/Grande Brière   *14,B2*

The **Marais Salants** of the Guérande peninsula is fed with salt water from the tongue of sea penetrating in at high tide from Le Croisic. The salt pans occupy some 2,000 hectares (5,000 acres). The sea water is brought up to them via canals and left to decant in increasingly shallow basins, until it reaches the so-called *œillets* (literally, "eyelets") a mere two inches deep, where the salt crystallizes.

Centre of the salt area is Saillé, built on a former island where 27-pound sacks of salt are stacked for sale beside every house. A **museum,** the Maison des Paludiers, illustrates the life of the marsh workers.

East of the town of Guérande begins **La Grande Brière,** a remote and strange marsh area where man lives in perfect but fragile harmony with nature—and where sky, water and earth achieve a precarious ecological balance. Twenty-one *communes* (villages) make up this nature park of 40,500 hectares (100,000 acres), of which 17,500 are covered by marsh. More than 90 kilometres (60 miles) of canals called *chalandières* criss-cross the marsh. No road cuts across the marsh: take a guided tour in a *chaland* (punt) from **Ile de Fédrun,** and spend an hour gliding around this extraordinary silent kingdom of reeds and rushes.

Nantes 15,C2

Anne de Bretagne would have turned over in her grave at the suggestion that Nantes wasn't firmly rooted at the southern end of her duchy. Nantes today is officially part of the Loire region, but, historically, sentimentally and culturally it's Breton.

The hazards of history have resulted in the two sides of the town being separated down the middle by a boulevard (Cours des 50 Otages) with to the east cathedral, castle and a little medieval city, to the west architectural ensembles, the homes of wealthy shipowners. This dichotomy parallels in effect closely the history and evolution of the city. The attachment of Brittany to France was signed within the castle walls in 1532. The Edict of Nantes, granting religious freedom, was signed here in 1598 by Henri IV. From then on Nantes turned to commercial maritime activities, and flourished throughout the 18th century with the so-called "triangular trade" whereby ships left Nantes for the Guinea coast loaded with beads and babioles, took on slaves to the Antilles, and returned to Nantes with spices and sugar that was then refined in Nantes. The slave trade was abolished and Nantes went into a steady decline in the 19th century.

A good place to start a visit would be on the old medieval side in the **cathedral.** It has had more than its fair share of disasters, fires, the latest in 1972 and has still not wholly recovered from them. The first church on the same spot was destroyed by the Normans in 843. Bishop Gohard was celebrating mass when the barbaric hordes broke in and cut off his head. But Brittany being Brittany, the legend took on another dimension when the saintly bishop picked up his head and walked away. The present church was designed by Mathurin Rodier in the 15th century

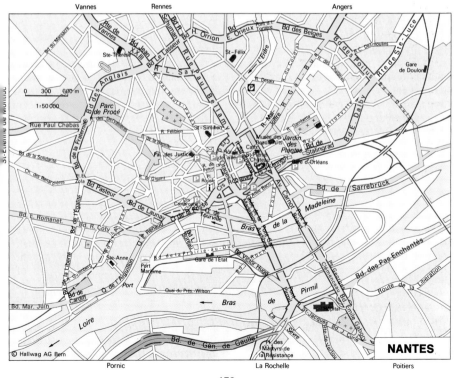

NANTES

© Hallwag AG Bern

179

in a very pure, Flamboyant Gothic style. Although its outside has been blackened by time and the disasters, note the fine portals of the façade and the statuary.

Anne de Bretagne inevitably had her role to play here; she commissioned from Michel Colombe the superb white marble tomb to her father, François II, the (last) independent Duke of Brittany, and her mother, Marguerite de Foix. At each end of the sarcophagus stands an allegorical statue symbolizing Justice, Prudence, Force and Temperance. Many see in Justice a portrait of Anne herself.

A short walk down cobbled Rue Mathurin Rodier leads to the **castle**; history was made and unmade, marriages, treaties, feasts and births and deaths took place within the walls of this massive, moated castle. Mostly built in the 14th century, before the tributaries of the Loire were blocked up, the castle stood beside the river—which must have given the place another feel. A four-storey building houses the **Museum of Decorative Art** and **Museum of Popular Art.**

At the feet of the castle over to the west, in the hurly-burly hive of little roads, it's easy to evoke the **medieval city** of Nantes, that centres round the **Eglise Sainte-Croix,** with its strange black-topped belfry with trumpeting angels. A few streets on, and the scene changes; with the **Cours des 50 Otages,** we are into a stately area of big bourgeois houses, chic shops, ordered squares, a part of the town that grew, flourished and developed on the fortunes gained by the shipbuilders and owners. It's a straight run through from the medieval to the grandiose: follow **Rue d'Orléans** which runs into **Place Royale,** then elegant **Rue Crébillon** to reach **Place Graslin,** modelled on Paris's Place de l'Odéon, with the Greek-style theatre dominating the square.

Although port activity is not what it used to be, the broad Bras de la Madeleine of the Loire gives a splendid harbour feeling. Particularly striking of the *hôtels* that used to line the river banks is the **Hôtel des Indes.** More intact are those on the Ile Feydeau; look first at the outsides, then peek into the courtyards behind (by Rue Kerguen).

One rich ship-owner donated his collection and his house to the city: it gives an idea of their amassed wealth. Thomas Dobrée's strange neo-Gothic manor house, **Musée Dobrée,** provides the setting for extraordinary collections. Next door, for the overspill, is the **Manoir de la Touche.** And, just to be complete, in a modern, glassy brick building next door is the **Museum de l'Histoire Naturelle.** Outside, scarcely inviting; inside it houses one of the most remarkable museums of its kind on natural history, presented in an attractive, clear fashion to be of interest to all.

S abots *or wooden clogs made their appearance in the 14th century, but are still made for the peasants of Brittany. Originally, they were an overshoe which people attached to their flimsy indoor slippers to get across a wet and muddy street. The soles achieved literally staggering heights, closer to stilts than shoes. In the French Revolution, sabots were as essential a part of a revolutionary's uniform as his Phrygian bonnet. A boy moved a step closer to adulthood when he got his first pair at first communion.*

Loire Valley *15,C,D,E2;16,AB2*

The Loire is the longest river in France—1,012 kilometres (628 miles) from its source in the Vivarais mountains south of Saint-Etienne to the estuary west of Nantes—but the region of the most interesting châteaux, from Chambord to Angers, covers barely a fifth of that.

The itinerary we propose for visitors coming from Paris goes first to Orléans by *autoroute* or the N20, to visit a small group of sites out to the east of Joan of Arc's city. It then heads west to Blois for the "heavyweights", most of them within easy access of the N152 to Angers. Just reverse the route if you're coming from Brittany.

Château-visiting can make heavy demands on feet and mind. Unless really pressed, don't try to see too many in too short a time. You'll cherish the memory of five or six of them far more than you would an ill-digested dozen.

For up-to-date information on opening times and entrance fees of châteaux and museums in the Loire Valley, you should obtain the handy brochure *Val de Loire, pays des châteaux* from the French Tourist Office in your country or from any tourist office on the spot.

The châteaux and museums charge entrance fees (not all cheap, and many visits can take a chunk out of one's budget), with reductions for children, students and groups. Some offer half-price entrance on Sundays and holidays. Most of the châteaux are open year-round, including Sundays, but some are closed for a month or two in winter. In off-season, several close once a week, generally on Mondays or Tuesdays.

For centuries, the Loire river, linking up with important tributaries such as the Indre and Cher, was a vital highway between the Atlantic and the heart of France, making Orléans a major distribution centre for exotic goods from the Orient. The gentry put their carriages on rafts, sort of precursor to the *wagon-lit*, and sailed to Brittany—six days from Orléans to Nantes. Commercial traffic declined in the 17th and 18th centuries, reviving briefly with the advent of the steamship in 1832, but finally succumbed to silting up and the onslaught of the railways.

Today, the Loire is a sleepy waterway, running deep only with the autumn rains or post-winter thaw, and turning its sandbanks and mud flats into veritable islands during the summer.

Orléans *16,C1-2*

The town remains famous for its deliverance from the hands of the dastardly English by Joan of Arc in 1429. The house which lodged the Maid of Orleans, **Maison de Jeanne d'Arc**, has been lovingly restored from the rubble left by a 1940 bomb, and stands on Place

*T*he walls of Chaumont are filled with all the malice that a fat and ugly widow could muster for her husband's beautiful mistress. Catherine de Médicis was 20 years younger than Diane de Poitiers but looked ten years older. Diane had maintained her influence during Henri II's reign by convincing him not to abandon his Florentine wife. She even befriended Catherine herself, but none of this helped when Henri died. As all-powerful regent in place of her sickly sons, Catherine forced Diane to give up Chenonceau for Chaumont. She herself came to Chaumont to hatch many of the murderous plots that characterized her regency.

du Général-de-Gaulle, that other great French saviour. Along with costumes and weapons of the period, there is an audio-visual account of the heroine's life. (During the week around the May 8 anniversary, fireworks, parades and illuminations celebrate the *Fêtes de Jeanne d'Arc*.) World War II bombs spared little of the city's past, but long before then, the **cathedral** had been destroyed by Protestants in the 16th-century Wars of Religion. An unhappy neo-Gothic edifice replaced the Romanesque original—still visible down in the **crypt**. Otherwise its principal interest is the fine 18th-century wood panelling of the **choir**.

The **Musée des Beaux-Arts**, Place Sainte-Croix, boasts a Velázquez masterpiece, *St. Thomas*, as well as major works by Correggio and Tintoretto. French painting is represented by Le Nain, Champaigne, Hubert Robert and Gauguin, while an interesting sculpture collection includes works by Houdon and Pigalle, Maillol, Auguste Rodin and Ossip Zadkine.

Saint-Benoît-sur-Loire   *17,C2*

The famous silhouette of its Benedictine **abbey-basilica**, with a gentle golden glow to the stone, lends an ineffable grace to Saint-Benoît from its commanding position at a bend in the river. This masterpiece of Romanesque architecture was built in the 11th century as a shrine for the founding saint's relics brought 400 years earlier from Monte Cassino and still preserved in the great **crypt**. In the **porch** beneath the delicately steepled belfry, notice the superbly sculpted capitals with their floral and animal motifs and scenes from the lives of Jesus and Mary. Inside, the nave, completed in the 13th century, is Gothic, but the Romanesque **chancel** (guided tours only) also has some fine sculpture in the chapels radiating from the ambulatory. If you want to rediscover the atmosphere of medieval religious fervour, attend an evening service (vespers) in the crypt.

A few minutes downriver, at **Germigny**, is one of France's oldest churches. Its **apse**, once one of four chapels in the church's original Greek-cross ground-plan, dates back to the year 800 and has a carefully restored Byzantine-style **mosaic** depicting the tabernacle of the covenant with angels and the hand of God.

Blois   *16,B2*

Built on a hill overlooking the Loire river, the town itself invites the visitor to linger a while in the narrow winding streets leading from the cathedral to the château, with handsome old houses situated on Place Saint-Louis and Rue Porte-Chartraine.

The entrance to the **château** is through the brick and stone gateway of the late Gothic Louis XII wing, completed in 1503. Across the courtyard on the right-hand side is the château's most distinctive feature, the splendid **François I wing**. It was built only a dozen years after the Louis XII wing but, reflecting the contrast between the debonair Renaissance prince and his dour predecessor, is a world apart in elegance and panache.

The open loggias of its magnificently sculpted octagonal stone **staircase** dominate the façade. They served as a kind of grandstand for courtiers watching important guests arriving on state occasions. The little beasts carved on the balconies and elsewhere around the château are the royal family's personal emblems, including Louis XII's porcupine, François I's salamander, Anne de Bretagne's ermine.

On the first floor of the François I wing, look out for the wood-panelled **cabinet** (study) of Catherine de Médicis, conniving queen mother and regent to three kings of France. Many of the 237 carved panels, each different, were believed to conceal poisons as well as jewels and state papers. On the second floor, in 1588, as guides never tire of telling, her son Henri III used not poison but a dozen men armed with swords and daggers to do away with his arch rival Duke Henri de Guise.

Chambord   *16,B2*

Upriver east of Blois in a huge densely wooded park surrounded by 32 kilometres (20 miles) of high walls, the brilliant white **Château de Chambord** is the most extravagant of all the royal residences in the Loire Valley. To have easy access to the wild boar and deer (still to be seen from observation platforms on D112 and D33), François I built himself this glorified 440-room hunting lodge. Later kings abandoned it as too big and unheatable (despite 365 fireplaces), though Louis XIV dropped by for the première performance of Molière's *Le Bourgeois Gentilhomme.* (He hated the first act, but found it picked up in the second.)

There is an astounding fantasy if not harmony in the arcaded towers and terraces, alternating storeys of arched and rectangular windows, and maze of turrets, stone lanterns and chimneys on the roof. The architects remain anonymous, but it's believed the central four-towered **donjon** that makes a dream palace out of a classically feudal castle keep may have been designed by Leonardo da Vinci, whom François brought to the Loire Valley in 1516. He's certainly the kind of fellow to have created the celebrated **double-ramped spiral staircase** in the dungeon's centre, which enables people to go up and down it without crossing each other.

Such aids to clandestinity were vitally important for the jolly shenanigans that went on among François' suite of 2,000 courtiers, as you can imagine for yourself up on the balustraded **rooftop terrace,** which affords a nice **view** of the forest. The nooks and crannies among the chimneys and turrets served as trysting alcoves for those who couldn't get one of the 440 rooms to themselves.

Cheverny   *16,B2*

Much more comfortable than most of its Loire neighbours, the **château** has been inhabited by descendants of the Hurault de Cheverny family almost uninterrupt-

Son et Lumière

It was the Loire Valley châteaux that started the craze for sound and light shows back in the 1950s. With their rich historical background of romance and murder most foul, they are still the ideal places for these English- and French-language dramatizations in a spectacular setting that at night takes on the quality of a fairy tale. Most of them run continuously throughout the summer months. The *syndicat d'initiative* at Blois (phone: 54.74.06.49) can give you details of the programmes. The best are at Chambord (the pioneer), Blois, Chenonceau and Azay-le-Rideau (see p. 53).

edly since the early 1600s. The public apartments are lavishly decorated in Italian Renaissance and French classical style. Most spectacular is the **Chambre du Roi** (King's Bedroom) kept ready, as was the custom, in case Louis XIV dropped by—but he never did. An equally illustrious visitor was Leonardo da Vinci's *Mona Lisa,* housed in the *orangerie* greenhouse for six months during World War II under the very noses of German troops billeted in the château.

Chaumont   *16,B2*

It is the setting that gives this **château** its charm, a beautiful hillside **park** graced with lovely old cedars. But that wasn't enough to keep the royal mistress Diane de Poitiers here after royal *wife* Catherine de Médicis pushed her out of Chenonceau (see p. 186). She found the place too grim and moved closer to Paris, leaving only her initials, a double D, embossed on the battlements. Catherine spent time here with her not very jolly companion Ruggieri, who made dire astrological predictions about her family and advised on the right poison to administer to enemies. The guided tour takes you through the celebrities' bedrooms. Horse-lovers admire the monumental 19th-century **stables.**

Amboise   *16,B2*

In contrast to the formidable Gothic fortress presented by its massive ramparts towering over the Loire, the **château** presents in its inner courtyards a more inviting palace with pretty pepperpot turrets and gabled windows. What you see now represents only a small portion of the vast original that embraced a menagerie and sprawling gardens where France grew its first peach and orange trees, brought back from Italy by Charles VIII in 1495.

Today's visitors enter by a somewhat forbidding narrow gateway, but guests of Charles VIII reached the castle terrace in style via a broad spiral ramp within the **Tour des Minimes**. From the 40-metre- (131 foot) high round tower, you look out on one side over the town's slate roofs and on the other over the castle grounds to a long balcony with rusty iron balustrade. This is the infamous **Balcon des Conjurés** (Plotters' Balcony) where Protestant nobles were hung, drawn, quartered and thrown into the river for their abortive 1560 plot to kidnap the young king François II. The latter watched the show from this very tower, together with his wife, Mary, the similarly unfortunate future Queen of Scots.

The Flamboyant Gothic **Chapelle Saint-Hubert** is decorated with stone reliefs of animals and trees honouring this patron saint of hunters. It is said to be the burial place of Leonardo da Vinci, brought to Amboise in 1516 to work for François I during the last four years of his life.

A short walk from the château, Leonardo's home in the manor of Clos-Lucé has been restored as a museum devoted to the genius's life and work, including models of his inventions and some frescoes attributed to pupils and perhaps a dab or two of the master.

Chenonceaux   *16,B2*

Raised on arches to span the Cher river, the château and its pretty gardens still evoke the romantic ghost of its beautiful chatelaine, Diane de Poitiers, mistress to Henri II. She owed her legendary health and complexion to regular washing and sensible eating—she swam nude in the river and grew her own artichokes in the gardens.

In the **apartments,** along with some fine 16th-century Flemish tapestries, French, Italian and Spanish furniture, you'll see Diane's neatly kept household accounts. It's not clear that Primaticcio's

---

Museums and Visits
Here's a list to help you choose. Museums are generally open from 10 a.m. to noon and from 2 to 4 p.m. and closed on Mondays or Tuesdays. Check first with the local tourist office.

Archaeology. Blois, Châteaumeillant, Le Grand Pressigny, Orléans, Romorantin, Thésée-la-Romaine, Tours.

Fine arts. Angers, Blois, Orléans, Tours, Saumur (china).

Hunting and fishing. La Bussière (fishing), Cère-la-Ronde, Gien, Cheverny.

Illusionists. Exhibits at Blois devoted to Robert Houdin, the 19th-century scientist and illusionist, from whom the American magician Harry Houdini took his name.

Local history, folklore, crafts. Amboise, Châteauneuf-sur-Loire, Chinon, Beaugency, Les-Ponts-de-Cé, Loches, Louresse-Rochemenier, Orléans, Plessis-lès-Tours, Romorantin, Saint-Laurent-de-la-Plaine, Tigy, Tours.

Military. Angers, La Flèche, Montsoreau, Saumur.

Natural history. Chaumont-sur-Tharonne, Doué-la-Fontaine, La Flèche (zoos), Angers, Ingrandes, Orléans.

Transport and cars. Amboise (postal), Briare, Le Mans, Montrichard, Villesavin.

Other visits. Cointreau and slate-works at Angers, Poulain chocolates at Blois, Gien chinaworks, Combier at Saumur, innumerable wine cellars large and small, waxworks at Tours.

ARCHITECTURE

Architecture in France as elsewhere is the reflection of the prevailing power, secular or ecclesiastic. The break-up of the Roman Empire left its mark with the dual influences of Rome and Byzantium. You'll find the centrally planned **Imperial Roman** style evident in the 5th-century baptisteries of Aix-en-Provence's Saint-Sauveur cathedral (p. 239) and Marseille's Saint-Victor basilica. The **Byzantine** Greek-cross influence can be seen in the Carolingian church of Germigny-des-Prés (p. 184) in the Loire Valley.

Romanesque abbey-church at Cluny (1088).

Amid the dispersion of political power during feudal times, the great monastic orders of Burgundy established the new building styles that became known as **Romanesque.** The Cistercians insisted on utter simplicity, seen in its finest surviving form at Fontenay (consecrated 1147), while the Benedictines of Cluny set a bolder pattern of apsidal chapels to accommodate more altars. Paray-le-Monial (begun 1109, p. 138) is a perfect example. More elaborate was the system of domed chapels radiating from an ambulatory around the choir, as can be seen in the elaborate chancels of Auvergne's Orcival or Saint-Nectaire (pp. 208 and 210). Frescoes (mostly disappeared) and sculpted capitals on arch columns were the major forms of interior decoration, telling biblical stories and the lives of the saints.

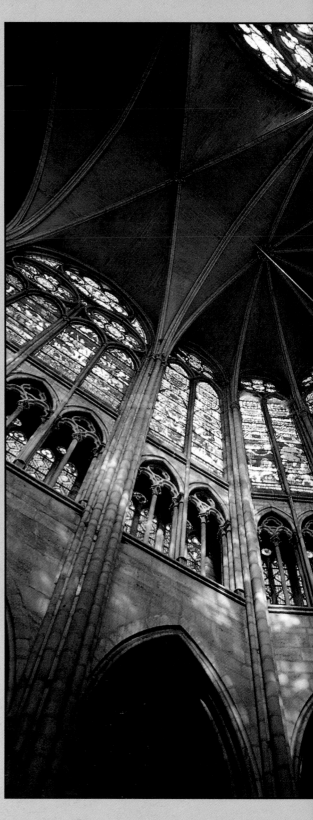

An important Romanesque innovation was Tournus's stone tunnel-vaulting (p. 141) instead of fire-prone wooden ceilings (as in the great Norman abbey-church of Jumièges, p. 154). It should be noted that the pointed arch, which many imagine to be the distinctive mark of Gothic architecture to achieve greater elevation than the rounded tunnel arch, was already a feature of Romanesque churches, as can be seen in Burgundy's Autun (p. 138). The loftiness of nearby Véze-lay's Sainte-Madeleine (p. 135) is achieved with groin vaulting and added the typical feature of stone tracery in its towers. Paris's huge Notre-Dame was perhaps the ultimate symbol of French royal power expressed through the church (see p. 83) while Beauvais overreached itself and could get only its gigantic 68-m.-high choir built (see p. 109).

Gothic architectural carving reached its high point with the stone tracery and elaborate but naturalistic foliage of Reims (1211, p. 120). By the end of the 14th century, the virtuoso craftsmanship earned the appropriate name of **Flam-**

Château de Chambord (1519)
< Gothic cathedral of Saint-Denis (1136).

(a ceiling of diagonally inter-locking arches).

The growing national power of the French kings found archi-tectural expression in the soaring **Gothic** style of their cathedrals, with slender columns sending their pointed arches up to an elaborate network of rib vault-ing. The greater height was supported externally by flying buttresses, and correspondingly elongated figures of saints and prophets appeared on the sculpted portals. (Compare them with the more squat figures of Romanesque sculpture.) With the opening up of the walls that the loftier structure per-mitted, stained-glass windows illuminated the interior. Saint-Denis and Sens (p. 103, 109), with their characteristic two-tower façades built in the 1140s, were the pioneering Gothic cathedrals. Laon (p. 116) achieved a four-tier elevation **boyant Gothic**, nicely exem-plified by Rouen's Saint-Maclou (p. 153) and, in the secular sphere, the nearby Law Courts.

Secular architecture devel-oped from the earliest simple castle-keep, square, oblong or round, to the more elaborate structures inspired by the Crusades in the Middle East. Fortifications comprised longer curtain walls, often forming a square with a tower at each corner, such as the original Louvre built by Philippe Auguste in 1200 (and recently excavated during the building of François Mitterrand's Pyramid). In the 15th century, the manor house replaced the castle, most notably the magnificent Flam-boyant Gothic house of Jacques Cœur in Bourges (p. 199).

French Renaissance blossomed in the Loire châteaux of François I, most notably Blois (1515) and Chambord (1519),

I. M. Pei's Pyramid for the Louvre (1988).

largely symmetrical compositions around a square main lodge, adding such fanciful features as a double-spiral staircase in the centre.

The great contribution of Henri IV was his Paris squares—Place des Vosges and Place Dauphine—with their elegant redbrick and white stone façades. The taste for airy city squares grew in the 17th and 18th centuries with Place Vendôme and Place des Victoires in Paris and Nancy's grand Place Stanislas.

Louis XIV's reign was marked by grandiose **Classicism.** Perrault built the graceful colonnaded east façade of the Louvre, but a more opulent tone was set by financier Fouquet's Vaux-le-Vicomte (pp. 49 and 104) with the combined work of **Baroque** architect Le Vau, painter Lebrun and landscape-architect Le Nôtre, co-opted by the Sun King for Versailles. As a reaction to Baroque excesses,

neo-Classicism brought a more sober elegance to the Place de la Concorde in the 1750s, with its Hôtel de Crillon and Ministère de la Marine. The masterpieces of this period include Bordeaux's Grand Théâtre and Paris's Panthéon (its dome inspired by London's St. Paul's). Out in the Jura, Ledoux was experimenting in urban industrial architecture with his Arc-et-Senans saltworks (p. 144). Under Napoleon, neo-Classicism became rhetorical and downright bombastic with the National Assembly (Palais-Bourbon), the Madeleine and the Bourse (Stock Exchange).

In the 19th century, Viollet-le-Duc led the movement inspired by writers Victor Hugo and Prosper Mérimée to restore the national monuments. In his own work, he shared with contemporaries an excessive taste for the **neo-Gothic,** but can be thanked for his restoration of Vézelay (p. 135), Notre-Dame and the Sainte-Chapelle. The

steel of the industrial age appeared in Baltard's market buildings of the now defunct Les Halles (1852, dismantled in the 1960s, but one *pavillon* is still preserved at Nogent-sur-Marne) and Eiffel's Tower (1889). The turn of the century was embellished by Guimard's florid **Art nouveau** designs for the métro stations.

France's modern age is notably cosmopolitan. Swiss-born Le Corbusier experimented both in mass public housing in Marseille and Nantes and a free-form pilgrimage chapel of Ronchamp (near Belfort). The factory-like Beaubourg (Centre Pompidou) was an Anglo-Italian effort by Richard Rogers and Renzo Piano, while Chinese-American I. M. Pei designed the new Pyramid for the Louvre and Danish architect Johan Otto von Spreckelsen conceived the gigantic hollowed-out marble cube for the Défense business district.

contemporary portrait of her as Diana goddess of hunting does full justice to her beauty.

After his death, Henri II's widow Catherine de Médicis took Chenonceau for herself and added the galleried floors of ballrooms and reception halls that complete the bridge across the river.

If the short walk from the main gate is too much for you, you can take an electric train in summer, and there are boat rides on the river when the water is deep enough.

Loches   16,B2

South-west of Chenonceau on the Indre river, the delightful medieval village of Loches is as much an attraction as the château itself.

The church of **Saint-Ours** is a fascinating piece of Romanesque architecture with two steepled towers at either end of the nave, which itself has two bizarre octagonal pyramids in place of a roof. In the interior, the **narthex**, or entrance hall, has some fine, if partially mutilated sculpture. Over the nave, the hollow pyramids appear to be designed in the style of chimneys for a castle kitchen.

Wander among the fine old houses along Rue Saint-Ours and Rue du Château and take a walk around the **ramparts**.

Particularly interesting is the 11th-century **donjon** (keep) which formed part of the fortified town's southern defences. Kids love the torture instruments. Two 15th-century additions served as prisons for royal enemies—most notoriously for the Duke of Milan, who was kept there in total darkness for eight years, only to drop dead on the day of his release, overcome by the blinding sunlight.

At the other end of the fortifications, the terrace of the **Logis royal** (Royal Lodge) affords a lovely view over the village and the Indre valley. Architecturally, the lodge offers an interesting transition from sober Gothic to more decorative Renaissance. Inside is a little gem of Gothic art: Anne de Bretagne's private oratory, the niches of its stone

walls finely carved with her ermine emblem and the symbolic cords of the Franciscan order.

Tours   16,A2

If the Loire Valley's capital has few great sightseeing attractions, it does have some excellent restaurants and bookstores around the university. And if you don't feel like hunting down the various châteaux on your list, it offers a wide range of guided bus tours (details from the tourist office, Place de la Gare). But the **Musée des Beaux-Arts**, 18 Place François-Sicard, is certainly worth a look for its European paintings: Quentin Metsys, Rembrandt and Rubens; Mantegna, Andrea del Sarto and Magnasco; Boucher and Delacroix.

Azay-le-Rideau   16,A2

If French life can still evoke an image of grace and elegance, the **château** at Azay is its epitome. This late Gothic treasure of dazzling white stone beneath grey slate roofs casts a serene reflection into the waters of the Indre river, 30 kilometres (19 miles) south-west of Tours.

It was erected in the early 16th century by François I's treasurer, Gilles Berthelot, partly on a Venetian-style foundation of wood piles close-driven into the river bed. Berthelot's wife Philippe supervised the design and the feminine delicacy of its forms, especially the slender conical turrets at each corner and the double-arched loggias of the **main staircase.** Notice inside how, with the château no longer serving the function of a fortress, the staircase innovated with straight flights and landings rather than the old spiral form that was designed to fend off invaders.

Madame Berthelot built the large vaulted **kitchen** almost on a level with the river, so that an indoor well provided the closest thing to running water and an unusually hygienic stone drain sent back the slops. You can see the kind of utensils and cake moulds her cooks would have used. At least, until the king confiscated

Emerging from his Austrian prison, Richard the Lion-Heart was furious to learn his brother John had given the fortified town of Loches away to the French. His surprise attack recaptured the fortress so quickly—three hours—that townspeople were convinced he had done it by magic.

Loches' most attractive resident was Agnès Sorel, nick-named the Dame de Beauté *both for her Château de Beauté east of Paris and personal charms for which she had a special wardrobe made. Mistress of Charles VII, she was condemned by the local clergy as a sinner and bizarrely rehabilitated centuries later during the French Revolution when godless soldiers destroyed her tomb, mistaking her for a saint.*

the castle because her husband was cooking the royal books.

Villandry   *16,A2*

The big attraction here is the castle's Renaissance **gardens**. They have been reconstructed with meticulous historical and botanical accuracy to reproduce their original appearance when the castle was built in 1532. The geometric harmonies are a joy for the eye: perfect ranks of espalier-trained fruit trees; lovingly sculpted box- and yew-trees; evergreen hedges clipped and shaped into delightfully infuriating **mazes**; cool, vine-covered arbours, fountains and canals. The **potager** (kitchen garden) is laid out with the same attention to aesthetics —but you'll find no tomatoes or potatoes here: they were unknown in Europe at the time. But spare some time for the château interior, furnished in Spanish style,

A Who's Who to Loire Valley History

St. Martin of Tours (316–97)	Soldier-turned-Priest, "Apostle of the Gauls", founded numerous monasteries. Universally remembered as a symbol of charity for cutting up his cloak to share with a pauper. Died at Candes; buried at Tours.
Charles VII (1403–61)	His name is forever linked to Chinon. There, as uncrowned King of France, he received Joan of Arc, who was to have him crowned at Reims almost despite himself. His reign saw the end of the Anglo-French Hundred Years' War.
Roi René (1409–80)	Duke of Anjou and King of Sicily. Popular figure known to contemporaries as Good King René. Cultivated, literate, a fine linguist, his interests were limitless. A true Renaissance ruler, he made Saumur and Angers cultural centres. Daughter Margaret married Henry VI of England.
Joan of Arc (1412–31)	Humble peasant girl with a mission, she saved France from English domination, freeing town after town along the Loire, including Orléans, and winning battle after battle. Captured and tried, she was burnt at the stake at Rouen by the English and declared a saint in 1920.
Louis XI (1423–83)	Son of Charles VII. Crafty, cruel and superstitious, yet a highly able ruler who reunified France by guile and diplomacy. Bitterest enemy of Charles the Bold of Burgundy. Built Langeais, often resided at Plessis-lès-Tours where he died. Buried at Cléry-Saint-André, near Orléans.
Charles VIII (1470–98)	Son of Louis XI. Married Anne de Bretagne in 1491, thereby adding independent Brittany to France. He rebuilt the château at Amboise and died there at the age of 28, due to an accident.
Anne de Bretagne (1477–1514)	Associated especially with Langeais, Amboise, Loches, and Blois where she died. Married Charles VIII, then his successor Louis XII, but tried to keep Brittany an autonomous duchy within France. Her arms, the ermine and cords of St. Francis, are frequently to be seen.
Louis XII (1462–1515)	Son of Charles, poet-Duke of Orléans. Born at Blois, lived there most of his life. His arms, the porcupine, are prominent at Blois and Amboise.
François I (1494–1547)	The Loire Valley's "star" king. Educated, charming, seductive, brave, fond of good living—and well over 6 feet tall! We owe him Chambord. Married Claude, daughter of Louis XII and Anne de Bretagne. His arms, the salamander, can be seen in many a Loire château.
Catherine de Médicis (1519–89)	Italian wife of Henri II of France, daughter-in-law of François I and mother of three French kings (François II, Charles IX, Henri III). An unscrupulous intriguer, she was personally involved in the St. Bartholomew's Day massacre of Protestants in Paris. Lived at Blois and Chenonceau, which she enlarged.

with an upstairs gallery of Spanish paintings and a 13th-century gilded **Moorish ceiling** transferred from a mosque in Toledo.

Langeais   *16,A2*

This greystone redoubt is every child's dream of what a castle should look like: massive drawbridge and portcullis, archers' slits in the battlements and covered catwalks with machicolations from which the defenders poured boiling oil and other nasty things on attackers trying to scale the walls with ladders. The 15th-century fortress encloses an original 10th-century square keep, now overgrown with trees. In the **guard room** *(Salle des Gardes)*, the 15th-century stone fireplace reproduces a castle's crenellated ramparts with soldiers' heads peering down at you. You can recapture the real soldiers' thrills along the **battlement walkway** *(chemin de ronde)*.

Chinon   *16,A2*

Although most of the **château** is now in ruins, the 400-metre (1,312-foot)-long **ramparts** are an impressive sight from the opposite bank of the Vienne river. The walls are famous for their echo when you yell from the foot of the north side. Home of the Plantagenets, most notably Henry II who died there, the fortress is in fact three castles in one: Fort Saint-Georges, the Château du Milieu and the Château du Coudray. In the last-named, the **Tour de Boissy** gives you a superb view over the town and river and across to the castle's original keep, the 12th-century **Tour du Moulin**. It was in the Château du Milieu that Joan of Arc met up with Charles VII in 1429 to push him into reconquering his throne. Only a large stone fireplace remains of the Great Hall where they met, but the **Tour de l'Horloge** (the visitors' entrance) houses a little museum commemorating the events. The tower's bell was cast back in 1399 and so would have been heard by Joan herself. A warren of tunnels burrows beneath the château and town.

In town, explore the historic atmosphere of the **Rue Voltaire**, brought to life by an annual medieval costumed street-fair in July.

Abbaye de Fontevraud   *15,E2*

Founded in 1099, the abbey was in fact a veritable spiritual village grouping five different monastic communities: monks dedicated to St. John, nuns to the Virgin Mary, lepers to St. Lazarus, invalids to St. Benedict, and repented women sinners to Mary Magdalene. It quickly became a refuge for the nobility's rejected wives and daughters and accumulated great wealth under the aristocratic abbesses who ran it—much to the chagrin of the monks.

While much was destroyed first by Protestants, then Revolutionaries, it became under Napoleon a prison (until 1963). After its years as a prison-dormitory, the 12th-century **abbey church** has returned to unadorned Romanesque simplicity. In the south arm of the transept are recumbent Plantagenet **tomb-monuments** *(gisants),* including Henry II and his unloved wife Eléonore d'Aquitaine. Note the fine ambulatory and radiating chapels beyond the choir.

The monumental **kitchens** are constructed on a similar principle, with each fireplace (three of the eight have been dismantled) built like a chapel leading off the central work-space under a great octagonal chimney-hood. The **nuns' cloisters** *(Cloître Sainte-Marie)* have elegant Renaissance vaulting around three sides with a Gothic gallery to the south. You will find 16th-century mural paintings of the most illustrious abbesses in the **salle capitulaire** (chapter house for religious readings).

Saumur   *15,E2*

This is a military town. It's famous for its **National Riding School** *(Ecole Nationale d'Equitation)*. Every Friday morning from October to June (with a gala *Carrousel* week added at the end of July), you can watch the superb horsemanship of the school's black-uniformed Cadre Noir. But for combat, of course, the cavalry has given way to tanks, and the **Tank School** *(Ecole d'application de l'Arme blindée)* puts on acrobatic displays, not on tanks, but motorbikes. Book your seats well in advance (details from the tourist office, 25, Rue Beaurepaire). Over by the river, the **Tank Museum** *(Musée des Blindés)* displays armoured vehicles—French, German, American, British and Soviet—from 1917 to the present day in rooms with evocative names like General Patton and Field Marshal Rommel.

Saumur's **château** is a grim-looking fortress that has served over its six centuries more as prison-dungeon than palatial residence. Today, it houses the **Equestrian Museum** *(Musée du Cheval)*, displaying the saddles, spurs, bits and harnesses of Japanese samurai, Indian princes, Russian Cossacks, Argentinian gauchos and Texan cowboys.

Angers   *15,D2*

The perfect base for exploring the Loire Valley from its western end, this bustling university town offers some first-class modern shopping in the pedestrian zone around the **Place du Ralliement**.

The ruins of the 13th-century Eglise Toussaint have been beautifully restored and converted into the town's **Musée des Beaux-Arts** (33 bis, Rue Toussaint) to house a unique collection of sculptures by David d'Angers. This Who's Who of the heroes revered in 19th-century France includes not only Balzac and Hugo, but also Gutenberg, Paganini and a plaster bust of George Washington, the bronze of which stands in the United States

Capitol. In the imposing 12th- and 13th-century Gothic **Cathédrale Saint-Maurice,** look out for the excellent **stained-glass windows** covering 800 years of the noble art.

If not the most beautiful, the **château** is certainly the most formidable in the Loire Valley, a real defensive fortress, its black ramparts still forbidding despite having had their towers decapitated at the order of Henri III. The château's proudest possession is the magnificent 14th-century **Apocalypse tapestry** narrating the gospel of St. John in moving detail.

Le Mans   *15,E1*

Most people know of the town for its famous 24-hour motor race in June. But others stopping off on their way to or from Brittany might like to visit the **Cathédrale Saint-Julien** with its fine Gothic chancel and the impressive sculptures of saints and biblical figures on its 12th-century porch. Inside, look for the Renaissance **monumental tombs** in the north transept chapel and some superb 13th-century **stained-glass windows** over the choir. South-west of the cathedral, stroll around the medieval and half-timbered Renaissance houses of the **old town.**

Out at the 13.63-kilometre-(8.45-mile-) long **24-hour circuit** south of the city (between N138 and D139) is a splendid **car museum** with an 1884 De Dion Bouton steam car, an 1896 Delahaye, vintage Ferrari, Ford GT 40 and Porsche winners of the great endurance race and an exciting array of motorcycles. The 4.24-kilometre (2.63-mile) Bugatti Circuit is now reserved for trial runs and motorcycles.

*T*he cavalrymen of Saumur's Cadre Noir have a tradition dating back to 1768. They served both the Ancien Régime and the French Revolutionary armies, before seeing action overseas in the colonies of Indochina and North Africa. The riding school's cadets distinguished themselves in 1940 with their heroic resistance to the German advance through the Loire Valley.

Quiet Days
Among the Volcanoes

Stretching down from the southern edge of the Loire Valley, the French heartland known to vote-hungry politicians as *la France profonde* is remote in geography and spirit alike from the vanities and preoccupations of Paris. The network of modern rail and motorway communications has been slow to link the region to the capital. This cramps the local economy, but keeps the landscape blessedly unspoiled.

The Berry flatlands rise gradually to the sprawling Massif Central plateau of the Limousin to the west and, in the centre, the haunting shapes of Auvergne's extinct volcanoes. It is a land of diligence in its craftsmen—Limoges porcelain, Aubusson tapestries—graceful honesty in its Romanesque churches—Orcival, Saint-Nectaire, Clermont-Ferrand's Notre-Dame-du-Port. The peasants, particularly the brooding Auvergnats, are renowned for their prudence and dour honesty. They offer you a France without frills.

Berry   *17,CD2-3*

The region's farmland embraces vast stretches of wheatfields around the cathedral city of Bourges, with the Sancerre vineyards to the north. To the south is the cattle-grazing Boischaut country of meadows surrounded by hedgerows like the Normandy *bocage*.

Sancerre   *17,D2*
The town stands in the middle of its river. Handsome Renaissance houses around the Nouvelle Place are a vestige of the town's 16th-century heyday when the local Huguenots fought their last stand in the Wars of Religion that left their castle in ruins. On the eastern edge of town, its one surviving tower, **Tour des Fiefs**, gives you a fine view down over the vineyards to the valley beyond.

Try the delicately fruity white wine or less celebrated but very fine red with the local Chavignol goat cheese—often served *toasted* on a bed of salad.

Bourges   *17,C2*
The Berrichon capital looms out of the plain with one of the greatest of France's Gothic cathedrals and the grand patrician architecture left by the 15th-century entrepreneur Jacques Cœur, Rothschild of his times. But the town also maintains a modern profile with schools of fine arts and experimental music. A very popular spring festival, Printemps de Bourges, is devoted to avant-garde and rock music.

Cathédrale **Saint-Etienne** owes its renown to the peculiar grace of its silhouette and the intricate harmony of the façade's five portals, each subtly different in dimension and design. The church is dominated not by its spireless towers but by the massive nave and the graceful double flying buttresses linking the five chapels to the chancel (viewed best from the archbishop's gardens behind the cathedral). The sculptures of the **façade** are a summit of 13th-century art. Outstanding on the steeply gabled centre portal is the monumental sculpture portraying the Last Judgment—Christ surrounded by angels bearing the instruments of the Passion, and St. Michael weighing the souls for the Resurrection. In the interior, note the magnificent vaulting and the **stained-glass windows,** also 13th-century, around the choir and chapels of the apse.

Palais Jacques-Cœur, a rare jewel of Gothic secular architecture with a rich interior heralding the Renaissance, was the residence of the merchant-prince who provided Charles VII with the financial counterpart to Jeanne d'Arc's moral support. Son of a modest furrier, Jacques Cœur built a commercial empire in fierce competition with Venice and Genoa. Behind a fortress-like western façade built along the town's old Gallo-Roman ramparts, the palace reveals its elegance in the inner courtyard, with its seven **turret-staircases** and handsome balconies. The merchant's two mottoes engraved around the windows proclaim the self-made man: *"A vaillans (cœurs), riens impossible"* ("To valiant hearts, nothing is impossible") and *"Dire, faire, taire"* ("Say, do and shut up"). Note the **pigeon-loft** from which, 400 years before Reuters and Associated Press, Jacques Cœur organized a private news service with carrier-pigeons to and from his offices in Montpellier and Marseille. Inside, look out for the **Chambre de l'Argentier,** a money-room protected by secret passages and armoured behind solid iron doors like the safe-deposit room of a modern bank.

Something of the graceful life of the Jacques Cœur era is also recaptured in the beautifully restored houses of the 15th and 16th centuries around **Place Gordaine.** For a colourful presentation of the region's town and country life—costumes, furniture, kitchen utensils—visit the **Musée du Berry** housed in the Renaissance mansion, Hôtel Cujas.

Boischaut 17,C3

Due south of Bourges, the N144 takes you through this pastoral region's rolling green meadows, home for the contented white Charolais cattle producing France's best beef. East on D92, in its own park, is the impressive **Château de Meillant.** If its southern façade presents the forbidding aspect of a medieval fortress, it becomes on its eastern façade a more graceful Italianate palazzo. Its lord in the 15th century was Charles de Chaumont, governor of Milan. The work of his Verona architect Fra Giocondo is evident in the elaborately carved stone tracery and sculptures around the windows of the **Tour du Lion.** The castle's interior is lavishly furnished, particularly the magnificent leather-tapestried **dining room,** its table set for a royal banquet. Bellicose kids will love the splendid weapons and armour in the **guard room.** Note in the chapel the 16th-century stained glass windows.

Back on N144, at the edge of the Meillant forest, the Cistercian **Abbaye de Noirlac** offers a sober contrast in the austere architecture of its 12th-century church, a transition from Romanesque to Gothic. Unlike the simple, unadorned pillars of the church's nave, the arcades of the **cloister** are richly carved. They were erected in the prosperous 14th and 15th centuries, when the monks had abandoned their frugal principles for the farm revenues from expanded land holdings. Declining under absentee abbots, the monastery was attacked by Protestants in the Wars of Religion and had only six monks by the time of the Revolution. It served as a porcelain factory in the 19th century and was restored after World War II.

Limousin
22,BC2

The wild, sparsely populated countryside of the Massif Central is less luxurious than the image the British and Americans might conjure up in a "limousine". (The vehicle derives its name from the early models' canopy similar to the hood of Limousin shepherds.) But the heathland and forests of pine, oak, beech and chestnut make for great hiking country, and fishermen are attracted to the salmon, trout, char and perch of the Vienne and Corrèze rivers. The region is famous for its craftsmanship—porcelain in Limoges and tapestry revived in modern forms at Aubusson, both worthwhile stops on your way to the Périgord and the Dordogne.

Aubusson
22,C2

Tucked in among green hills down by the Creuze river, the historic centre of the French tapestry industry still demonstrates the ancient art brought here from Flanders in the 14th century. Among the fine Renaissance houses of the old city centre, the weavers' workshop in the **Maison du Vieux Tapissier** on Rue Vieille recreates the atmosphere of its 16th-century heyday. Manufacture declined when Louis XIV's Edict of Nantes sent into exile the Protestant Huguenots, who formed the backbone of the industry here. But at the modern **Centre culturel et artistique Jean-Lurçat** (Avenue des Tissiers), you can see where the noble art has been revived in the 20th century by Lurçat and his followers, Gromaire, Prassinos and Wogensky. Watch the weavers at work, producing one square metre of tapestry in a month. In summer, exhibitions of traditional and modern tapestries are held at the Hôtel de Ville (city hall).

Limoges
22,B2

The region's capital is also French capital of porcelain manufacture, providing fully half of the nation's production.

The town has two distinct centres. The oldest part, known as the **Cité**, lies to the south-east down by the Vienne river, where medieval houses cluster around the Cathédrale **Saint-Etienne**. Six centuries in the building, the church is most notable for its Flamboyant Gothic portal. Inside, see the handsome 16th-century choir-screen now at the western end of the nave beneath the organ loft.

Housed in the bishop's palace nearby, the **Municipal Museum** (in addition to a couple of paintings by Limoges-born Auguste Renoir) has a remarkable collection of fine enamels. These ornaments, made of brilliant blue, red, green and white metal oxides fused to gold, silver or copper plate, were the city's glory from the Middle Ages to the 18th century.

You can watch the time-honoured craft in **enamellers' workshops** around Place Wilson in the modern city-centre, known as the **Château**. Stroll around the timbered houses in the lively old market area of **Rue de la Boucherie**.

West of the Château district, the **Musée Adrien-Dubouché**, 8 bis, Place Winston-Churchill, has the country's second largest collection of porcelain—after the Sèvres museum outside Paris

Flaying for Keeps
Ruler of western France, Richard was mortally wounded while besieging his vassal, the Viscount of Limoges, for refusing to give up some treasure found on his land. Before he died, Richard pardoned the captured crossbowman who had shot him, but the king's men skinned the poor fellow alive anyway.

(see p. 313). Its 10,000 pieces cover the history of porcelain manufacture from all over the world—china from China, Dutch Delft, Italian Faënza, German Meissen, English Chelsea, Derby, Worcester and Wedgwood. Besides French Sèvres, Rouen, Lille and Strasbourg work, pride of place goes naturally enough to local production, which began in 1771 after the discovery of the white china clay known as kaolin at Saint-

Yrieix-la-Perche just south of Limoges. A few companies demonstrate the hand-decoration of porcelain, including Pastaud, 36, Rue Jules Noriac, and Limoges Castel, Avenue Kennedy.

If you're heading down to the Périgord on N21, stop off at **Château Châlus-Chabrol** where Richard the Lion-Heart died in 1199. The castle's massive 11th-century dungeon-tower survives near traces of the chapel where Richard was buried before his heart was transferred to Rouen cathedral. A 17th-century addition to the castle lodge documents Richard's life.

Vallée de la Corrèze   *22,B2*

The N89 from Tulle south-west to Brive-la-Gaillarde makes a pleasant drive along the Corrèze river as it rushes through a narrow winding valley of steep cliffs widening occasionally into sunny cattle pastures.

Sprawling along the river with its old houses clinging to the valley's slopes, **Tulle** has for three centuries been a centre of arms manufacture. A more pious tradition is the colourful procession along the town's heights honouring the June birthday of John the Baptist. It starts out from the Romanesque-Gothic cathedral whose graceful belltower dominates the medieval quarters known as L'Enclos. (Manufacture of the famous silk lace fabric to which the town gave its name moved up to Calais in the 19th century.)

Before continuing down the valley, take a side trip to the spectacular waterfalls at Gimel-les-Cascades and see the splendid 12th-century gold and enamelled reliquary casket of Saint Stephen in the local church.

The busy market-town of **Brive-la-Gaillarde** is as cheerful as its name, distribution-centre for the fruit, vegetables, truffles and *foie gras* of the Limousin and neighbouring Périgord. On your walk through the old part of town behind the church of Saint-Martin, peep into the courtyard of the superb Renaissance mansion, **Hôtel de Labenche** in the Rue Blaise-Raynal.

Auvergne   *23,CDE1-3*

The province has a place apart in the national consciousness. The rough, tough climate has created a rough, tough, but ultimately highly respected peasant. As careful with his *sous* as a Scotsman with his pennies, the Auvergnat is also proud of having produced many national leaders —from the Gallic chieftain Vercingetorix to two presidents of the Fifth Republic: Georges Pompidou and Valéry Giscard d'Estaing. The Auvergnat's sober dignity is reflected in the great Romanesque churches in and around the provincial capital of Clermont-Ferrand, monuments of the region's strong religious tradition. Its seclusion attracted many monasteries, while pilgrimage churches sprang up along the route to Santiago de Compostela in Spain. It was at Clermont that Pope Urban II preached in favour of the First Crusade in 1095. Le Puy remains a major centre for the cult of the Virgin Mary.

The region's dominant geographical feature is its chain of 200 volcanoes. They stopped erupting some 3,500 years ago but remain as fascinating testimony to the different forms—domes, pyramids and needle-like pillars—produced by the earth's upset stomach. Appropriately enough, a continuing by-product of this volcanic activity is the hot springs and mineral waters that offer cures for gastric disorders, among other ills. The major spas include Vichy (good for liver, bile and digestive tract), Royat (heart and arteries), Saint-Nectaire (kidneys) and Le Mont-Dore (respiratory ailments). The mineral waters, along with the fruity Beaujolais-like local Côte d'Auvergne wines, are good accompaniments to the hearty cuisine of hams, tripe and sausages, often served with cabbage, and the local cheeses—the soft Saint-Nectaire, blue Fourme d'Ambert and savoury Cantal.

We propose here a roughly north-south itinerary beginning in Vichy and revolving around the capital, Clermont-

Ferrand, before moving down to the Cantal mountains.

Vichy 23,D1

The "queen of spa resorts" by the Allier river is famous for its bottled mineral water but infamous, too, as the seat of the French collaborationist government during World War II. Even if nothing ails you, there's something here for history buffs and amateur anthropologists alike. Sportsmen will appreciate the summer horse-racing, sailing on the artificial lake and, in a palace looking a little like Versailles' Trianon, casino gambling without which no spa is a spa.

For the hot springs still lure those who wined and dined too well in their youth to come and fix their liver, while genteel melancholics are invited to nurse their migraines. In the grand Byzantine-domed **Halle des Sources**, they gather around the *buvette* drinking fountain, designed like a Greek love-temple in a décor of gilded mosaic tiles, and sip natural spring waters that range in temperature from 27° to 42.5°C. (Outside in the park are cold springs in the low 20s.) The waters are heavy in bicarbonate of soda and carbonic acids. Between gripes, they stroll around the plane trees, chestnuts and the bandstand of the **Parc des Sources** dressed in their Sunday best, even on Wednesdays. However you feel, you've got to *look* good.

Even more attractive are the English gardens down by the river, the **Parc de l'Allier**, with its rockeries and duck ponds and a special place for the grandchildren to play. There are several elegant hotels, but the grandest, a true monument, is the **Pavillon Sévigné**, near the river. Much remodelled, it was the home of the 17th-century literary lady, Marquise de Sévigné, who came here for her rheumatism. Known in the 1940s as the Hôtel du Parc, it became the headquarters of Marshal Pétain.

Among the many excursions out of Vichy, take the N209 west towards the spectacular **Gorges de Chouvigny**. The D915 follows the winding Sioule river to a heather-covered ravine towering over the rapids. Climb the stairway cut in the cliff face to the **Roc Armand** for a view over the sharp pyramids of granite to the 13th-century Chouvigny **castle**, once a family home of American Revolutionary hero La Fayette. On your way back, stop off at **Ebreuil** to visit the ancient Benedictine abbey-church of **Saint-Léger**. The nave and transept date back to the 10th and 11th century, but a Gothic choir was added and the whole has been heavily restored in the last 150 years. In the gallery surrounding the nave are some remarkable Romanesque **frescoes** recounting the saints' lives. The remains of St. Léger are kept in a handsome 16th-century copper **reliquary** behind the high altar. Just 4 kilometres (2½ miles) north of Ebreuil, try to see the little Romanesque church of **Veauce** at noon to appreciate the white stone (rare in volcanic Auvergne) of its

---

Comeuppance

On July 2, 1940, less than two weeks after signing France's capitulation to Hitler's Germany, the 84-year-old Marshal Philippe Pétain installed himself in Vichy's Hôtel du Parc to run the French government in the unoccupied zone. From time to time during the next four years he would make a ritual appearance on his balcony to salute parades of schoolchildren singing the propaganda song: *Maréchal, nous voilà!* (Marshal, here we are!) Several times a day he took a brisk walk through the park along the Allier river, greeting admirers with a nod and a twinkle—he was a notorious lady's man, even in his eighties.

On August 20, 1944, amid rumours that French Resistance fighters were plotting to kidnap him, 35 S.S. troops stormed into his hotel in the middle of the night. With a slightly less cheerful German version of *Maréchal, nous voilà,* they kicked his door down and carried him off as Hitler's prisoner to Sigmaringen in Baden-Württemberg. Pétain returned to France in 1945 to be tried for treason. His death-sentence was commuted to life imprisonment, and Vichy renamed two streets where he used to walk down by the river Boulevard des Etats-Unis and Avenue Eisenhower.

*F*rom their castle north of Le Puy, the Polignac barons lorded it over the surrounding country from the Crusades to the French Revolution. In 1181, one of them overdid his brigandry and was ordered to go barefoot to the abbey of Saint-Julien de Brioude to be beaten by a monk as a penance. The amazing thing about this brute was that he actually went.

noted that 15 minutes before his death, he was still alive, an observation henceforth known as a Lapalissade and cited whenever a modern politician launches into similar profound truths. Visit the fine tapestried Renaissance dining room and, upstairs, the gilded **Salon Doré** reception-room with its grand coffered ceiling.

Riom
23,D2

Long a rival of Clermont-Ferrand for Auvergne's political and cultural leadership, the town reveals something of its heyday from the 16th to the 18th century in the elegant Renaissance and neo-Classical mansions, notably on **Rue d'Horloge** and **Rue de l'Hôtel-de-Ville**. Look out, too, for the many ornamental **fountains** of the same period.

The town acquired a certain notoriety in 1942 as the scene of the Vichy government's abortive show-trial of prime ministers Léon Blum and Edouard Daladier, blamed for causing the war with Germany.

The **Regional Museum** *(Musée régional d'Auvergne)* housed in an 18th-century mansion at 10 bis, Rue Delille gives you a good introduction to traditional Auvergnat rural life–old farm implements, the paraphernalia of beekeeping, fishing and hunting, country games and musical instruments. The **Musée Francisque-Mandet**, 14, Rue de l'Hôtel de Ville, has a display of Egyptian and Etruscan bronzes, local medieval sculpture, and a small collection of European painting, including early Italians of the 13th century, Dutch and Flemish (Teniers and Van Goyen) and French (Natoire and Regnault). But many art-lovers make straight for the Eglise de **Notre-Dame-du-Marthuret** just for its exquisite 14th-century Gothic statue of the Virgin and Child playing with a bird (in the first chapel right of the entrance).

Compare it with an equally admired 12th-century sculpture, the so-called **Black Virgin** in the adjoining village of **Marsat**. In the 19th century, the statue's

graceful chancel. It stands at the edge of a beautiful **park**, the grounds of a medieval fortress.

A half-hour's drive north-east of Vichy is the **Château de Lapalisse**, originally built in the 12th century, but remodelled 400 years later in the Florentine style. It commands the affection of the French as the home of Jacques de Chabannes, lord of Lapalisse killed at the battle of Pavia in 1525. His men composed a song which

clothes were gilded and the faces of the Virgin and Child painted black to conform with the widespread Auvergnat cult of Black Virgins.

The village of **Mozac**, immediately north-west of Riom, is definitely worth a visit for the 12th-century Romanesque **church** and its magnificent **sculpted capitals,** regarded as among the finest in Auvergne. This once-prominent abbey church attached to the powerful Benedictine order of Cluny lost its chancel and most of the transept after four earthquakes in the 15th century. The imposing columns and arcades of the main nave attest to its ancient authority. The nave-capitals are carved with lively centaurs, dragons, goats and monkeys. The masterpieces are two capitals salvaged from the chancel and placed at the entrance to the nave: the Resurrection, portrayed in the old tradition, not with Christ, but with three Holy Women carrying phials of perfume for his embalming and greeted by a youthful angel at the entrance to the empty tomb; and Atlantes, four men kneeling in the position of world-bearers. The church's other treasure, in the south arm of the rebuilt transept, is the enamelled bronze **reliquary** of its 7th-century founder, St. Calmin, portraying the Crucifixion and enthronement of Christ and, on the rear side, the life of Calmin with his wife Namadie, in the days before monks were celibate.

Before heading into Clermont-Ferrand, stop off at **Châteaugay**, where they grow some of the best Côte d'Auvergne wine. You can taste it in the Gay Cœur **wine-cellars** on the ground floor of the town's 14th-century castle.

Clermont-Ferrand   *23,D2*

The capital of Auvergne, joining the two towns of Clermont and Montferrand in the 18th century, stands on a foothill of the Puy-de-Dôme volcanoes. At first sight, the black lava stone of its major monuments and older houses gives it a dark, even foreboding aspect. But the eye soon grows accustomed, and the sombre

hues serve to underline the medieval character of the town's historic centre.

Any introduction to the old city, however, begins naturally enough amid the modern bustle of the **Place de Jaude**, heart of a multi-level shopping centre. Statues on the square pay homage to two Auvergnat warriors: Vercingetorix, sculpted in the heroic manner by Auguste Bartholdi (creator of New York's Statue of Liberty), and Louis Desaix, a general of the French Revolutionary army. Head into the old town north-east of the square along the **Rue des Gras**. This pilgrimage street, now a pedestrian zone lined with houses of the 16th and 17th centuries, was once a processional stairway leading up to the cathedral (*gras* meant steps). Set in the wall of the corner house on Place des Gras is a medieval sculpted frieze of Jesus washing the feet of the disciples.

The Gothic **cathedral** was begun in the 13th century, but its distinctive spires and façade are the work of restorer-architect Viollet-le-Duc in the 1880s. Inside, the black Volvic stone, hard as ordinary granite but more workable, proves an admirable material for the slim Gothic pillars and arches. The fine **stained-glass windows** in the chapels beyond the choir are the work of four centuries, from the 12th to the 15th, depicting in vivid scarlets and blues the lives of Jesus and the saints.

Behind the cathedral, among the old houses in the lively shopping district along the **Rue Pascal** and **Rue du Port**, take a peep at the attractive little arcaded inner courtyards. This was ever a centre of Clermont's commercial activity, *port* meaning trading counter and giving its name to the town's noblest edifice, the 11th-century basilica of **Notre-Dame-du-Port**. Ignore the restorers' ugly bell-towers and black lava stone slabs replacing the original roof-tiles to concentrate on the splendours of the interior, if possible bathed in the noonday light. Stand in the narthex at the western end of the church to admire the harmony of the nave's arcades, a masterpiece of Romanesque simplicity. The church's greatest treasure is its **sculpted capitals** on the chapel columns leading off from the ambulatory beyond the choir. Signed "Rotbertus" (Robert), the sculptures tell worshippers of the Book of Life, the struggle between vice and virtue from the fall of Eve to salvation achieved through Mary, each scene carved with touching detail, particularly eloquent in the hand-gestures.

Make your way back west on the Rue Claussmann alongside a broad esplanade to the Place de la Poterne and the grand Renaissance **Fontaine d'Amboise**. Built in 1515 by the free-spirited Bishop of Clermont, his Amboise family arms are carried by the Hercules on top of the monument while some cheeky little stone cherubs piddle into the fountain below.

Two museums deserve your attention: the **Musée Bargoin**, 45 Rue de Ballainvilliers, displaying locally excavated prehistoric and Roman remains, and the **Musée du Ranquet**, 1, Petite Rue Saint-Pierre, devoted principally to medieval and Renaissance art. The Ranquet reserves for philosopher-scientist Blaise Pascal, born in Clermont-Ferrand in 1623, a room of memorabilia including the calculating machine he invented at the age of 19—he was also much involved with barometers and wheelbarrows.

Puy de Dôme and the Volcano National Park   *23,CD2*

The province's rolling green volcano country, organized now as a vast national park that runs 120 kilometres (75 miles) from the Monts Dôme (or Chaîne des Puys) to the southern edge of the Cantal mountains, is great for ramblers. You can get detailed maps of easy-going itineraries *(sentiers de petites randonnées)*, most of them circuits ranging from 1 to 6 hours, from Clermont-Ferrand's tourist office, 17, Place Delille.

The D68 west of the city takes you through the smart residential suburb of Chamalières (former mayor, ex-President Giscard d'Estaing) and the spa resort of **Royat**, which offers treatment for tired blood and cellulitis. Those preferring to work off their fatty tissue with a good walk in the mountains can stop off for picnic supplies of local cheeses and hams at the small market behind the 11th-century **Eglise Saint-Léger**. Beside the south wall of this sturdy battlemented fortress church, take a look at the little Breton-style **stone calvary** carved with the figures of Adam and Eve, Abraham and Isaac, and the Crucifixion.

Le Puy de Dôme (1,465 metres or 4,806 feet), is the highest of the Monts Dôme range and its easily accessible peak affords a magnificent panorama of the other volcanoes. A road (open from the spring to the first winter snowfalls) forks right off the D68 to spiral up to within a half-hour's walk of the summit. On the southern slope of this once-sacred mountain, you will see **Roman ruins** of a 1st-century temple to Mercury built on the orders of the Emperor Nero (more remains are exhibited in Clermont-Ferrand's Musée Bargoin). After supplanting an earlier sanctuary to the Gallic god Lug, the temple was in turn replaced in

Where's the Battlefield?
Four kilometres (2½ miles) south of the city, the Plateau de Gergovie is believed by some historians to be the site of the great victory in 52 B.C. when Vercingetorix led his Gallic armies against Julius Caesar (before ultimate defeat later the same year at Alésia, in Burgundy [see p.135]). This successful alliance of otherwise warring Gallic tribes is traditionally cited as the exemplary first act of French national unity. Despite topographical similarities with the place described as Gergovia by Caesar himself, no archaeological finds have so far confirmed the plateau as the actual battlefield. (Other historians put it north-west of Clermont-Ferrand at Chanturgue.) But the site, marked by a monument, does provide a fine view of the Allier valley and surrounding mountains. And it prompted Napoleon III to give the proud name of Gergovie to a village once less happily known as Merdogne.

the Middle Ages by a Christian chapel to St. Barnaby, that has completely disappeared. The modern religions of science and technology now top the mountain with a television antenna and observatory. (An alternative route to the summit, if the approach-road is closed, starts out from the Col de Ceyssat further along the D68. This is the old Roman road and if it takes you an hour's hard but not unmanageable slog to the top, just think what it was like lugging the masonry up to build that temple.)

The **view** from the observation area beyond the TV antenna is particularly impressive at sunset or on a partly overcast day when the peaks loom out of the low-lying cloud. Notice how the volcanoes to the north are mostly, like this one, craterless dome-topped cones, while those to the south have craters scooped out of their tops like soft-boiled eggs. A plaque on the TV antenna building commemorates a scientific experiment of barometric pressure organized on the mountain-top in 1648 by Pascal to prove that air is not weightless.

Orcival   23,D2

South-west of the Puy de Dôme, this charming village beside the Sioule river nestles in a tranquil green valley in the foothills of the Monts-Dore. Climb up the wooded hillside of the Bois des Bourelles on the north-east side of the village for a delightful view over the houses' steeply sloping stone-tiled roofs clustered around its 12th-century church.

The Basilica of **Notre-Dame-d'Orcival,** built of light grey volcanic stone, is considered one of the five jewels of Auvergnat Romanesque (the others being Clermont-Ferrand's Notre-Dame-du-Port, Saint-Nectaire, Saint-Austremoine of Issoire and Saint-Saturnin). The tiered domes of its characteristic chancel rise above the apsidal chapels to a belltower whose steeple was slightly truncated in the Revolution. The church's great treasure, a beautifully gilded statue of the **enthroned Virgin and Child,** also 12th-

century, was saved by walling it up in the gallery of the narthex entrance-hall (along with the bells) before the vandals arrived. The revered statue (now behind the high altar) made the basilica a major pilgrimage church, and Ascension Day still brings worshippers overflowing into the church-square for the festivities (torchlit procession and Midnight Mass the day before). Notice the prisoners' **irons and chains** hung on the outside wall

*I*nside the lovely Romanesque village church of Saint-Nectaire, the sculpted capitals teach us practically all we can glean about the life of the 4th-century missionary after whom it is named. He worked miracles raising the dead, crossed the Tiber to Rome with the devil as his boatman and later himself was resurrected from the dead to witness the construction of his church.

of the southern transept as a symbol of Mary's liberating powers. If the morning or late afternoon sun provides the best light for a Gothic church's stained glass windows, the midday sun is the best for the play of light and shade among the pillars and arcades of a Romanesque interior. This is especially true for the Orcival basilica's unusually lofty arcades, bringing light flooding into the barrel-vaulted main nave. While the nave's capitals are mostly decorated only with foliage motifs, the **capitals** of the ambulatory behind the choir are more lively, with eagles and fish, griffins and monkeys, and a debauched devil riding a goat.

A few minutes' drive north of Orcival on D27 is the elegant **Château de Cordès**, an aristocratic manor built in various stages from the 13th to the 17th centuries with pretty pepperpot towers. The fine gardens were designed by Versailles' André Le Nôtre.

Le Mont-Dore   23,D2

This popular spa and winter sports resort lies in a wooded valley of beeches and pines near the source of the Dordogne river. Its clear mountain air and hot springs (38° to 44°C, 100° to 111°F) offer tried and tested cures for respiratory ailments, but it also attracts a hale and hearty younger crowd to its many summer sporting activities: tennis, golf and hiking. Nearby **Lake Guéry** is popular either for some contemplative trout-fishing or more vigorous windsurfing.

Even if you don't intend to "take the waters", it's worth paying a visit to the spa's ornate 19th-century **Etablissement thermal**—for which the British, no doubt influenced by the royal Hanovers, preferred the German word *Kursaal*. The grand red-tile and enamel-brick décor makes an honourable successor to the ancient Roman baths of which traces remain in the main hall and the park. For your first serious breath of fresh mountain air, a funicular railway and easy half-hour walk take you up to the **Salon du Capucin**, a clearing in the middle of the

pine forest. From there, you can wander back down or continue to the top of the Capucin mountain (1,465 m./4,806 ft.) for an extended view over the resort and the whole Monts-Dore range. The winding hillside path to the sparkling waterfall of the **Grande Cascade** makes a leisurely two-hour walk on the south-east side of town. In spring, look out for the wild flowers—crocus, jonquil, narcissus and alpine anemone.

Just 4½ kilometres (3 miles) south of the resort on D983 is the **Puy de Sancy**, at 1,885 metres (6,184 feet) the tallest peak in Auvergne. The summit is within easy reach by cable-car and a 20-minute walk, providing a spectacular view—on clear days across the Rhône Valley to the Alps.

Another popular excursion is the winding D996 mountain road east over the Monts-Dore to the sandy beaches and limpid volcanic waters of **Lake Chambon**. It has good public camping facilities in clearings of the pine forest surrounding the lake. Perched up on a rock above the Couze river are the imposing ruddy lava rock ruins of the **Château de Murol**.

Saint-Nectaire   23,D2

The sleepy little town is better known for its cheese than the hot springs that give it a pleasant air of quiet gentility. But visit it above all for the splendid 12th-century Romanesque **church**, to which the wind, the rains and the lichen have given a glorious golden patina in its lush green setting of wooded hills. This small but monumental gem is dedicated to an evangelist preaching Christianity in pagan Auvergne at the beginning of the 4th century. To escape the fussy details of 19th-century "improvements" to its façade, take the road that winds up around to the south-east corner of the church for a view of the magnificent **chancel** with half-domed and gabled chapels grouped around the taller dome over the apse. Inside, the lively sculpture of the **capitals** on the pillars surrounding the choir tell the story of Christ's Passion—the flagellation, carrying the Cross, the descent to hell and the soldiers guarding the tomb—and the life of Saint Nectaire, including a stylized view of the church itself. In the left arm of the transept is a superb gilded bronze **bust** of St. Baudime, a companion of Nectaire on his evangelizing mission.

Issoire 23,D2

Besides its famous 12th-century Benedictine abbey-church, aluminium manufacture has made the town an important centre of the aviation industry. At the aerodrome south-east of town, gliding and delta-plane enthusiasts from all over the world are attracted by the exceptional atmospheric conditions, with currents lifting gliders to altitudes of up to 10,000 metres (33,000 feet).

The **Eglise Saint-Austremoine**, named after the leader of the 4th-century evangelists who Christianized Auvergne, is the largest of the province's major Romanesque churches. On your tour of the exterior, bypass quickly the ugly 19th-century towers and façade (replacing the porch of an older edifice on the same site), to admire the handsome proportions of its **chancel**. Notice the subtle interplay of pure geometrical shapes in the chapels' cylinders, cone-shaped roofs, fronton triangles and semi-circular blind arches around the windows. An intricate mosaic of stars and diamond shapes decorates the cornices and window-arches, together with 12 finely sculpted cosmic symbols of the zodiac.

Inside, be prepared for the shock of the columns and capitals garishly repainted during restoration. The carvings themselves have been heavily restored over the centuries with putty, stucco and cement, but on the north side of the choir, spare a moment for the cunning composition on the first capital: the **Last Supper** portraying Jesus and his 12 Disciples sitting three by three at a table encircling the pillar. From the ambulatory, look back over the nave with its spacious aisles especially designed for large monastic processions. Down in the **crypt** (en-

trance in the north arm of the transept), you can get an idea from the unadorned simplicity of its massive cross-vaults of the upper church's dignity before the restorers got at it. On your way out, look out for a 15th-century **fresco** of the Last Judgment in the chapel south of the entrance.

If you're heading back to Clermont-Ferrand on the N9, stop off at the enchanting little village of **Saint-Saturnin** at the entrance to the Monne gorge on the Veyre river. Rough-stone houses and the tower of a medieval castle nestle up against the smallest, simplest, but perhaps most charming of Auvergne's major Romanesque churches. The noble octagonal **bell-tower** is one of the few to have escaped the vandalism of revolution, civil war or official restoration. The decoration of the church interior is similarly sober, with only simple foliage motifs and a few birds decorating the capitals. In the crypt is a stone **Pietà** of Mary, St. John and Mary Magdalen.

The Brivadois 23,DE2

A joy for ramblers and fishermen alike, the Brivadois country (taking its name from the town of Brioude) is some of the most attractive—and unspoiled—in all Auvergne: the rocky gorges of the fast-running Allier river, and to the east, along its more tranquil Sénouire tribu-

The Politics of Cheese
As one of his many gimmicks in periodic attempts to regain popular favour, ex-President Giscard d'Estaing hands out packets of creamy Saint-Nectaire made by his local constituents. This yellow-skinned cow's milk cheese is actually manufactured throughout the *départements* of the Puy-de-Dôme and Cantal, but it did originate in Saint-Nectaire and first captured national attention in the 17th century. At that time it served as a means of currying not popular but royal favour when the town's feudal lord, Henri de Sennectère, presented it at the table of Louis XIV.

tary, highland forests of pine, oak, birch and beech.

Brioude is a popular holiday-base for salmon fishermen wading into the waters of the Allier. It also boasts a superb Romanesque church, begun in the 11th century, the **Basilique Saint-Julien-de-Brioude**. A morning sun on the magnificent chancel of five radiating chapels brings out the full beauty of the local basalt stone's brown, golden and ruddy patina. Notice the rich mosaic decoration around the windows of the raised apse. The interior has a similar warm blend of colour—ochre, rose, grey and white stone—in the nave's majestic pillars and columns soaring in a single sweep to the 13th-century Gothic vaults. You'll find great variety, religious and pagan, in the **sculpted capitals** of the narthex and nave: angels, sirens, centaurs, an ass playing the lyre, soldiers in battle, a shepherd carrying his sheep. See the fragments of fresco at the entrance to the nave, depicting Christ with a choir of angels. In the south aisle are a moving 15th-century *Christ lépreux,* carved at the nearby Bayasse colony to show the body with a leper's deformities, and a polychrome Gothic sculpture of the rarely treated theme of the Virgin pregnant.

South-east of Brioude, in a wooded valley on the banks of the Sénouire river, is the charming if somewhat derelict farming village of **Lavaudieu**. Visit the 11th-century **monastery**, the only one in Auvergne left intact by the Revolution. Climb up the gallery of the two-storeyed **cloister** to appreciate the proportions of the single- and double-pillared arcades. Among the sculpted capitals, a little worn by time and weather, look out for the portrayal of Lechery, a woman suckling salamanders.

Further up the Sénouire, through the pretty Lamandie forest, is **La Chaise-Dieu**, once one of France's most powerful abbeys. At the height of its prestige, during the papacy's exile in Avignon, a Chaise-Dieu monk became Pope Clement VI (1342–52) and began building the Gothic **Eglise Saint-Robert** (the abbey's 11th-century founder). The pope's **tomb**, a white marble statue on a black sarcophagus, lies in the choir. Notice the fine carving of the 15th-century oak **choir-stalls** and the Flemish **tapestries** depicting biblical themes from Adam and Eve to the Resurrection. In the north aisle, a celebrated **Danse Macabre** (Dance of Death) fresco depicts Death requesting the pleasure of the dance with a pope,

*R*ising above the pious city of Le Puy are the cast iron statue of the Virgin Mary on top of the Rocher Corneille and the little 12th-century Chapelle Saint-Michel on its needle-like hillock. As a major pilgrimage destination on the route to Santiago de Compostela, Le Puy benefitted both from the influence of church-craftsmen from Burgundy and, on the way back, of Moslem sculptors from Spain.

emperor, cardinal and aristocracy in the first panel, lady, poet, canoness and gentry in the second, and humbler troubadour, monk-philosopher and artisans in the third. Everybody gets to dance.

Follow the **Gorges of the Allier** south from the junction of N102 and D585 at Vieille Brioude. Dark tree-covered cliffs and organ-like columns of rock close in across the ravines to create an eery atmosphere of fairytale foreboding— Grimm rather than Disney. **Saint-Ilpize** is a medieval village with a fortified 14th-century chapel clinging to the overhanging cliff in the grounds of a ruined castle. Down on the river bank, beside a splendid 900-year-old donkey-backed bridge, **Lavoûte-Chilhac** has an elegant 18th-century Benedictine priory built around its Gothic church. Take a look inside at the huge wooden **crucifixion** (12th century) opposite the pulpit. Across the river, you can see the striking octagonal belltower of **Saint-Cirgues**. Visit the little Roman-

esque chapel above the village of **Peyrusse**, before the gorges open up into the bright and fertile valley of cattle-pastures, pig-farms and vineyards of **Langeac**, a town of handsome old houses and a ruined castle.

Le Puy   23,E3

Encompassing a spectacular landscape of steep pillar-like volcanic mounds rising out of the Loire river plain, Le Puy (from a dialect word *puech* meaning heights) is renowned in Auvergne for its deep religiosity. Its strategic position on the route from Burgundy to Santiago de Compostela made it throughout the ages the object of massive pilgrimages. Le Puy boasted France's most revered Black Virgin, a cedarwood statue of a black-faced mother and child—in fact, Isis, the Egyptian goddess of fertility—brought back from the Crusades by Louis IX in 1254. It was burned in the Revolution and replaced by a grotesque replica during the 19th-century revival of the Mary cult.

To this day, besides its numerous churches, including two true jewels of Romanesque architecture, it abounds in convents, monasteries, seminaries and religious hospices for the old and poor. On the eve of Good Friday, Maundy Thursday is the occasion for a torchlit procession by the formidable hooded order of the White Penitents. They reappear at the centre of a larger celebration for the Assumption of the Virgin Mary (August 15). There is on these and other holy days an ambiance of devotion and fervour comparable to the great occasions in Naples, if somewhat less flamboyant. Quite apart from the more sober character of the Auvergnats, this is perhaps because the deliberate placing of the religious sanctuaries on the town's heights imposes a sense of mortification on the worshippers making their way up.

In the doorways of the old houses in the **Rue des Tables** leading up to the cathedral, you can still see old ladies (and a few daughters) practicing the

---

Keeping Their Spirits Up

The White Penitents are a religious fraternity of laymen seeking to expiate their sins by penitence and mortification. Barefoot in white robes and pointed hoods masking their whole face, they symbolically re-enact the Passion of Christ through the streets of Le Puy every Maundy Thursday—for the past four centuries and still some 40 strong. The man in the role of Christ is always a sturdy fellow as the Cross, even though it is hollow, is very heavy. An understudy stands by in case he falters, and a "Simon" gives a hand at the rear. Behind "Christ", follow Penitents carrying hammer, pincers, heart pierced with nails, club, cockerel, vinegar-soaked sponge, ladder, crown of thorns, and Veronica's veil (replica of the shroud imprinted with the face of Christ).

Citizens observing the solemn torchlit procession, from the chapel around the cathedral and back, have a hard time keeping a straight face as the penitents singing hymns, not exactly a Gregorian choir, are notorious for their loud and terrible voices. Nonetheless, they are rewarded at the end with a good hot shot of grog back in their chapel.

traditional art of **lace-making**. Le Puy is considered the country's oldest centre of lacework, dating back at least to the 11th century when Spanish-Arab craftsmen from Cordova came here to build the cathedral, together with their lacemaking wives. For a closer look at the art, visit the **Centre d'Initiation à la Dentelle** (Lace Handicraft Centre), 2 Rue Duguesclin, which demonstrates the various techniques and exhibits French, Belgian and Venetian lacework done by needle and bobbin, as well as Oriental embroidery and Irish crochet work. The **Musée Crozatier**, in the Jardin Henri-Vinay, also has a large collection of local lacework, as well as some fine medieval sculpture from churches of the region.

Begun at the end of the 11th century, the **cathedral** soon had to be extended to accommodate the ever-increasing numbers of pilgrims and now juts out over the top of its hill, supported on a staircase passing under the church. The fine tapering **belltower** manages to withstand the unfortunate neo-Byzantine dome added in the 19th century. The polychrome façade's three cavernous round-arched portals form together a crypt-like porch through which the stairs from the Rue des Tables lead on up to the original entrance into the church at the middle of the nave. It is now closed off by a grill at the foot of which is an ancient dolmen, the **Fever Stone**, bereft of its original powers to heal since being moved from the high altar where the sick and maimed lay overnight to rise the next day cured of their fever and paralysis.

More authentic are the Arabic influences brought in from Spain, hinted at in the striped masonry of the façade, but quite emphatic in the interior with cusped, trefoil and horseshoe arches and octagonal cupolas in the nave. In the transept left of the high altar (with its garishly gilded Black Virgin) are some fine Romanesque **frescoes** of the 12th century, depicting the Holy Women at Christ's tomb and St. Catherine with the wheel of her martyrdom.

The Muslim influence is again clear in the lovely **cloister**, with the polychrome masonry of its arches, delicate tracery carving on the capitals and lacework motifs in the wrought-iron gate leading to the church. In the **Chapelle des Reliques** is a beautifully restored 15th-century mural painting, possibly Burgundian, depicting the Liberal Arts (grammar, logic, rhetoric and music).

Behind the cathedral is the 17th-century **Chapelle des Pénitents blancs** (Chapel of the White Penitents), worth a look inside for its coffered ceiling with its central painting of the Assumption, very fine but perhaps not quite justifying the name given by local admirers: "Le Puy's Sistine Chapel". The museum displays the implements of Christ's Passion used in the procession on the Maundy Thursday before Easter.

The most visible and popular of Le Puy's religious monuments, on top of the **Rocher Corneille** (altitude 757 metres [2,484 feet], but just 132 metres [433 feet] above the city's main square), is also artistically the most hideous. The gigantic russet-coloured statue of the Virgin Mary was erected in the 19th century. Anticipating victory at Sebastopol in the Crimean War, the Bishop of Le Puy asked Napoleon III for the melted-down metal of the canons captured from the Russians. He was expecting bronze, but got cast iron, which has to be repainted every ten years to avoid rust. A stairway leads right up inside the statue to Mary's crown, which offers a fine view of the surrounding countryside; it's also one place from which you cannot see the statue.

If you have to choose between two climbs, take the 268 steps spiralling up around the 80-metre (262-foot-) high Mont d'Aiguilhe (Needle Hill) to the fine little 12th-century **Chapelle Saint-Michel**. The Muslim influence is again strong, with an elaborately ornamented polychrome façade, trefoil-arched portal and minaret belltower. Like the Puy de Dôme (see p. 207), the hill was originally crowned by a Roman temple to Mercury.

Monts du Cantal
23,CD2-3

The Cantal lies at the southern end of the Parc naturel régional des Volcans d'Auvergne (see p. 207). Its mountains are believed to be the remains of one gigantic 3,000-metre (9,800-foot-) high volcano that exploded in prehistoric times. It's still a relatively untamed countryside inviting hikers to explore the wind-blown pine-forests and rolling green meadows with just an occasional shepherd's hut or isolated village.

Start out from the town of **Murat**, a good place to try the Cantal cheese, much tangier here than those you may have tried in Paris restaurants. The grey stone houses and slate roofs are an attractive feature. The **Rocher de Bonnevie** basalt outcrop west of the town gives you a first glimpse of the Cantal mountains and the valleys of the Alagnon and Chevade.

To get to the mountains, follow the N122 towards **Le Lioran**, but avoid the tunnel by taking the D67 up to the winter sports resort of **Super Lioran**. Here a cable-car and short walk take you to the top of the **Plomb du Cantal**, 1,855 metres (6,086 feet), for a magnificent view across the volcanic peaks north to the Mont-Dore (see p. 210). **Thiezac** is a pleasant summer resort in the Cère valley, within easy reach of two very pretty **waterfalls**—the Faillitoux, 3 kilometres (2 miles) north on D59, and the Roucolle, just off the N122 plunging into the Cère river. At **Vic-sur-Cère**, visit the handsome 15th-century home of the princes of Monaco. The medieval **Château de Pesteils** overlooking the village of Polminhac has some fine 17th-century Aubusson tapestries. **Aurillac**, a major centre for the local cheeses, makes a good overnight stop. The **Maison des Volcans** housed in the Château Saint-Etienne offers a well-documented explanation of volcanoes and earthquakes.

The Cantal cheese wielded by this fellow is best eaten in the region if you want to enjoy the full authentic flavour. There is apparently a general feeling that people north of the Loire river do not like their cheeses as pungent as the tougher folk down south. Similarly, blue Roquefort served in Paris is much milder than the one the locals eat.

Bracing Alpine Hike before the Mediterranean Siesta

Travelling through the south-east of France from the Alps, or down the Rhône Valley from Lyons through Provence to the Côte d'Azur (French Riviera) is like strolling out of your hotel on a crisp sunny morning and walking slowly down to the beach for a dip in the sea or a lazy sunbathe. It's one long exercise in self-indulgence.

In the Savoie Alps, the resorts around the Mont-Blanc, Western Europe's highest mountain, can be as exhilarating for the outdoors life in summer as they are for their superb winter sports facilities (see p. 57), and unrivalled *après-ski* attractions. Life is less energetic but equally refreshing down on the lovely lakes of Annecy and Le Bourget.

The Rhône Valley region around Lyon is the epicentre of French gastronomy, so loosen your belt—and your purse-strings. But first work up a healthy appetite wandering around Lyon's charming back streets and alleyways and checking out the meat and vegetables in the early-morning street markets.

In Provence, you take your jacket off and undo a few buttons and do some serious basking among the olive trees and vineyards. On energetic days, there are Roman theatres and amphitheatres to explore, the papal palace at Avignon and a feudal fortress at Les Baux. By which time you'll be ready to do nothing, in great style, in the fleshpots of the Côte d'Azur, or some desultory shopping and museum-seeing in the back country.

We also suggest a couple of resorts and excursions on wild, beautiful Corsica.

Savoie
19,CD2-3;25,CD1-2

Like many mountain regions, the province of Savoie remained, despite occasional invasions, proudly independent of its more powerful neighbours, cannily playing off Italy and France against each other over the centuries until finally voting by plebiscite to throw in its lot with France in 1860.

Except for a few smugglers, geologists and botanists, the French steered clear of the Alps until the mountain-climbing craze was launched by the conquest of Mont-Blanc in 1786. It wasn't until 1924, with the first Winter Olympic Games at Chamonix that skiing—at the time only cross-country—attracted international attention and a demand for ski resorts. As a result, most French resorts are 20th-century creations with first-class winter sports facilities, but lacking the quaintness and old traditions that people associate with their longer-established counterparts in Austria and Switzerland. Chamonix and Megève are among the most attractive resorts, with something of a real town life, and serve as good bases for summer hikes and excursions into the mountains.

219

Annecy, Chambéry and Aix-les-Bains are all towns with considerable history and character to make them worth exploring in their own right before embarking on tours of their lakes.

Chamonix   25,D2

The neighbourhood around the church has enough old-fashioned charm to retain something of the town's 19th-century pioneering atmosphere. For a fuller sense of what it was like when mountain-climbing and skiing were in their infancy, spend an hour in the **Musée alpin**, tracing the history of the region, its heroes and their exploits, in photos and displays of equipment.

For your summer excursions by cable car and rack railway, don't forget to take a sweater, sunglasses and binoculars for the sudden change in altitude, brilliant sunlight and fabulous panoramas. And go carefully until you're used to the rarefied atmosphere.

The cable car *(téléférique)* ride up to the **Aiguille du Midi** (3,800 metres/ 12,470 feet) is the most spectacular in the French Alps, for its view of the **Mont-Blanc**'s snow-covered peak, altitude 4,807 metres (15,770 feet), and the surrounding landscape. For some easy hiking, stop off at the lower station of Plan de l'Aiguille (2,310 metres/7,580 feet).

The cable car to **Le Brévent** (2,525 metres/8,284 feet), north-west of Chamonix, lets you take in the whole north face of the Mont-Blanc and the Aiguille du Midi, too. For a close-up view of a glacier and formidable ice caves, take the rack railway up the Montenvers to the dazzling **Mer de Glace** (Sea of Ice).

Megève   25,D2

This perennially fashionable resort is particularly popular for families. The slopes provide sufficient challenge without being breakneck, so that instructors can pay special attention to children. For summer visitors, in addition to superb facilities for tennis and swimming, the town's attractive setting of grassy alpine meadows and pine, spruce and larch forest is ideal for hikes.

A cable car takes you to **Mont d'Arbois** (1,833 metres/6,014 feet) for a great view of the Aravis peaks and the Mont-Blanc. Hikers continue to **Mont Joly** (about five hours to and from Mont d'Arbois cable-car station) for an even more spectacular view.

Few resorts in France, bar Megève and Val d'Isère, have much tradition or village life. Inveterate skiers head for modern, highly specialized *stations* such as Les Arcs, Tignes, La Plagne and Avoriaz, with challenging pistes and frenetic discos but little character.

*M*ountaineers insist you cannot "climb" Mont-Blanc on the French side, from Chamonix. The route to the top is just too easy, little more than a bracing walk. The real challenge, they say, is on the darker, more precipitous Italian side of the mountain, from Courmayeur. Nonetheless, hikers need a lot of stamina, good equipment and are not averse to an occasional little boost via cable-car.

Val d'Isère
25,D2

The weather-beaten granite houses give the old village a rare charm among Savoie ski-resorts. In summer, the great attraction is the **Vanoise National Park**, for which the local tourist office can advise you on hiking itineraries and guided tours.

The D902 road from Val d'Isère up to the **Col de l'Iseran** (2,770 metres/9,088 feet) is the highest motorable road in the Alps. For superb views of the Isère valley, look out en route for the pleasant sign-posted walk (45 minutes each way) to the **Tête du Solaise** and—a little further on and much closer to the road—the **Belvédère de la Tarentaise**. The road continues down to the pretty medieval village of **Bonneval-sur-Arc**. Notice the handsome old chalets, roofed not with slate tiles, but overlapping slabs of rust-coloured stone strong enough to bear enormous weights of winter snow.

Annecy
25,D2

This is one of those gracious towns that are still the quiet joy of provincial France. Cross the **Parc du Pâquier** to a waterfront observation platform for a first view of the lake and its backdrop of mountains. The lakeside promenade back towards town takes you over the self-explanatory Pont des Amours and west to the 15th-century Dominican **Eglise Saint-Maurice**. Inside, in the choir, look out for a fine painting of Jesus' descent from the Cross, by 16th-century Flemish artist Pieter Pourbus.

In the middle of the Thiou river (whose source is the lake itself), stands the 12th-century prison, **Palais de l'Isle**. Explore the **old town** and its handsome 15th- and 16th-century houses along Rue Perrière and Rue Sainte-Claire.

The imposing **château**, former home of the Counts of Geneva, houses an interesting museum devoted to local archaeology and folklore and a natural history of the Alps. The castle terrace is the best vantage point for pictures of the old town.

The cruises around **Lake Annecy** start out from the Thiou river. Some of them include a cable-car ride to the top of **Mont Veyrier** (1,291 metres/4,236 feet) and its spectacular panorama of the Alps, but all give you a marvellous swan's-eye view of the jagged snow-capped peaks of the Dents de Lanfon and the rugged La Tournette to the east, and gentler Entrevernes and Taillefer mountains to the west. If you decide to drive, take the

Many of the sheep grazing in the Alps of the Dauphiné in the summer have come all the way from Provence in search of more luxuriant pastures. In the old days, herds of several thousand sheep made the journey on foot over mountain routes marked by centuries of seasonal migration. Now those tracks are fading as the sheep are brought in by train or lorry, up to 400,000 a year.

D909 east to the Mont Veyrier cable car, continuing on to the pretty town of **Menthon-Saint-Bernard** and its medieval castle high above the lake. The D42 takes you up to the **Col de la Forclaz** (1,157 metres/3,796 feet), while the lake-front road leads to a gastronomic temple at Talloires.

Evian and Lac Léman   *19,CD2*

Shared by France and Switzerland, the deceptively calm and quite sizeable Lake Léman or Lake of Geneva is instantly recognizable to almost every calendar-user with its dramatic mountain backdrop. This is the Savoy Alps (usually photographed from the Swiss side); nestling beneath them lie the spa towns of Evian and Thonon.

Evian's mineral water is known and drunk, as well as used as skin-cleanser, the world over. The sleepy little town with its cosy villas ensconced in greenery springs to life in summer. The constitutional along the lakeside (Boulevard Baron de Blonay), passing in front of the active **casino,** is a must. Drop by the former **thermal buildings** in Rue Nationale—delightfully art déco.

Thonon has a small lower port-town beside the lake, while the old part above has taken on a new lease of life when the central area became pedestrian-only. It retains a genuine Savoy feel, as does nearby **Yvoire** with its beautifully preserved medieval houses, bedecked with geraniums.

Aix-les-Bains   *24,C2*

This spa town on the edge of the Lac du Bourget has for centuries offered cures for rheumatism and broken hearts. Ever since 4th-century Roman Emperor Gratianus took his natural hot bath here, people have been plunging into what they call the *bouillon* or "hot broth" at 42 °C (107.6 °F). In the 19th century, Romantic poet Alphonse de Lamartine stopped off to fix his liver and a bout of melancholia with a lyric tribute, *Le Lac*, that had his fans weeping enough tears to flood the lovely chestnut trees and poplars on its banks.

There's a respectable casino, and the **Musée du Docteur Faure** (Villa des Chimères, Boulevard des Côtes) exhibits some excellent Rodin bronzes and watercolours, Corot landscapes and works by Degas, Sisley and Cézanne. But by and large, the great pleasure here is to do nothing at all, siesta, take the waters, siesta, stroll along the **Boulevard du Lac** and siesta.

The major attraction is the **lake cruise**, starting out from the Grand Port. With its "harmonious waves... moan of the wind, sigh of the reeds, light perfume of the balmy air", the lake is truly as romantic and dreamy as Lamartine claimed. One of the destinations of the cruise is the neo-Gothic **Abbaye de Hautecombe**, a little over-restored but well worth a visit if you can attend a mass performed with the Gregorian chant.

Chambéry   *24,C2*

Along its elegant streets arcaded in the Italian style, the town radiates a restrained good humour, typified by its favourite monument, the **Fontaine des Eléphants**. The stone tuskers of this 19th-century monument, minus their rear ends, pay tribute to Count Boigne, old India hand, soldier and local benefactor.

At the other end of the lively **Rue de Boigne** is the old castle, rebuilt in the 18th century and now housing the prefecture, of which one massive round tower, the **Demi-Ronde**, survives from the medieval dungeon. The best people-watching spot in town is **Place Saint-Léger**, with its fountains and pretty lanterns.

A five-minute drive south of Chambéry, uphill, is the charming 18th-century country house of **Les Charmettes**, home of writer-philosopher Jean-Jacques Rousseau for five happy years as guest of his mentor, the Baroness de Warens. Visit the gardens in which the young romantic climbed the cherry tree and tossed the cherries down his girlfriend's décolleté.

Dauphiné
24-25,B-D2-3

Historic bone of contention between Provence and Burgundy, this more southerly of the Alpine provinces was ceded to the French crown in the 14th century. Some 200 years earlier, the count's English wife gave birth to a boy she called Dolphin, which became in French *Dauphin,* subsequently adopted as the title of all royal heirs and the source of the province's name.

Grenoble
24,C2

This bouncy, thoroughly modern Alpine metropolis lies in a broad valley-basin at the confluence of the Isère and Drac rivers. Skyscrapers have mushroomed in apparent challenge to the surrounding mountains, epitomizing the town's forward-looking spirit with its university at the spearhead of modern sciences and technology and museum renowned for its avant-garde art.

For a **view** of the town's spectacular mountain setting, take the cable car from Quai Stéphane-Jay up to the the rocky spur of the **Fort de la Bastille**. From the observation-deck above the restaurant you can see the peaks of **Belledonne** (2,978 metres/9,770 feet) to the east, **Taillefer** (2,857 metres/9,373 feet) to the south-east and the **Moucherotte** (1,901 metres/6,237 feet) to the south-west.

The town's historic centre is the **Place Grenette**, dominated by the **Palais de Justice** (once seat of the Dauphiné provincial parliament), with its intriguing mixture of Flamboyant Gothic and Renaissance architecture. Townspeople still like to gather on the square, walking to see and be seen with something of that self-consciousness described by local boy Stendhal in his novel, *Le Rouge et Le Noir*. His birthplace is nearby at 14, Rue Jean-Jacques Rousseau.

Over on Place de Verdun is the great **Musée de Peinture et de Sculpture**. Its exceptionally rich collections devote three galleries to European art from the 16th to the 18th century, including works by Perugino, Tintoretto and Veronese; Zurbaran and Ribera; Rubens' masterly *St. Gregory*; and Georges de la Tour, Delacroix, Courbet, Sisley and Gauguin. But it is especially appreciated for its modern collections—Matisse, Bonnard, Picasso, Max Ernst, Klee and Giacometti —and avant-garde Americans such as Sam Francis, Ellsworth Kelly, Sol Le Witt and Louise Nevelson.

Briançon
25,D3

Claiming to be the "highest town in Europe" at a respectable 1,326 metres (4,350 feet), Briançon guards the frontier with Italy. Predictably, it's a real Alpine town of steeply sloping streets; less predictably, however, at that height, it's a walled city, with the ubiquitous Vauban having created a citadel, ramparts and all the trappings of an easily defensible town in 1692 for Louis XIV. The **Main Street** *(Grande-Rue)* of the old town above a busy shopping thoroughfare is pedestrians-only; a stream rushing down the middle gets rid of the snow in winter— and anything else all year long. Note the **Porte Pignorol** on the way out, celebrating the heroic resistance in 1815. Modern engineers are full of admiration for the 1754 **Pont O'Asfelt** straddling the Durance at over 50 metres (160 feet).

First Blood

For Grenoble, the French Revolution started a year earlier with their *Journée des Tuiles* (Day of the Tiles), June 7, 1788. Under a boiling hot sun, thousands of Grenoblois vented their rage at Louis XVI's decree disbanding the Dauphiné provincial parliament. From the rooftops the people pelted the royal troops with heavy tiles, while others down in the streets, in a tradition that continued to 1968, dug up paving stones for missiles. A hat-maker bayoneted to death became the Revolution's first victim. From his grandfather's window, 5-year-old Henri Beyle witnessed the killing that he was later to record under the pen-name of Stendhal.

Rhône Valley

24;30

From its source high in the Swiss Alps, the Rhône courses down to the Mediterranean, bending southwards at Lyon. It has always been France's vital central artery for river, road and rail traffic between the north and south. Its valley was the main path of the Roman conquest of Gaul, the key to Lyon's medieval commercial wealth. Today it is the most direct route from Paris to the Mediterranean.

Located at the crossroads between north and south, Lyon was the ideal choice as the Roman capital of Gaul. It has become the natural capital of French gastronomy: at the conjunction of Atlantic and Continental climates, the farmers get the best out of a subtle mixture of the cooler and damper north with the first hints of Mediterranean warmth and light. The regions around Lyon produce some of the best food in the country: poultry from Bresse, freshwater fish from the Savoie lakes, Charolais beef, and splendid orchards of pears, apples and cherries north of town and peaches and apricots to the south. The blossom of those orchards is one of the great delights of a spring drive through the valley.

The fruit industry started in earnest in the 1880s as a reaction to the dreaded phylloxera disease that struck the local vineyards. Today, the Beaujolais country thrives as never before, and wine-lovers on the way down to Lyon detour through such sweet-sounding places as Juliénas, Chénas, Morgon, Brouilly—and Saint-Amour. Continuing south, opposite Tournon, they may like to sample a celebrated Côtes-du-Rhône at Tain-l'Hermitage.

Lyon

24,B2

Prosperous since the Middle Ages for its trade fairs, banking and silk manufac-

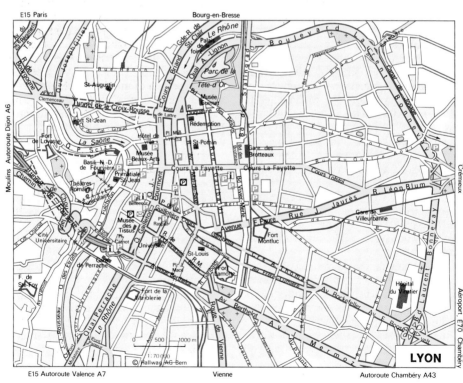

ture, Lyon still has a bouncy pride and taste for the good life.

Besides the great shrines of *haute cuisine* in and around the city, appropriately sumptuous in décor and price, you should also seek out the little bars and cafés and the old-fashioned bistros that the Lyonnais call *bouchons* (after the bunches of straw or foliage that served as a sign for the restaurant). But it's not easy to make your way around town to find them. The city is built across the looping confluence of the Saône and Rhône rivers, with hills on either side and a peninsula in the middle. A street map is a must.

So head first for the tourist office on the huge **Place Bellecour**, in the middle of the peninsula between the two rivers. The square has a pretty flower market, and you know you're approaching the south of France when you see your first game of *boules* there.

Cross over the Pont Bonaparte to stroll around the fine Renaissance houses of Lyon's **old town** between the Saône river and the Fourvière hill. Some of the best are along the Rue Saint-Georges, Rue Saint-Jean and Rue Juiverie.

The handsome **Hôtel de Gadagne** (Rue de Gadagne) houses a museum on the history of Lyon and the marionettes of the town's celebrated Guignol theatre. If your French is up to it, you may enjoy the plays of traditional folklore, parodies of opera or contemporary satire performed at the Palais du Conservatoire—details at the tourist office.

To take in the full sweep of the city, ride the funicular railway from Gare Saint-Jean up the hill to the **observatory** at the church of Notre-Dame-de-Fourvière.

The town's **Musée des Beaux-Arts**, housed in a 17th-century Benedictine abbey (20, Place des Terreaux), has a rich collection of European paintings and sculpture. Most notable are three Rodin bronzes in its cloister, and works by Perugino, Veronese, El Greco and Rubens, Courbet, Manet and Matisse.

Pérouges 24,B2

A short (36 kilometres/25 miles) drive north-west of Lyon provides a delightful sidetrip, even though outside Dauphiné.

The well-preserved medieval atmosphere of Pérouges made it a natural location for one of the many films of the *Three Musketeers*. Double ramparts recall the brutal fights of the Kingdoms of Dauphiné and Savoie.

Centre of the enclosed town, **Place du Tilleul** is clustered around an ancient lime-tree. Note the interesting sundial and pop into the **Musée du Vieux Pérouges** for a view of the past. The cobblestoned Rue des Rondes leads you round the ramparts. The Rue du Prince once had the most well-heeled shops and artisans. And the local sparkling white wine will buck up any flagging spirits.

Ardèche 24,AB3

Heading down the Autoroute du Soleil towards Provence or the Côte d'Azur, look up at the series of apparently forbidding hills on the opposite (right) side of the Rhône. This is the Ardèche. Though it is the name of a *département,* in loose parlance it refers to the **Gorges de l'Ardèche,** a dramatic stretch of country running 60 kilometres (38 miles) from Vallon-Pont-d'Arc to Pont-Saint-Esprit.

Followed by a corniche road of sometimes hair-raising hairpin bends, the river twists and turns through grandiose landscapes of untaméd nature. At Vallon-Pont-d'Arc, you can rent a canoe for the strenuous descent beneath a huge natural arch 34 metres (112 feet) high, after which grottos, cliffs, belvederes, chapels and views speed by in succession. But be careful, the rapids require practice and skill. At Vallon visit one of the last silk farms *(magnanerie)* still operative.

Elsewhere, the Ardèche offers rest, relaxation and solitude amid orchards, vineyards, ruins of feudal castles, villages precariously holding onto hilltops, narrow passes and gorges and plenty of summer sun.

The historic centre of Lyon has a certain Italian flavour to it, dating back to the presence in the city in Renaissance times of a powerful Florentine colony heavily involved in banking and the silk trade. The Médicis were there in strength and the Guadagni, richest merchant family in Europe in their day, left the French version of their name on the city's grandest Renaissance mansion, Hôtel de Gadagne.

Provence   30-31,B-D2

Though much of France is cool and green and rational, it likes to think of itself as a Mediterranean country, warm, golden and passionate. Blame it on the seductive charm of Provence. On those rare occasions when the Frenchman seeks to be loved, he seems to be trying to pass as a Provençal, a jovial, generous fellow with a colourful, pleasant-sounding, but not necessarily profound, gift of the gab.

Understandable in a region where the sun is the most benevolent of dictators. The monuments of the Roman Empire still stand proudly in Orange, Arles and Nîmes, like the medieval strongholds in Les Baux and Avignon, but the most important pleasure of Provence remains the sensuality of its landscape. Squat little vineyards stretch to the foot of the rugged Alpilles, cypresses loom like signposts to the sea above the twisted olive trees and almond groves, while the sweet-smelling umbrella pines provide a natural shelter for your siesta.

Sweet-smelling Provence... As you drive through the scrubland they call *garrigue*, keep your window rolled well down to let in the fragrance of lavender, and the wild rosemary, thyme and savory to which local market gardeners add sage, tarragon and marjoram for the famous *herbes de Provence*. Even the garlic and onions are sweet in Provence.

The accent is on unabashed indolence, but Provence bristles with cultural activity in the summer months, each town using its ancient amphitheatre, cathedral or palace as a magnificent setting for festivals of music, theatre and the other arts (see p. 55).

The itinerary we propose deals in turn with different layers of Provençal life: the "Roman" towns of Orange, Nîmes and Arles; the medieval bastions of Les Baux and Avignon; the essence of Provençal landscape in the Lubéron mountains; finishing in exhilarating style in Aix-en-Provence, the city most Frenchmen would choose to live in, if they could.

Orange   30,B1

The grandiose ancient monuments of this once prosperous Roman trading centre on the road from Arles to Lyon strike a delightfully incongruous note in the peaceful Provençal backwater of today.

Since this is the gateway to Provence, make an appropriate entrance into town from the north, at the great three-arched **Arc de Triomphe**. Built in A.D. 21, it stands on a traffic island across the old

*The Pont du Gard aqueduct offers matchless
testimony to the engineering genius of the Romans, and French stone-
masons have visited it over the centuries as an essential part of their
education. They pay homage to their venerable predecessors by carving
in the stone their initials and an emblematic tool of their trade.
Less respectful were medieval wagoners who used it as a road-bridge.
They hacked away at the supports of the aqueduct's second tier of
arches to make way for their carts and nearly brought the whole thing
tumbling down into the Gardon river, a threat averted by masonry
added in the 18th century.*

N7, which here traces the route of the ancient Via Agrippa. The friezes of battling soldiers, weaponry and naval equipment sculpted on the north side celebrate Julius Caesar's victories over Gallic tribes of the region and the merchant fleet of the Greek colony in Marseille.

The town's other great Roman monument, the **Théâtre antique**, is on the south side of town. Historians regard this as the finest and best preserved of all the surviving theatres in the Roman Empire, unique for its towering scenic wall still standing, with a statue of Emperor Augustus to greet you. Originally, 7,000 spectators came from all over Provence to watch a circus, Greek tragedy, Latin comedy or lottery draw. It still provides a wonderful stage for the July festival's opera and symphony concerts. Out of season, test—even with a whisper—its exceptional acoustics.

From the top of Colline Saint-Eutrope, you get a good bird's-eye **view** of the theatre in relationship to the triumphal arch and the Rhône valley beyond.

Vaison-la-Romaine *30,B1*

A pretty excursion 30 kilometres (19 miles) north-east of Orange along the D975 takes you to the site of one of the most important towns of Roman Provence, excavated north of Vaison's modern and medieval quarters. To understand better the layout of the ancient town, its streets, houses, shops, fountains and theatre, visit the **museum** on the Puymin hill. It houses some superb marble sculpture of the 2nd century A.D., most notably a Venus, the Emperor Hadrian and his wife Sabina.

Climb up, too, to the medieval houses of the **Haute Ville**, overlooking the Ouvèze river.

Mont Ventoux *30,B1*

The mountain derives its name from the high winds that buffet its 1,909-metre (6,263-foot) peak (one pass is known as the *Col des Tempêtes*). But don't let that put you off a drive to the top, on D974, from the pretty village of **Malaucène**, with its 16th-century clock-tower, through delightful lavender fields and sheep meadows dotted with groves of larch and cedars of Lebanon. It is also popular hiking and biking country, but take it easy—British cyclist Tom Simpson met a tragic end on the mountain during the Tour de France of 1967. Offer yourself a rest at the little waterfall and café beyond the octagonal domed **Chapelle Notre-Dame du Groseau** before starting the climb up to the Observatory and the spectacular **view** of the surrounding Provençal countryside from the top. Down the other side of Mont Ventoux, pay a visit to delightful **Carpentras** with a busy, compact centre and fine synagogue.

Pont du Gard *30,B2*

Take the A9 *autoroute* south-west from Orange to the Fournès-Remoulins exit and follow the D981 to the parking lot in front of the "bridge".

In the Gardon valley's wonderful natural setting of forest and river, this gigantic 2,000-year-old **aqueduct** is without doubt the most impressive of all Roman monuments preserved from ancient Gaul. It carried spring water from near Uzès to the town of Nîmes, over a distance of 35 kilometres (22 miles).

Quite apart from its historic impact, it's worth the visit for what is likely to be one of the more memorable picnics of your French tour, well away from the crowds (avoid the dreadful local restaurants). But first, hold the hand of your little ones (vertigo victims abstain) and take the easy marked path up to the roof of the aqueduct, 49 metres (160 feet) above the river.

Built of huge granite blocks joined without mortar in three tiers of arches, 6 at the base, 11 at the middle level and 35 at the top, this highly functional construction is also remarkably beautiful, in total harmony with its landscape. The roof walkway is 275 metres (300 yards) long, not too difficult to negotiate with a minimum of care. The best **view** of the ensemble is from the river bank near the Château Saint-Privat, beyond the aqueduct.

Nîmes 30,A2

Emperor Augustus made a gift of this town to the veterans of his victorious battle over Antony and Cleopatra in Egypt, commemorated to this day in the Nîmes coat-of-arms with the chained crocodile of the Nile. The grand **amphitheatre** *(arènes)* was built for gladiator battles; later it was used for the less equal combats between lions and Christians. Having served as a fortress for the invading Visigoths in the 5th century and a communal residence for the poor in the Middle Ages, it has now resumed the ancient bloody tradition with summer bullfights.

The more pacific Greek-style temple known as the **Maison Carrée** is an elegant monument of the same period (1st century B.C.), noted for the finely sculpted Corinthian capitals on its columns. After a varied history as town hall, residence, stable and church, it was saved from a project of Louis XIV's minister Colbert to move it stone by stone to Versailles. Today it houses a small **museum** of Roman sculpture and mosaics.

The **Jardin de la Fontaine,** a pretty tree-shaded 18th-century park on the slopes of the Mont Cavalier at the northwest edge of town, offers a refreshing respite from the summer heat—and a good **view** of the surrounding mountains. The park is built around the spring of Nemausus that gave the town its name; it includes a ruined temple attributed to the hunting goddess Diana and a Roman tower of no known significance at all.

Arles 30,B2

An important town in Roman Gaul, replacing Lyon as capital towards the end of the Empire, it boasts a powerful **amphitheatre** *(arènes)*, seating over 20,000 in the days of the gladiators. For the most spectacular view, climb up to the broad path that runs along the roof of the

arches on its perimeter. Less fortunate than the one at Orange, Arles's **Théâtre antique** has been reduced to ruins over the centuries as builders carted away masonry for their houses, churches and town walls, but the remains in a pleasant park are quietly eloquent of its noble past.

In the **Eglise Saint-Trophime** (on Place de la République), you can see the Roman influence recurring in the triumphal-arch design of its splendid porch. This masterpiece of Provençal Romanesque sculpture depicts the Last Judgment in the tympanum above the doors, surrounded by statues of the saints. Nearby, the church cloister, **Cloître Saint-Trophime**, with its beautiful sculpted capitals on the pillars, is a haven of peace.

South-east of town, cut off by a railway track, you'll find the melancholy remains of the **Alyscamps,** famous Roman and medieval burial grounds that were a favourite subject of Van Gogh when he came to live in Arles in 1888. Today, just a few sarcophagi remain in an avenue leading to the ruins of the Eglise Saint-Honorat. The abbey-church of **Saint-Gilles** (20 kilometres/13 miles away) has Romanesque sculpture around three doorways that rivals even Saint-Trophime.

Looking for the Ghost of Van Gogh

Van Gogh wrote in a letter from Arles: "Oh, the beautiful sun of midsummer! It beats upon my head, and I do not doubt that it makes one a little queer." It inspired his most fertile period, but also triggered the frenzy in which he cut off an ear and had himself committed to an asylum in nearby Saint-Rémy. He died a year later back up in the Paris outskirts. Today, the tourist office in the Boulevard des Lices provides a map tracing 30 of the sites he painted while in Arles. His house and favourite café have both gone, bombed in 1944, but, beside the last stones of the Alyscamps and the town park, the sun is as strong as ever. You can find surrounding fields filled with the sunflowers and olive trees he loved to paint, and still imagine the painter tramping the road to Tarascon in the inadequate shade of the plane trees.

La Camargue   *30,AB2*

At the delta of the Rhône, where its two arms spill into the Mediterranean, the Camargue has been reclaimed from the sea to form a national **nature reserve,** with modern resorts along the coast. The region is famous for its white horses, which you can hire to ride along the sandflats and some paths of the interior, and for the black bulls that race through the streets of Provençal towns to the bull-fight.

With permission from the Directeur de la Réserve, La Capelière, Arles, you can visit the nature reserve, popular with birdwatchers for its wild duck, herons and pink flamingos.

It's curious to think that **Aigues-Mortes** once stood right by the sea, and yet the pious Louis XI embarked from outside its walls on the Seventh Crusade in 1248. Today in the haunting landscape of the Camargue, silting has left the rectangular fortified city 8 kilometres (5 miles) inland from the Mediterranean, its grid system of streets, its walls and for-tifications miraculously preserved.

Begin by investigating the **Tour de Constance,** that used to be a watchtower and lighthouse, but that with decline in maritime activity was turned into a pri-son for Templars and Huguenots *(Cami-sards)* in turn. Then take a stroll along the **ramparts** to admire the extraordinary foresight and technique of the 13th-cen-tury city-planners. Beside the very good craft shops on the central square, Place Saint-Louis, is the church in which Louis reputedly prayed before setting out for the Holy Land.

At the Camargue's southern tip, the town of **Saintes-Maries-de-la-Mer** comes as something of a mirage after the re-gion's flat, yet curiously disturbing land-scape. Legend has it that the Virgin Mary and Mary Magdalene plus their black servant Sara landed on this spot before setting off to evangelize Provence; one Mary stayed on with Sara, and was buried in the church of Saintes-Maries-de-la-Mer. The ensuing cult's first pilgrims

were gypsies and nomads and gypsy tra-dition continues today. In the crypt of the extraordinary **fortress-church** are a reliquary and strange costumed statue of Sara. Each May, after a night vigil in the crypt, the statues of the saints in their little boats are carried aloft by the gypsies of the world to the sea. Go up to the church roof for a superb view of the sea and the town, including the seaside bull-ring *(arènes).*

234

The proud greys of the Camargue gallop at liberty, powerful, spirited and courageous. Their hoofs are tough enough to make horseshoes superfluous when the time comes for them to be trained for use in herding the Camargue bulls for branding. The mane and tail are particularly abundant to deal with the region's pesky mosquitoes.

*O*ne of the most colourful moments in the winter
calendar of Les-Baux-de-Provence is its Shepherds' Festival (Fête
du Pastrage) on Christmas Eve. For centuries the church has striven
to impose a religious tone on the celebrations in which a lamb
is paraded through the streets in a bullock-cart, but the shepherds
continue to dance around their shepherdesses with pagan abandon
and everybody seems to have entirely too much fun.

236

autumn or, best of all, on a brilliant crisp winter's day can be a rare moment invested with all the romantic magic of the Middle Ages.

The barons of Les Baux put the star of the Nativity on their coat-of-arms, claiming to be descendants of Balthazar, lord of the treasury among the Three Wise Men. It was with that brazen pride that they ruled 79 towns of medieval Provence, and their impregnable redoubt became a centre of courtly love much prized by travelling troubadours. For centuries they defied the papal authority in Avignon and the kings of France, offering refuge to rebellious Protestants during the Wars of Religion until Louis XIII ordered the destruction of the fortress in 1632—and made the residents pay the costs.

The **village** of Les Baux is an attractive mixture of boutiques and galleries in medieval and Renaissance houses, many of them with delightful flower gardens.

The demolition of the citadel was clearly a half-hearted job, as you can see when you stroll through the **Ville morte** (Dead City), entrance at the Musée lapidaire, Hôtel de la Tour-du-Brau. The ramparts, castle walls and ruined chapels each reveal their own startling view over the sheer ravines to the surrounding mountains.

The jagged peaks of the Alpilles are the last gasp of the great Alpine chain that sweeps in a 1,200-kilometre (750-mile) arc from Vienna. If you're tempted by a hike or bike ride around the valleys, drive on into the charming town of **Saint-Rémy-de-Provence**, where the *syndicat d'initiative* provides detailed itineraries and advice on renting a bicycle—and on "Van Gogh itineraries".

Les Baux-de-Provence   30,B2

The astounding natural location of this medieval citadel, a single massive outcrop of rock cut adrift from the Alpilles mountains like a ship of war separated from its fleet, exerts a unique grip on the popular imagination.

The invasion of the tourist buses in high season has made the little village surrounding the old fortress unbearably crowded. But a visit in early spring,

Avignon   30,B2

The City of the Popes is today a proud cultural centre, home of one of Europe's greatest arts festivals and all year round a lively and cheerful town of good cafés, art galleries and fashionable shops. They no longer dance on the Pont d'Avignon, but there's plenty going on in the discotheques.

The opulence and luxury have disappeared from the **Palais des Papes**, but your visit will still give you an idea of the grandeur and above all the embattled situation of these maverick popes entrenched behind the ramparts of a feudal fortress. The entrance is on the west side, through the Porte des Champeaux, and the guided tour takes you across the Grande Cour (transformed into an open-air theatre for the summer festival) to the **Palais vieux**. Its formidable, even forbidding design reflects the pious austerity of its builder, Benedict XII, quite out of keeping with his high-living successors.

East of Benedict's cloister is the **consistory**, where the pope met with his cardinals, today decorated with the superb **frescoes** of Simone Martini, transferred from the porch of Notre-Dame-des-Doms cathedral. The process of raising the frescoes from the porch walls revealed Martini's original drawings, which are now displayed beside the finished

Popes, Pro and Anti

Imagine the secretary-general of the Soviet Communist Party deciding to leave Moscow and build a new Kremlin in Krakow. That's what it was like in 1309 when Pope Clement V moved his Holy See from the turmoils of Italy to Avignon. Seven popes, all French, made their home beside the Rhône. Like Rome, Avignon became a city of pomp and intrigue. It attracted great Italian artists, such as the poet Petrarch and Sienese painter Simone Martini, but was soon decried as "an unholy Babylon" of gaudy luxury and vicious riffraff. Not at all to the liking of the pious mystic, Catherine of Siena, who brought Pope Gregory XI back to Rome in 1377.

But a year later, more power struggles caused the Great Schism—doctrinal problems were not uppermost in papal deliberations in those days. Rival popes, known as anti-popes, set up shop back in Avignon for another 40 years. The Schism ended, the infighting returned once and for all to Rome, but Avignon remained part of the papal lands in Provence until the French Revolution.

paintings. Other frescoes, by Simone Martini's disciple Matteo Giovannetti, can be seen in the Chapelle Saint-Jean and, upstairs, in the Chapelle Saint-Martial.

In Clément VI's more decorative **Palais nouveau**, Giovannetti has painted frescoes of the Old Testament prophets on the ceiling of the Grand Audience Hall.

Beyond the much-remodelled cathedral, north of the palace, is the pleasant garden of the **Rocher des Doms**, extending to the outer ramparts and giving you your best view of the **Pont d'Avignon**, more properly named the Pont Saint-Bénézet, broken off halfway across the Rhône river. In fact, they used to dance *under* the bridge, on a little island.

The **Petit Palais**, at the northern end of the Place du Palais, houses, together with Gothic sculpture and frescoes of the Avignon School, a magnificent collection of Italian painting from the 13th to the 16th century, including major works by Taddeo Gaddi, Veneziano, Botticelli and, the museum's masterpiece, Carpaccio's *Holy Conversation*.

Centre of the bustling life of the modern town is the airy **Place de l'Horloge**, surrounded by cafés and a pedestrian zone of smart shops along the Rue des Marchands. At the far end is the Place Jérusalem with its old synagogue.

For a walk through the **old town**, start at the 14th-century **Eglise Saint-Didier**, with its excruciatingly painful altar sculpture *Jesus Carrying the Cross* by the Dalmatian artist Francesco Laurana. The Rue du Roi-René takes you past some handsome 17th- and 18th-century houses. On the pretty cobblestoned **Rue des Teinturiers**, you can see where the dyers used to work the paddlewheels for their Indian-style cloth in the little Sorgue river emerging here from its underground course.

Hop over the Rhône to the town's opposite number, **Villeneuve-lès-Avignon**—both for superb views down over Avignon and the remarkable **gardens** up around the Chapelle Notre-Dame de Belvézet. The **charterhouse** below is huge and bare, much like the monks' cells themselves, but the tomb of Innocent IV is admirable. Many of the charterhouse's art treasures are housed in the museum of the Hôtel du Luxembourg, the masterpiece being the 1453–54 *Couronnement de la Vierge* (Crowning of the Virgin) by Enguerrand Quarton.

Lubéron and Vaucluse   30,BC2

Starting out from Cavaillon, home of France's, nay, the world's, most succulent cantaloupe melons, head east to the Lubéron mountains, the heart of the Provençal countryside and now a protected regional park. Whole valleys are carpeted with lavender, and the *garrigue* scrubland is ashimmer with every colour and fragrance of the sunny Mediterranean. The villages have been lovingly restored, a few of them so recently that they need a little time for the stone of the houses to recapture its subtle patina, but the Provençal sun and wind weather things fast.

Perched on a spur of rock, the village of **Oppède-le-Vieux** has been rescued from its ruins by writers and artists seeking a residence off the beaten track. The best-intentioned visitor respects the peace of the writer and buys a canvas or two from the painter. **Ménerbes** is also up on a hill, with a medieval fortress that served as the Protestants' last redoubt in the 16th-century Wars of Religion. Behind the church on the outskirts of town, you have a fine **view** over the mountains to the Vaucluse plateau and the distant peak of Mont Ventoux.

Bonnieux juts out over the Coulon valley. From its terrace up on the hill behind the town hall, look north-west to the rust-coloured ravines surrounding Roussillon. To set off that startling red, the villagers of **Roussillon** paint their houses with every imaginable variation of ochre from the nearby quarries.

Its dramatic location looking across to the Lubéron from the southern edge of the Vaucluse plateau has made **Gordes** one of the most prosperous villages in the region, popular for its boutiques and little galleries, and its **Vasarely Museum,** a panoramic collection of the Hungarian painter's Op and Pop works. Its houses hug the hillside on steep, winding streets, leading to a 12th-century castle at the top. A couple of kilometres south-west of Gordes is the strange little **Village Noir,** consisting of *bories*, old dry-stone cabins grouped around a baker's oven and serving as a museum of rural life in Provence. Their origins disappear into the mists of history.

A short drive north-west of Gordes on D177 takes you to the exquisite 12th-century Cistercian **Abbaye de Sénanque,** nestling in a bewitching valley of lavender fields. The Romanesque **cloister** has been beautifully restored for summer artshows, while the refectory provides an audio-visual guide to monastic life. The 17th-century **kitchens** are now a little museum of Romanesque architecture.

Aix-en-Provence   30,C2

It was the first Roman town in Gaul, a citadel and spa founded in 125 B.C. as Aquae Sextiae, but there's nothing left of that. Aix is one of those blessed towns that win the affection of their visitors without the aid of spectacular monuments, grand cathedrals or richly endowed museums. Elegant, charming and cheerful, it forces a grateful smile out of the most world-weary traveller.

The town's great treasure is a street. There are few more refreshing experiences than to arrive in Aix at the end of a hot afternoon and walk along the majestic green arbour formed by the plane trees arching across the **Cours Mirabeau** and its fountains. One side of the street is a quiet row of gracious buff-coloured 17th-century mansions, abandoned by their aristocratic owners to banks or genteel pastry shops dispensing *calissons*, the celebrated local delicacy made from ground almonds and candied melon. The other side is a bustle of cinemas, bou-

The particular charm
of Provençal villages like Gordes
owes much to the subtle variations in the colour and texture
of the distinctive stone used in the
houses. When first quarried, the
limestone is easy to work, to hew
into large or small slabs according
to need, before it hardens with
age. It takes on a patina of buff,
rose or silver hue, enhanced or
changing with the seasons or time
of day.

tiques and cafés, a rendezvous on the terrace of the Café des Deux Garçons being one of the few obligations that Provençal life imposes.

People still come to take the waters—the moss-covered fountain in the middle of the Cours Mirabeau spurts water with a natural heat of 34 °C (93.2 °F). But the university keeps the spirit of the town young, and cosmopolitan—Aix being one of the few provincial towns where non-French films are shown in original versions. You'll find fountains and little squares scattered all over the old town north of the Cours Mirabeau, one of the most attractive being the tranquil **Place d'Albertas**.

The cathedral is less worthy of your attention than its exquisite little Romanesque **Cloître Saint-Sauveur,** a peaceful refuge for a quiet read. Chamber music and choral recitals are held there during the summer music festival. The operas are performed behind the cloister, in the Palais de l'Ancien Archevêché. Don't go, however, without first a look at the Flemish tapestries, the 1465 triptych by Nicolas Froment, *The Burning Bush,* and the Baptistry, some of it 7th century.

Paul Cézanne spent most of his life in Aix, and his studio (*Atelier de Cézanne,* 9, Avenue Paul-Cézanne), on the hills outside Aix proper, has been preserved as a little **museum** including his palette, his cape and beret and other personal belongings. The musty smells of dried herbs and flowers, of fruit laid out as Cézanne would have had it, and the untidy artistic look of the place make one expect the artist to step in at any moment. But the best way to evoke his memory is to make the pretty drive out to the subject of his most famous landscapes, the **Montagne Sainte-Victoire**, 14 kilometres (9 miles) east of Aix on the D10. You'll enjoy a short hike round "his" territory.

Grand Canyon du Verdon   *31,D2*

This is Provence's answer to Arizona, perhaps not as big but the vistas are just as spectacular and the food in the little villages on the way is much better. The rock-strewn, emerald waters of the Verdon river run 170 kilometres (106 miles) through ravines sometimes only 6 metres (20 feet) wide but as much as 700 metres (2,300 feet) deep. To explore the canyon bottom, enquire at the tourist offices of Castellane or Moustiers-Sainte-Marie about guided tours, four days on foot, two days by canoe, the latter especially hazardous for beginners because of the rock-strewn stream. Starting out from Castellane, the D952 winds along the top of the canyon past well-marked *belvédères* (look-outs) such as **Point Sublime** near the village of Rougon, the **Mayreste** and the **Galetas**.

*N*ear the tunnel of Tusset, the Grand Canyon *du Verdon dwindles to a narrow gorge known as Samson's Corridor* (couloir de Samson). *At this point, a gigantic pillar of rock looks as if it is holding up the south wall of the canyon, waiting for the Israelite hero to pull it away.*

Côte d'Azur

31,DE2

When the British invented this playground in the 19th century, they called it the French Riviera, distinguishing it from the Italian one that begins round the corner at Ventimiglia. Nowadays, it's considered more chic to use its French name, the Côte d'Azur.

In summer, it's overcrowded, but that's the fun of it. You can always head back into the hills for a moment's peace. It's the country's safest bet for good weather, hot days and balmy nights. Apart from an occasional unsightly modern apartment block, the coastline outside the resorts still has considerable charm. The native umbrella pines share the landscape with acacia, eucalyptus and palm trees, imported by the British for the inevitable gardens they built around their villas. For years they came only for the mild winter to cure their chilblains, going home for the summer when, in those days, the coast was infested by hordes of mosquitos.

Most of the beaches are great, the boys and girls gorgeous, and the older set have a Fellini-esque charm that makes for very entertaining people-watching.

Nobody knows any more where the Côte d'Azur begins and ends. Purists restrict it to the stretch of coast from Cannes to Menton. That takes in only the original, more expensive resort towns: Juan-les-Pins, Antibes, Nice and Monte Carlo, with Menton dismissed as a pretty but too sleepy retirement community. In recent years, the tourist industry has extended the "Côte" westwards to include popular family-style resorts like Saint-Raphaël and Sainte-Maxime, and the special glamorous phenomenon of Saint-Tropez.

You have to really stretch your imagination to include Marseille, too, but this tough and gritty metropolis is hard to overlook, particularly for the *bouilla-*

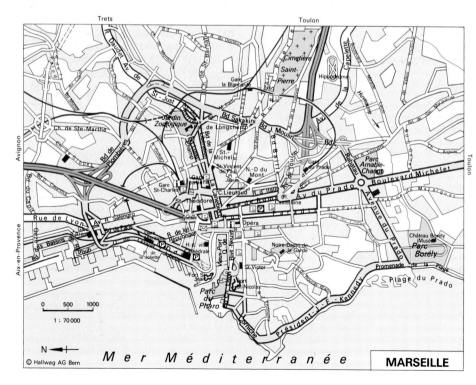

MARSEILLE

© Hallwag AG Bern

Mer Méditerranée

1 : 70 000

0   500   1000

244

baisse fish soup. The Marseillais insist it's the best, and it's not wise to argue with the Marseillais. In fact, to keep them happy, we'll start with Marseille and work our way east.

Marseille   30,BC2

This noisiest and most boisterous of ports is not exactly a tourist attraction. But as France's oldest city, founded by Greek colonists 2,500 years ago, it's not to be ignored.

Its pushy, gabby citizens have more personality in their little finger than most provincials in their whole body. They play the meanest game of *boules*. The politicians make their Boston, Chicago or Liverpool counterparts look like choirboys, and endless police raids have still not broken the French Connection.

Soak up the atmosphere along the main thoroughfare of the **Canebière**, where sailors the world over have broken their hearts and noses. Excellent shopping is to be had in the pedestrian streets leading off it.

The **Vieux Port** marks the spot where the Phocaean-Greek merchants of Asia Minor docked to create their western Mediterranean trading post. It's so perfect you'll soon see why. Today, it's a colourful harbour for yachts and motor launches. From the Quai des Belges, take a cruise out to the **Château d'If**, the island prison that was the scene of Alexandre Dumas's *Count of Monte Cristo*. It also offers a great view of the harbour and town, putting it all into perspective.

Côte des Calanques   30,C2-3

The limestone coastline between Marseille and Toulon is riddled with deep, uneven inlets *(calanques)*. This stretch, backed by the green scrub growth of the *maquis,* has inevitably spawned holiday developments. But you can still find attractive natural sites.

The port of **Cassis** may seem familiar—paintings of it by artists like Vlaminck, Matisse and Dufy hang in museums all over the world. Today you'll see the same

gaily-coloured stucco houses and crisp little triangular sails bobbing on the clear blue water, with the rocks of La Gardiole or the tree-covered Cap Canaille hovering in the background.

Cassis is mainly known for its incomparable shellfish, its *bouillabaisse* (fish soup) and its white wine, appreciated all over the south.

One of the world's largest shipyards, **La Ciotat** has managed to retain a small bit of its original charm. Against the background of towering cranes and steel hulls of the busy modern shipyard, the old fishing port holds out doggedly—typically Provençal with nets, small boats and colourful houses.

Bandol takes honours as the area's leading resort. It has a mild climate and long beach lined with housing developments, and is known for its vineyards which produce some very respectable red and white wine.

Toulon   31,C3

Formidable modern naval installations have replaced most of the historic fortifications after the town was devastated in World War II. But the proud **old port** remains the most interesting part of town. Excursion-boats can be found along **Quai Stalingrad**. The town's military history, where Bonaparte won his general's braid with his action against the British in 1793, can still be traced with ship-models, prints and documents in the **Musée de la Marine**, Place Ingénieur-Monsenergue. The remains of the old town are south of the busy Boulevard de Strasbourg. Head for **Place Puget**, a charming Provençal square with dolphin fountain and refreshing greenery. The colourful morning market stretches out its stalls under the plane trees of the **Cours Lafayette**.

High above the city-bustle, the 542-metre (1,778-foot) **Mont Faron** offers a fine view of the port, coast and surrounding mountains (take the cable-car at the beginning of the Corniche du Mont Faron.

Iles d'Hyères   *31,CD3*

The three islands make a pleasant ferry-excursion from Hyères or Toulon. The narrow rocky **Ile du Levant** attracts voyeurs and spies. Peek discreetly at the Héliopolis nudist camp to the west, but they'll ship you off to Devil's Island if you're caught gawking at the rocket-launchers on the naval base covering the rest of the island. Next door, the little **Ile de Port-Cros** is a protected national park area of steep hills covered with myrtle and heather and an abundance of bird life. Enjoy the flamingos, turtledoves, cormorants and puffins, the orchids and groves of holly-oaks, but camping, campfires (or even smoking outside the villages) are not allowed. The largest island, **Porquerolles** (8 kilometres [5 miles]) long, 3 kilometres [2 miles]) wide) is most popular as a beach resort with fine sands along the north coast east of the port.

The harbour of Saint-Tropez remains as glamourous as ever. Cruise into port at the end of the afternoon—if you are lucky enough to have rented a mooring—and you are guaranteed a rapturous reception of envious eyes, many of them pretty. Ignore them. Mess about with your forestay and jib, lanyards and tiller, while the cabin-boy is getting the champagne out of the cooler.

Saint-Tropez 31,D2

The town made famous by the film and rock stars of the 1960s, and whose popularity has been perpetuated by fashion photographers, their models and sundry groupies of the good life, is still going strong. People have always complained that this colourful little fishing port was being "ruined" by its celebrity. Saint-Tropez deserted in wintertime has an undeniably enchanting melancholy, but only for *habitués* who have known the summer madness.

The essence of Saint-Tropez has always been the crazy paraders along the **Vieux Port,** nipping in and out of boutiques with their ever more audacious fashions, on and off the flashy yachts and table-hopping through the cafés. Like the Deux Magots in Paris or the Deux Garçons in Aix, the **Sénéquier** might almost be consecrated by the

Ministry of Culture as a national people-watching monument where, lounging in their scarlet canvas chairs, the pretty watch the beautiful, and others.

It's unlikely you'll find any masterpieces among the paintings of the harbourside artists, but the **Musée de l'Annonciade** (Place Charles-Grammont) has a quite outstanding collection of works from 1890 to 1940—many of them studies of Saint-Tropez itself. In a handsomely renovated 16th-century chapel, blessed with that wonderful natural Mediterranean lighting, they include important canvases by Bonnard, Van Dongen, Matisse and Braque.

Away from the harbour, the town keeps its Provençal character intact on the **Place des Lices**, shaded by plane trees for the morning market, a late afternoon game of *boules* or sunset apéritif at the *Café des Arts*. For a view over the port, climb up to the 16th-century **Citadel**, from which a community of families from Genoa used to defend the town on a coast under constant attack from pirates.

Drive out of town south along the D93, signposted *Route des Plages*, to Tahiti or Pampelonne for the best **beaches**—fine sand shaded by lovely umbrella pines, but beware of the occasional stinging jellyfish. Part of the beach is traditionally given over to nudists—of all shapes. Other areas are more or less discreet and more or less chic. Each has its own style. The same goes for beach-bars.

Port-Grimaud, 6½ kilometres (4 miles) downhill on the bay of Saint-Tropez, opened in 1964, is a fanciful—and commercially highly successful—pastiche of Venice. The artificial canals built on marshland are lined with pleasant little houses and terraces painted in the same colours as Saint-Tropez.

On the way north-east, you'll pass through the attractive little town of **Sainte-Maxime,** with a casino, a minute beach and a wide promenade. In the summer it's packed with people who would love to be in Saint-Tropez but can't find a hotel room there.

Fréjus

31,D2

Little remains of the busy Roman market town of Fréjus (Forum Julii) founded in 49 B.C. The big harbour, built by Augustus into a great naval base and shipyard, has been completely filled up with silt deposits and replaced by modern Fréjus. A good part of the town was rebuilt after the 1959 catastrophe, when a dam upstream over the River Reyran broke, killing over 400 people.

Nearly razed by Saracens in the 10th century, Fréjus was revived in 990 by Bishop Riculphe, who established a fortified **episcopal city** here with a cathedral, baptistry, cloister and bishop's palace.

One of the oldest religious buildings in France (late 4th to early 5th century), the octagonal **baptistry** is punctuated by handsome black granite columns with Corinthian capitals (from the ancient Fréjus forum). The terra-cotta baptismal bowl, the original, was unearthed in the course of archaeological research.

In the **cloister,** a double-deckered arcade surrounds a garden of roses and cypress trees. The ceiling of the upstairs arcade is decorated with some amusing 14th-century creatures—imaginative scenes from the Apocalypse. An archaeological museum adjoining the cloister has Gallo-Roman remains.

The 10th- to 12th-century **cathedral,** with its "broken cradle" vaulting, exemplifies the early Gothic style of the region. It was built on the site of a Roman temple dedicated to Jupiter.

Most impressive of the Roman vestiges remains, however, the **arena** that could seat 10,000 spectators.

Saint-Raphaël

31,D2

Best known now as the railway stop for nearby Saint-Tropez, Saint-Raphaël had its heyday a century ago.

The town's centre is a palm-lined modern seafront (the old one was destroyed during World War II) with an ornamental fountain and pyramid commemorating Napoleon's debarkation after the 1799 Egyptian victories.

FILM IN
FRANCE

The inauguration of the Cannes International Film Festival was originally planned for September 1, 1939, but that was the day Hitler chose to invade Poland. At the opening seven years later, prizes went to David Lean's *Brief Encounter* and René Clément's *La Bataille du Rail* (The Railway Battle). Michèle Morgan and Ray Milland won the acting awards. Since then, the Cannes event has been the natural Gallic counterpart to the glamour of Hollywood.

It was just along the coast at La Ciotat in 1895 that brothers Auguste and Louis **Lumière** projected the world's first real films in their industrialist father's château. Much to the chagrin of Thomas Edison with his less effective kinetoscope, the Lumière brothers created moving pictures with the ingenious idea of perforating the film to sprocket it through a cinematograph combining camera and projector. The first films lasted just a minute or two—*Baby's Meal, The Waterer Watered* and *Arrival of the Train at La Ciotat*

Station. The latter created a sensation at the historic first public show December 28, 1895, in Paris's Grand Café on Boulevard des Capucines (now the Hôtel Scribe). Beginning as a small black speck, the train grew larger and larger until it filled the screen and scared the audience out of their seats. Box office receipts were 33 francs, at 1 franc a ticket. The press was invited but didn't turn up. After all, Auguste said: "The cinema is an invention without any future."

Georges **Méliès,** appropriately an amateur conjuror, realized the possibilities of "special effects" and rearrangement of reality to tell a story. After *Cinderella* in 1900 and the screen's first science-fiction, *A Trip to the Moon*, in 1902, he also specialized in historic events, reconstituting *The Dreyfus Affair* in what television would now call a docu-drama. Like many an innovative director after him, he came to a sad end, selling toys at a Paris railway station.

Simone Signoret
Previous page
MICHEL SIMON/ARLETTY

JEAN GABIN/BRIGITTE BARDOT

Louis **Feuillade** championed commercial cinema with hugely successful adventure serials, but one of his actors, René **Clair,** who went on to direct often brilliant and even profitable fantasy and satire (*A nous la liberté* and *Le million*), was already lamenting in 1925: ''Cinema as an art is dying, devoured by its double, the cinema industry.''

Abel **Gance,** an ambitious one-man industry all to himself, gave a new dimension to extravagant spectacle with his *Napoléon* (1928) projecting simultaneously three images across three screens. Comic Max **Linder,** considered an important influence on Charlie Chaplin with gags such as the asthmatic patient who overdid his cure by blowing down a wall, proved you could make art pay. The short, bitter life of anarchist filmmaker Jean **Vigo** suggested the opposite. His surrealist masterpieces, *Zéro de Conduite* and *L'Atalante* made him no money at all and he had to sell his camera to pay the doctor's bills, dying at 29.

Jean **Renoir,** son of painter Auguste, financed his first films with his inheritance and brought his own painterly vision to warm personal studies of French gesture and behaviour—*Une Partie de Campagne* and *La Règle du Jeu*. If Sacha **Guitry** was unabashedly theatrical, he did emphasize the value of scintillating dialogue, most notably in *Le Roman d'un Tricheur*.

The light and dark of the immediate post-war period were epitomized in the comedies, alternately gentle and mordant, of Jacques **Tati** *(Jour de Fête* and *Monsieur Hulot's Holiday)* and the awesome austerity of Robert **Bresson** *(Diary of a Country Priest* and *A Man Escaped)*.

GERARD PHILIPPE

PIERRE FRESNAY/GINETTE LECLERC

and mediocrity prevailed in the 50s until the arrival of the New Wave, most of them originally film critics with the prestigious magazine, *Cahiers du Cinéma*. Jean-Luc **Godard,** with *Breathless* and *Pierrot le Fou*, and François **Truffaut,** with *400 Blows* and *Jules and Jim*, adopted a fresh and often insolent tone to demonstrate their hostility to an *ancien régime* they deemed conventional, unimaginative and stereotyped. Since then, the contemporary French cinema has been heavily influenced by the techniques of TV commercials, with new talents like Jean-Jacques **Beneix** *(Diva* and *Betty Blue)* and Etienne **Chatiliez** *(La Vie est un Long Fleuve tranquille).*
But French cinema is also its film stars. Among the men,

Philippe to Alain Delon; all-round talents from Pierre Brasseur to Gérard Depardieu. And actresses that filled the dreams of any red-blooded male: from Michèle Morgan, Danielle Darrieux and Simone Signoret to Brigitte Bardot, Jeanne Moreau, Romy Schneider, Catherine Deneuve and Isabelle Adjani.

superb character actors like Raimu, Michel Simon and Fernandel; elegant, almost aristocratic figures like Louis Jouvet and Pierre Fresnay; tough guys with hearts of gold, Jean Gabin, Lino Ventura and Jean-Paul Belmondo; heart throbs

JEAN-PAUL BELMONDO

ROMY SCHNEIDER

In days gone by, there was a small holiday resort here for Romans based in Fréjus. It stood more or less on the site of the present casino—if you can substitute in your imagination the clicking roulette tables for luxurious tile baths and fish ponds.

Between Cannes and Saint-Raphaël lie a mass of porphyry rocks worn down and chipped by streams. This is the Esterel, now not much more than 2,000 feet at its highest, though the landscape seems abrupt and impressive. In the spring, the scrub-herb hills are golden with mimosa.

The coastal route—the **Corniche d'Or** (the Golden Corniche)—is pretty. Reddish porphyry rocks tumble into the dark blue sea making a jigsaw pattern of colours and shapes, tempting you to stop at every outcrop to admire the view.

Cannes   31,D2

Pure piece of hedonism, this luxury resort offers a magnificent beach front, the most elegant of boutiques and jewellery shops, the ultimate in grand hotels. Exquisite destiny for a sleepy little fishing village that was "made" by a nearby cholera epidemic in 1834. That's what stopped British law reformer Lord Brougham on his way to Italy. He fell in love with Cannes's climate, built himself a villa, and his aristocratic pals soon followed.

Overlooking the fine white-sand beaches, the **Croisette** is the resort's grand palm tree-lined promenade, from the Palm Beach casino past the great hotels—obligatory stop for an extremely expensive drink on the Carlton terrace—to the old port and the gigantic new **Palais des Festivals**. This is the venue of the International Film Festival in May and recorded music festival in January. If you like a mob scene, these are good opportunities to gawk at the stars of show business, but don't expect to get in to any of the galas unless you have professional accreditation—security is very strict.

Up on the hill above the port, **Le Suquet** preserves something of the old fishing village, and gives you a fine **view** of the coast. This may whet your appetite for a boat cruise (from the port's Gare Maritime) out to the peaceful little **Iles de Lérins** where you can stroll through groves of pines and eucalyptus and beautiful flower gardens.

A few kilometres north of Cannes are two towns renowned for their craftwork. At **Vallauris**, the ceramics and pottery industry was revived almost single-handedly by Picasso, who worked there after World War II. He also decorated its Romanesque chapel with murals entitled *La Guerre et la Paix* and left a bronze statue on Place Paul-Isnard. **Biot**, worth visiting for its nicely preserved 16th-century centre, is popular for its heavy tinted glassware with tiny champagne-like bubbles. And for the airy **Musée National Fernand Léger**, which documents the artist's lifework.

The famous old highway N7 that used to take holidaymakers from Paris to the Côte d'Azur before the *autoroute* was built becomes the coast-road east of Cannes, passing through the celebrated resorts of **Juan-les-Pins** and **Antibes**. Launched by American magnates and the Scott and Zelda Fitzgerald gang in the twenties and thirties, these high-class beach towns cater today to a family crowd, affluent young sun-soakers and disco-dingbats.

If it ever dares *rain*, Antibes has an excellent **Picasso Museum**, housed in the Château Grimaldi on Place Mariéjol. Built around the collection bequeathed by the artist in gratitude for the opportunity to work there in 1946, it includes a superb group of works by Nicolas de Staël and other 20th-century artists, Picabia, Miró and a great Modigliani portrait of Picasso.

On the pine-covered **Cap d'Antibes** promontory separating the two resorts, millionaires and Hollywood brats—often indistinguishable—hide out in the cabanas of the venerable but sparkling white Eden-Roc hotel, its swimming pool set in the rocks high above the sea.

Grasse 31,D2

The world's perfume capital won't bowl you over with heady scents; but you can't miss the enormous signs inviting you to visit the factories.

Although the Grassois were distilling essential essences from local flowers as far back as the 13th century, the industry didn't bloom until the Médicis family launched the fashion of scented gloves in the 16th century (Grasse made gloves as well).

Nowadays the manufacturers use at least 10,000 tons of flowers—violets (January to March), mimosa (February), daffodil (April), rose and orange-flowers and so on—to produce their essence. The gleaming brass cauldrons, alembics and other trappings displayed in the factories, though mainly for show, do give an idea of the first steps in making perfume and soap.

Built on a steep hill, Grasse was already renowned for its good air in the 19th century, and invalids and people on holiday flocked here. The most charming spot in town is the friendly, crowded **Place aux Aires,** with its fountains, arcades and sculptured 18th-century façades. The morning market is a palette of brilliant colours (flowers and vegetables) under the blue shade of lotus *(micocoulier)* and plane trees.

A few blocks downhill, the Place aux Herbes has an even larger food market. Several steps away is the sober, ochre-stone **cathedral,** begun in the 12th century and restored in the 17th. Inside you'll find cradle-vaulting and a rare religious canvas by Honoré Fragonard, *The Washing of the Feet.*

The **Musée Fragonard,** on the Boulevard Fragonard, occupies the village where the painter spent a year during the French Revolution. He brought with him a series of love-scene paintings which had been turned down by Madame du Barry. Most of the collection has ended up in the Frick Collection in New York, but the excellent, sensuous *Three Graces* remains.

The **Musée d'Art et d'Histoire de Provence** in the Rue Mirabeau is housed in an elegant 18th-century town house once owned by the Marquise de Cabris. Her furniture is in remarkably good condition. Among the less conventional articles on display are a nicely carved wooden bidet-chair with shell-shaped basin and a pewter bathtub on wheels.

Grasse is a good starting point for delightful side trips. **Gourdon** and the Loup Valley are off to the north-east; to the south-east you have the Tanneron range and the man-made lake of Saint-Cassien, a popular place for windsurfing.

Saint-Paul-de-Vence 31,E2

This feudal fortified village is magnificently situated amid colourful terraces of vineyards, bougainvillea and mimosa, with cypresses as their sentinels. For the **view** over the valley, take a drink on the terrace of the *Colombe d'Or* restaurant. If you stop for dinner, you can see the restaurant's famous collection of paintings by Matisse, Derain and Utrillo.

*H*igh in the hills behind the Riviera, the little medieval village of Sainte-Agnès commands magnificent views down to the Bay of Menton and all the way over to Italy.

An even more impressive collection of modern art awaits you at the splendid **Fondation Maeght,** on a grassy hill just outside the town. Here, sculpture takes pride of place, with an imposing black stabile by Alexander Calder at the entrance, some monumental pieces by Miró in the gardens and a matchless array of Giacometti statues in their own courtyard.

Nice 31,E2

An ancient Greek trading post, the town manages to combine the atmosphere of a bracing resort with a gutsy, bustling city life. The people are by nature highly independent—Nice was not incorporated into France until 1860—and tend to look down on the indolence of neighbouring Cannes. The good shopping and first-class restaurants more than make up for the pebble beach.

Instead of sprawling on sand, natives and visitors alike take the air on the grand **Promenade des Anglais,** financed by the town's English colony in 1822 to replace a wretched little footpath. Its most remarkable landmark is the **Hôtel Negresco,** a classified national monument whose domes are said to be modelled after the breasts of la Belle Otéro, mistress of the future King Edward VII. The promenade ends with a spectacular display of flowers and fountains in the **Jardin Albert-Ier.**

The **vieille ville** is at its best at the early morning **fish market** on Place Saint-François. Find out what's good that day for your evening meal. The **port** is worth a visit for a genteel waterside dinner or, more amusing, a drink at the rough-and-ready sailors' taverns.

For a good view over the port and the Baie des Anges, climb up through "old" Nice to the little park on top of the hill still known as **Le Château,** even though its castle was destroyed nearly 300 years ago. The ruins you can see are the

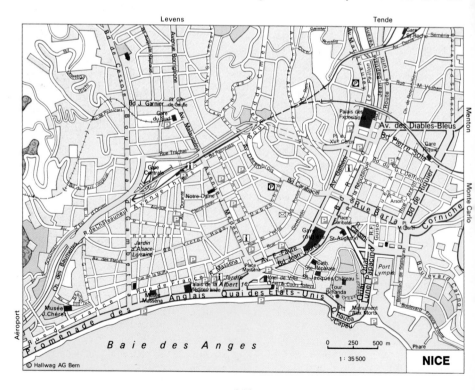

remains of the town's 11th-century cathedral. And the fountain's just what you need after the climb.

Les Corniches   *31,E2*

The route from Nice to Monaco, along the precipices of the Maritime Alps' southern slopes, offers one of the most spectacular drives in the country. There are actually three winding roads or Corniches, all safe but exciting—*Grande*, the high road, starting out from the Avenue des Diables-Bleus in Nice, *Moyenne*, in the middle, beginning at Place Max-Barel, and *Inférieure*, along the coast from Boulevard Carnot, but nearly always traffic-jammed.

The **Grande Corniche**, built by Napoleon, follows the route of the ancient Roman road, Via Julia Augusta. Stop off at **Belvédère d'Eze** and **La Turbie** for great views of the coast, especially at night for the lights of Monaco. In La Turbie, climb up to the remains of a curious 2,000-year-old Roman monument, the towering, slightly crumbling **Trophée des Alpes** built by Emperor Augustus to celebrate victories over 44 Gallic tribes, named in the inscription on the base.

Highlight of the **Moyenne Corniche**, the best road of the three, is the hilltop village of **Eze** hanging at a dizzying angle above the sea, once the fortress of Ligurian brigands. In summer, it's a bit of a tourist trap, but take a look at the cacti, tropical flowers (and ruins of a 14th-century castle) in the **Jardin exotique**. Its terrace affords the best view of the coast.

Villefranche   *31,E2*

Six kilometres (4 miles) east of Nice, Villefranche is one of the most sheltered Mediterranean harbours. It derives a certain charm from its yellow, pink and red stucco or brick houses packed against the hill, the plunging alleyways and staircases and the covered **Rue Obscure** that snakes down to the sea.

On the right, below the town's old citadel, is the 14th-century Chapelle Saint-Pierre, also known as the **Cocteau chapel**. Writer-artist Jean Cocteau decorated it in 1956 with his pastel, boldly outlined scenes of fishermen and the life of St. Peter.

Monaco   *31,E2*

The cliché is the truth, a phenomenon deserving close examination. It really is a millionaire's paradise. Ever since the roulette wheel and baccarat tables began earning enough money to do away with taxes in the 19th century, the minute principality has attracted the cream of dethroned Eastern European monarchs, tired American moguls and Nordic striplings resting their tennis elbow and athlete's foot.

Surrounded by **exotic gardens** to provide a little sweet-scented breathing space, gleaming skyscrapers have sprung up to pack all that wealth into the tiny area between mountain and Mediterranean. North of the square-shaped port, **Monte-Carlo** is the centre of the prin-

Table For One
One evening back in the Belle Epoque, James Gordon Bennett didn't like being kept waiting for his usual table at Monte-Carlo's Café Riche. So the multimillionaire American newspaper publisher bought the café, fired the manager and gave it to Ciro, his favourite waiter.

cipality's luxury. The world's most celebrated **Casino** was designed by Charles Garnier, architect of the Paris Opera House, and has the same grandiose nonsense all over the façade, foyer and gambling-rooms. Don't miss the lovely nude nymphs smoking cigarillos on the ceiling of the Salon rose.

Across the square, the **Hôtel de Paris** is another monument of unabashed ostentation. In the lobby, gamblers in search of luck have stroked Louis XIV's bronze equestrian statue until the horse's fetlock shines like the gold they lose next door. The outrageous Second Empire décor of the dining-room provided the perfect

In the casinos of Monte Carlo, they have brought one-armed bandits in from Las Vegas to join the more sedate two-armed variety who already have residence status in the otherwise immaculate principality. The gentle whirl and click of the roulette wheel and aristocratic murmurs at the baccarat and chemin-de-fer tables are drowned out these days by the boisterous excitement of the crap-game.
Rien ne va plus?

setting for famed chef Auguste Escoffier to create his outrageously elaborate sauces.

The **Palais du Prince** up on Monaco Rock is a fairy-tale affair, neo-Renaissance and neo-Baroque, with a quaint **changing of the guard**, fife, drums and all, at 11.55 a.m. every day.

On more serious matters Monaco is a music capital with an orchestra, opera house and festival of its own.

Menton

Hot-point of the Riviera for climate, milder for fun and games, Menton is a favourite of retired people, particularly railway employees for whom this is the end of the line.

Lemons flourish in this sunny spot. In February, they even hold a lemon festival.

A long pebble beach and Promenade George-V lead to a 16th-century bastion, now a **Cocteau museum.**

After a stop at the **Place aux Herbes,** with its arcades and three huge plane trees, go uphill to the heart of the **old town.** It has a decidedly Italian air. Here the 17th-century church of **Saint-Michel** occupies a charming square with a view over to Italy.

Cocteau painted some bold and fanciful allegorical frescoes in the marriage room of the Town Hall, popular with last-time-around sunset couples.

Corsica

32,AB1-2

In every sense a region apart from the rest of France, this rugged island offers dramatic coastlines and a wild interior of densely forested hills. Still largely unspoiled, it is the ideal place to escape the Riviera crowd. The population of less than a quarter of a million is concentrated mainly in the two major towns of Bastia (industrial and noisy) and the more attractive Ajaccio. The people are less fierce than they look and give you a simple, unaffected welcome.

Alternate indolent days on the beach with some of the Mediterranean's best deep-sea diving, boat excursions around pirate coves, canoeing and fishing on inland rivers or hikes and picnics in the mountains. For the holidaymaker, the best resorts are along the indented shorelines of the western and southern coasts, for which Ajaccio's airport or harbour (for the car ferry from Nice, Toulon or Marseille) provides the ideal gateway. Give yourself plenty of driving time, as the roads are narrow and tortuous.

Ajaccio

32,A2

At the head of the Gulf of Ajaccio, Napoleon's birthplace is the liveliest of Corsican towns, but tourists impatient to get out to the seaside resorts are usually content with a stroll around the **port** and a pilgrimage to the **Maison Bonaparte**
(Rue Saint-Charles). A guided tour will tell you how, on Assumption Day (August 15), 1769, pious mother Letizia was rushed out of church with her first birth pains. She made it no further than a first-floor sofa to bring little Nabulio kicking and screaming into the world he was soon to conquer. The sofa you see there now is a replica, the original having been stolen during the Revolution. You can also see paintings of Napoleon's parents and officers, the sword he wore as lieutenant-colonel and other memorabilia.

South of Ajaccio, the major seaside resorts are **Porticcio** and **Propriano**, both with sandy beaches and good opportunities for sailing and deep-sea diving.

Sartène

32,A2

Constant prey in olden days to the pirates of North Africa, this heavily fortified town has preserved its medieval appearance around the massive granite **Hôtel de Ville**, once the palace of the Genoese governors. There are strange perspectives to be discovered from the narrow streets, staircases and archways suddenly opening out to a view of the sea below on one side or the Rizzanese valley on the other.

Bonifacio

32,A2

This proud port city occupies a narrow peninsula surrounded by towering white chalk cliffs, in striking contrast to the red granite predominant in the rest of the island.

*T*he port of Bonifacio, more peaceful now than in its turbulent days of pirates and innumerable sieges, turns its back on the rest of Corsica. Its Ligurian dialect is quite unlike anything spoken in the rest of the island and the people themselves remain proudly aloof, having once formed a miniature republic of their own, with separate currency, parliament and laws.

The best way to appreciate the spectacular location of the old town perched high on the cliffs is to take a **boat cruise** from the marina at the entrance to Bonifacio. The cruise takes you deep into the limpid blue waters of the **Sdragonato cave**. The "skylight" in its roof is shaped exactly like a map of Corsica. As the boat passes along the southern side of town, notice the **Escalier du Roi d'Aragon**, a staircase cut diagonally into the cliff face, used by the soldiers of the Spanish king in an abortive siege of the town in the 15th century. When visiting the old town on foot, take an exhilarating walk down the staircase to the base of the cliffs and along the water's edge, climbing gradually back up to the southern end of town.

Porto-Vecchio   32,A2

Surrounded by a pretty forest of cork oaks and sweet-smelling eucalyptus, the gulf surrounding Porto-Vecchio has an ever-expanding series of luxury resorts, the best being out on the fine sandy beaches of **Cala Rossa**.

Inland, there are some beautiful excursions to be made into the **forests** of l'Ospedale and Zonza. The cork oaks are stripped of their valuable bark every ten years or so, baring a russet-brown trunk until the cork grows back again.

For a picnic up on the wild, lovely mountain pass of **Bavella**, take some of the great local tomatoes, smoked liver sausage *(figatelli)* and ewe's or goat's milk cheese *(broccio)*. The most enjoyable of Corsican wines are the *rosés*.

Cap Corse   32,B1

This rugged peninsula forming the northern tip of the island offers the wildest of Corsica's many wind- and sea-buffeted landscapes—slate-grey and pale-green cliffs set off against the deep blue of the Mediterranean.

Start your tour from **Bastia**. This tough commercial town with its Chicago-style politics spearheads the island's perennial independence movement. Something of the earthy Corsican spirit can be sensed in the cafés on the long esplanade of **Place Saint-Nicolas** or in the banter to be heard over the click of the *boules* under the palms and plane-trees. Along the waterfront of the **old port**, you'll catch the bustle of the town at work.

Some Hero

You wouldn't believe, from all the statues and souvenirs, and the streets named after them, that Corsica once heartily hated the whole Bonaparte clan.

In the 1760s, when nearly 500 years of rule under the city republic of Genoa was coming to an end, Carlo Maria Buonaparte fervently supported Corsican independence. But the island was ceded to France in 1768, and Carlo Maria promptly became an equally fervent supporter of Louis XV. His son Napoleon, born a year later, became a Corsican nationalist but went on with brother Lucien to champion the French Revolution's opposition to the island's separatism. The family house in Ajaccio was plundered to cries of "Death to the traitors of the fatherland!" Things didn't improve when Napoleon crowned himself Emperor. The city celebrated his abdication by tossing his statue into the Mediterranean.

262

The D80 coastroad takes you north to the pilgrimage town of **Lavasina**. The devout pay homage to a 16th-century Italian portrait of the Virgin Mary and Child, believing it to have miraculous properties. Beyond **Erbalunga**, a characteristic little fishing-village with some colourful old houses around the harbour, the heather-covered landscape grows dramatically wilder. You'll find the coast still dotted with sturdy **lookout towers** built by Genoan merchants, mostly around the 15th century, to warn against pirates.

A gentler breed of sailors steer their yachts into the port of **Macinaggio** and you'll get a good bird's-eye view of their activities out at sea as you drive inland to **Rogliano**, up on Monte di u Poggio. A short walk from the Col de Serra, the **Moulin Mattei**, a restored windmill, commands an impressive panorama of the peninsula's mountains and rocky west coast. Making your way back south on the D35, **Centuri-Port** is a favourite base for deep-sea diving and fishing, and well worth a look for its tiled houses with roofs of green serpentine stone clustered around the harbour. In one of the peninsula's most spectacular sites, the medieval fortified town of **Nonza** is perched on a cliff with a massive lookout tower even higher above the stone-tiled houses. In the 16th-century **church** is an altar painting of St. Julia, an early Christian martyr crucified here for rejecting the local pagan cult and thus became Corsica's patron saint.

Calvi   *32,A1*

This family beach resort is also popular with sailing enthusiasts, and the cafés and quays of the lower town's marina, **La Marine**, provide a lively gathering-place to watch the yachts and fishing boats. You'll welcome the shade of the umbrella pines on the long **beaches**. But to really cool off, explore the narrow shady streets of the upper town inside the old **citadel** high on the town's rocky promontory. The Genoans built the mas-

sive granite ramparts in the 15th century. Accepting that Christopher Columbus was of Genoan stock, locals insist he was born in Calvi, even identifying one of the houses on Rue Colombo as his birthplace. Historians are not convinced.

Golfe de Porto   *32,A1*

Some of France's most grandiose panoramas of sea and landscape are clustered around this gulf 70 kilometres (43 miles) north of Ajaccio.

Piana is the most delightful of its sleepy village resorts, unspoiled by commercialization and blessed with the nearby natural wonders of **Capo Rosso** and the **Calanche**. These craggy red granite cliffs and boulders have been hurled down to the sea by volcanic eruptions and eroded there by wind and water into the most bizarre and fanciful shapes. Some of the Calanche boulders are hidden in a forest of sea pines, lying there like sleeping monsters. Over the centuries, they have been nicknamed Dog, Eagle or Turtle, but you'll recognize your own big-nosed geography teacher or even, along the well-marked walk of the chemin du Château-fort, an unmistakably bouffant-hairstyled prime minister. Thick-soled shoes are recommended for your walks over the rocks.

Be sure to take a **boat cruise** from the little resort town of Porto. The best one goes out to the cliff caves on the northern edge of the gulf, to the isolated fishing village of **Girolata**, and the marvellous nature reserve of **Scandola**, a coastal haven for eagles, bald buzzards and other rare species nesting on the peaks of the jagged volcanic rocks.

In the interior, drive along the winding mountain road to Evisa and the cool, quiet **Forêt d'Aïtone**. Off the D84 road just 3 kilometres (2 miles) north-east of Evisa is a sign reading *Piscine*. Follow the path: it's not a municipal chlorine-saturated swimming pool, but a series of clear, clean, natural pools formed in smooth slabs of rock by the **Cascades d'Aïtone** (waterfalls). A sheer delight.

Did Cro-Magnon Eat Foie Gras?

From the southern edge of the Loire Valley to the Pyrenees, from the Atlantic to the Mediterranean, this area encompasses peoples and landscapes as varied as their histories. From the Atlantic across to the Mediterranean, the south-west corner of France is a rich mixture of Catalan, Basque, Protestant and Cathare "heretic" and even British traditions.

Uniting the area is a mood akin to that of the *Midi*—as the locals themselves say, *midi-moins-le-quart* (a quarter to twelve, playing on *midi's* double meaning of south and noon).

In and around the lovely valley of the Dordogne, the Périgord beckons with its rich cuisine, fortified towns, fascinating cave paintings and other prehistoric remains. From the Basque country to the Mediterranean, you can explore the sunny mountains of the Pyrenees, country of France's most popular king, happy-go-lucky Henri IV. And in between, the historic towns of Montpellier, Albi, Carcassonne and Toulouse. The sun-drenched Languedoc coast, particularly the Côte Vermeille, has character and culture, with inland mountainous areas less known such as the mysterious, tragic but touchingly beautiful Cévennes.

The Atlantic coast remains the preserve of the country's most independent-minded ports, the Protestant stronghold of La Rochelle and proud and prosperous Bordeaux, with its hinterland of great vineyards. Poitou-Charente, its neighbour, offers a certain stately rural peace and harmony with one or two cities of exceptional artistic interest.

Périgord

21,DE2-3;22,AC2-3

This rich and fertile country is densely forested and crisscrossed by rivers flowing from the plateau of the Massif Central out to the Atlantic. Of these, the Dordogne has carved out through the centre a beautiful winding valley of gentle greenery.

In the village markets, the fruit and vegetables, mushrooms and nuts of every description bear witness to the region's self-sufficiency in food. Gourmets lament the dwindling supply of truffles snuffled out by the pigs under a special kind of oak tree, but the *pâté de foie gras* and slowly roasted *confit* of goose and duck are as succulent as ever. Even the salads of the Quercy region are all the more subtle for their dressing in walnut oil.

If so many Stone Age relics have been found here rather than elsewhere in France, it's thanks to the unique combination of abundant fish supplies in the rivers, and dwellings safe from wild animals in the myriad caves and grottos riddling the valley cliffs.

With a similar concern for self-protection, the proliferation of ramparts and fortresses throughout the Périgord is a vestige of the many wars against the English, between Protestant and Catholic, and resistance to marauding bands of brigands left behind at the end of each battle.

Brantôme 21,D2

On a strenuous driving tour, few places are more refreshingly welcome than this sleepy little town of flower-bedecked houses, weeping willows and graceful lime trees beside the Dronne river. Wade in for some great trout-fishing down by the old 16th-century bridge. Apart from its grand 11th-century Romanesque belfry, Brantôme's Benedictine **abbey** has been remodelled over the centuries and now houses the town hall, a couple of schools and a little **museum** of Fernand Desmoulin's sketches of famous Frenchmen.

Vallée de la Vézère 22,AB2-3

Exploring the valley that shelters the earliest signs of European civilization and man's artistic awakening is by no means a dry and dusty archaeological tour of fossils and bones. The region in any case would be idyllic for hikes and picnics. Around the caves that pockmark the cliffs overhanging the Vézère river is a green and pleasant countryside of meadows, vineyards and orchards and a profusion of graceful willows and poplars at the water's edge.

Montignac, a likeable enough village in its own right, is the departure point for your visit to the world-famous cave paintings of **Lascaux.** Concealed and protected against atmospheric changes for 17,000 years, these awe-inspiring frescoes and engravings of bulls, horses, ibex, bison and deer were discovered in 1940—by four boys chasing their dog down a hole. Within a few years, the humidity of human bodies and the exhaust fumes wafted in from passing traffic caused a rapid deterioration, and the caves had to be closed to the general public.

Now, the original caves (four galleries of 200 paintings and 1,500 engravings) can be seen only by special appointment. An authoritative guided tour in French or English is available for a maximum of *five* people each day. Write to: Directeur des Antiquités préhistoriques d'Aquitaine, 26–28, Place Gambetta, 33000 Bordeaux.

Although the thrill of seeing the original work of these prehistoric artists is undeniable, the astonishingly realistic replica created at **Lascaux II** makes a very satisfying alternative. Anthropologists and artists have reproduced the *Salle des Taureaux* (Hall of Bulls) with 100 pictures of the animals that shared the environment of Stone Age man.

Complete your visit with a side trip to **Le Thot,** where the museum has some excellent audio-visual exhibits and models of cave life; the nearby park has been turned into a zoo devoted to descendants of the animals portrayed at Lascaux.

Back on the river, you pass the handsome 16th-century **Château de Losse** (visitors can admire its fine Italian Renaissance furniture and tapestries) on your way to **Saint-Léon-sur-Vézère.** Surrounded by beautiful poplars and willows, the town's buff-stoned 11th-century church, with its stone-slabbed roof

---

Stone Age Art

Because no household tools or weapons were found near the paintings of the deep galleries, scholars have deduced that most of the French caves were not dwellings, but sanctuaries where Stone Age man depicted the beasts he hunted and probably worshipped. For his home, he preferred cave entrances or the shelter of a cliff overhang. Some of the frescoes show animals pierced with arrows or spears, perhaps a form of sympathetic magic to promote success in the hunt.

The artists depicted their potential game with red and yellow oxidized iron, powdered ochre, black charcoal and animal fats. They blew powdered colour on to the walls of the caves through hollow bones or vegetable stalks, basically the same technique as aerosol-graffiti artists in the latterday caves of a modern subway.

and graceful windowed steeple, is a characteristic example of Périgord Romanesque. For a wonderful view of the valley, climb to the top of **La Roque Saint-Christophe**, a spectacular long cliff 80 metres (262 feet) high and honeycombed with caves inhabited 20,000 years ago.

The French taste in grandiloquent epithets for its cultural centres is fully indulged, and not totally unjustified, at **Les Eyzies-de-Tayac**, *"capitale de la préhistoire"*. Besides its important **museum** housed in the remains of a medieval castle, the village is at the centre of literally dozens of major palaeolithic excavation sites, explored only since the 19th century by the French pioneers of studies in prehistory.

The Cro-Magnon shelter *(Abri de Cro-Magnon)* on the north side of town is the spot where railway workers uncovered in 1868 three 30,000-year-old human skeletons beside their flint and bone tools. The forefathers of the painters of Lascaux were the most advanced of our direct prehistoric ancestors. Anthropologists say that these tall, large-brained men, with high foreheads *(homo sapiens sapiens),* were of a physical type still to be seen in parts of south-western France.

For cave paintings, all accessible by guided tour only, the most attractive site is the **Grotte de Font-de-Gaume**, reached by an easy walk up on a cliff above the eastern edge of town. The pictures of mammoths, bison, horses and reindeer are between 15,000 and 40,000 years old. The **Combarelles** cave, further east, is a long winding gallery where the pictures are engraved rather than painted, and very often superimposed on each other.

The caves of the **Grotte du Grand Roc** north-west of Les Eyzies are a natural rather than historical phenomenon, but well worth a visit for the weirdly shaped stalagmites and stalactites and the panorama of the Vézère valley.

Périgueux   *21,D2*

The region's capital is naturally enough a market-town for Périgord truffles and *foie gras*. Try them out in the local restaurants or hoard them for your first banquet when you get home. The five domes and forest of stone lanterns adorning the **Cathédrale Saint-Front** emphasize the Byzantine influence of its ancient Greek-cross ground plan, but they are largely 19th-century bastard additions of Paul Abadie, who perpetrated Paris's Sacré-Cœur.

Visit the **Musée du Périgord**, 22, Cours Tourny, for its important exhibits of the region's many prehistoric findings, but also fascinating artefacts from Polynesia, New Caledonia, the Solomon Islands, Australia and pre-Columbian America.

Vallée de la Dordogne   *22,AB3*

This valley is so beloved by British and Dutch holidaymakers that cunning travel agents quite happily extend its name to the whole Périgord region. For the British in particular, its rolling green countryside of river, meadow, copse and hedgerow, fertilized with the blood of their ancestors in the Hundred Years' War, is a "home from home", with the bonus of a ruined castle or two, roast goose and walnut liqueur.

The river is good for fishing and canoeing, and if you haven't brought your own bike to explore the back country, you can rent one at Sarlat.

Start at the confluence of the Vézère and Dordogne rivers, where the hilltop village of **Limeuil** affords a fine view of both valleys and their bridges meeting at right angles down below. Drive south away from the river to **Cadouin**, with its impressive 12th-century Cistercian **abbey**, a major Périgord Romanesque church with wooden belfry on a remarkable split pyramidal cupola. The soberly designed church contrasts with the more decorative Gothic and Renaissance sculpture of the cloister.

Back on the river, perched above a 150-metre (490-foot) ravine, the redoubt of **Beynac-et-Cazenac** is a splendid fairytale castle, much frequented by English troublemakers in the Middle Ages. The barons of Beynac lost it in turn to King Richard the Lion-Heart and Simon de Montfort, Norman-born Earl of Leicester, before turning it into a handsome Renaissance palace. Across the river, you can see Beynac's rival, **Castelnaud**, in ruins, and the 15th-century castle of **Fayrac**, with drawbridge, battlements and pepperpot towers nicely restored.

You get a magnificent view of all three castles from **La Roque-Gageac**. It has won a prize as one of the most beautiful villages in the country, especially true when the late afternoon sun catches the houses' stone-tiled roofs. It's also an antique-collectors' paradise (amateurs beware).

South of the river, the fortified town of **Domme** sits on a promontory overlooking the valley. Built in 1281 during the Hundred Years' War, it later served the Protestant cause in the 16th-century Wars of Religion. Two vantage-points offer great views, the *Promenade des Falaises* (cliff-walk) and the *Belvédère de la Barre*. For a reminder of the troubled past, visit the subterranean grottoes in which citizens sheltered during the wars, and the ramparts with soldiers' graffiti still scrawled on the inner walls.

Sarlat, capital of the Périgord Noir, is a lovely old town, bustling in high season but of unrecognizable quiet charm in spring and autumn, as French *cinéastes* know whenever they need "authentic" locations for a period film. The Saturday **market** on the Place du Marché-aux-Oies is a joy. As are the narrow streets of the old town east of the busy Rue de la République. Look out for the fine old Gothic and Renaissance houses on Rue Fénelon, Rue des Consuls, especially **Hôtel Plamon**, and Place du Peyrou's grand **Maison de La Boétie**, across from the cathedral. An open-air summer festival is held on Place de la Liberté. And don't leave town without trying that humblest and most magnificent delicacy: *pommes sarladaises*, thin-sliced potatoes sautéed in goose fat with garlic and parsley, the sweetest death known to Western man.

Rocamadour 22,B3

Since the 12th century, sightseers and religious pilgrims alike have been flocking to this spectacularly situated fortified town up on its cliff top above the Alzou river (best appreciated from the eastern vantage point of L'Hospitalet on D673). Founded on the tomb of a hermit, St. Amadour, believed to have mystic curative powers, Rocamadour attracted Henry II of England and many French kings after him.

The modern mob scene buzzing around the souvenir shops and the **Chapelle miraculeuse de Notre-Dame** captures something of the medieval frenzy. The secular visitor may prefer to get there by the elevator rather than the 216 steps of the Via Sancta, which reformed heretics and other penitents were obliged to negotiate on their knees with heavy chains around their neck and arms.

The great chasm *(gouffre)* of **Padirac**, 16 kilometres (10 miles) north-east of Rocamadour, is one of the Périgord's most exhilarating natural wonders. Elevators take you 100 metres (328 feet) down to a subterranean river for a delightfully spooky boat ride past huge stalactites and stalagmites formed by the calcite residue and deposits of thousands of years of dripping water.

Vallée du Lot 22,BC3

The Lot river meanders through steep limestone cliffs with an occasional ruined castle or old village perched precariously on overhanging crags. **Capdenac-le-Haut** (south of Figeac on the N140) is just such a town, old redoubt of the Cathar rebellions and the Wars of Religion, still medieval in look with its Gothic half-timbered houses. Down below is its modern railway-town from which you start a picturesque drive along a river bank lined with poplars and groves of oak trees. The Lot's relatively tame waters make canoeing a more leisurely proposition here than on the Dordogne. At **Saint-Cirq-Lapopie**, centuries-old traditions of carpentry and other crafts are still practiced along its steeply sloping streets. And modern artists have turned its wood-beamed gabled houses into studios and galleries. Look out over the valley from the terrace beside the 15th-century church with its sturdy clocktower, but the grandest view of all is above the village among the remains of **La Popie castle**.

Cross the river and turn north-west past the village of Cabrerets to visit the Grotte du **Pech-Merle** and its fascinating prehistoric cave paintings. Some 60 animals—bisons, mammoths and horses—and a dozen human figures were painted or etched on the walls about 20,000 years ago (discovered only in 1922). At the cave entrance is the **Amédée Lemozi Museum**, named after the local curate who led the researches and assembled the region's prehistoric artifacts, including a 40,000-year-old stone dagger and bronze axes and swords. A film places the cave in its prehistoric context.

Cahors   *22,B3*

Home of a lusty red wine (which its former archbishop promoted for communion when he became Pope John XXII in Avignon), this fortified town is surrounded on three sides by a loop of the Lot river. Spanning the river on the west, the sturdy 14th-century turreted **Pont Valentré** was a self-contained military bastion, strong enough to keep the English out in the Hundred Years' War.

Massive **ramparts** with an imposing guardhouse and lookout tower protect the town's northern approaches. The double-domed Gothic **cathedral** is another fortress in its own right. The north **portal** has a splendidly sculpted 12th-century tympanum showing the Ascension of Jesus and life of St. Stephen (Etienne), to whom the cathedral is dedicated. A door to the right of the choir leads to the finely carved Flamboyant Gothic arcades of the **cloister.**

Moissac   *28,B1*

Just north of the Bordeaux–Toulouse *autoroute* A62, the town's 12th-century abbey-church of **Saint-Pierre** makes a rewarding side-trip for lovers of Romanesque sculpture. The *Apocalypse* of the magnificent **tympanum** on the southern belltower-porch depicts a most authoritarian Jesus enthroned with 24 elderly musicians looking up at him in awe. He is flanked by the bull of St. Luke and winged man of St. Matthew, the eagle of St. John and lion of St. Mark. In the doorway, noteworthy for the Spanish-Moorish influence of its indented curves, stand St. Peter and the prophet Isaiah. Inside, in the chapels to the right of the entrance, are fine 15th-century polychrome wooden **sculptures** of the *Pietà,* the *Flight to Egypt* and *Descent from the Cross*. Notice in the elegant single- and twin-columned marble arcade of the **cloister** the sculpted capitals of scenes from the Old and New Testaments.

The nice little **Musée Moissagais**, 4, Rue de l'Abbaye, is devoted to local arts and crafts.

Montauban   *28,B2*

The home-town of painter Jean-Auguste-Dominique Ingres (1780–1867) houses a marvellous collection of his art in the 17th-century bishop's palace. The **Musée Ingres** covers every aspect of this virtuoso draughtsman and master of Classicism. Most celebrated painting here is the monumental *Dream of Ossian,* commissioned in 1812 for Napoleon's bedroom in Rome, but many prefer the austere, cool vitality of his portraits. The museum makes a revolving choice from its collection of over 4,000 drawings. Compare Ingres' work with representative paintings of his classical master, Jacques-Louis David, and romantic contemporary, Eugène Delacroix. Memorabilia of Ingres' life include his legendary violin, which he nearly preferred to his paintbrush. On the ground floor is a bust of Ingres by Bourdelle, another local boy.

The most colourful spot in town is the **Place Nationale** with its red-brick arcades, at its best during the morning market.

Atlantic Coast

Decidedly more businesslike than those of the Mediterranean, the major Atlantic coastal towns are notable for their civic pride, and the resorts appeal more to the sailor than the beach-lover. What the vineyards around Bordeaux lack in attractive landscape and villages (apart from Saint-Emilion) they make up for in the quality of their wines, with good possibilities for tasting.

La Rochelle *20,B1*

Without doubt the most handsome of France's ports, this historic bastion of Protestantism seduces the visitor with its quiet charm and dignity.

Surrounded by lively cafés, with an avenue of trees along one quay, the old harbour still serves the fishing fleet and small sailing boats. Its entrance is guarded by two 14th-century towers remaining from the town's fortifications. To the east, the **Tour Saint-Nicolas** served as fortress and prison. At the foot of the **Tour de la Chaîne**, a gunpowder storehouse, lies the huge old chain slung across to Saint-Nicolas to bar passage at night. The grand old lighthouse (and second prison), **Tour de la Lanterne**, now stands inland at the end of the ramparts of the Rue Sur-les-Murs. You'll find prisoners' graffiti on the walls of the graceful octagonal steeple, as you climb up to the balcony for its view over the old city and the islands in the bay.

The Gothic tower gate and belfry, **Porte de la Grosse-Horloge,** leads into the prosperous old merchant quarters. Note the gracefully vaulted shopping arcades and galleries of the 16th- and 17th-century houses. On the Rue des Merciers, don't miss the handsome Gothic **Hôtel de Ville,** with its Italian-style courtyard, staircase and belfry. Another elegant house is the double-gabled **Hôtel de Pontard** hidden away at the rear of a garden at the savings bank (Caisse d'Epargne, 11, Rue des Augustins).

The **Musée des Beaux-Arts** (28, Rue Gargoulleau) includes an important portrait of Martin Luther by Lucas Cranach and notable canvases by Giordano and Ribera.

Ile de Ré *20,B1*

Gleaming white villas and smart little hotels, a sunny microclimate, pine-shaded beaches, good oysters and mussels—this cheerful island is much appre-

La Rochelle's harbour was the focus of a brutal siege (1627–28) with which Cardinal Richelieu crushed the town's Protestant resistance to national unity under a Catholic monarch. With their British allies prevented by sea-blockade from bringing relief, the population was decimated by famine, only 5,000 surviving from the original 28,000.

ciated as a holiday resort, especially for the sailing possibilities from the harbour of its "capital", **Saint-Martin-de-Ré.** Visit the lighthouse, **Phare des Baleines**, at the west end of the island (257 steps to the view at the top). A new, controversial bridge now links the island to the mainland, making it infinitely more convenient to get there, but taking the "adventure", the charm, and, no doubt, some of the seclusion away for good and ever.

Bordeaux   21,C3

Useful as an obvious base of operations for wine-enthusiasts, this commercial metropolis may be too busy for other holiday-makers.

Ship folk will head for the great **port** to see the freighters and tankers from Asia, Australia, Africa and the Americas. Guided tours by launch depart from the landing stage *(Embarcadère Vedettes)* of the vast Esplanade des Quinconces.

Landlubbers prefer the cafés, shops and galleries around the **Place de la Comédie**, a main centre of city life. The square is dominated by the **Grand Théâtre**, the jewel of Bordeaux's many 18th-century buildings. It is a temple-like structure of 12 Corinthian columns, its entablature adorned with the statues of the Greek muses and the goddesses Juno, Venus and Minerva. The majestic double staircase inside inspired Charles Garnier for his design of the Paris Opera House.

South of the imposing Place de la Bourse, the old **Quartier Saint-Pierre** around the church of the same name is a masterpiece of urban renewal. The once ill-famed slum has grown into a lively neighbourhood of art galleries and quaint little shops, with an open-air market on Place Saint-Pierre. On the beautifully renovated houses along Rue Philippart

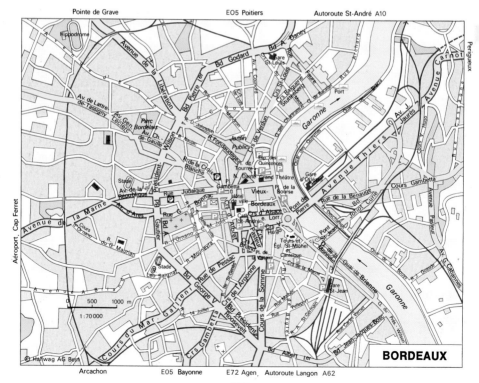

and Rue Bahutiers, notice the grotesque masks and winged angels sculpted over the doorways.

The dimensions of the Flamboyant Gothic **Cathédrale Saint-André** rival those of Notre-Dame de Paris, which is only 6 metres (20 feet) longer and 4 metres (13 feet) wider. It has some remarkable sculpture over the porches. Inside, the unusual, almost blasphemous Renaissance **bas-reliefs** on the organ loft show Jesus ascending to heaven on an eagle like a Greek god, and descending to Limbo among diabolical figures of the Underworld.

The **Musée des Beaux-Arts** (Cours d'Albret) includes works of Veronese, Perugino, Rubens and Van Dyck and major paintings by Delacroix and Matisse.

For a guided **wine tour**, write to the Maison du Vin, 1, Cours du 30-juillet, 33075 Bordeaux. This wine-growers' association also organizes tastings.

Saint-Emilion   *21,C3*

At the western end of the Dordogne valley, this is undoubtedly the most attractive of the Bordeaux wine villages, enhanced by the golden-tinted stone of the medieval houses around its sleepy Place du Marché. Unique in Europe, the 1,000-year-old church known as the **Eglise Monolithe** was carved out of the solid rock on which the village was built. After wandering around the old ramparts and narrow streets, take a rest in the ivy-covered ruins of the·14th-century **Cloître des Cordeliers**. The local Maison du Vin can advise you for your tour of the surrounding vineyards.

Arcachon   *20,B3*

Cashing in on the 19th-century railway boom and new-fangled craze for bathing in the sea, the Bordeaux financier brothers Emile and Isaac Péreire created this seaside resort in 1857. The European aristocrats who made the place fashionable have disappeared, but their villas, strange mixtures of neo-Gothic and Moorish or English Tudor architecture surrounded by pine trees, are still there in the elegant *ville d'hiver* (literally, winter town). The "summer town" is of course along the **sea front,** with its tamarisks lining the promenade above a fine sandy beach. With oysters fresh in from the bay, you'll find excellent seafood restaurants—and a shining white **casino**—on the Boulevard de la Plage. In the **Aiguillon** quarter behind the port, you'll see the fishermen's cabins and drawn up on the shore the last of the *pinasses*, long narrow pinewood fishing smacks.

South of town, beyond the smart suburbs of Pyla-sur-Mer and Pilat-Plage, is the much-vaunted **Dune du Pilat**, at 114 metres (344 feet) the tallest sanddune in Europe (with a stairway to the top).

A Prince of a Fellow

Was the Black Prince in fact a white knight, a proper English gentleman or a brutal bandit, a scoundrel, a blackguard? As was usual in the so-called age of chivalry of the 14th century when the black-armoured Edward, Prince of Wales, ruled Aquitaine from his court in Bordeaux, he was all those things. After distinguishing himself at the battle of Crécy, he burned, pillaged and raped his way through south-west France with an army half English, half French, all (according to French historians) perpetually drunk on the local wines. For rest and recreation, the prince returned with his spoils to Bordeaux and wife Joan the Fair Maid of Kent to enjoy the quieter life of a brilliant, elegant court. He massacred the defenceless civilian population of Limoges, but at Poitiers in 1356, when he captured France's king Jean le Bon, he personally served him dinner at table. Back in London, the French king rode in the victory procession on a grand white horse while the Black Prince chose to trot humbly behind on a mangy-looking black nag. There are times when the French would prefer the English not to be so bloody polite.

Poitou

15,DE3;16AB3

The region's plains sweeping over to the Atlantic have historically laid it open to invasion—Visigoths from the east, Arabs from Spain and English from the north. Today, it is appreciated above all for the Romanesque architecture of its churches and abbeys—and excellent *chaudrée* fish-soup.

Poitiers

15,E3

The town is famous for the battle of 732 in which Charles Martel beat back the northern advance of the Arabs, a major step in the unification of the French nation. This university town of many centuries' standing is particularly lively in the historic centre around the grand **Palais de Justice**, which incorporates the medieval castle of the Dukes of Aquitaine. In the baptistery of **Saint-Jean**, Poitiers possesses one of France's earliest surviving church buildings, dating back in part to the 4th century. The elaborately sculpted 12th-century façade of the church of **Notre-Dame-la-Grande**, depicting scenes from the Old and New Testaments, set the characteristic style of Poitou Romanesque.

Saintes

21,C2

This airy town of bright white-washed houses makes a pleasant stop on the road south to Bordeaux. The bustling street life gives it a distinctly southern tone. The church of the **Abbaye aux Dames** is a notable example of Saintonge Romanesque, with its graceful cone-shaped belfry centrally placed over the transept crossing. Of the great **Saint-Eutrope** pilgrimage church, crippled by 19th-century restorers, only a fine Romanesque **crypt** remains. The **Musée des Beaux-Arts**, Rue Victor-Hugo, housed in a handsome 17th-century mansion, has fine paintings by Primaticcio, Rigaud and Pourbus. Down by the Charente river, stands the 1st-century **Arc de Germanicus.** The lovely gardens of **Château de la Roche-Courbon** make a pleasant excursion 16 kilometres (10 miles) north-west of town.

Cognac

21,C2

The world-famous tipple is distilled privately from white-wine grapes in surrounding vineyards, but you can visit major manufacturers along the riverside **port** to observe the all-important blending and bottling (details from the local tourist office).

You'll notice that the town's houses have been blackened by a microscopic fungus nurtured by the alcohol fumes. Nobody complains. The Dutch developed the great drink as *brandewijn*, which English merchants dubbed brandy. It is the latter who give the supreme accolade of V.S.O.P.—"Very Superior Old Pale."

The rich decoration on the Romanesque façade of Poitiers' church of Notre-Dame-la-Grande reflects the Byzantine and Oriental influences brought back from the Crusades. The corner turrets formed by a bundle of shafts with a cone-shaped pinnacle became a characteristic feature of the Poitou region, spread through the Périgord and reappeared in the 19th century on Paris's Sacré-Cœur.

Pyrenees
26-27,B-E2-;28,AB3

The mountains that form France's natural barrier with Spain present for the most part a landscape of gentle rolling greenery, in marked contrast to the more formidable Alps. Snow-capped peaks are few and distant, and rugged "moonscapes" an exception. Even the mountain streams tend more to the babbling brook than the turbulent torrent. The coastal resorts range from the venerable aristocratic playground of Biarritz to the picturesque fishing port of Saint-Jean-de-Luz.

Inland, tourism is less developed, but cross-country skiing is greatly favoured. As a result, the mountain scenery is unspoiled by pylons and chair lifts. The Pyrenees are ideal for hiking and camping, one of the rare regions still open to "discovery".

Biarritz
26,B2

Anyone feeling nostalgic will appreciate the patina of faded grandeur of this resort, where Queen Victoria once promenaded along the front, Bismarck fell madly in love with the wife of a Russian ambassador, and the Prince of Wales took care of all the others.

Today, hortensias and tamarisks still ornament the seafront gardens. But the **Grande Plage** is no longer considered a hazard, unlike in 1900 when it was known

---

King Pong

It has often been told that his grandfather, determined to make a man of the future Henri IV as fast as possible, rubbed the new-born babe's lips with a clove of garlic and a few drops of the local Jurançon wine. The garlic habit stuck, and Henri, indefatigable horseman and infrequent bather, made a point of honour of cultivating a pungent body odour as a badge of virility. On the rare occasions when he slept with his own wife, who did care for personal hygiene, she complained she had to change the sheets two or three times a night.

---

as the *Plage des Fous* (Madmen's Beach). And fewer suicidal shots ring out from the casinos. The Villa Eugénie, from which the wife of Napoleon III made Biarritz fashionable, has become the **Hôtel du Palais**, an extravagant monument of idle luxury where the barmen tell you stories of the heiresses who seduced their grandfathers. Dare all and take tea beside the fantastic swimming pool.

The easy beach walk is from the lighthouse of **Cap Saint-Martin** (good view of the Pyrenees) out to the rugged **Rocher de la Vierge**. Beyond, at the foot of impressive cliffs, the big waves of the Plage de la Côte des Basques are more suitable for expert surfers and windsurfers than for desultory bathers.

When you're a little sun-silly, cool off at the aquarium of the **Musée de la Mer**. Or take a pleasant day trip to nearby **Bayonne** where the **Musée Basque**, in a 16th-century mansion, offers a valuable introduction to the folklore of the region.

Saint-Jean-de-Luz
26,A2

Less famous than Biarritz, this charming little fishing village has converted from whale to tuna (tunny) and anchovy, and similarly has small-scale but delightful attractions around its sheltered **harbour.** The cafés, galleries and boutiques are lively, the artist's colony not at all phony and the timbered houses of the shipbuilders' old **Quartier de la Barre** tastefully preserved.

The town's great claim to fame is the wedding of Louis XIV to the Spanish Infanta Maria Theresa in 1660; the houses that lodged them, **Maison de Louis XIV** and **Maison de l'Infante**, still stand by the port. The austere exterior of the 15th-century **Eglise Saint-Jean-Baptiste**, where the wedding was celebrated, doesn't prepare you for the characteristic Basque ornament inside: carved oak galleries to separate the classes of worshippers on three sides of a single nave, with polychrome wooden vaulting and a grandiose three-tiered gilded and crimson Baroque altar.

Pays Basque   26,B2-3

The fierce regional pride of the Basques is nourished in the most serene and restful landscape imaginable. Amid sunny valleys and rolling green hills, their gabled houses are immaculately maintained, gleaming white, set off by russet brown timbering. The Basques are as pious as the Bretons, and decorate the timbered interiors of their churches with meticulous carpentry.

From Saint-Jean-de-Luz, take the D918 south to **Ascain**. Its village square is surrounded by handsome 17th-century houses, and there's a typical wooden-galleried church. A rack railway at Col de Saint-Ignace carries you 900 metres (2,950 feet) up to the top of **La Rhune** for an exhilarating view of the Atlantic Ocean and the western Pyrenees.

With its pretty forest and warm hospitality, **Sare** is a favourite stop for gourmets and hikers—or a healthy combination of the two. You can measure the villagers' religious fervour by the grand Baroque altar in the church. And there's no more attractive demonstration of the Basques' independent-minded nature than the main street of **Aïnhoa**, where each sturdy-beamed whitewashed house is of a different height, jutting out at a different angle. The church, too, is worth visiting for the gilded timbers of its choir.

Saint-Jean-Pied-de-Port became important in the Middle Ages as the last stage before crossing into Spain on one of the main routes of pilgrimage to Santiago de Compostela. Follow the pilgrims' path around the **ramparts**, up a stairway through Porte Saint-Jacques to the **Ville Haute**. Note the charming red sandstone houses along the **Rue de la Citadelle** leading to an old bridge across the Nive river (good fishing), with a pretty view of the town's Gothic church. For the panorama across the Nive valley, climb up to the **citadel** which Louis XIV had built to fend off a potential Spanish invasion.

Leave the D933 at Larceveau to cut east across the **Col d'Osquich**, delightful walking and picnic country with a con-

stant view of the Pyrenean peaks to the south. End your tour of the Pays Basque at **Oloron-Sainte-Marie**, with a visit to its 13th-century **Eglise Sainte-Marie**, notable for the remarkable sculpture of medieval life on its Romanesque portal in white Pyrenees marble.

Don't Put All Your Basques In One Exit

The origins of this people settled on the Spanish and French sides of the Pyrenees, in the old kingdom of Navarre, remain a mystery. Their language is known to be older than the invasion of the Indo-Europeans and is still spoken in the mountains.

The 80,000 French Basques are less militant than their 600,000 Spanish cousins, but they lovingly cultivate the traditional arts, particularly their songs and dances, imbued with a strange melancholy passion. In times of hardship, to avoid the scattering of the family wealth, one child was designated heir to the house and land, not necessarily the eldest, while the others emigrated, most often to the Americas. The Basque ball-game of *pelota* turns up around Miami, for instance, as *jai alai*.

Pau   27,C2

The town holds a special place in French hearts as the birthplace of their beloved Henri IV in 1553. More recently, after their victorious campaigns against the French in the Pyrenees, the Duke of Wellington's veterans appreciated its balmy climate and retired there to make it something of a British colony. The British provided two mayors—Taylor and O'Quinn—and left their mark with the country's first golf club, horse racing and fox hunting, all still going strong.

Today, the **Château de Pau**, more Renaissance palace than fortress, heavily restored in the 19th century, remains an interesting museum of Gobelins tapestries and paraphernalia from the early life of the country's most popular king. Difficult to distinguish legend from fact in the life of this lusty womanizer. But it's doubtful whether Henri IV actually did sleep in the great tortoiseshell said to be his cradle.

Stroll along the terrace at the foot of the château, known as the **Boulevard des Pyrénées,** for the region's most spectacular view of the snow-capped peaks lining the southern horizon like a white crystal necklace. The chief treasure of the **Musée des Beaux-Arts** is a fascinating Degas, *The New Orleans Cotton Exchange,* but it also has an important Spanish collection: El Greco, Ribera and Zurbarán.

Lourdes *27,C2-3*

Ever since Bernadette Soubirous, 14-year-old daughter of a local miller, saw the Virgin Mary in 1858 at a grotto on the western edge of town, millions of pilgrims flock here every year for the healing powers of its waters. They include thousands of halt, lame and blind who, if they are not all cured, at least draw solace from the town's all-pervasive spirituality. Centre of attraction is the **Massabielle grotto,** site of the miraculous spring that Bernadette scratched from the ground. Three churches have been built around it to hold the faithful. The millhouse where Bernadette was born, **Moulin de Boly,** has also become a popular shrine.

Saint-Bertrand-de-Comminges *27,D3*

Pleasant detour off the Pau–Toulouse road, this fortified hilltop town has a fine Romanesque-Gothic **cathedral** that merits an extended visit. Inside, the superb 16th-century wooden sculptures of the **choir stalls** make up a cheerful compendium of Pyrenees characters, high and low. Look out, too, for the Renaissance pulpit and organ (recitals throughout the summer). The open Romanesque arcades allow the peaceful little **cloister** to take full advantage of the mountain backdrop —notice the four Apostles carved in the middle of the western arcade.

Luchon *27,D3*

We're not far from the Spanish frontier way up in the Pyrenees at one of the smartest thermal resorts in the region. Eighty springs provide sulphuric waters

at 22 °C (71.6 °F) or more. Teachers, public speakers, lawyers, singers, politicians (who sometimes perhaps overindulge the treatment) come here to look after their vocal chords and respiratory ailments in the flowery, well-ordered spa. The rest of the time, they hike—or, for the less energetic, drive—around the beautiful valleys of the region. Skiers prefer **Superbagnères;** so, in summer, do hanggliders.

*B*eyond the green pastures of the Basque Country, the snow-capped Pyrenees beckon, but after a lunch of the spicy local Basque cuisine and heady Jurançon wine, the balmy air is more likely to tempt you to take a siesta under a tree. The lamb here is especially succulent and try the sheep's milk cheese (fromage de brebis), *too.*

Midi-Pyrénées

27,DE2; 28-29,A-D1-2

The three (or really four) musketeers of Gascony aptly epitomize the region's highly independent-minded people. In the Middle Ages, it had taken a full-scale crusade to crush the militant Cathar heresy centred around Albi, Toulouse and Carcassonne, leaving a legacy of castle-like red-brick churches or massive fortifications.

Toulouse

28,B2

Centre of the national aerospace industry, with a vigorous local culture and bright and breezy street life, the city has an infectious enthusiasm to it. The charm works quickly if you hang out at the cafés on **Place Wilson** or shop in the boutiques in the nicely refurbished old houses of the **Rue des Changes** and **Rue Saint-Rome**, and the second-hand book shops around the church of Saint-Sernin.

The red brick of its major monuments and old houses, the dominant building material of the region, has won Toulouse the name *la ville rose*. The structural prowess of its architects in this medium can be seen in the magnificent 11th-century **Basilique Saint-Sernin**, a true masterpiece among France's Romanesque churches. On the south side of the church, note the 12th-century **Porte Miègeville** and the vigorous sculpture of the Apostles gazing up at the Ascension of Jesus on the tympanum.

Dedicated to the first bishop of Toulouse, the church served as a major gathering place for the pilgrimage to Santiago de Compostela, which explains the need for such a vast nave and the eight doors to let the masses in and out. Be sure to see the seven beautiful 11th-century marble **bas-reliefs** on the wall of the ambulatory beyond the choir. They portray

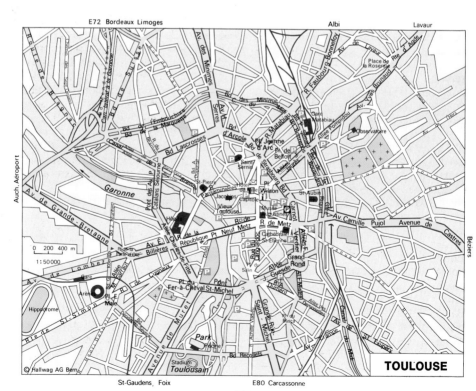

TOULOUSE

Jesus triumphant, flanked by angels and two apostles.

L'Eglise des Jacobins, burial place of philosopher and theologian Thomas Aquinas, is a Gothic fortress-church comparable to Albi's cathedral, with a noble tower and elegant twin-columned **cloister**. For years it suffered many indignities, even serving as a stable for Napoleon's artillery corps. Modern restoration has retrieved the polychrome beauty of its interior—subtle dark reds, pink and buff—illuminated by the 20th-century stained glass. The relics of Thomas Aquinas are kept beneath the altar.

The town's civic pride is given concrete expression in the grand Gothic and Renaissance houses of merchants who made their fortune in woad for the textile industry. They proclaimed their success with the highest tower they could build. The **Hôtel de Bernuy** (1, Rue Gambetta), now a high school, reveals its splendours once you are inside the gates. The first courtyard has a monumental Renaissance stone loggia and arcade, while a second courtyard is in traditional red brick and boasts an octagonal tower for its staircase. At the equally splendid **Hôtel d'Assézat**, set back from the Rue de Metz and home of various scholarly academies, you can climb the lanterned tower for a panoramic **view** of the city.

At the corner of Rue de Metz and Rue d'Alsace-Lorraine, the **Musée des Augustins** houses in a converted medieval monastery one of the richest collections of religious sculpture in France—treasures recovered from the cloister of Saint-Sernin and the monastery of Notre-Dame de la Daurade, both destroyed in the 19th century, and from the cathedral of Saint-Etienne, reduced today to an ungainly hodge-podge. Among the Romanesque sculptures, look out for King David tuning his harp and the death of John the Baptist. Most important of the Gothic pieces is a Madonna and Child known as *Notre-Dame-de-Grâce*. The paintings in the converted church include works by Rubens, Van Dyck and Murillo.

Auch   27,D2

Two hundred steps lead from the lower to the upper town, that beams down on the Gers river. Capital of Gascony, Auch has—predictably—a statue to the region's most famous son, d'Artagnan. In fact, Dumas based *his* musketeer on Charles de Baez, who hailed from the nearby château de Castelmore. Above the town towers the **Cathédrale Sainte-Marie**, boasting a twin-towered Renaissance façade. The real joy, however, lies inside: the 113 wooden stalls carved with more than 1,500 biblical and mythical figures, sculpted with vivid detail. Started in the early 16th century, they took some 50 years to complete—three generations of wood-carvers. Equally striking are the **stained-glass windows** by Arnaud de Moles. The cathedral's great 1694 **organ** built by Jean de Joyeuse, comes into its own during the Auch musical festival.

Carcassonne   28,C2

This is the town for all who like fairytale castles. It has served as a fortress for the Gallo-Romans, Visigoths, Franks and medieval French; you can see layers of their masonry in the ramparts.

You'll get your best overall view of the town from the *autoroute*—most dramatic with the night-time illuminations. Try to slow down without causing a traffic jam. Most people park on the east side of the old town *(la Cité)* and walk over the drawbridge of the **Porte Narbonnaise**, convenient for the *syndicat d'initiative* and the souvenir shops of Rue Cros-Mayrevieille.

But you'll get a better feel for the medieval atmosphere of a fortified town, its ramparts and lookout towers, if you park on the west side, by the church of Saint-Gimer, and walk up around the old **Château Comtal**. After a look at the ancient sarcophagi and medieval sculpture in the castle's little museum, take the guided tour around the parapets.

If the battlements and pepperpot towers, the dungeons, moats and draw-

Linked to the Garonne river, the 240-km. Canal du Midi enables you to sail clear across south-west France from the Mediterranean to the Atlantic. Brainchild of a Béziers tax collector,

Pierre-Paul Riquet, who persuaded Louis XIV to start construction in 1666, the canal still has many of the original locks, beautifully designed works of art in their own right.

bridges strike you as a bit too much, put some of it down to the romantic imagination of Viollet-le-Duc. Much is authentic, but the great 19th-century architect who performed the restoration work had a somewhat fanciful idea of feudal architecture and stuck on all kinds of frills and furbelows if he lacked the original plans. The most blatant example of this is the Romanesque-Gothic **Basilique Saint-Nazaire**, which Viollet-le-Duc thought was originally part of the fortifications, so he added battlements to the west façade. Inside the church are some fine 13th- and 14th-century **stained-glass windows** and sculptures in the choir. Summer concerts are held in the amphitheatre beside the church.

Castres   28,C2

Like much of the area, the wool-weaving town of Castres was embroiled in the violent religious struggles of the mid-16th century. Today, the older houses of this busy industrial town reflect their handsome façades in the Agout river. The major attraction is the albeit slightly musty **Musée Goya,** housed in the former bishopric, now Hôtel de Ville. The paintings, particularly the huge 1816 *Junta of the Philippines,* and some 80 caustic prints from the series the *Caprichos* make Castres an important stop. Then stroll round the formal gardens of the bishopric laid out by Versailles' André Le Nôtre.

Albi   28,C2

This serene and cheerful town, built like Toulouse with red brick and so known as *Albi la Rouge,* was once the scene of brutal religious persecution.

The grandiose Gothic **Cathédrale Sainte-Cécile** bears witness to that turmoil. In the Middle Ages, Albi provided a controversial refuge for the Cathare "heretics", also called Albigeois or Albigenses, whose austere doctrines of simple opposition of good and evil were an im-

plicit reproach to the luxurious life of the Church in Rome. In 1208, Pope Innocent III sent a military crusade to wipe out the movement that had spread to Toulouse, Carcassonne and Béziers. Twenty-five years later, the first Inquisition was established to take care of the remnants. To impress the citizens of Albi with the reasserted power of the Roman Church, the cathedral was built in 1282 as a red brick "fortress of the faith", massive enough to resist any heresy.

While the square tower reinforces the cathedral's castle-like character, the stone canopied **porch** makes a more decorative contrast. Inside, the ornamental effect is carried further with the Flamboyant Gothic stone tracery and statuary of the choir's magnificent **rood screen**. Most of the original statues were destroyed when the "fortress" succumbed to the Revolution of 1789, but Judith on the south side and Esther on the north survived.

In the bishop's 13th-century residence, Palais de la Berbie, the **Musée Toulouse-Lautrec** honours the painter (who was born in Albi in 1864) with the country's largest collection of his works and sketchbooks. You can follow the artist's tragic life from the first paintings of his aristocratic youth—a self-portrait, his mother, a ride in a dog-cart—to his brothel days in Montmartre with *Au salon de la rue des Moulins, A la toilette,* and the Paris music hall stars Jane Avril and Yvette Guilbert.

Cordes   28,C2

Its splendid isolation high above the Cérou valley made it a natural choice for the Cathars' fortified refuge built by the Count of Toulouse in 1222. The heretics prospered in the textile and leather trades, and today the town's remoteness still keeps it delightfully unspoiled for a new race of "refugees"—weavers, engravers, painters and sculptors. They work in the grey-pink stone Gothic houses in and around the steeply sloping **Rue Droite**. Take a tour of the **ramparts** along the Chemin de Ronde.

Rodez
28,C1

Out of the way but worth the detour (90 kilometres [56 miles] north-east of Albi), this hilltop town boasts a fine fortress-style cathedral. Note in particular its 74-metre (243-foot) belltower, a superb example of Flamboyant Gothic, and inside, the purity of line and proportion. Other points of interest are the **Holy-Sepulchre altar,** the vast **rood screen** and the **organ.** Around the Place du Bourg and the cathedral, numerous old houses and medieval mansions, the Maison d'Armagnac, Maison Benoît and Maison de l'Annonciation, give an appealing picture of an affluent town in Renaissance times.

Conques
28,C2

One of the "essential" pilgrimage stops on the way south to Santiago de Compostela, the village derives its name from the conch-shaped hollow formed here by the ravines at the confluence of the Ouche and Dourdou rivers. Far from "everywhere", Conques' strategic importance meant that it was endowed with treasures out of proportion to its modest size.

Solidly embedded in the hillside rock, the ochre stone of the superb 11th-century Romanesque **Eglise Sainte-Foy** is best seen in the late afternoon sun. This is especially true for the splendidly sculpted **tympanum** of the Last Judgment over the western entrance. With his raised right arm, Jesus enthroned blesses the saved, while casting his left arm down towards the demons and their damned. In the sober interior, unornamented pillars accentuate the elevation of the nave, but in the northern aisle and transept are some **sculpted capitals** of St. Foy's martyrdom, the Annunciation and, near the high altar, Abraham's sacrifice of Isaac. Originally behind the altar but now housed in the old cloister, along with other reliquaries of the 9th and 10th century, is the church's greatest treasure, the **statue-reliquary of St. Foy,** a seated wooden sculpture covered with gold leaf and jewels and said to contain the martyr's skull. The mystery of her decidedly unfeminine air was recently solved by art-historians ascertaining that the statue's head is in fact that of a 4th-century Roman emperor.

Get a view of the Ouche valley from the church-cemetery and spare time to stroll among the silvery stone-tile-roofed houses clustered around the village's 16th-century Château d'Humières.

Pézenas
29,D2

Molière made two stays at Pézenas where he was much appreciated by the Prince de Conti, Duke of Languedoc. The playwright lodged in **Gely's barber shop.**

Back behind the cobblestoned Place Gambetta, take a look inside the splendid *hôtels* of the town's 16th- and 17th-century heyday. Look out in particular for the **Maison des Consuls** with its fine façade and staircase, the **Hôtel d'Alfonce,** the **Hôtel de Lacoste,** and the **Tribunal de Commerce.** Jacques Cœur, the financier from Bourges (see p. 199), had his *hôtel* in this busy trade centre (the town grew wealthy with a liberal tax system). **Rue de la Foire** emerges straight from the Middle Ages. Unusual is the 16th-century Jewish **ghetto** still enclosed by its walls.

Monastic Mole

Off the beaten track with infertile lands, things were quiet for Conques' Benedictine abbey in the 9th century. What it needed to perk things up was a good religious relic. So Ariviscus was dispatched to Agen, famous for its prunes and the remains of St. Foy, a Christian girl martyred in 303 for refusing to sacrifice to pagan gods. Ariviscus joined the monastery and went underground for 10 years until he got the job of guarding the saint's tomb. While his brother monks were at supper in the refectory, he smashed Foy's sarcophagus and whisked her bones off to Conques. Miraculous powers attributed to the relics attracted thousands of pilgrims, their donations paying for the statue-reliquary and a new basilica to house the traffic.

Gorges du Tarn

29,D1

The limestone plateaux south of the Massif Central, known locally as *causses,* are split by dramatic ravines and canyons, none more spectacular than the 50 kilometres (30 miles) of the Tarn valley from pleasant **Florac** meandering downriver to Le Rozier. Drive along the D907 *bis* to take in the landscape of broad canyons narrowing down to the river below and, along the way, picturesque villages like **Ispagnac** and **Castelbouc** carved out of the rock beneath the ruins of medieval fortresses.

Sainte-Enimie nestles in a green "oasis" of vineyards and groves of almond and peach trees. Wander around the old town and its **Halle au Blé** (corn market) and take in the fine view of the valley from the monastery. You can rent canoes here to paddle down to the rock-strewn **Pas du Souci,** a good place to stop as it does not mean "no worry" but rather the opposite for any but the hardiest canoer. If you prefer somebody else to do the work, hire a punt *(barque)* with boatsman at **La Malène** through the Société Coopérative des Bâteliers des Gorges du Tarn. An all-in fee covers four passengers for a 90-minute round-trip, return by taxi. Glide through the towering cliffs of **Les Détroits** (straits), ready to topple down on you, to the ruddy rocks of the **Cirque des Baumes,** with trees and bushes sprouting from impossible niches.

At **Le Rozier,** energetic ramblers will enjoy the well marked hiking-trail that starts out from behind the church up to the aptly named lookout, **Belvédère du Vertige,** giving you a dizzying view (from behind a protective barrier) down a sheer 400-metre (1,320-foot) drop to the river.

From here on to **Millau,** a former glove-making centre that has hit upon hard times, the landscape loses some of its drama when the Tarn meets up with the Jonte. However, by following the D996 in the other direction, and wending your way along the Gorges de la Jonte to **Meyrueis,** you'll find scenery scarcely less exhilarating.

Languedoc–Roussillon

29,DE1-3

This is the land of tough-and-tumbling rugby. But after the match, *camaraderie* knows no bounds, much enhanced by a bottle or two of full-bodied Madiran or robust Roussillon. In summer, enjoy the genteel pleasures of the fine arts at Montpellier or scrummage on the beaches of the Côte du Languedoc.

Montpellier

29,E2

This is a lively university town at the Mediterranean end of the South-West, with a good TGV link back to Paris.

The centre of city life—theatre, cafés and cinemas—is around the airy, bustling **Place de la Comédie.** For a quieter coffee, try the pretty **Place du Marché-aux-Fleurs,** shaded by plane trees around a Henry Moore sculpture. You'll discover handsome 17th- and 18th-century **mansions** on the Rue des Trésoriers de France and Rue des Trésoriers de la Bourse, with imposing stairways in the inner courtyards.

The **Musée Fabre** (13, Rue Montpellieret) is admired for its important works by Courbet and Delacroix, as well as Veronese and Zurbarán.

For many, the most attractive spot in town is the classical late 17th-century **Promenade du Peyrou,** spacious gardens with triumphal arch, equestrian statue of Louis XIV and, on a mound at the far end, a hexagonal *château d'eau* (water tower) that looks more like a love temple, providing a fine view south to the Mediterranean and north to the Cévennes mountains.

Cévennes

29,DE1-2

This powerful mountain range provided just the cover needed for the *Camisards,* the Huguenot resistants brutally suppressed in 1704 and vividly documented at the **Musée du Désert** near Anduze. It also offers one of the most beautiful (but difficult) drives in France, the **Corniche**

des Cévennes, from Florac over to Saint-Jean du Gard, about 50 kilometres (30 miles). Robert Louis Stevenson donkeyed through this glorious but secretive countryside in 1878; organized (donkey) tours follow the same route.

Côte du Languedoc   29,DE2

The long fine sandy beaches of the Mediterranean coast south of Montpellier have been developed since the 1960s as a whole new series of resorts for popular tourism. **La Grande Motte** was created lock, stock and barrel in 1967, offering holidaymakers horse-riding, sailing-schools and every imaginable water sport. Pyramidal blocks of hotels and holiday-apartments surround the port and 4 kilometres (2½ miles) of beaches, while holiday-villages of more intimate Provençal villas and campsites cluster around broad fishing ponds.

Sète has 300 more years of charm—unpretentious charm—to its credit, especially around the **harbour** where the nautical joust in August is its proudest tradition. The **Musée Paul-Valéry** celebrates the great modern poet along with popular singer Georges Brassens, both local boys buried here. Climb the **Mont Saint-Clair** (175 metres/574 feet) for a splendid view west to the Pyrenees and, out over the Mediterranean, east to the distant Alpilles of Provence. The town's beaches stretch clear down to **Cap d'Agde,** another newly created resort on a promontory at the mouth of the Hérault river. Besides sailing, tennis is the big sport here—and nudism at **Port Nature.**

Narbonne   29,D2-3

Until the Aude river's change of course turned its bay into a pond in the 14th century, the ancient capital of Roman Provence was a major seaport. Now the distribution centre for the local Corbières and Minervois wines some 12 kilometres (7½ miles) from the sea, it maintains a classical Mediterranean atmosphere in the old town around the 13th- and 14th-

century **Cathédrale Saint-Just.** Left unfinished because town-fathers did not want to destroy the ramparts to make way for a nave and transept, this imposing edifice boasts a soaring choir with magnificent flying buttresses worthy of the best Gothic cathedrals of the north. In the **Palais des Archevêques** (archbishops' palace), an archaeological museum covers the region's history from the Stone Age through its years of Roman glory. A collection of paintings in the luxurious apartments on the second floor includes works by Tintoretto, Veronese and Jordaens.

South-west of town, off the A61 *autoroute,* the **Abbaye de Fontfroide** is tucked away in a beautiful setting of cypresses and lovingly tended flower gardens in the Corbières valley. The Gothic cloister and sober abbey-church of yellow-pink sandstone (abandoned in the Revolution) offer a rare moment of meditation for the tired tourist-pilgrim.

Perpignan   29,D3

In this most Spanish of French towns, once capital of the kingdom of Majorca and part of France only since 1659, the atmosphere in its cafés along the **Quai Vauban** and around the **Place Arago** is almost as Catalan as Barcelona. In the **Castillet,** 14th-century fortress gate-tower and town symbol, the folklore and history of Catalonia are celebrated in the **Casa Pairal** museum. Look for the *Croix aux Outrages*, a primitive crucifixion displaying the instruments of Christ's suffering.

You can visit the Majorcan kings' severe but handsome **royal palace** now ensconced in the 16th-century citadel. The **Musée Hyacinthe-Rigaud,** 16, Rue de l'Ange, has a superb collection of Spanish-Moorish ceramics dating back to the 12th century, but also modern works by Maillol and Picasso. Fans of Surrealist painter Salvador Dalí make a pilgrimage to the remarkably unremarkable **railway station** to wonder why he called it the "centre of the world".

Côte Vermeille   *29,D3*

Literally the Vermilion Coast, this last enchanting gasp of the Pyrenees offers a rugged rocky shoreline, more ochre in colour than red. Orchards, vineyards and fragrant groves of eucalyptus and sea-pines add to the charm of the beaches.

With a population close to 250,000 in high summer, the tented villages of **Arge-lès-Plage** make it the self-proclaimed camping capital of Europe. More pop-ular with painters (in the past, Braque, Matisse and Derain), is the Catalan fish-ing-village of **Collioure**, with its lovely harbour divided into two ports by an old castle of the kings of Majorca. Stroll around the old **Mouré** district before visiting the 17th-century **church** with its nine gilded altarpieces, characteristic works of Catalan Baroque. The resort of **Banyuls** is famous for its sweet dessert wines and excellent fish.

S̀ète is France's most important Mediterranean fishing port—bringing in 139 different varieties of seafood. The fish is sold off by public auction (criée) at the harbour on Quai Général-Durand, where the Japanese are top customers for high-quality tunny (tuna) fish. Red mullet, sole, hog fish (rascasse), whiting, sea bass and every imaginable crustacean are also much in demand. As you might imagine, the quayside fish soup is divine.

How to Avoid an Overdose of Sightseeing

With such a weight of culture, of monuments and natural sights, it would be easy to forget that France is also a country where the good life is still to be enjoyed far from the châteaux and cathedrals. Sports are popular, the self-indulgent shopper is pampered, and night life is cultivated with a special care. Sightseeing is only the beginning of a visit to France.

Sports

After years of excessive attention to intellectual pursuits, the French have turned increasingly to outdoor sports. Everybody and his grandmother are out running, jumping, hiking and biking. For skiing and spectator sports, the most modern facilities have been installed, greatly enhanced by the Winter Games in the Savoie. The enormous diversity of climate and geography means that every imaginable kind of sport is available.

Jogging seems to have turned from fad to daily habit, and there's always a park or river bank where you can get away from the car fumes. Large hotels increasingly have saunas and gyms to complete your work-out. Paris organizes a spring marathon along the Seine and around the Bois de Boulogne.

No better sport than **hiking** to get the most out of the French countryside. Every little *syndicat d'initiative* can provide you with itineraries, many of them marked in red or blue on trees or lampposts along the trail. Good exercise without being exhausting, some of them are guided tours for botany or geology enthusiasts. More ambitious hikers can try the challenging routes known as *grandes randonnées* marked out through the Alps, the Pyrenees and the Lubéron mountains in Provence (details from the Fédération française de randonnées pédestres, 8, Avenue Marceau, 75008 Paris). Even for the most modest hike, be sure to equip yourself with proper footwear, not just skimpy tennis shoes. French manufacturers have specialized in lightweight boots for summer hiking to replace the heavy clodhoppers of old.

Mountaineering novices can get training through the Club alpin français (7, Rue La Boétie, 75008 Paris) while the club's local branches in resort towns of the Alps and Pyrenees dispense advice and information to experts and novices alike.

Whether your main means of transport is car, train or even boat, **cycling** is ideal for excursions. Take off into the hills on a bike rentable at some 250 railway stations throughout the country. It's an especially pleasant way to visit the vineyards of Champagne, Alsace or Burgundy.

Horse riding is a delight in the forests of the Ile-de-France and Brittany or around Pau in the Pyrenees, among many other possibilities. The *loisir–accueil*

(leisure and hospitality) department of major regional tourist offices can tell you where to rent a horse for the day. For a prolonged riding holiday with accommodation and meals included, write to the Association nationale pour le tourisme équestre, 15, Rue de Bruxelles, 75009 Paris.

For ecological reasons, **hunting** is declining in popularity these days, but the best "shoots" for experienced hunters (with a 48-hour licence from the local prefecture) are still available in Sologne, the Vosges and the Périgord. The season is generally from mid-September to the end of January.

Fishing is going as strong as ever: freshwater for trout and pike in the Annecy and Le Bourget lakes, trout, carp, shad and bream in the Burgundy rivers, the Dordogne, and tributaries of the Loire. Get your licence through the local

Galloping along the beaches of Cabourg is one of a hundred sporting delights in Normandy. The golf and sailing here are excellent, too, but the region's horses remain its special pride, from the grand old Percheron warhorses to the brilliant thoroughbreds on display at the yearling sales in Deauville.

société de pêche (fishing association). Sea fishing is better in the Atlantic than the Mediterranean. Good deep-sea expeditions are usually advertised down at the port, most notably along the Brittany coast and at La Rochelle.

Water sports are amply catered for. The Côte d'Azur has cleaned up most of its polluted beaches so that **swimming** is much safer there these days, but you'll find the Brittany and smaller Normandy resorts much less crowded. The pollution count is tested regularly, and the percentage is displayed at local town halls. Watch out for the occasional stinging jellyfish *(méduse)* in the Mediterranean. Be careful at some of the more secluded Atlantic beaches where there are no lifeguards on regular duty. Municipalities

---

Piglets and Pétanque

Perched on a borderline between sport and folklore, the grand Provençal game of *boules* or *pétanque* is the perfect expression of regional character. At a distance, all seems tranquil in the gravelly village square, where half a dozen or more convivial fellows lob heavy metal balls along a shady avenue of plane trees. But draw nearer and you'll discover a ferocious combat, in which the ambient good humour barely conceals the high passions fuelled by mutual scorn, recrimination and *pastis.*

The object of the game is quite simply to get the maximum number of balls as close as possible to a little wooden jack, the *cochonnet* (literally piglet). Good *boules*, each with a distinctive pattern of stripes, acquire the patina of medieval cannonballs. Players form teams of two *(doublettes)*, three *(triplettes)*, or four *(quadrettes)*. They may be meticulous *pointeurs*, aiming close to the jack, or debonair *tireurs*, bombing the opponent's ball out of the way. *Pétanque* is properly the short-distance game in which the player stands feet together at a mark in the gravel. In *la longue*, the players can take a couple of strides to build up momentum.

The most important piece of equipment is a piece of string, to determine the distance between the *boules* and the *cochonnet* and who pays the next round of *pastis.*

---

have excellent Olympic-size pools, and more and more hotels are catching up with the American habit.

The **windsurfing** craze has calmed down a little, but enthusiasts can still rent a board *(planche à voile)* in all the major resorts. Straight **surfing** is a strictly Atlantic sport, best at Biarritz.

Sailing continues to grow in popularity. If price is no object, you can hire a 30-metre vessel with ten-man crew down at Cannes or Antibes, and, on the Atlantic coast, at the equally well-equipped Saint-Malo, La Baule or La Rochelle. For those with their own boat, berths may be easier to find in Atlantic ports than on the Côte d'Azur. Inland, the great boating adventure is **canoeing**, particularly in the Périgord and the Ardèche. For details of nationwide facilities and a list of navigable rivers, write to the Fédération française de canoë-kayak, 17, Route de Vienne, 69007 Lyon.

Back on dry land, possibilities to play **tennis** are endless, so pack a racket. Tennis courts are hard surface, in municipal parks or attached to hotels. The latter can often help you with temporary membership to private clubs.

For **golf**, bring your own home club membership card for easier access to the best courses in the major seaside resorts —Le Touquet, Cabourg, Deauville, La Baule, Biarritz and Mandelieu (Cannes). Around Paris, there are international-class courses at Saint-Nom-la-Bretèche, Saint-Cloud, Chantilly and Fontainebleau.

Generally speaking, the Alps are best for downhill **skiing** *(descente)* and the Pyrenees for cross-country *(ski de fond)*. For the latter, you might also consider Corsica. The Berlitz *Ski Guide to France* will help you make your choice.

France, unlike Austria or Switzerland has little in the way of cozy chalets; its resorts are recent creations, designed to provide effective and efficient skiing and facilities, and are thus less strong on tradition and character—with a few outstanding exceptions, such as Megève and

Val d'Isère that both offer appealing village life to supplement activity on the slopes. These are best for families who want first-class ski schools for kids and other beginners. Write, too, to the Association des maires des stations de sports d'hiver, 6, Boulevard Haussmann, 75008 Paris, for a list of other mountain villages in the Alps, and also the Pyrenees, where hotel and skiing facilities are more modest but where village life is not completely submerged by ski and *après-ski*.

Excellent facilities, hi-tech equipment, the most challenging *pistes* and frenetic discos are found at the modern, highly-specialized stations, such as Flaine or Avoriaz, Tignes or Alpe d'Huez. Wherever you go for your skiing, if you're not travelling with children, try to go outside the school holidays.

Of the spectator sports, **bicycle racing** remains very popular. The Tour de France in July, with its grand finale along the Champs-Elysées in Paris, is as important as a Cup Final for English football or a World Series for American baseball. Each stage of the race, most strenuous and exciting in the Alps or Pyrenees, resembles a local festival with each village considering it a (highly lucrative) privilege to be blessed with the cavalcade of grimacing, groaning stars.

If **football** (soccer) is a national sport, with Bordeaux, Nantes and Paris regularly providing championship teams, **rugby** is at its best in the south-west—Béziers, Narbonne, Toulouse and Agen being among the most famous teams. For once, the rough and tumble are all on the field rather than among the vociferous but good-natured spectators.

Pelote is a Basque speciality, along the lines of squash, but played with a leather-bound ball hurled at the wall with an elongated basket-glove known as a *chistera*.

The Roman amphitheatres of Arles and Nîmes make dramatic settings for the annual summer **bullfights**.

Monte-Carlo has a major **tennis** tournament in May, important warm-up for the French Open at Paris's Roland-Garros Stadium in June, just before Wimbledon. See if your hotel concierge can get you tickets.

In **motor racing**, the most spectacular events, in late May or early June, are the Grand Prix at Monaco and the 24-hour race at Le Mans (a day trip from the Loire Valley or Normandy).

Horse-racing enthusiasts in Paris go to Auteuil for the steeplechase and Longchamp for flat racing, June and early October being the months for the great classics. Chantilly (in June) and Deauville (in August) claim equally prestigious events.

Shopping

To shop seriously in France, you need a clear plan of attack. Unless you're buying things you want to use during your vacation, such as clothes or sports equipment, it doesn't make sense to shop right at the beginning of the trip and have to lug the stuff around the country.

Paris is still a shopper's paradise, not only for the fashions, perfumes and other luxury goods for which it has always been famous, but also for a comprehensive selection of handicrafts and gourmet delicacies that at one time could be found only in the provinces. If possible, divide your Paris stay in two, the major part at the beginning, to see the town, with a couple more days at the end of the tour to do your shopping. Try to compare price and quality—you can't always be sure it will be cheaper "on the spot" than in Paris.

Paris: The Big Stores

The department stores best equipped for dealing with foreigners are Galeries Lafayette and Printemps, next door to each other on the Boulevard Haussmann. Both have hostesses to help non-French-speaking customers, as well as the convenience of grouping selections from the major designers in their clothes departments. The Galeries probably has the edge in the fashion and perfume departments, china and household goods, while Printemps leads in its lingerie and vast toy and adult gift departments.

For those who like dressing up in baker's overalls, waiter's jackets, butcher's aprons and plumber's pants, the Samaritaine at the Pont-Neuf has an enormous selection of professional uniforms—52 trades represented.

FNAC is a chain of breezy, new-style department stores (Rue de Rennes, Forum des Halles and Avenue Wagram) specializing in books, discount records, cameras, hi-fi, electronics and sports goods.

Fashion

These days, the fashion pendulum occasionally swings to New York, Rome or Tokyo, but the capital for all of them, the showplace for their talent, remains Paris. From the Right Bank, around the Rue du Faubourg-Saint-Honoré, the Avenues Montaigne and George-V and over to Place des Victoires and Les Halles, the *haute couture* houses and their *prêt-à-porter* (ready-to-wear) boutiques have spilled over to the Left Bank, around Saint-Germain-des-Prés.

Look out not only for the "old school" of Dior, Givenchy, Lanvin, Saint-Laurent, Ungaro and Louis Féraud, but the new generation of Gaultier, Mugler, Montana and their foreign competitors, Yamamoto, Issey Miyake, Valentino and Missoni—as well as the scores of cheaper satellite boutiques that turn out clever variations on the innovators' designs. For the designers' perfumes, you'll probably get a better deal in the duty-free shop at the airport, though the selection may not be as comprehensive as in the perfume departments of Printemps and Galeries Lafayette.

For leatherware, in addition to its fabled silk scarves, Hermès (Rue du Faubourg-Saint-Honoré) is an institution all on its own, catering for the well-heeled horseman, globetrotter and man-and-woman-about-town, with high-quality luggage, saddles, stirrups and boots, and the ultimate diary and address book.

While Paris fills practically every clothes need you can imagine, you might find good old-fashioned stuff out in the provinces—oilskins *(ciré)* or the sturdy windproof dufflecoat *(kabig)* in Brittany or a heavy woollen sweater *(chandail breton)*. And Saint-Tropez is still famous for sexy, imaginative casual wear.

Antiques

Astronomic prices for the genuine article should not frighten you away from antique-hunting in the exquisite Left Bank shops of Paris's 6th and 7th *arrondissements*. The Carré des Antiquaires, a little rectangle bounded by the Quai Voltaire and the Boulevard Saint-Germain, the Rue du Bac and the Rue des Saints-Pères, constitutes a veritable museum of ancient Egyptian and Chinese art, pre-Columbian, African and Polynesian, as well as Louis XV, Second Empire, Art nouveau and art déco. It has the advantage that here, you're allowed to touch the objects—and pay for breakages.

The prices are more manageable at the weekend **flea markets**, although many of their stalls are manned by professional antique dealers. The *Marché aux puces* of Saint-Ouen at Porte de Clignancourt (tough to park, but an easy walk from the Métro station) groups half a dozen markets. Vernaison specializes in musical instruments, lead soldiers, old toys, buttons, brass and tinware; Biron has mostly antique furniture; Malik is a great favourite with the young for its *Belle Epoque* dresses, World War I military uniforms, 1920s hats and an amazing assortment of Americana. Paul Bert might have that undiscovered masterpiece that every flea-market addict dreams of—but get there early, practically at dawn, before the professionals rummage among the unloading trucks. Jules Vallès is the smallest and cosiest, especially good for

Perfume

A Perfume Primer

In the perfume trade, contrary to the famous claim of Gertrude Stein, a rose is a rose is not only a rose, but also a nose.

A multimillion-dollar business depends on the olfactory organ of experts who daily sniff out the ideal blend of roses and other flowers with various natural and artificial elements for bottling as an essence of seduction.

If the price of catching a partner's fancy, even duty free, is so high, blame the delicate and costly process of producing a perfume's essential oils and "absolutes" (concentrated flower oils). It takes two tons of rose petals to provide just one kilo of rose essence. The scent is distilled and condensed, often producing a "natural" fragrance only when recombined with chemicals.

How it's done

Let's start in the Provençal fields around Grasse, France's perfume capital. Masses of blossoms—mainly May rose, jasmine, orange blossom, lavender and lily of the valley—are gathered from early spring to late autumn.

Besides petals, manufacturers collect essences from across the world, sandalwood from India and Australia, bergamot (an inedible citrus-like fruit) from southern Italy, nutmeg, ginger and vetiver (an aromatic grass) from the Caribbean or the Orient. Add to these the perfume's musk, an animal element—castoreum from the beaver or ambergris from the sperm whale—which on its own is quite foul-smelling but acts as a fixative to provide greater lasting power.

Enter the noses. Adopting a resolutely musical jargon, perfume-maestros in white lab coats potter around a gamut of fragrances in a work area known as the "organ" or "keyboard" (like chefs who call their range of kitchen-stoves the "piano"). With an array of pincers holding slim strips of blotting-paper *(mouillettes)*, they dip into the assembled essences, seeking a new harmony, eliminating a discord, daring a subtle syncopation, working towards the effect of a subdued sonata or bold concerto.

For the perfect harmony of ingredients, the nose is alert first to the "top note", what you smell as the perfume comes out of the bottle, then the main theme or "heart note" revealed after a few minutes, culminating in the "end" or "base note" that underlines the whole.

The right scent for you
All the noses and roses and beavers and sperm whales are as nothing compared with the ultimate factor, the individual skin chemistry of the customer. A perfume that creates an overpowering cloud on one woman may have an exquisitely delicate impact on another.

Women who like to play it safe stick to one perfume, a personal signature. But just as clothes change from summer to winter or even time of day, so there's a scent for each season, for morning as well as evening.

Summer scents appropriate for women of all ages are sporty, flowery, light, notable for fruity and citrus tones, for vetiver and freshness. The headier, lingering smells such as Yves Saint-Laurent's *Opium* or Guerlain's *Shalimar* are better worn in winter, but even these have a lighter impact if you buy the fragrance as *eau de cologne* or *eau de toilette*.

To find the most appropriate scent, seek advice in a small perfume boutique—not a department store where each brand has its own counter, making it difficult to compare one with another. Apply fragrance to pulse points like the wrist and neck.

Smell it immediately, for that "top note", but don't decide till you smell it again a few minutes later, for the "heart note". If it's at all possible, a man buying perfume for a woman without knowing her favourite brand should seek out among the sales-women her closest physical type for the crucial test.

Don't try more than three samples at once, otherwise your nose will get confused. Narrow the field to one of the basic fragrance groups: single floral, floral bouquet, spicy citrus, Oriental, modern blend, green, woody-mossy, fruity, amber, leather. (If your French can't handle it, check in your local perfume shop at home which brands fit each category before heading for France.)

Use it. As with stylish clothing, perfume shouldn't be hoarded for Sunday best. In fact, if you don't use it within a reasonable time of opening, it might lose or change its fragrance.

Keep it in a cool, dark place. Light and heat create harmful oxydation. Some experts recommend the refrigerator, but only if you can keep the smoked salmon and Chanel well apart and hermetically sealed.

Be careful when applying perfume to certain fabrics or furs. It might alter their colour.

Art nouveau lamps, military souvenirs, theatre costumes and old dolls.

The **bouquinistes** (second-hand book sellers) along the Seine, most of them between the Pont Saint-Michel and the Pont des Arts, still turn up the odd rarity in periodicals as well as old books, along with a lot of weird stuff from the period of the German occupation.

In the provinces, apart from what you come across by chance in little out-of-the-way villages, your best bets for antiques are in historic cities like Strasbourg, Colmar, Dijon, Rouen, Lyon or Avignon. The Loire Valley has good flea markets, especially at Angers on Saturdays.

Household Goods

In a country where cooking is so highly prized, kitchenware is obviously particularly good. The old Paris food-market district of Les Halles has held on to its restaurant-supply shops, offering an astonishing array of pots and pans, kitchen knives and other utensils at the venerable Dehillerin (18, Rue Coquillière) and MORA (13, Rue Montmartre).

Normandy and Brittany are both known for their rustic pottery, while Gien, in the Loire Valley, and Limoges (the only reason for stopping there) produce excellent chinaware. In the back country behind the Côte d'Azur, Vallauris is a major centre for ceramics and nearby Biot for glassware (see p. 253). If you don't want to risk breakables, consider the superb Provençal olive-wood salad bowls and fruit plates that you'll find in the Lubéron.

Gourmet Delicacies

While you can probably get almost everything in Paris, food and wine are things which it's more fun and more often (but not always) cheaper to get where they're produced. Every region has a wealth of specialities, well displayed and easy to find.

But if you do prefer to do your food shopping in Paris, the most famous luxury grocery shop is Fauchon (26, Place de la Madeleine). Despite its aristocratic reputation, the service is friendly, courteous and multilingual. Salespeople only become (mildly) annoyed if you suggest they might not have what you're looking for. You'll also find groceries specializing in regional delicacies, with self-explanatory names like *Aux produits de Bretagne* or *Aux produits de Bourgogne*. There are street markets all over town, particularly good if you want to take some cheese or sausage back on the last day. The most colourful are on the Rue Mouffetard, Place Maubert and Rue de Seine on the Left Bank and Rue des Martyrs and Avenue du Président-Wilson on the Right Bank.

For wine, the best bargains in Paris are at the Nicolas chain. One of the largest selections is at Lucien Legrand (1, Rue de la Banque)—bankers and stock-brokers being notorious connoisseurs. The more adventurous will want to stalk the vineyards of Alsace, Burgundy, the Loire Valley and Bordeaux. You'll get a better price on Champagne in Reims or Epernay than back in Paris.

The strong alcohols may be better bargains at the duty-free shop, but the choice will be limited. Cognac and Armagnac, and other local *liqueurs* and *eaux-de-vie* are best bought in their region.

Entertainment

After something of a lull in the seventies, the performing arts are booming again in France. The cultural decentralization has worked faster than the political. While Paris is still the undisputed major focus for theatre and music, you'll find plenty going on in the provinces, particularly in summer when even the tiniest Provençal or Périgord village stages some kind of arts festival.

There's something for every kind of brow, from the highest to the unashamed low.

Paris After Dark

The Paris night scene has lost none of the glitter and bounce that Toulouse-Lautrec made famous at the turn of the century. The Moulin Rouge (Place Blanche) still puts on one of the great boisterous floor shows of Europe. The rest of Pigalle is indeed sleazy, but it always was. Exceptions to the rule, Chez Michou (Rue des Martyrs) remains a witty cabaret of talented transvestite imitators, and the Folies-Bergère (Rue Richer), the music hall that launched the careers of Joséphine Baker, Maurice Chevalier and Mistinguett, is still going strong.

Over on the Champs-Elysées, the Lido continues the grand tradition of girls wearing nothing but feathers and balloons, while the Crazy Horse Saloon (Avenue George-V) relies just on cunning patterns of light to clothe the most beautiful naked ladies in Paris (very few of them actually French).

On the Left Bank there are two floor

Festivals

Although small villages in the religious regions of Brittany, Alsace and the Basque country still celebrate the old Christian festivals, folklore and tradition have dwindled since World War II. In their place, there has been a veritable explosion of arts festivals, drawing on local, national and international talent, performed in the wonderful historic settings of palaces, châteaux, cathedrals, monasteries and Roman amphitheatres.

We offer here a far from exhaustive list of both the traditional events and new cultural festivals.

January: *Avoriaz* (Savoie) science-fiction film festival; *Champagne* and *Burgundy* village processions for wine-growers' patron Saint Vincent.

February (or early March): *Nice* Mardi Gras carnival.

March: *Cluny* chamber music.

April: *Bourges* rock music; *Strasbourg* choral music; *Arles* Easter bullfights in Roman amphitheatre.

May: *Cannes* International Film Festival; *Saint-Tropez* "Bravade" religious procession; *Amiens* jazz.

June: *Versailles* chamber music at the château; *Normandy* D-Day memorial ceremonies at Sainte-Mère-Eglise and Sainte-Marie-du-Mont (Utah Beach); *Strasbourg* music; *Honfleur* Whitsuntide Fête des Marins (sailors, at harbour); *Nîmes* Whitsuntide bullfights, in Roman amphitheatre; *Paris* Festival du Marais (music and theatre); *Paris* air show at Le Bourget airport (biennial); *Dijon* (until August) music and theatre, especially street theatre.

July: July 14 (Fête Nationale), celebrated all over the country. Also in July: *Avignon* international theatre (in Palais des Papes), music, opera, dance and cinema; *Aix-en-Provence* opera; *Arles* international photography seminars, exhibitions and audio-visual shows in amphitheatre; *Montpellier* music, opera and dance (starts last week in June); *Orange* opera in the amphitheatre; *Nice* jazz; *Bayonne* folklore; *Sarlat* theatre (till August); *Albi* (music in cathedral and palace); *Paris* Festival Estival, music and theatre (till September).

August: *Annecy* fireworks by the lake; *Chartres* organ recitals in cathedral; *Chartres* (August 15) Assumption Day procession and mass; *Aix-en-Provence* jazz; *Colmar* wine fair; *Le Touquet* chamber music.

September: *Lyon* Dance Biennale; *Deauville* American film festival; *Paris* Festival d'Automne, music and theatre, till December; *Dijon* wine festival; *Saint-Jean-de-Luz* music; *Mont-Saint-Michel* procession and mass for Saint Michael.

October: *Angers* avant-garde music; *Nancy* jazz.

November: *Burgundy* (Beaune, Nuits-Saint-Georges, Meursault and Chablis) wine festivals; *Dijon* gastronomy fair; *Cannes* dance.

December: *Les Baux-de-Provence* Christmas Eve Fête des Bergers (shepherds) and Midnight Mass.

shows that combine pretty girls and pretty transvestites in a nonstop riot of pastiche and satire: the Alcazar (Rue Mazarine) and Paradis Latin (Rue du Cardinal-Lemoine).

Music

For lovers of **classical music**, the Paris Opéra once more attracts international stars, and the Orchestre de Paris is thriving under musical director Semyon Bychkoll. If you haven't booked ahead, it's worth going directly to the Opéra and the Pleyel or Gaveau concert halls for tickets, since agencies add at least 20 per cent to the price, and cancellations are returned directly to the hall.

In the provinces, Lyon, Strasbourg, Toulouse and Lille all have first-class orchestras, and the festivals (see p. 310) bring top performers from all over the world.

The French seem to take their **jazz** much more seriously these days than Americans do. Paris has some 15 clubs; in summer the action moves down to the Côte d'Azur. Of the Paris clubs, the New Morning (Rue des Petites-Ecuries) attracts all the major American and European musicians, while Le Dunois (Rue Dunois) is a modest, intimate place cultivating the avant-garde. You can hear good mainstream jazz at the Bilboquet (Rue Saint-Benoît), Le Furstemberg (Rue de Buci) and the bars of the Méridien hotel (Boulevard Gouvion-Saint-Cyr) and Concorde-Lafayette (Place du Général-Koenig).

Rock music concerts are held at the spectacular new Zénith (La Villette, métro Porte de Pantin).

Discothèques go in and out of fashion as fast as the music that's played in them. The expensive and exclusive Paris discos hide out around the Champs-Elysées, notably on the Rue de Ponthieu and Avenue Matignon, while the younger crowd haunts exhilarating eardrum-bust-

*A*fter years of suffering from an inferiority complex vis-à-vis New York, the Paris dancing scene has experienced a great burst of new creativity. Beyond the "establishment" theatres of the Paris Opera, Théâtre de la Ville and Beaubourg, the main focus is on small theatres around the Bastille, with a fresh stimulus coming from the new Opéra-Bastille itself. In the summer, the action moves down to the festivals of Montpellier, Aix-en-Provence, Orange and Avignon.

ers around les Halles. At the coastal resorts, the expensive discos are often attached to the casino and the big hotels, with a more relaxed atmosphere in the smaller backstreet places.

Theatre

The Comédie-Française (Rue de Richelieu) is the high temple of French classical drama—Molière, Racine and Corneille—while slowly expanding its repertory. On the Left Bank, the Odéon (Place de l'Odéon), in keeping with its new title as the Théâtre de l'Europe, puts on international works, with prestigious guest companies performing in English, German and Italian. Even with a minimum of French, playgoers can enjoy the innovative contemporary theatre under the direction of Peter Brook at the Bouffes du Nord (Boulevard de la Chapelle), Patrice Chéreau at the suburban Théâtre des Amandiers (Nanterre) and Ariane Mnouchkine at the Cartoucherie de Vincennes (Avenue de la Pyramide).

Some of the major centres of provincial theatre are Nancy, Strasbourg, Toulouse, Lyon, Avignon and Montpellier.

Cinema

For serious movie fans, Paris is an unrivalled treasure island, a film-crazy town where directors and screenplay writers achieve a celebrity equal to that of star actors and actresses. Not even Los Angeles or New York can match the French capital's average of 300 different films showing each week. Practically all of them are available in at least one cinema in *VO*, an original, undubbed version with French subtitles. Study the weekly entertainment guides, *Pariscope* or *L'Officiel du Spectacle*, especially for the obscure little jewels offered by the town's two *cinémathèques* (Palais de Chaillot and Centre Pompidou).

Don't be intimidated by the queues; you nearly always get in. The usherettes *(ouvreuses)* expect to be tipped, it's their only income. Give them at least one franc.

Themes and Variations

France is so rich in churches, castles, paintings, palaces, museums, ruins—and landscapes—that you scarcely know where to begin. One way to avoid cultural indigestion is to choose a theme or take your favourite hobby and organize your trip around it. No need to neglect everything else, but you can head straight for the things you most want to see and take in anything else along the way.

We round up below a certain number of ideas and suggestions, scattered all over the country, from which you will make your selections according to your tastes, the time available and where you are heading.

Crafts and Trades

Nothing made France so unique as its incredible wealth of artisans and craftsmen. Many workshops are still kept up so you watch demonstrations; other trades that have disappeared or are disappearing bring the past to life.

Aiguines (Var), Musée des Tourneurs. Wood carving.

Baume-les-Messieurs (Jura), Musée d'Art et de Traditions populaires, Abbaye de Baume. Blacksmith's workshop and others being reconstituted.

Bédarieux (Hérault), Maison des Arts de Bédarieux et des hauts centres héraultais, Avenue Abbé-Tarroux. Evocation of past crafts.

Caen (Calvados), Musée de Normandie, Logis des Gouverneurs, Château. Big and varied collection of objects relating to crafts, with many reconstitutions of workshops, as well as pottery, etc.

Caromb (Vaucluse), Musée des vieux outils Noël-Morard, Cave Saint-Marc. Agricultural tools of Provence.

Clion (Charente-Maritime), Musée rural. 400 worktools of old.

Cruzille-en-Mâconnais (Saône-et-Loire), Musée de l'Outillage. 3,500 objects relating to 30 rural trades that have since gone.

Dompierre (Orne), Musée de l'Artisan local au musée des Métiers d'autrefois, Place de l'Église. Trades and crafts that have disappeared.

Fumay (Ardennes), Musée de l'Ardoise, Rue des Fusillés. Documents about, and tools used in, slate quarrying.

Molsheim (Bas-Rhin), Musée de la Metzig, Place de l'Hôtel-de-Ville. Tools of trades of times past.

Montignac (Dordogne), Musée Eugène-Leroy et du Vieux-Périgord, Place Betran-de-Born. Picturesque museum, reconstituting trades of the time of Jacquou le Croquant, a local "Robin Hood".

Nans-Sainte-Anne (Doubs), Musée de la Faulx, La Taillanderie. A fascinating visit of a scythe and sickle-making works; forge and bellows in working state.

Paris, 5ᵉ arrondissement, Musée des collections historiques de la Préfecture, 1 bis, Rue des Carmes. Most unusual view showing the *petits métiers* of Paris, plus a number of historical documents of great interest.

Poncé-sur-le-Loir (Sarthe), Musée ethnographique et folklorique sarthois. The château brings crafts to life.

Le-Puy-en-Velay (Haute-Loire), Centre d'initiation à la Dentelle, 2, Rue Duguesclin. Lace-making throughout Europe and in particular in the Puy region.

Troyes (Aube), Maison de l'Outil et de la Pensée ouvrière, 7, Rue de la Trinité. Wood, stone, iron-work crafts.

Curiosities

There are museums and collections of everything from babies' bottles (Musée de l'Assistance publique, Paris) to Graffiti (Musée du Graffiti at Verneuil-en-Halatte, Oise). Here are just a few of the unusual and curious collections of objects or activities scattered round the country.

Auriac-du-Périgord (Dordogne), Ecomusée de l'Abeille. Bees and beehives, honey and honeymaking with audio-visual show.

Bergerac (Dordogne), Musée du Tabac, Place du Feu. Nicot, of nicotine fame, was French, and here you'll find an astonishing array of the different aspects—social, artistic and industrial—of tobacco.

Champagney (Haute-Saône), Maison de la Négritude et des droits de l'homme, 1, Rue Léopold S.-Senghor. Small museum dealing with the Blacks in France, discrimination and human rights.

Charenton-le-Pont (Val-de-Marne), Musée du Pain, 23 bis, Rue Victor Hugo. Most curious museum of the development of bakery and bread-making.

Gien (Loiret), Musée international de la Chasse, Château. Pictorial art and the art of hunting.

Paris, 16ᵉ arrondissement, Musée des Lunettes et des Lorgnettes, 2, Avenue Mozart. 3,000 objects with every kind of device to improve one's sight including examples belonging to the famous.

Romans (Drôme), Musée de la Chaussure et d'Ethnographie régionale, 2, Rue Sainte-Marie. In the capital of French shoe-making, some rare and fascinating specimens of what we had on our feet through the centuries.

Saint-Cyr-au-Mont-d'Or (Rhône), Musée national de la police. By written request only to the director (Ecole nationale de la Police at Saint-Cyr-au-Mont-d'Or). From famous murders to weapons of all sorts, a fascinating panorama of police action.

Saint-Hilaire-Saint-Florent (Maine-et-Loire), near Saumur, Musée du Champignon, "La Houssay". Guided tours round some fascinating underground caves where mushrooms are produced, plus the background story to their cultivation.

Sorges (Dordogne), Ecomusée de la Truffe. Truffles museum; explanation and documents.

Thiers (Puy-de-Dôme), Musée de la Coutellerie, 58, Rue de la Coutellerie. Living museum of the art of knife-making, with demonstrations in the traditional capital of French cutlery.

Verderonne (Oise), Musée de la Magie, Château de Verderonne. Magic in all its forms, from posters to the magicians' stock in trade.

Famous Frenchmen
Many of the great men and women of France who have forged the history of the country have houses, museums or collections devoted to them.

Figures of State
Jeanne d'Arc (1412–31). — *Chinon* (Indre-et-Loire), Musée Jeanne d'Arc, Tour de l'Horloge. *Domrémy-la-Pucelle* (Vosges), Musée de la Maison natale de Jeanne d'Arc. *Orléans* (Loiret), Maison de Jeanne d'Arc, 3, Place de Gaulle. *Rouen* (Seine-Maritime), Musée de Jeanne d'Arc, 33, Place du Vieux-Marché. *Vaucouleurs* (Meuse), Musée municipal, Rue des Annonciades.

Napoléon Bonaparte (1769–1821). — *Ajaccio* (Corsica), Musée napoléonien de l'Hôtel de Ville, Place Maréchal-Foch — Musée national de la maison Bonaparte, Rue Saint-Charles. *Antibes* (Alpes-Maritimes), Musée naval et napoléonien, Boulevard J.-F.-Kennedy. *Auxonne* (Côte d'Or), Musée Bonaparte, Tour Notre-Dame. *Boulogne-Billancourt* (Hauts-de-Seine), Bibliothèque Marmottan, 19, Rue Salomon-Reinach. *Brienne-le-Château* (Aube), Musée Napoléon Ier, 34, Rue de l'Ecole-Militaire. *Fontainebleau* (Seine-et-Marne), Musée napoléonien d'Art et d'Histoire militaires, 88, Rue Saint-Honoré — Musée national du Château. *Ile-d'Aix* (Charente-Maritime), Musée national napoléonien, Rue Napoléon. *Monaco,* Musée des Souvenirs napoléoniens, Place du Palais. *Rueil Malmaison* (Hauts-de-Seine), Musée national du Château de Bois-Préau, 1, Avenue de l'Impératrice-Joséphine.

Charles-Maurice de Talleyrand (1754–1838). — *Saint-Chéron* (Essonne), Musée Talleyrand, Château du Marais.

Richelieu, Louis, Cardinal (1696–1788). — *Richelieu* (Indre-et-Loire), Musée du XVIIe siècle.

De Gaulle, Charles (1890–1970). — *Colombey-les-Deux-Eglises* (Haute-Marne), La Boisserie.

Science and Research
Ampère, André-Marie (1775–1836), physician and mathematician. — *Poleymieux-au-Mont-d'Or* (Rhône), Musée André-Marie-Ampère.

Champollion, Jean-François (1790–1832), Egyptologist, decipherer of Rosetta Stone. — *Figeac* (Lot), Musée Champollion, Impasse Champollion.

Favre, Jean-Henri (1832–1915), Entomologist. — *Sérignan-du-Comtat* (Vaucluse), Harmas de Jean-Henri Favre, Route d'Orange.

Pasteur, Louis (1822–95), Chemist and biologist. — *Arbois* (Jura), Musée de la maison paternelle de Pasteur. *Dole* (Jura), Musée de la maison natale de Pasteur. *Paris,* 15e arrondissement, Musée Pasteur, 25, Rue du Docteur-Roux.

Schweitzer, Albert (1875–1965), Theologian, philosopher, musician, mission doctor. — *Kaysersberg* (Haut-Rhin), Musée Albert Schweitzer, 126, Rue du Général-de-Gaulle.

Fashion
Paris's new Musée de la Mode only confirms the French passion for fashion and dress; following its history and development, be it folkloric and local or *haute couture* and national, makes one realize how inbred and instinctive style in dress is—and always has been—in the French.

Amiens (Somme), Centre d'exposition du costume "Hier le Costume", 3, Rue de Condé.

Arles (Bouches-du-Rhône), Muséon Arlaten, 29, Rue de la République.

Château-Chinon (Nièvre), Musée du Costume et Folklore, Rue du Château.

Lourdes (Hautes-Pyrénées), Musée pyrénéen, Châteaufort.

Lyon (Rhône), Musée historique des Tissus, 34, Rue de la Charité.

Paris, 1er arrondissement, Musée des Arts de la Mode, 109, Rue de Rivoli.

Quimper (Finistère), Musée départemental breton, 1, Rue du Roi-Gradlon.

Saint-Rémy-de-Provence (Bouches-du-Rhône), Musée des Alpilles Pierre-de-Brun, Place Favier.

Flowers and Gardens

The French garden tends to be more formal than the English but again it's an art in which France satisfies all tastes. And with its varied but hospitable climate, the country boasts even tropical plants growing in natural surroundings.

Anduze (Gard), Prafrance. Exotic park with over 100 kinds of bamboo—giant, dwarf, black, yellow, spotted, striped—with reconstruction of an Asian village. A bit of the Orient in the heart of the Cévennes.

Boulogne-Billancourt (Hauts-de-Seine) Collections Albert-Kahn. English-, French- and Japanese-style gardens, among others. Superb arrangements.

Caen (Calvados), Jardin des Plantes. A living conservatory of regional and foreign flora, with rock garden, cacti, aromatic and medicinal plants.

Cagnes-sur-Mer (Alpes-Maritimes), International Flower Exhibition, spring.

Eze (Alpes-Maritimes), Jardin Exotique. Set around the ramparts of a ruined château, with marvellous view over the Mediterranean.

Gérardmer (Vosges), Daffodil Festival.

Giverny (Eure), Fondation Claude Monet. The beloved flower beds of Monet; the Japanese bridge covered in wisteria and the pond filled with water lilies will be familiar from Monet's paintings.

L'Haÿ-les-Roses (Val-de-Marne), Roseraie et Musée de la Rose, Rue Albert-Watel. The prince of flowers in every shape and size and put to every imaginable "use".

Menton (Alpes-Maritimes), Les Colombières. A series of décors representing an artist's memories of his travels; spectacular view over the Mediterranean.

Menton (Alpes-Maritimes), Villa "Vall Rahmeh". Superb exotic garden created by Lord Radcliffe at the beginning of the century.

Mézidon (Calvados), Parc de Canon. Gardens conceived before the Revolution; French- and English-style arrangements, statue-ornamented promenades.

Orcival (Puy-de-Dôme), Jardins de Cordès. Designed by Le Nôtre and hidden behind hedges, a surprise of flower beds on two elevated terraces, forming an oval ensemble—unique in France.

Paris, 5e arrondissement, Botanical gardens (Jardin des Plantes). Opened to the public in 1640. Tropical and alpine gardens, zoo, reptiles, as well as mineral, fossil and insect galleries.

- Bagatelle (Bois de Boulogne). Azaleas, roses.
- Vincennes. Rhododendrons, tulips, dahlias.
- Open-air flower market at Place L.-Lépine.
- Flower Market, Conciergerie and Place de la Madeleine.

Saint-Jean-Cap-Ferrat (Alpes-Maritimes), Fondation Ephrussi-de-Rothschild, Villa "Ile-de-France". A wonderful collection of furniture and paintings amid equally wonderful gardens.

Samoëns (Haute-Savoie), La Jaÿsinia. Winding pathways on a hillside amidst ravines, water cascades, outcrops of rock; alpine and other flora.

Saverne (Bas-Rhin), Jardin Botanique du Col de Saverne. Profusion of colours featuring bamboo, orchid, azalea, even carnivorous plants!

Sélestat (Bas-Rhin), Flower Parade, second Sunday in August.

Strasbourg (Bas-Rhin), Jardin Botanique. Haven of peace in city centre, with rock gardens featuring iris and veronica around a lake, tropical plants.

Vic-le-Comte (Puy-de-Dôme), Buséol. Hanging gardens in 12th-century style, featuring medicinal and medieval-style ornamental plants and Mediterranean flora.

French Literary Figures

Get familiar with the giants of French literature in their own context during your tour of France. They come to life as people, and such visits bring their writings closer, make them more direct, more real.

Balzac, Honoré de (1799–1885). — *Saché* (Indre-et-Loire), Musée Balzac, in the château. *Paris,* 16ᵉ arrondissement, Musée Balzac, 47, Rue Raynouard.

Cocteau, Jean (1889–1963). — *Menton* (Alpes-Maritimes), Musée Jean-Cocteau, Quai du Vieux-Port. *Milly-La-Forêt* (Seine-Maritime), Chapelle.

Corneille, Pierre (1606–84). — *Rouen* (Seine-Maritime), Musée Corneille, 4, Rue de la Pie.

Daudet, Alphonse (1840–97). — *Font-vieille* (Bouches-du-Rhône), Musée Alphonse Daudet, Avenue des Moulins.

Dumas, Alexandre (1802–70). — *Villers-Cotterêts* (Aisne), Musée Alexandre Dumas, 24, Rue Demoustier.

Flaubert, Gustave (1821–80). — *Croisset* (Seine-Maritime), Pavillon Gustave Flaubert, 18, Quai Gustave Flaubert. *Ry* (Seine-Maritime), Galerie Bovary – Musée d'Automates, Place Gustave-Flaubert.

Hugo, Victor (1802–85). — *Besançon* (Doubs), Musée populaire comtois. *Paris,* 4ᵉ arrondissement, Maison de Victor Hugo, 6, Place des Vosges. *Villequier* (Seine-Maritime), Musée Victor-Hugo, Rue Ernest-Binet.

La Fontaine, Jean de (1621–95). — *Château-Thierry* (Aisne), Musée Jean-de-La-Fontaine, 12, Rue Jean-de-La-Fontaine.

Molière, Jean-Baptiste Poquelin (1622–73). — *Meudon* (Hauts-de-Seine), Musée. *Pézenas* (Hérault), Musée de Vulliod Saint-Germain, 3, Rue Albert-Paul Alliès.

Pascal, Blaise (1623–62). — *Magny-les-Hameaux* (Yvelines), Musée national des granges de Port-Royal. *Clermont-Ferrand* (Puy-de-Dôme), Musée du Ranquet, 1, Petite-Rue Saint-Pierre.

Proust, Marcel (1871–1922). — *Illiers-Combray* (Eure-et-Loire), Musée Marcel-Proust, 4, Rue du Docteur-Proust.

Rabelais, François (1494–1553). — *Seuilly-la-Devinière* (Indre-et-Loire), Musée Rabelais, La Devinière.

Racine, Jean (1639–99). — *Magny-les-Hameaux* (Yvelines), Musée national des granges de Port-Royal. *Saint-Cyr-l'Ecole* (Yvelines), Musée du Collège militaire de Saint-Cyr, 2, Avenue Jean-Jaurès.

Rimbaud, Arthur (1854–1891). — *Charleville-Mézières* (Ardennes), Musée Municipal; Musée de l'Ardenne – Musée Rimbaud, Vieux-Moulin.

Stendhal (Henri Beyle) (1783–1842). — *Grenoble* (Isère), Musée Stendhal, 1, Rue Hector-Berlioz.

*T*he *Musée d'Orsay, which opened in 1986, has quickly become one of the most popular museums in France. Its vocation being the 19th century or, more precisely, the period from 1848 to World War I, it provides a logical bridge between the classical collections of the Louvre and the resolutely modern exhibitions of Beaubourg. Covering the height of France's industrial revolution, the converted railway station provides, beyond its painting and sculpture collections, fascinating insights into the history of photography, the cinema and industrial architecture.*

Horse Racing

Racing in France holds a special place of its own, where elegance, style and excitement compete on an equal footing and the atmosphere is uniquely French, in spite of the international nature of the gatherings.

Paris and Ile-de-France

Auteuil. Known for its jumps, especially a 28-ft water jump. Paris Grand Steeple Chase, third Sunday in June.

Longchamp. Opened by Napoleon III in 1857. Paris Grand Prix, last Sunday in June.

Saint-Cloud. Spring Grand Prix, Whit Monday.

Vincennes. America Stakes in January and Summer Grand Prix in September.

Elsewhere

Cagnes-sur-Mer (Côte d'Azur). Racing at the Hippodrome de la Côte d'Azur, 13 km. (8 mi.) from Nice.

Chantilly (Oise). Prix de Diane, June.

Deauville (Normandy). The racing season culminates in the Grand Prix de Deauville run on the fourth Sunday in August. Races are held at La Touques or the Hippodrome de Clairefontaine. The sale of yearlings takes place at the end of August and November.

Music Festivals

Music festivals take place all over the country, mostly in the sunny south.

Aix-en-Provence (Bouches-du-Rhône), from mid-July. For nearly a month this gracious gateway to the Côte-d'Azur concentrates on opera, with concerts and art exhibits in historic indoor and outdoor settings.

Avignon (Vaucluse), mid-July. Magnificent medieval architecture—this was the papacy's 14th-century redoubt—provides the backdrop for a festival more heavily weighted towards theatre and ballet than concerts.

Bordeaux (Gironde). This industrial city in western France, with a prized two hundred-year-old opera house, calls its festival Mai Musical International, since it begins the first week in May.

Evian (Haute-Savoie). By the shores of Lake Geneva, chamber music of a high standard in May.

Lourdes (Bouches-du-Rhône), an Easter festival of music and sacred art.

Lyon (Rhône). Starting the second week in June, the Festival International de Lyon covers symphonic music, ballet, and jazz. In mid-September, in *odd* years, the Hector Berlioz Festival devotes a week to the local composer and his music; in *even* years, modern dance festival alternates agreeably with it.

*E*mperor Augustus presides over the Roman theatre at Orange, understandably proud of his magnificent setting for an orchestral concert at the ancient city's summer music festival.

Menton (Alpes-Maritimes), August. In the centre of a lovely old town, an open-air concert of high-quality classical or romantic chamber music; day at the beach and night at the casino.

Nice (Alpes-Maritimes) plays host to a jazz festival in the second and third week of July, with performances in the venerable Cimiez Gardens, at several sites.

Orange (Vaucluse), late July and early August. A great Roman theatre is the site for Chorégies d'Orange. The emphasis is on choral music and opera.

Photography and Cinema

Cradle of photography (Nicéphore Niepce was French, so was Daguerre), France makes a particular effort to give the art its rightful place. It is excellently documented throughout the country's museums, often grouped with the cinema (another French first).

Arles (Bouches-du-Rhône), Musée Réattu, 10, Rue du Grande Pierre. Collection of works from some of greatest French and world photographers.

Beaune (Côte-d'Or), Musée des Beaux-Arts et Musée Marey, Rue de l'Hôtel-de-Ville. Chronophotography was invented here by Etienne-Jules Marey; documents and inventions.

Bièvres (Essonne), Musée français de la Photographie, 78, Rue de Paris. Very important general collection of early records of the art.

Boulogne-Billancourt (Hauts-de-Seine). Collections Albert-Kahn, 10, Quai du 4-Septembre, (72,000 photos from every corner of the world and 140,000 m. of film—not all on show—in a collection called by the collector "archives of the Planet").

Chalon-sur-Saône (Saône-et-Loire), Musée Nicéphore-Niepce, 28, Quai de Messageries. The inventor of photography was born here and the first camera ever made is displayed.

Lyon (Rhône), Fondation nationale de la Photographie, 25, Rue de Premier-Film. A little museum devoted to the Lumière brothers who "invented" the cinema.

Paris, 3e arrondissement, Musée national des techniques, 292, Rue Saint-Martin. Some interesting early cameras of Niepce, Daguerre, Marly and Lumière.

Toulon (Var), Musée de Toulon, 113, Maréchal-Leclerc. Very important store of contemporary photos of famous photographers.

And, of course, for cinema-lovers, France has the Cannes Film Festival and for the lovers of science-fiction and horror films, the Avoriaz Festival, in its lovely Alpine setting.

Porcelain, Faïence and Ceramics

A subject where so many museums have something to show, it seems invidious even to make a choice. If, however, you only choose one, it should probably be Sèvres where so much is represented.

Aix-en-Provence (Bouches-du-Rhône), Musée bibliographique et archéologique Paul-Arbaud, 2, Rue du 4-Septembre.

Bailleul (Nord), Musée Benoît-De-Puydt, 24, Rue du Musée.

Barr (Bas-Rhin), Musée de la Folie-Marco, 30, Rue du Docteur Sultzer.

Carcassonne (Aude), Musée des Beaux-Arts, 2, Rue de Verdun.

Limoges (Haute-Vienne), Musée national Adrien Dubouché, 8 bis, Place Winston-Churchill.

Lunéville (Meurthe-et-Moselle), Musée du Château, Chateau.

Le Mans (Sarthe), Musée de la Reine Bérangère, 7-13, Rue de la Reine-Bérangère. Musée de Tessé, 2, Avenue de Paderborn.

Marseille (Bouches-du-Rhône), Musée Cantini, 19, Rue Grignan.

Montluçon (Allier), Musée du Vieux-Château, Rue du Château.

Moulins (Allier), Musée d'Art et d'Archéologie, 3, Place du Colonel-Laussedat.

Moustiers-Sainte-Marie (Alpes-de-Haute-Provence), Musée de la Faïence, crypte romane, under the presbytery.

Nevers (Nièvre), Musée municipal, 16, Rue Saint-Genest.

Paris, 1er arrondissement, Musée du Louvre–Musée des Arts décoratifs, 107, Rue de Rivoli. 8e arrondissement, Musée Nissim-de-Camondo, 63, Rue de Monceau.

Perpignan (Pyrénées-Orientales), Musée Hyacinthe Rigaud, 16, Rue de l'Ange.

Quimper (Finistère), Musée des faïenceries de Quimper, Faïenceries HB et Henriot, Rue Haute.

Roanne (Loire), Musée Joseph-Déchelette, 22, Rue Anatole-France.

Rouen (Seine-Maritime), Musée de la Céramique, 1, Rue Faucon.

Samadet (Landes), Musée de la Faïencerie, Rue de l'Eglise.

Sarreguemines (Moselle), Musée de Sarreguemines, 15-17, Rue Poincaré.

Sèvres (Hauts-de-Seine), Musée national de Céramique, Place de la Manufacture.

Don't forget the special Porcelain Exhibition held annually in Limoges in summer.

Study Groups

To get the most out of France, why not be active; do a course in painting, in the French language or in cooking or a multitude of others (pottery, archaeology, etc.). There's even more fun to be had when you participate.

French Language Courses

The French speak foreign languages grudgingly; it really helps your enjoyment to have at least a minimal grasp of French to take advantage of what's going on around you.

Language schools are to be found all over France. They may be combined with sports, sightseeing, arts and crafts, or even cooking. Lodging can also be arranged with local families if desired. Write the French Tourist Office for the brochure "Cours de Langue française", specifying the region, the type of course (intensive, etc.) and other relevant requests.

Cooking Classes

After tasting the incomparable French cuisine, why not try your hand at preparing it yourself?

France abounds in cooking courses all over the country, given in specialized schools, by chefs of famous restaurants, or in the homes of knowledgeable housewives. Courses vary in length from a single morning to a year's training.

In the countryside, the classes are usually part of a complete package providing lodging and meals, and may include visits to restaurants in the region and sightseeing.

For complete documentation, write to the French Tourist Office and ask for the brochure "Apprenez la cuisine française", NDF No. 202.

Additional courses not included in the above literature, in Lyon and on the Côte d'Azur, are described in the booklets "Vallée du Rhône, Balade du Gourmet" (Comité Régional du Tourisme, 5, Place de la Baleine, 69005 Lyon) and "Cuisine Azur Loisirs" (Côte d'Azur Loisirs, Lycée d'Etat Jacques Audiberti, Bd. Wilson, 06600 Antibes-Juan les Pins).

Those who want to take their research further into the historical side of French cuisine and its development should pay a visit to Villeneuve-Loubet (Alpes-Maritimes) to the Fondation Auguste-Escoffier. A fascinating cookery museum.

Painting Classes

Head for Paris, Provence or the Côte d'Azur to enroll in a vacation-time painting course.

Select one from the booklet "Métiers d'art et stages" published by the Centre National d'information et de documentation sur les métiers d'art, available at Dessain et Tolra, 10, rue Cassette, 75006 Paris. Courses are held at Calvisson near Nîmes, Vieil Antibes, and Morillon in the Haute-Savoie, to name only a sampling.

Workshops in the countryside usually quote a price inclusive of lodging, and some have apartments available suitable for the whole family.

"Everything is a Pretext for a Good Dinner."

There are some tourists who come to France without visiting a single museum or church and who would not dream of "wasting" their time shopping. And yet they come away with tales of adventure, excitement, poetry and romance—and the feeling they know the country inside out.

The onslaught of fast food and *autoroute* cafeterias has not staled the infinite variety of France's regional cuisines, and you can enjoy anything from a gorgeous feast to a simple selection of piquant sausage and pâté in the knowledge that eating and drinking are not just a means of satisfying hunger and thirst.

Even if you were so inclined, not all budgets or waistlines would permit such single-minded dedication to eating your way across France. Nonetheless, reserve at least a couple of evenings to that unique institution, a great French meal. As playwright Jean Anouilh once said, "Everything ends this way in France—everything. Weddings, christenings, duels, burials, swindlings, diplomatic affairs—everything is a pretext for a good dinner."

Where to Eat

In the big cities, you have a wide choice: gourmet restaurants, relatively expensive; large, family-style *brasseries* or intimate little *bistrots*, more moderately priced; cafés or wine bars for a cheaper snack. Fast-food chains are very successful and need no introduction.

The fixed-price *menu* (appetizer, main course and dessert) is often the best deal, particularly in the major gourmet establishments, where you get a first-class introduction to the restaurant's specialities without paying the much higher *à la carte* prices. Look, too, for the house wine *(réserve de la maison)* usually served in carafe by the *quart* (quarter) or *demi* (half) litre.

In that lovely insular phrase which even the American continent seems to have adopted, the typical "continental" **breakfast** *(petit déjeuner)* is still croissant, brioche or bread and butter with coffee, tea or chocolate. Increasingly, orange juice is offered as an extra, but you must insist on *orange pressée* if you want it freshly squeezed. Big hotels offer English- and American-style breakfasts. But we recommend you go out as often as possible to the corner café—it's great to watch a town getting up in the morning when you don't have to go off to work. Traditionally, a French **lunch** *(déjeuner)* is as important as dinner, but you may not want to handle two big meals a day when you're travelling. A good alternative is a café salad, or a cheese, ham or pâté sandwich in a long *baguette*. Or else a picnic. *Charcuteries* and *traiteurs* (caterers) pack complete meals, hot or cold. A corkscrew is more important than a credit card—don't leave home without it.

The **evening meal** *(dîner)* in the provinces is served early—8 or 8.30 p.m., compared with 8.30 or 9 p.m. in Paris and such favourite Parisian resorts as Deauville, Saint-Tropez or Cannes. The French are much more relaxed than you might have expected about how you dress for dinner, and if the smart places expect a jacket, only a very few insist on a tie.

What to Eat

There are some general notions to French eating habits that you'll find all over the country. First things first. Forgoing the **starter** *(entrée)* does not necessarily mean that the main course will be served more quickly. Besides, it's worth trying some of the simplest dishes that do work genuinely as appetizers: *crudités*—a plate of raw vegetables, green pepper, tomatoes, carrots, celery, cucumber; or just radishes by themselves, served with salt and butter; *charcuterie*—various kinds of sausage and other cold meats, notably the *rosette* sausage from Lyon, *rillettes* (a soft pâté of pork or goose) from Le Mans and ham *(jambon)* from Bayonne or Auvergne; vegetable soups *(potage)* or fish soups served with *croûtons* and a Provençal sauce of garlic and chilli pepper *(rouille)*.

Most big cities get their **fish** fresh every day except Monday. Trout *(truite)* is delicious *au bleu* (poached absolutely fresh),

meunière (sautéed in butter) or *aux amandes* (sautéed with almonds). At their best, *quenelles de brochet* (pike dumplings) are much lighter and airier than their English translation. Sole and turbot take on a new meaning when served with *sauce hollandaise*, that miraculous blend of egg yolks, butter and lemon juice with which the Dutch have only the most nominal connection.

For your **main dish**, expect the meat to be less well done than in most countries —extra-rare is *bleu*, rare *saignant*, medium *à point*, and well done *bien cuit* and frowned upon. Steaks *(entrecôte* or *tournedos)* are often served with a wine sauce *(marchand de vin)*, with shallots *(échalotes)*, or—rich sin—with bone marrow *(à la moelle)*. A la bordelaise means with wine sauce, shallots *and* bone marrow. Roast leg of lamb *(gigot d'agneau)* is also served pink *(rose)* unless you specify otherwise.

General de Gaulle once asked a *Newsweek* magazine interviewer how one can be expected to govern a country that has 246 different cheeses. French dairy farmers boasted that the General was understating the problem and that the actual number was closer to 400. While each region favours its specialities, the most famous **cheeses** are available everywhere: the blue Roquefort, soft white-crusted Camembert or Brie (the crust of which you can safely remove without offending true connoisseurs), and countless goat cheeses *(fromage de chèvre)*.

Desserts are the most personal choice

Handling the Waiter

Because French restaurants are regarded as secular temples, tourists sometimes feel they must treat waiters and maîtres d'hôtel like high priests and cardinals. First rule: never be in awe of them. They will not bite. If they bark, bark back. These people are not ogres by nature. They grow testy only when you show you are frightened or aggressive—much like the rest of us. Remember that being a waiter is a respected profession in France, and they like nothing better than when you call on their expertise.

If you are not satisfied with the wine or the meat is too rare, say so. If you do it with a smile, the waiter will be too surprised to argue. In any decent restaurant, surreptitious tipping to get a table is rarely a good idea. But if you are pleased with the service, an extra tip (on top of the 15% in the bill) *after* the meal will be greatly appreciated and get you good service if you return. Amazing how human the French can be.

of the meal, the moment you plunge back into childhood. Try a heavenly *mousse au chocolat* or diabolical *profiteroles*, little ball-shaped éclairs filled with vanilla ice cream and covered with hot chocolate sauce. Or water ice *(sorbet)*—blackcurrant *(cassis)*, raspberry *(framboise)* or pear *(poire)*. And fruit tarts—apricot *(tarte aux abricots)*, strawberry *(aux fraises)*, and most magical of all, *tarte Tatin*, hot caramelized apples baked under a crust, attributed to the Tatin sisters of Sologne after one of them accidentally dropped the tart upside down on the hotplate when taking it out of the oven.

Regional Cuisine

Once acquainted with these basics, you're ready to start your tour of the regional specialities. There's no specifically "Parisian" cuisine; but the capital can offer a sample of almost everything you'll find around the country.

Picardy, for those coming in from the north, offers its speciality, *flamique à porions*, a leek pie best served piping hot. This, with one of the region's great vegetable soups, will keep you going all the way into Paris and beyond. In Amiens, try the traditional *pâté de canard* (duck pâté).

Flanders makes good use of its North Sea fish—mackerel and herring—and a pronounced taste for beer in its cooking. Try the *soupe à la bière* (beer soup with chicken bouillon, cream and breadcrumbs) or eel *(anguilles)* cooked in beer. Sour herring salad with beetroot and potatoes makes a savoury hors d'œuvre, while *craquelots* (herring doused in milk and then grilled) are a Dunkirk speciality. Not to be confused with Roubaix's *craquelins*, a crusty sweet biscuit. *Hochepot* is the Flemish version of *pot au feu*, with oxtail and vegetables. In Lille, look for the *lapin à la flamande* (rabbit with prunes and grapes).

Lorraine is justly famous for its *quiche*, a ham and egg pie that takes its name from the German *Kuchen*, but is known as *féouse* in Nancy. Ham and pork are prominent in local cooking— *soupe au jambon fumé* (smoked ham soup), *potée* (pork and vegetable stew)— while Nancy is proud of its *boudin* (blood sausage) and Epinal of its *andouillettes* (tripe sausage). The forests of the Vosges produce great mushrooms and bilberries *(myrtilles)*.

Champagne cuisine does not live up to its wine, *champenoise* being a nationwide style of cooking in (cheap) champagne. But in Reims, try the *gâteau champenois*, a dessert of pink biscuits, raisins and other dried fruit doused in champagne brandy *(marc)*.

Alsace is rich in freshwater fish and game, and makes a subtle mixture of French, German and even Jewish cooking —*carpe à la juive* will be recognized as gefilte fish. Wonders are performed with cabbage. *Choucroute* cooked in Riesling with juniper berries, with a cup of kirsch tossed in at the end, makes poetry out of sauerkraut. *Civet de lièvre* is jugged hare fit for a king, and braised goose with apples *(oie braisée aux pommes)* warms the cockles of the coldest heart. The prince of Alsatian cheeses is the pungent Munster.

Burgundy, inspired by the high life led by its grand old dukes, is ideal for those with solid appetites. This wine-growing region produces the world's greatest beef stew, *bœuf bourguignon*: beef simmered in red wine for at least four hours, with mushrooms, small white onions and chunks of bacon. The corn-fed poultry of Bresse is the aristocrat of French fowl —enjoy it at its simplest, roast or steamed. Charolais beef, from the lovingly tended white cattle of southern Burgundy, produces the tenderest steaks. *A la dijonnaise* will usually mean a sauce of Dijon's mustard, distinctively flavoured by the sour juice of Burgundy grapes. *Jambon persillé* (parsleyed ham) is another Dijon speciality. *Escargots* (snails) are mostly imported from Eastern Europe these days to meet the heavy demand, but Burgundians still make the

THE BIG
CHEESES

French cheese is not unlike Shakespeare's Cleopatra—
''Age cannot wither her nor custom stale her infinite variety.''
A whole mystique surrounds the preparation of the country's
400-odd different types of cheese made
from cow's, ewe's and goat's milk, many of them good
only at certain times of the year.

Take Normandy's Camembert, Livarot and Pont-l'Evêque. The success and world-wide demand for Camembert has led inevitably to ''industrial'' production, but that's been true since 1880. The streamlining of traditional methods does not mean a boring, homogenized product.

It's still a painstaking process. Milk straight from the cow (pasteurized only for export) with rennet, from a calf's stomach, as a curdling agent, is heated at 30 °C (87 °F) for two hours. The curds are put in flat cylindrical moulds: 2.2 litres for one Camembert, drained for 6 hours, left overnight, coated with salt and left a further 24 hours. It's then put on wattle racks in a drying room for 10 days and occasionally turned to achieve a uniform coating of white mould for its ''skin''. It stays another 10 days in a maturing cellar to take on that characteristic faint yellow hue and supple texture before being wrapped and boxed. A ripe Camembert should ''give'' to thumb pressure, without the skin puncturing, the texture inside soft and creamy, but not ''runny''. Good all year round.

Whereas Camembert is made with cow's milk from all over Normandy, Livarot production is limited to the narrow area of its canton in the Auge. It takes 5 litres to make 1 Livarot, and it is matured over a month (3 to 6 months before ''industrialization''). The ruddy-skinned Livarot encircled with straw is still pungent but no longer takes the roof off your mouth. At its best from April to November.

The square-shaped aromatic Pont-l'Evêque is the oldest of Normandy's Big Three (originally known as Augelot, dating back at least to the 13th century). Three litres of milk go into each cheese, ending up a little drier than the other two. Best from November to April.

The distinctive character of Roquefort, king of France's blue cheeses and for many the king of all cheeses, derives from the unique conditions in which it's matured—for 90 days. A mountain landslide around the village of Roquefort-sur-Soulzon in the Tarn Valley created natural chalky caves that provide the

ewe's-milk cheese with the necessary cool, damp, fungus-laden draughts of air. The fungus that gives the creamy cheese its special punch bears the scientific name of *penicillium roqueforti*. It's an old cheese: Roman writer Pliny the Elder tried some in the 1st century A.D.; it was Charlemagne's favourite; and the village has had an exclusive royal charter since 1411. With butter on your bread and a glass of sturdy red Madiran, Roquefort is at its best from June to December.

Two of the best-known goat cheeses *(chèvres)* come from the Loire Valley. Produced in the Sancerre wine country, the flattened little ball known as Crottin de Chavignol emphasizes the easy-going relationship between French cuisine and the barnyard, *crottin* meaning a horse-dropping. When not ideally pungent and almost dry,

it can be perked up by toasting and serving it on a salad. In the shape of a pyramid with the top lopped off, the Valençay may be almost black in appearance when powdered with (edible) charcoal dust or light grey with a coat of mould. It is firm but not dry and has a slight taste of hazelnut to it.

To get a Frenchman to smile for the camera, it's no good asking him to say *fromage*. Try ''Brie''. This great flat wheel of soft-crusted cow's-milk cheese is manufactured in and around three villages east of Paris—Meaux, Melun and Coulommiers. It's at its best from May to October, with a red Burgundy. During the Revolution of 1789, it became a symbol of the new human rights when it was said that, ''loved by rich and poor alike, Brie preached equality before we ever imagined such a thing was possible.''

*M*aster chef Alain Chapel keeps a watchful eye
on his staff in the kitchens of his restaurant in Mionnay, north-west
of Lyon. In an era when the great French chefs seem to spend a lot
of time on public relations in Tokyo or New York, Chapel prefers
to hang around his own ovens.

are also cooked in white wine. Soups are popular mountain dishes, with sorrel *(oseille)*, pumpkin *(potiron)* or vitamin-rich nettles *(orties)*, while dandelions with bacon and cream make up the refreshing *mouraillons* salad. *Potée savoyarde* is a stew of pork, sausage, vegetables and chestnuts. For dessert, try the rhubarb or bilberry tarts, apple bread, and with your coffee or tea, the little *suisses*, orange-flavoured pastry mannikins.

Normandy makes full use of its prolific dairy farms. Cream and butter are staples of the cuisine, the secret behind the sumptuous *omelette de la mère Poulard* that you'll find at Mont-Saint-Michel. The rich, slightly sour, *crème fraîche* also makes the perfect accompaniment to a hot apple pie. The local Reinette apples turn up with flambéed partridge *(perdreau flambé aux reinettes)* and in chicken with apple-brandy sauce *(poulet au Calvados)*. The Normandy capital is famous for its *caneton à la rouennaise*, a duckling of unusually deep red meat with a spicy red-wine sauce thickened with minced duck livers. Tough guys and dolls who tackle *tripes à la mode de Caen* should know it contains all the various compartments of a cow's stomach, plus the trotters, stewed in a bouillon. Beside the Camembert cheese, be sure to sample the stronger Livarot and square Pont-l'Evêque.

Brittany is best for its magnificent sea-food, served fresh and unadorned on a bed of crushed ice and seaweed, a *plateau de fruits de mer*. It will include oysters *(huîtres)*, various kinds of clam *(palourdes, praires)*, mussels *(moules)*, scallops *(coquilles Saint-Jacques)*, large prawns *(langoustines)*, periwinkles *(bigorneaux)* that you winkle out with a pin, large whelks *(bulots)* and chewy abalones *(ormeaux)*. Purists prefer their lobster *(homard)* steamed or grilled to retain the full, undisguised flavour. Lobster *à l'américaine* (or *à l'armoricaine*) swims in a shellfish stock enriched with tomato, cognac, cream and herbs.

The **Loire Valley** has some excellent

best butter, garlic and parsley sauce, also used with *cuisses de grenouilles* (frogs' legs) from the Dombes region. Among the great Burgundy cheeses are the moist orange-crusted Epoisses and Soumaintrain.

Savoie, so close to Switzerland, has its own version of *fondue*, a hot dip of Beaufort cheese laced with white wine and kirsch. The little local *diot* sausages

freshwater fish (eel, perch, trout and pike) in a light *beurre blanc* (white butter sauce). A major delicacy is *matelote d'anguille* (eel stewed in red wine). Angers and Tours each insists it makes the best *andouillette* (tripe sausage), while *rillettes* of duck, goose or pork meat make another fine starter. For a lusty main dish, try *noisette de porc aux pruneaux* (pork tenderloin with prunes). One of the best goat cheeses in the country is the Valençay, shaped like an Aztec pyramid.

Lyon, the gastronomic capital of France, is renowned for the quality of its pork, wild game, vegetables and fruit, while giving the common or garden onion its letters of nobility. Onion soup *(soupe à l'oignon)* is a local invention; *à la lyonnaise* most often means sautéed in onions. If you have a robust stomach, try *grasdouble* (tripe) or *andouille*, a sausage

---

A Few Pearls about Oysters

In Brittany, oysters can be eaten all year round, and increasingly, with modern refrigerated transportation, in most other major regions, too. The comma-shaped ones in rough, ruffled greyish shells *(creuses)* are broadly classified as *Portugaises* (so called because of a ship wrecked on the Atlantic coast in 1868 with a cargo of Portuguese oysters of this type). These days, they're usually cultivated rather than wild and can be quite salty. The consistency is fatty. You'll often see them listed as *fines de claires* (which denotes the kind of pen or *clairière* in which they're raised) and *spéciales*, a type of *fine de claires*. On menus, numbers after names denote the weight, from 5 (lightest) to 1, 0 or even 000 (heaviest of all). Thus, *fines de claires N°2* would specify average-size Portugaise oysters.

Belon and *Marenne* oysters have flat and comparatively smooth shells. Highly esteemed for their quality and commonly found in Brittany, they are less fatty and salty than *Portugaises*. With an accompaniment of brown bread *(pain bis)* and butter, purists eat their oysters raw, with just a touch of lemon juice. Others like a red-wine vinegar with chopped shallots. But some inventive chefs may propose poached oysters with a butter and white-wine sauce or even sandwiched in the middle of a beefsteak after it's been flambéed in cognac!

---

made of chitterlings. More "genteel" dishes include, for starters, artichoke hearts *(cœurs d'artichaut)* with *foie gras,* or *gratin de queues d'écrevisses* (baked crayfish tails); as main dishes, seven-hour braised leg of lamb *(gigot d'agneau)* and *poularde demi-deuil*—chicken in semimourning, because of the white meat and black truffles.

Poitou is rich both in seafood—shellfish, oysters and mussels—and meat dishes. In the *Marais poitevin* region, the frogs *(grenouilles)* and snails *(lumas)* are served in garlic or a wine sauce. The local fish soup *(chaudrée)* comes thick with skate, sole, cuttlefish and eel cooked in Muscadet wine, butter, thyme, bay and garlic. For a glorious local version of the hamburger, try the *bifteck poitevin*, chopped beef with egg, beef-marrow, breadcrumbs, onions and white wine. *Gigorit* is a pungent concoction of pig's offal and chicken giblets. Look, too, for the *pirot*, wild goat sautéed with green garlic and sorrel. As a dessert, try the *grimolles* fruit crêpes.

Bordeaux cooking naturally enough also exploits its wines, the *bordelaise* sauce being made with white or red wine, shallots and beef marrow, served variously with *entrecôte* steaks, *cèpes* (boletus mushrooms) or lamprey eels *(lamproies)*. A surfeit of them may have killed a few medieval kings but the right amount never hurt anyone. Oysters and mussels from nearby Arcachon are excellent. Try the region's Pauillac lamb *à la persillade* (with parsley).

Provence, embracing the **Côte d'Azur**, marries Mediterranean seafood with garlic, olives, tomatoes and the country's most fragrant herbs. But for a starter, have the local fresh sardines, just grilled and sprinkled with lemon. More spicy is *tapenade*, a mousse of capers, anchovies, black olives, garlic and lemon—delicious on toast. From the coast between Marseille and Toulon comes the celebrated *bouillabaisse*, a fish soup that might contain *rascasse*, John Dory, eel, red mullet, whiting, perch, spiny lobster, crabs and other shellfish, seasoned with garlic, olive oil, tomatoes, bay leaf, parsley, pepper and (not authentic without it) saffron. Provençal cooks also do a fine *daube de bœuf* (beef stew with tomatoes and olives).

Corsica makes a judicious combination of Provençal and Italian cuisine, except for its frequent use of mint. The great delicacy is *cabri*, roast leg of goat. The prized local *charcuterie* includes smoked liver sausage *(figatelli)* and pork loin *(coppa)*. They make a lusty mutton stew known as *stufatu*, while *ziminu* is the Corsican *bouillabaisse* whose superiority to the Marseillais version is best not debated. The famous *Broccio* cheese is widely used in desserts such as the lemon-flavoured *fiadone* flan and fritters *(fritelles)*.

Limousin is great hunting country and has excellent hare and partridge dishes to show for it. A speciality is the *lièvre en cabessal*, hare stuffed with its liver and garlic and marinated in onions, carrots, shallots, spices and red wine. For a lusty soup, have the *bréjaude*, with cabbage, leeks, potatoes, salt pork and beans and the local *miques* (dumplings). The region's best-known dessert is the *clafoutis,* thick-crusted cherry pie.

Auvergne has a cuisine as solid and robust as its landscape—*soupe au Cantal* (cheese-soup) and *mourtayrol*, a saffron-flavoured pot-au-feu of beef, ham, chicken and vegetables. The freshwater fish are first-rate—trout, carp, pike, eel, perch and salmon, the last delicious baked in a *tourte* (pie). The ham *(jambon d'Auvergne)* has a national reputation and is the chief ingredient of the *omelette brayaude*, with potatoes, cheese and cream. *Gigot brayaude* is leg of lamb braised in garlic and white wine. Look out, too, for the *pounti*, a savoury flan of bacon, onions, beets, raisins and prunes. *Picoussel* is a local dessert of plum flan.

Périgord is famous for its *pâté de foie gras, truffes* (truffles), in ever dwindling supply, and for all the richness of goose and duck, most notably *confit d'oie* or

confit de canard. The bird is cooked slowly in its own fat and kept for days, weeks and even months in earthenware jars. The *confit* is the base of the hearty Toulouse or Castelnaudary *cassoulet*, with beans, pork, mutton, and sausage. And don't forget *pommes sarladaises*, potatoes sautéed in goose fat, garlic and parsley; dandelion salad *(salade de pissenlit)* dressed with walnut oil and bits of bacon, and cabbage, green or red, simmered for hours in red wine and chestnuts.

Wine

What is for many people the most intimidating of experiences—ordering a French wine—has in fact far fewer rules than you think. If you happen to like red wine more than white, you can safely and acceptably order red with fish; a chilled Brouilly, Morgon or Chiroubles of the Beaujolais family goes well with both fish and meat. Dry Burgundy or Loire Valley whites are indeed exquisite with fish and you can drink Alsatian whites with everything, with impunity. Remember, in a French restaurant, *you* are king. You prefer beer? Go ahead, it goes especially well with Toulouse sausage and Alsatian *choucroute*.

But the connoisseurs do have preferred accompaniments and make subtle distinctions—discerning hints of all kinds of fruit and nuts in the taste and flowers in the bouquet. So before opening that often formidable *carte des vins*, you might like to take a look at our thumbnail guide to France's more important wines.

Burgundy

The vineyards south of Dijon divide into two distinct regions, Côte de Nuits, grouping most of the region's top reds, and Côte de Beaune, with reds only slightly less prestigious, but not to be sneezed at, and what locals insist are the world's greatest whites. Best years for reds: 1947, 49, 55, 61, 69, 71, 78, 83, 85; for whites: 47, 61, 78, 79, 82, 83, 85.

Côte de Nuits: the reds of **Gevrey-Chambertin** are a little tannic (acid) when young, but grow firmer with age, acquiring a hint of liquorish as they are kept in the cellar up to 20 years. Ideal with pheasant. **Chambolle-Musigny** produces the region's most delicate reds, with aromatic hints of raspberry and spices. Its "feminine" reputation is most present in the celebrated *Les Amoureuses*. Keeps 6 to 12 years, good with duck and other game birds. **Clos de Vougeot** is rich, generous and full-bodied, keeps 3 to 15 years and is fine with venison or *coq au vin*. When regiments marched past the vineyards of Clos de Vougeot (illustration opposite), the order rang out to salute. Today, awe-inspired connaisseurs need no such order—the salute takes place at table. **Vosne-Romanée** is the rarest (and most expensive) of Burgundies, with a unique velvety texture and spicy aroma. Keeps 5 to 15 years, great with roast beef, lamb and chicken. **Nuits-Saint-Georges**, rich and heady, keeps 2 to 10 years, perfect for *bœuf bourguignon*.

Côte de Beaune: Voltaire cherished his **Aloxe-Corton** so much that he hid it from guests. Powerful and rich without going to your head, it keeps 3 to 10 years, good with roast beef and venison. **Savigny-les-Beaune**, light and tender with a heady bouquet, can be drunk young, with pigeon or veal. **Beaune**, elegant and easy on the palate, keeps 2 to 10 years, good with pâté and quail. **Pommard**, powerful and more tannic than other Côte de Beaune

reds, is renowned for its Epenots and Rugiens vineyards. Keeps 3 to 10 years, good with beef and game. **Volnay** has a delicate bouquet and rounded elegance. Keeps 2 to 6 years, ideally light for veal. **Santenay**, tannic and tough when young, develops with age (3 to 10 years) a deeper aroma of violets and hints of strawberry and chestnut. Goes with *bœuf bourguignon* and *coq au vin*. **Puligny-Montrachet** is the greatest of the Burgundy whites, golden in colour, rich and generous in flavour, with touches of almond, hawthorn and honey. Keeps 10 years and more and crowns the most delicate seafood dishes. **Meursault** is the region's other noble white in which connoisseurs detect hints of brioche, hazelnut and almond, lime-tea and quince. Keeps 2 to 12 years, good with seafood and veal, ideal for curries.

The splendid white **Chablis** comes

from northern Burgundy, east of Auxerre. The best of this vigorous, fruity wine keeps 10 years, while others can be drunk young, with fish and poultry.

Mâcon

If its own reds are rather undistinguished, the region's **Pouilly Fuissé** is a much appreciated rich, full-bodied and aromatic white that keeps 3 to 10 years and is ideal for fish, pork and veal, and the local snails.

Beaujolais

"Three rivers flow through Lyon," says a local adage, "the Rhône, the Saône and the Beaujolais." The major industry that has been carved out of the annual *"Beaujolais-nouveau-est-arrivé"* slogan should not blind you to the region's more noble red wines that happily age 5 to 10 years, each adding to the grape its own distinctively subtle fruitiness: **Saint-Amour** (a hint of peach and apple); **Juliénas** (raspberry and peach); **Chénas** (fragrance of peony); fuller-bodied **Moulin-à-Vent** (raspberry and strawberry); **Chiroubles** (bouquet of violets), best drunk young; robust, generous **Morgon** (black cherry, even kirsch); **Brouilly**, biggest producer, cheerful "wine of love". Served chilled, they're all fine with fish, or *chambré* (at room temperature) with practically anything.

Bordeaux

In the Middle Ages, the vineyards were the preserve of the English, who loved the light red "claret". Now most of the reds are a much deeper hue and rich in variety, from the châteaux of Médoc and Saint-Emilion on either side of the Gironde river, to those of the Graves, beside the Garonne. The nearby Sauternes vineyards produce celebrated mellow whites. Best years for reds: 1945, 47, 49, 55, 61, 66, 70, 75, 78, 82, 85; for whites: 45, 47, 53, 55, 59, 61, 70, 75, 85.

The king of the **Médoc** wines is the **Margaux**, delicate, sumptuous and sensual, with an aroma suggesting violets or roses. Keeps 5 to 20 years, divine accompaniment to beef, lamb, and veal sweetbreads. Of the nearby **Saint-Julien** vineyards, *Château Beychevelle* is most celebrated: velvety, fragrant, keeping 5 to 15 years and good with game, lamb and the local lamprey eels. **Pauillac** wines are appreciated for their classic vigour, a fruity freshness and an oak-like dryness. The most famous are the *Mouton-Rothschild* and *Lafite-Rothschild*, both keeping 5 to 20 years and superb with beef, lamb and light game. **Saint-Estèphe** is the biggest Médoc producer, its renowned *Château Calon-Ségur* supple and heady, but lighter than Pauillac. Keeps 5 to 15 years, good with goose *cassoulet* and *confit*.

Saint-Emilion is a deep garnet-red with a powerful aroma of truffles and autumn leaves, warm and generous in taste. Keeps 4 to 25 years, fine with venison, beef and lamprey eels. **Pomerol**, most notably the *Château Pétrus*, is full-bodied, warm and aromatic. Keeps 4 to 15 years, ideal with poultry. **Fronsac**, robust with a spicy bouquet, keeps 4 to 15 years, and is good with roast beef and lamb.

Best known of the **Graves** reds is the American-owned *Château Haut-Brion*, delicate and elegant. Keeps 5 to 10 years, great with poultry, veal and pork.

Of the sweet **Sauternes** whites, served with *foie gras*, white fish and desserts, the **Barsac** are much appreciated, full and subtle, with a vital hint of acid, keeping 5 to 25 years. The monumental *Château d'Yquem* must age at least 10 years and keeps getting better. Connoisseurs are almost frightened to open it.

Alsace

Traditionally, Alsatian white wines are categorized not by specific locality but by the three main grapes used in their production, the best keeping up to 20 years. Their distinctive flavour comes from a continental climate, unique among French vineyards, of particularly cold winters and hot, stormy summers.

Look out for the quality notation on the label, *vendanges tardives* (late-harvesting), or *sélection de grains nobles* (selection of noble grapes).

Most prestigious are the wines from **Riesling** grapes, producing an elegant and vigorous blend of sweet and acid with a bouquet hinting of lime-tea. Serve with hors d'œuvres, seafood and *choucroute* (Sauerkraut). **Gewürztraminer** grapes produce a more aromatic wine, both dry and fruity, with a heady hint of faded rose in the bouquet, splendid with Strasbourg *foie gras*, roast veal and slightly tart desserts. **Sylvaner** is the mass-production grape, simple, light and lively. Good with seafood, salami sausage and *choucroute*.

Champagne

Beyond the mystique of the world's most wonderful bubbles (see p.117), remember that *brut*, absolutely dry, is the best quality, followed by *extra-sec* (extra dry). Deceptively, the labelling of merely *sec* implies a hint of fruitiness; *demi-sec* is sweet and *doux* is very sweet. In the unending battle over which is best, **Ruinart** and **Roederer** each has its champion, but **Dom Pérignon** remains the most prestigious. Since 1969, only 72, 77, 81 and 84 have not been vintage years *(millésimés)*.

Try the rosé coloured with addition of red wine and Champagne's own red, **Bouzy**, superbly delicate but a bad traveller, so drink it on the spot.

Loire Valley

The dry white **Muscadet** is pale yellow, with a refined elegance that goes well with the local pike and other fish, good up to 5 years. The **Rosé d'Anjou** may be dry or semi-dry, lively, fruity, always drunk young, with sausage and ham, pork and veal. **Saumur** produces bubbly whites *(mousseux)* and light reds. The reds of **Bourgueil** and **Chinon** are heavily tannic but supple, good wines for cheese. **Vouvray** whites, both dry and sweet, need aging 5 to 10 years, good with poultry and fish. **Sancerre** produces one of the region's most admired dry whites, good with the local Chavignol goat cheese, but also an excellent rosé, subtly fruity with a grassy bouquet. The renowned **Pouilly Fumé** is a dry white Sauvignon, slightly greenish golden in hue, with a smoky aroma, best in its second year, served with shellfish.

Côtes du Rhône

These generous reds are grand with beef, lamb and game. One of the finest, **Hermitage** is purple with a rich, velvety, smoky flavour, a hint of blackberries, aroma of peony. Keeps 4 to 30 years, grand with beef, lamb and game. But the best known is **Châteauneuf-du-Pape**, named after the summer residence of the 14th-century Avignon popes, a powerful, sunny wine with spicy, heady bouquet. Keeps 4 to 10 years. The **Gigondas** has a warm, plummy flavour with a hint of liquorish. Keeps 2 to 5 years, very good with poultry and game birds.

Jura

One wine stands out, the heady *vin jaune* of **Arbois**, maturing six years for its rich amber hue and nutty flavour of hazel, almond and walnuts. Perfect for sausage, pâté and siestas.

Provence

Summer wines for lazy days on the beach or under the olive trees. Of the **Côtes de Provence** rosés, the best is the *Estandon* of Saint-Tropez. **Bandol** produces a full red, with all the fragrance of the *garrigue* heathland, and an amber-coloured rosé with a spicy tang to it.

South-West

The deep garnet-red **Madiran** is emphatically tannic, but elegant in its strength, fine for roasts, game, Roquefort and other blue cheeses. At the eastern end of the Pyrenees, **Languedoc** and **Roussillon** are sturdy picnic reds. **Banyuls** sweet reds, rosés and whites are splendid with *foie gras* and desserts, especially chocolate.

The Right Place at the Right Price

While hotels and restaurants throughout the world are becoming more the same and more easily "forgettable" day by day, in France they usually continue to provide a unique experience, something that stays in the mind long afterwards, that is discussed on cold evenings back at home with nostalgia and pleasure.

To help you choose a hotel or restaurant we have tried to make a selection based on the criteria of price, attraction and location.

We do not list crêperies, pizzerias, fast food outlets and brasseries where prices will be lower. Many of the restaurants chosen are indeed well known and have received distinctions for the quality of their cuisine. Even here, a fixed menu at a lower price is often offered at lunchtime on weekdays.

KEY

⊯ **Hotel**
⇌ **Restaurant**

Hotels (*for a double room with bath*)
▯▯▯ Higher-priced: above 1,000 F
▯▯ Medium-priced: 500–1,000 F
▯ Lower-priced: below 500 F

Restaurants (*for a three-course gourmet meal*)
▯▯▯ Higher-priced: above 400 F
▯▯ Medium-priced: 200–400 F
▯ Lower-priced: below 200 F

MF$: coupon in companion volume *More France for the $* providing a rebate, benefit or gift.

Paris and Vicinity
* *Postal or zip code. The final one or two figures represent the arrondissement or district.*

PARIS AND VICINITY

Paris

Ducs d'Anjou ⊯▯
1, rue Sainte-Opportune
75001 **Paris**
Tel. 42.36.92.24
38 rooms. Restored hotel. Small, quiet rooms.

Hôtel Lotti ⊯ ⇌▯▯▯
7, rue de Castiglione – 75001 **Paris**
Tel. 42.60.37.34; tlx. 240066
126 rooms. Smallest of the grand hotels with comfortable rooms furnished in period style. MF$

Ritz ⊯ ⇌▯▯▯
15, place Vendôme – 75001 **Paris**
Tel. 42.60.38.30; tlx. 220262
164 rooms. Pleasant luxury hotel. Interior garden.

Westminster ⊯ ⇌▯▯▯
13, rue de la Paix – 75002 **Paris**
Tel. 42.61.57.46; tlx. 680035
84 rooms. Completely renovated hotel with modern amenities but also many Louis XIV antiques. Restaurant closed in Aug., Sun. and Mon. MF$

Lutèce ⊯▯▯
65, rue Saint-Louis-en-l'Ile
75004 **Paris**
Tel. 43.26.23.52
23 rooms. Restored hotel. Tastefully decorated rooms.

Miravile ⇌▯▯
25, quai de la Tournelle – 75005 **Paris**
Tel. 46.34.07.78
Good cuisine. Intimate little restaurant on the banks of the Seine. Closed Sat. lunch and Sun. MF$

La Tour d'Argent ⇌▯▯▯
15, quai de la Tournelle – 75005 **Paris**
Tel. 43.54.23.31
Outstanding cuisine. Exceptional view of Notre-Dame. Historical wine display in the cellar. Closed Mon.

Abbaye Saint-Germain ⊯▯▯
10, rue Cassette – 75006 **Paris**
Tel. 45.44.38.11
45 rooms. Quiet hotel. Tastefully decorated rooms. Garden.

Angleterre ⊯▯▯
44, rue Jacob – 75006 **Paris**
Tel. 42.60.34.72
29 smart, renovated rooms. Flowered patio. Bar. Salon.

Lutétia ⊯ ⇌▯▯▯
45, bd Raspail – 75006 **Paris**
Tel. 45.44.38.10; tlx. 270424
282 rooms. Decorated in Art Deco style. MF$

Le Muniche ⇌▯
27, rue de Buci – 75006 **Paris**
Tel. 46.33.62.09; tlx. 201820
Popular restaurant. Open late at night.

Lenox ⊯▯
9, rue de l'Université – 75007 **Paris**
Tel. 42.96.10.95; tlx. 260745
32 rooms. Small, tastefully decorated rooms.

Saint-Dominique ⊯▯
62, rue Saint-Dominique
75007 **Paris**
Tel. 47.05.51.44; tlx. 206968
36 rooms. Small but well-equipped rooms, in a 17th-century building with a garden for breakfast. MF$

Varenne ⊯▯
44, rue de Bourgogne – 75007 **Paris**
Tel. 45.51.45.55
24 rooms. Quiet hotel. Charming patio.

Baumann Marbeuf ≈ ▯
15, rue Marbeuf – 75008 **Paris**
Tel. 47.20.11.11
Alsatian specialities. Near the Champs-Elysées. Closed mid-July to mid-Aug., Sat. lunch and Sun. MF$

Le Boeuf sur le Toit ≈ ▯
34, rue du Colisée – 75008 **Paris**
Tel. 43.59.83.80
Popular restaurant. Afternoon tea. Cocktails. Open late at night.

Concorde Saint-Lazare ≈ ≈ ▯▯▯
108, rue Saint-Lazare – 75008 **Paris**
Tel. 42.94.22.22; tlx. 650442
324 rooms. Comfort and tradition in luxury hotel. Lobby listed as a national monument. Edwardian billiard room. MF$

Hôtel de Crillon ≈ ≈ ▯▯▯
10, place de la Concorde – 75008 **Paris**
Tel. 42.65.24.24; tlx. 290204
146 rooms. Pleasant luxury hotel. Outdoor dining.

La Fermette Marbeuf ≈ ▯▯
5, rue Marbeuf – 75008 **Paris**
Tel. 47.20.63.53
1900s decor. Stained-glass windows.

Fouquet's ≈ ▯▯
99, av. des Champs-Elysées
75008 **Paris**
Tel. 47.23.70.60; tlx. 648227
Good cuisine. Closed mid-July to end Aug., Sat. and Sun.

Lucas-Carton ≈ ▯▯▯
9, place de la Madeleine – 75008 **Paris**
Tel. 42.65.22.90; tlx. 281088
Outstanding cuisine. 1900s decor. Closed 3 weeks in Aug., 2 weeks in Dec.–Jan., Sat. and Sun.

Royal Monceau ≈ ≈ ▯▯▯
37, av. Hoche – 75008 **Paris**
Tel. 45.61.98.00; tlx. 650361
180 rooms. Luxury hotel with fitness centre, indoor swimming pool and low-calory restaurant. Business club with full secretarial service. MF$

Taillevent ≈ ▯▯▯
15, rue Lamennais – 75008 **Paris**
Tel. 45.63.39.94
Outstanding cuisine. Closed Feb. school holidays, 4 weeks in Jul.–Aug., Sat. and Sun.

Ambassador-Concorde ≈ ≈ ▯▯▯
16, bd Haussmann – 75009 **Paris**
Tel. 42.46.92.63; tlx. 650912
300 rooms. Recently renovated and comfortable. MF$

Hôtel Moulin Rouge ▯▯
39, rue Fontaine – 75009 **Paris**
Tel. 42.82.08.56; tlx. 660055 ·
50 rooms. Charming hotel.

Au Petit Riche ≈ ▯
25, rue Le Peletier – 75009 **Paris**
Tel. 47.70.68.68
19th-century decor. Closed Sun.

Scribe ≈ ≈ ▯▯▯
1, rue Scribe – 75009 **Paris**
Tel. 47.42.03.40; tlx. 214653
217 rooms. Large luxury hotel. Furnished in period style. MF$

Brasserie Flo ≈ ▯
7, cour des Petites-Ecuries
75010 **Paris**
Tel. 47.70.13.59
1900s-style restaurant. Open late at night.

La Coupole ≈ ▯
102, bd du Montparnasse – 75014 **Paris**
Tel. 43.20.14.20
Popular restaurant. 1920s decor. Open late at night. Closed Aug.

Bistro 121 ≈ ▯▯
121, rue de la Convention
75015 **Paris**
Tel. 45.57.52.90
Good cuisine. Closed mid-July to mid-Aug., last week of Dec., Sun. evening and Mon.

Le Petit Victor-Hugo ≈ ▯
143, av. Victor-Hugo – 75016 **Paris**
Tel. 45.53.02.68
Popular restaurant.

Raphaël ≈ ≈ ▯▯▯
17, av. Kléber – 75116 **Paris**
Tel. 45.02.16.00; tlx. 610356
88 rooms. Small luxury hotel with antique-furnished rooms. MF$

Résidence du Bois ▯▯▯
16, rue Chalgrin – 75116 **Paris**
Tel. 45.00.50.59
16 rooms. Tasteful decor. Garden.

Robuchon (Jamin) ≈ ▯▯▯
32, rue de Longchamp – 75116 **Paris**
Tel. 47.27.12.27
Outstanding cuisine. Closed July, Sat. and Sun.

Centre Ville Etoile ▯▯
6, rue des Acacias – 75017 **Paris**
Tel. 43.80.56.18; tlx. 206968
16 rooms. Comfortable hotel in a quiet street, near the Champs-Elysées. Modern and tastefully decorated rooms. MF$

Epicure 108 ≈ ▯
108, rue Cardinet – 75017 **Paris**
Tel. 47.63.50.91
Modern decor. Closed Sat. lunch and Sun.

Le Manoir de Paris ≈ ▯▯
6, rue Pierre-Demours – 75017 **Paris**
Tel. 45.72.25.25
Excellent cuisine. Closed 3 weeks in July, Sat. and Sun. MF$

Regent's Garden ▯▯
6, rue Pierre-Demours – 75017 **Paris**
Tel. 45.74.07.30; tlx. 640127
40 rooms. Large rooms. Rustic furnishings. Flowered garden.

Terrass'Hotel ≈ ≈ ▯▯
12, rue Joseph-de-Maistre
75018 **Paris**
Tel. 46.06.72.85; tlx. 280830
95 rooms. Splendid view over Paris from the 7th-floor terrace. MF$

Ile-de-France

Hostellerie les Pléiades ≈ ▯
21, rue Grande – 77630 **Barbizon**
Tel. 60.66.40.25; tlx. 692131
15 rooms. Quiet restaurant/hotel with outdoor dining and garden.

La Belle Epoque ≈ ▯▯
10, place de la Mairie
78117 **Châteaufort**
Tel. 39.56.21.66
Good cuisine. Rustic inn overlooking the valley. Closed 3 weeks in Aug.—Sep., 2 weeks in Dec.—Jan., Sun. evening and Mon.

Relais Sainte-Jeanne ≈ ▯▯
95830 **Cormeilles-en-Vexin**
(Cergy-Pontoise)
Tel. 34.66.61.56
Excellent cuisine. Outdoor dining. Garden. Closed Feb. school holidays, 3 weeks in Aug., Sun. evening, Mon., Tues. evening (except Apr. to Aug.).

Auberge de Condé ≈ ▯▯
1, av. de Montmirail
77260 **La Ferté-sous-Jouarre**
Tel. 60.22.00.07
Excellent cuisine. Closed Mon. evening and Tues.

La Vieille Fontaine ≈ ▯▯
8, av. Grétry
78600 **Maisons-Laffite**
Tel. 39.62.01.78
Excellent cuisine. Outdoor dining. Garden. Closed Aug., Sun. and Mon.

Cazaudehore et ☒ ⇌ ▯▯
La Forestière
1, av. du Président-Kennedy
78100 **Saint-Germain-en-Laye**
Tel. 34.51.93.80
24 rooms. Good cuisine. Outdoor dining. Rustic decor. Garden. Restaurant closed Mon.

Les Trois Marches ⇌ ▯▯
3, rue Colbert – 78000 **Versailles**
Tel. 39.50.13.21
Excellent cuisine. 18th-century villa with view of the Palais de Versailles nearby. Attractive decor. Outdoor dining. Closed 2 weeks in Feb., Sun. and Mon. MF$

Trianon Palace ☒ ⇌ ▯▯▯
1, bd de la Reine – 78000 **Versailles**
Tel. 39.50.34.21; tlx. 698863
110 rooms. Quiet hotel in large park. Outdoor dining. MF$.

NORTH-EAST

Flanders

Château de La ☒ ⇌ ▯
Motte Fénelon
Square du Château – 59400 **Cambrai**
Tel. 27.83.61.38; tlx. 120285
29 rooms. Quiet hotel. Park, indoor swimming pool, tennis. Closed Sun. evening.

Bellevue ☒▯
5, rue Jean-Roisin – 59800 **Lille**
Tel. 20.57.45.86/64; tlx. 120790
80 rooms. Spacious, comfortable rooms.

Le Flambard ⇌ ▯▯
79, rue d'Angleterre – 59800 **Lille**
Tel. 20.51.00.06
Excellent cuisine. 17th-century building. Closed first week in Jan., Aug., Sun. evening and Mon.

La Meunerie ⇌ ☒ ▯▯
174, rue des Pierres
59229 **Teteghem (Dunkerque)**
Tel. 28.26.14.30; tlx. 132253
Good cuisine. Elegant restaurant. 8 rooms. Closed end Dec. to mid-Jan., Sun. evening and Mon.

L'Albéroi ⇌ ▯
(Buffet de la Gare)
59300 **Valenciennes**
Tel. 27.46.86.30
Good cuisine. Closed Sun. evening.

Picardy

La Faisanderie ⇌ ▯▯
45, Grand-Place – 62000 **Arras**
Tel. 21.48.20.76
Good cuisine. In 17th-century wine cellar. Closed Feb. school holidays, 3 weeks in Aug., Sun. evening and Mon.

Hostellerie du Château ☒ ⇌ ▯▯
02130 **Fère-en-Tardenois**
Tel. 23.82.21.13; tlx. 145526
14 rooms. Quiet hotel in attractive 16th-century residence with park and view. Good cuisine. Tennis. Closed Jan. and Feb. MF$

Manoir Hôtel ☒ ⇌ ▯▯
Av. du Golf – 62520 **Le Touquet**
Tel. 21.05.20.22; tlx. 135565
42 rooms. Quiet, pleasant hotel. Comfortable rooms. View, outdoor dining, swimming pool, garden and tennis. Closed Jan. and Feb.

Champagne

Royal Champagne ☒ ⇌ ▯▯
Champillon – 51160 **Ay (Epernay)**
Tel. 26.52.87.11; tlx. 830111
25 rooms. Renovated hotel dominating the Champagne vineyards near Epernay. Garden. Good cuisine. Closed Jan. MF$

Le Cheval Blanc ☒ ⇌ ▯
Sept-Saulx
51400 **Mourmelon-le-Grand**
Tel. 26.03.90.27; tlx. 830885
23 rooms. Good cuisine. Charming hotel. Park, tennis. Closed mid-Jan. to mid-Feb.

Boyer (Les Crayères) ⇌ ☒ ▯▯▯
64, bd Henry-Vasnier – 51100 **Reims**
Tel. 26.82.80.80; tlx. 830959
Outstanding cuisine. Outdoor dining. 15 rooms. Tasteful decor. Elegant building facing a park. Tennis.

Le Chardonnay ⇌ ▯▯
184, av. d'Epernay – 51100 **Reims**
Tel. 26.06.08.60
Good cuisine. Bustling, popular restaurant. Closed Aug., Sat. lunch and Sun. MF$

Le Florence ⇌ ▯▯
43, bd Foch – 51100 **Reims**
Tel. 26.47.12.70
Good cuisine. Elegant decor. Outdoor dining. Closed Feb. school holidays, end July to mid-Aug. and Sun. evening. MF$

La Paix ☒ ⇌ ▯
9, rue de Buirette – 51100 **Reims**
Tel. 26.40.04.08; tlx. 830974
105 well-equipped rooms. Swimming pool, sauna, fitness club.

Lorraine

Les Vannes et ⇌ ☒ ▯
sa Résidence
6, rue Porte-Haute – 54460 **Liverdun**
Tel. 83.24.46.01
Good cuisine. Panoramic view of the Moselle. 11 rooms. Closed Feb. and Mon. MF$

Château d'Adoménil ⇌ ☒ ▯▯
54300 **Lunéville**
Tel. 83.74.04.81
Good cuisine. Outdoor dining. 4 luxury rooms. Park. Closed 4 weeks in Jan.—Feb., Sun. evening and Mon.

Le Goéland ⇌ ▯
27, rue des Ponts – 54000 **Nancy**
Tel. 83.35.17.25
Good cuisine. Attractive, modern restaurant. Elegant decor. Seafood specialities. Closed Sun. evening and Mon. MF$

Grand Hôtel de la Reine ☒ ⇌ ▯▯
2, place Stanislas – 54000 **Nancy**
Tel. 83.35.03.01; tlx. 960367
44 rooms. Comfortable luxury hotel in 18th-century palace. Period furnishings. MF$

Alsace

Aux Armes de France ⇌ ☒ ▯▯
Grand-Rue 1 – 68770 **Ammerschwihr**
Tel. 89.47.10.12
Excellent cuisine. 8 rooms. Closed Jan., Wed., and Thurs. lunch.

Hostellerie Saint-Barnabé ☒ ⇌ ▯
Murbach – 68530 **Buhl**
Tel. 89.76.92.15; tlx. 881036
27 rooms. Flower-decked hotel in a valley. View, tennis. Closed mid-Jan. to early Mar., Sun. evening and Mon. (out of season).

Terminus-Bristol ☒ ⇌ ▯▯
7, place de la Gare – 68000 **Colmar**
Tel. 89.41.10.10; tlx. 880248
70 rooms. Quiet, renovated hotel. Good cuisine.

Schillinger ⇌ ▯▯
16, rue Stanislas – 68000 **Colmar**
Tel. 89.41.43.17

Excellent cuisine. Elegant restaurant.
Closed Sun. evening and Mon.

Chambard ⇒🛏️🍴
rue du Gal-de-Gaulle
68240 **Kaysersberg**
Tel. 89.47.10.17; tlx. 880272
Good cuisine. 20 rooms. Nice, comfortable little hotel. Closed 3 weeks in Mar., 2 weeks in Dec., Sun. evening and Mon.

Hostellerie du Cerf ⇒🛏️🍴
30, rue du Gal-de-Gaulle
67520 **Marlenheim**
Tel. 88.87.73.73
Excellent cuisine. Outdoor dining. 20 rooms around a typical Alsatian courtyard. Closed Feb. school holidays, Mon. and Tues.

L'Auberge de l'Ill ⇒🍴
Illhaeusern – 68150 **Ribeauvillé**
Tel. 89.71.83.23
Outstanding cuisine. Elegant restaurant on the banks of the Ill. Outdoor dining. Superb garden. Closed Feb., first week in July, Mon. (except lunch in summer) and Tues.

Les Vosges ⇒🛏️🍴
2, Grande-Rue
68150 **Ribeauvillé**
Tel. 89.73.61.39
Good cuisine. 18 rooms. Closed Dec. to mid-Mar. and Mon.

Château d'Isenbourg 🛏️⇒🍴
68250 **Rouffach**
Tel. 89.49.63.53; tlx. 880819
37 rooms. Graceful hotel surrounded by vineyards. Good cuisine. Outdoor swimming pool, garden and tennis. Closed early Jan. to mid-Mar. MF$

Cathédrale Dauphin 🛏️🍴
12, place de la Cathédrale
67000 **Strasbourg**
Tel. 88.22.12.12; tlx. 871054
28 rooms. Small, renovated hotel. View of the cathedral. Modern, comfortable.

Crocodile ⇒🍴
10, rue de l'Outre
67000 **Strasbourg**
Tel. 88.32.13.02
Excellent cuisine. Closed 4 weeks in July–Aug., Sun. and Mon.

Hilton 🛏️⇒🍴
Av. Herrenschmidt
67000 **Strasbourg**
Tel. 88.37.10.10; tlx. 890363
247 rooms. Modern, well-equipped hotel. Outdoor dining. Restaurant closed in Feb., Aug. and Sat. lunch.

Maison Kammerzell ⇒🍴
16, place de la Cathédrale
67000 **Strasbourg**
Tel. 88.32.42.14
16th-century Alsatian building across the square from the cathedral. Closed Feb. MF$

Monopole-Métropole 🛏️🍴
16, rue Kuhn
67000 **Strasbourg**
Tel. 88.32.11.94; tlx. 890366
94 rooms. Friendly hotel furnished with Alsatian antiques. Indoor swimming pool, sauna, fitness centre. MF$

Burgundy

Chez Camille ⇒🛏️🍴
21230 **Arnay-le-Duc**
Tel. 80.90.01.38
13 rooms. Good cuisine. Beautiful furnishings. Sauna. Closed Jan.

Le Jardin Gourmand ⇒🍴
56, bd Vauban – 89000 **Auxerre**
Tel. 86.51.53.52
Good cuisine. Outdoor dining. Closed Feb. school holidays, first 3 weeks in Nov., Sun. evening and Mon.

Moulin des Ruats 🛏️⇒🍴
Vallée du Cousin
89200 **Avallon**
Tel. 86.34.07.14
23 rooms. Charming hotel with view. Garden at the water's edge. Outdoor dining. Open end Feb. to end Nov. Closed Mon., and Tues. lunch.

L'Ermitage de Corton ⇒🛏️🍴
Rte de Dijon
Chorey-lès-Beaune – 21200 **Beaune**
Tel. 80.22.05.28; tlx. 351189
Good cuisine. 5 rooms. 5 suites. Comfortable, luxury hotel with excellent service and facilities. View, garden. Closed 4 weeks in Jan.–Feb., Sun. evening and Mon. MF$

Jacques Lainé ⇒🍴
10—12, bd Foch – 21200 **Beaune**
Tel. 80.24.76.10
Good cuisine. Outdoor dining. Closed Tues., and Wed. lunch out of season.

Auberge Bressane ⇒🍴
166, bd de Brou
01000 **Bourg-en-Bresse**
Tel. 74.22.22.68
Good cuisine. Outdoor dining.

Hostellerie des Clos ⇒🛏️🍴
Rue Jules-Rathier – 89800 **Chablis**

Tel. 86.42.10.63
Good cuisine. 26 rooms. 18th-century inn remodelled in pleasant modern style. Garden. Restaurant closed Jan. and Wed., and Thurs. lunch (Oct. to May). MF$

Lameloise ⇒🛏️🍴
Place d'Armes – 71150 **Chagny**
Tel. 85.87.08.85; tlx. 801086
Outstanding cuisine. Elegantly decorated old Burgundy house. Closed mid-Dec. to mid-Jan., Wed. and Thurs. lunch.

Le Moulin de Martorey ⇒🍴
Saint-Rémy
71100 **Chalon-sur-Saône**
Tel. 85.48.12.98
Good cuisine. Outdoor dining. Closed Feb. school holidays, 3 weeks in Aug.–Sep., Sun. evening and Mon.

Chapeau Rouge 🛏️⇒🍴
5, rue Michelet – 21000 **Dijon**
Tel. 80.30.28.10; tlx. 350535
30 rooms. Quiet, old building in the centre of Dijon. Good cuisine. MF$

Jean-Pierre Billoux ⇒🍴
14, place Darcy – 21000 **Dijon**
Tel. 80.30.11.00
Excellent cuisine. Outdoor dining. Closed Feb., Sun. evening and Mon. MF$

Thibert ⇒🍴
10, place Wilson – 21000 **Dijon**
Tel. 80.67.74.64
Excellent cuisine. Closed 3 weeks in Jan., 2 weeks in Aug., Sun., and Mon. lunch.

La Rôtisserie
du Chambertin
21220 **Gevrey-Chambertin**
Tel. 80.34.33.20
Excellent cuisine. Former wine cellar. Closed Feb., first week in Aug., Sun. evening and Mon.

La Côte Saint-Jacques ⇒🛏️🍴
14, fg de Paris – 89300 **Joigny**
Tel. 86.62.09.70; tlx. 801458
Outstanding cuisine. 14 tastefully decorated rooms in two buildings, joined by a tunnel. Indoor swimming pool. Closed Jan. MF$

La Côte d'Or ⇒🛏️🍴
37, rue Thurot
21700 **Nuits-Saint-Georges**
Tel. 80.61.06.10
Excellent cuisine. 7 rooms furnished with antiques. Closed 3 weeks in July, Wed., and Sun. evening. MF$

La Côte d'Or ⇒ 🛏️ ▥▥▥
2, rue d'Argentine – 21210 **Saulieu**
Tel. 80.64.07.66; tlx. 350778
Outstanding cuisine. 15 rooms. Tastefully decorated suites.

L'Abbaye Saint-Michel ⇒ 🛏️ ▥▥
Rue Saint-Michel – 89700 **Tonnerre**
Tel. 86.55.05.99; tlx. 801356
Excellent cuisine. 10 rooms in rustic style. Quiet situation. View, park, tennis. Closed early Jan. to mid-Feb., Mon., and Tues. lunch (Oct. to Apr.).

Greuze ⇒ ▥▥
1, rue Albert-Thibaudet
71700 **Tournus**
Tel. 85.51.13.52
Excellent cuisine.

Le Rempart 🛏️ ⇒ ▥▥
2, av. Gambetta – 71700 **Tournus**
Tel. 85.51.10.56; tlx. 351019
28 rooms. Good cuisine. MF$

L'Espérance ⇒ 🛏️ ▥▥▥
Saint-Père – 89450 **Vézelay**
Tel. 86.33.20.45; tlx. 800005
Outstanding cuisine. 21 tastefully furnished rooms. Country garden. Closed early Jan. to early Feb. Restaurant also closed Tues., and Wed. lunch.

Jura

Le Paris ⇒ 🛏️ ▥
9, rue de l'Hôtel-de-Ville
39600 **Arbois**
Tel. 84.66.05.67; tlx. 361033
Good cuisine. 18 rooms. Garden. Closed mid-Nov. to mid-Mar., Sep., Mon. evening and Tues.

Château de Divonne 🛏️ ⇒ ▥▥
01220 **Divonne-les-Bains**
Tel. 50.20.00.32; tlx. 309033
23 rooms. Quiet, pleasant hotel with superb view of the lake and Mont-Blanc. Garden. Good cuisine. Closed early Jan. to mid-Mar.

Château de Rigny 🛏️ ⇒ ▥
Rigny – 70100 **Gray**
Tel. 84.65.25.01; tlx. 362926
24 rooms. Quiet, pleasant hotel in a park on the banks of the Saône. Swimming pool, tennis. Closed last 3 weeks of Jan.

Valentin ⇒ ▥
Ecole Valentin
25480 **Miserey-Salines (Besançon)**
Tel. 81.80.03.90
Good cuisine. Outdoor dining. Closed 2 weeks in Aug.

NORTH-WEST

Normandy

Le Lion d'Or 🛏️ ⇒ ▥
71, rue Saint-Jean – 14400 **Bayeux**
Tel. 31.92.06.90; tlx. 171143
29 rooms. Old posthouse with flowered courtyard. Good cuisine. Closed Jan. MF$

La Bourride ⇒ ▥▥
15, rue du Vaugueux – 14000 **Caen**
Tel. 31.93.50.76
Excellent cuisine. Old-Caen-style building. Closed 3 weeks in Jan., last 2 weeks in Aug., Sun. and Mon.

Normandy 🛏️ ⇒ ▥▥▥
38, rue Jean-Mermoz
14800 **Deauville**
Tel. 31.88.09.21; tlx. 170617
298 rooms. Charming luxury hotel. View of the beach, indoor swimming pool. Outdoor dining.

La Mélie ⇒ ▥
2, Grande-Rue-du-Pollet
76200 **Dieppe**
Tel. 35.84.21.19
Good cuisine. Closed Feb., Sun. evening and Mon.

La Ferme Saint-Siméon 🛏️ ⇒ ▥▥▥ et son Manoir
Rue Adolphe-Marais
14600 **Honfleur**
Tel. 31.89.23.61; tlx. 171031
33 rooms. Pleasant hotel in park overlooking the estuary. Outdoor dining, tennis. MF$

Château du Molay 🛏️ ⇒ ▥▥
Rte d'Isigny – 14330 **Le Molay-Littry**
Tel. 31.22.90.82; tlx. 171912
38 rooms. Quiet hotel. Park, outdoor swimming pool, tennis. Outdoor dining. Open early Mar. to end Nov.

Hôtel de la Cathédrale 🛏️
12, rue Saint-Romain – 76000 **Rouen**
Tel. 35.71.57.95
24 rooms. Delightful hotel. Flowered courtyard.

Gill ⇒ ▥▥
60, rue Saint-Nicolas
76000 **Rouen**
Tel. 35.71.16.14
Good cuisine. Closed 2 weeks in Feb., end Aug. to mid-Sep., Sun. and Mon. lunch.

Brittany

Castel Marie-Louise 🛏️ ⇒ ▥▥▥
1, av. Andrieux – 44500 **La Baule**
Tel. 40.60.20.60; tlx. 700408
29 rooms. Attractive hotel in a park. View. Good cuisine. Outdoor dining.

L'Hermitage 🛏️ ⇒ ▥▥▥
Espl. François-André
44500 **La Baule**
Tel. 40.60.37.00; tlx. 710510
228 rooms. Luxury hotel. View, park, outdoor swimming pool, tennis, private beach, sauna. Outdoor dining. Open mid.-Apr. to mid-Oct.

Restaurant de Bricourt ⇒ 🛏️ ▥▥
1, rue Duguesclin – 35260 **Cancale**
Tel. 99.89.64.76
Excellent cuisine. 6 rooms. Open mid-Mar. to mid-Dec. Closed Tues., Wed.

Lann-Roz 🛏️ ⇒ ▥
36, av. de la Poste – 56340 **Carnac**
Tel. 97.52.10.48
14 rooms. Charming restaurant and hotel with simple comfort. Swimming pool, flowered garden. MF$

Le Galion ⇒ 🛏️ ▥▥
15, rue Saint-Guénolé
29110 **Concarneau** – Tel. 98.97.30.16
Good cuisine. Pleasant restaurant. 5 rooms. Closed end Jan. to early Mar., end Nov. to early Dec., and Mon.

Château de Locguénolé ⇒ 🛏️ ▥▥
Rte de Port-Louis – 56700 **Hennebont**
Tel. 97.76.29.04; tlx. 950636
Excellent cuisine. 31 rooms. Quiet hotel by the river. Swimming pool, tennis. Open early Mar. to mid-Nov. MF$

Le Golf de la Breteshe 🛏️ ⇒ ▥
44160 **Missillac**
Tel. 40.88.30.05
27 rooms. View, park, outdoor swimming pool, tennis, golf. Closed Feb.

Restaurant de l'Europe ⇒ 🛏️ ▥
1, rue d'Aiguillon – 29210 **Morlaix**
Tel. 98.62.11.99
Excellent cuisine. 66 rooms. Closed mid-Dec. to mid-Jan.

L'Hôtel 🛏️
6, rue Henri-IV – 44000 **Nantes**
Tel. 40.29.30.31
31 charming, well-decorated rooms.

Les Maraîchers ⇒ ▥▥
21, rue Fouré – 44000 **Nantes**
Tel. 40.47.06.51
Excellent cuisine. Closed Sat. lunch and Sun.

La Plage
Sainte-Anne-la-Palud
29127 **Plomodiern**
Tel. 98.92.50.12; tlx. 941377
30 rooms. Quiet, attractive hotel. View. Garden, tennis, outdoor swimming pool. Good cuisine. Open early Apr. to mid-Oct.

Moulin de Rosmadec
29123 **Pont-Aven**
Tel. 98.06.00.22
Good cuisine. Pleasant restaurant in former mill, Breton decor. 4 rooms. Closed Feb. and last 2 weeks in Oct.

Georges Painaud
13, rue Saint-Michel
56230 **Questembert**
Tel. 97.26.11.12
Excellent cuisine. 6 rooms. Closed early Jan. to early Mar., Sun. evening and Mon. (except July and Aug.)

Altea
Place du Colombier – 35000 **Rennes**
Tel. 99.31.54.54; tlx. 730905
140 rooms. Pleasant, bright rooms. Good cuisine.

Le Palais
7, place du Parlement
35000 **Rennes**
Tel. 99.79.45.01
Good cuisine. Closed Feb. school holidays, last 3 weeks in Aug., Sun. evening and Mon.

Duchesse Anne
5, place Guy-La Chambre
35400 **Saint-Malo**
Tel. 99.40.85.33
Good cuisine. 1920s decor. Outdoor dining. Closed Dec.—Jan. and Wed.

Mercure
2, chaussée du Sillon
35400 **Saint-Malo**
Tel. 99.56.84.84; tlx. 740583
70 rooms. View over the port and old town.

Loire Valley

Le Manoir Saint Thomas
Place Richelieu – 37400 **Amboise**
Tel. 47.57.22.52
Good cuisine. Renaissance building. Outdoor dining. Garden. Closed mid-Jan. to mid-Feb.

Le Quéré
9, pl. du Ralliement –49100 **Angers**
Tel. 41.87.64.94
Excellent cuisine. Closed Feb. school

holidays, first 2 weeks in July, Fri. evening and Sat.

Le Grand Monarque
Place de la République
37190 **Azay-le-Rideau**
Tel. 47.45.40.08
30 rooms. Charming hotel. Simple comfort. Outdoor dining. Garden. MF$

Auberge du XIIe Siècle
Saché – 37190 **Azay-le-Rideau**
Tel. 47.26.86.58
Good cuisine. Medieval setting. Garden. Closed Feb. and Tues. MF$

Le Bocca d'Or
15, rue Haute – 41000 **Blois**
Tel. 54.78.04.74
Good cuisine. Closed end Jan. to early Mar., Sun., and Mon. lunch.

Le Relais
1, av. de Chambord – 41250 **Bracieux**
Tel. 54.46.41.22
Excellent cuisine. Closed end Dec. to early Feb., Tues. evening and Wed.

Château de Teildras
Cheffes-sur-Sarthe
49125 **Châteauneuf-sur-Sarthe**
Tel. 41.42.61.08; tlx. 722268
11 rooms. 16th-century residence in a park. Open early Apr. to end Oct. Restaurant closed Tues. lunch. MF$

Au Plaisir Gourmand
2, rue Parmentier – 37500 **Chinon**
Tel. 47.93.20.48
Good cuisine. Charming old building. Closed last 3 weeks in Jan., last 2 weeks in Nov., Sun. evening and Mon.

Domaine de Beauvois
37230 **Luynes**
Tel. 47.55.50.11; tlx. 750204
28 rooms. Quiet, pleasant hotel. View, park, outdoor swimming pool, tennis. Good cuisine. Closed mid-Jan. to mid-Mar.

Château d'Artigny
Route d'Azay-le-Rideau
37250 **Montbazon**
Tel. 47.26.24.24; tlx. 750900
46 rooms. Luxurious hotel in large park with superb view over the Indre river, outdoor swimming pool, putting green and tennis. Good cuisine. Closed end Nov. to mid-Jan. MF$

Domaine de la Tortinière
37250 **Montbazon**
Tel. 47.26.00.19; tlx. 752186
14 rooms. Good cuisine. View of the Indre valley. Park, outdoor swimming

pool, tennis. Open early Mar. to mid-Nov. Closed Tues.lunch and Wed.

Auberge des Templiers
Les Bézards
45290 **Nogent-sur-Vernisson**
Tel. 38.31.80.01; tlx. 780998
Excellent cuisine. 22 rooms. Attractive hotel in a park. Outdoor swimming pool, tennis. Outdoor dining. Closed mid-Jan. to mid-Feb.

Domaine des Hauts-de-Loire
Rte de Herbault – 41150 **Onzain**
Tel. 54.20.72.57; tlx. 751547
22 rooms. Former 1840 hunting lodge. Good cuisine. Outdoor dining. Tennis. Closed Dec. and Jan. MF$

La Crémaillère
34, rue N.-D.-de-Recouvrance
45000 **Orléans**
Tel. 38.53.49.17
Excellent cuisine. Closed Aug., Sun. evening and Mon.

Jackotel
18, rue Cloître-Saint-Aignan
45000 **Orléans**
Tel. 38.54.48.48
39 rooms. Charming hotel. Tastefully decorated, small rooms. Garden.

Lion d'Or
69, rue Georges-Clemenceau
41200 **Romorantin-Lanthenay**
Tel. 54.76.00.28; tlx. 750990
Excellent cuisine. 10 rooms. Pleasant hotel with flowered terrace. Closed early Jan. to mid-Feb.

Barrier
101, av. de la Tranchée – 37100 **Tours**
Tel. 47.54.20.39
Excellent cuisine. Closed Feb. school holidays, Sun. evening and Mon.

Jean Bardet
57, rue Groison – 37100 **Tours**
Tel. 47.41.41.11; tlx. 752463
Excellent cuisine. 9 rooms. Pleasant hotel in a park. Swimming pool.

Le Royal
65, av. de Grammont – 37000 **Tours**
Tel. 47.64.71.78; tlx. 752006
35 rooms. In the heart of Tours. Comfortable, charming rooms.

Hôtel d'Espagne
9, rue du Château – 36600 **Valençay**
Tel. 54.00.00.02; tlx. 751675
10 rooms. Quiet hotel in former coaching inn with flowered terraces. Good cuisine. Closed Jan. and Feb. MF$

CENTRE

Berry

La Cognette ⌦ ⌦ ▯▯
2, bd Stalingrad – 36100 **Issoudun**
Tel. 54.21.21.83
Good cuisine. 11 rooms. Closed Jan., last 2 weeks in Aug., Sun. evening and Mon.

Limousin

Château de Castel Novel ⌦ ⌦ ▯▯
Varetz
19240 **Allassac (Brive-la-Gaillarde)**
Tel. 55.85.00.01; tlx. 590065
33 rooms. Ancient residence in a large park, outdoor swimming pool, tennis. Good cuisine. Open early May to mid-Oct.

Royal Limousin ⌦▯
1, place de la République
87000 **Limoges**
Tel. 55.34.65.30; tlx. 580771
75 rooms. Good situation. Bright, spacious rooms.

Auvergne

Hôtel Radio ⌦ ⌦ ▯
43, av. Pierre-Curie
63400 **Chamalières**
Tel. 73.30.87.83; tlx. 530955
27 rooms. Good cuisine. Renovated hotel. Art Deco furnishings. Most rooms with view. Garden. Open early Mar. to mid-Nov. Restaurant closed Sun. evening and Mon. MF$

Hôtel de Paris ⌦ ⌦ ▯▯
21, rue de Paris – 03000 **Moulins**
Tel. 70.44.00.58; tlx. 394853
27 rooms. Good cuisine. Restaurant closed Sun. evening and Mon. Oct. to May).

La Belle Meunière ⌦▯▯
24, av. de la Vallée – 63130 **Royan**
Tel. 73.35.80.17
In the upper part of town. Belle Epoque restaurant. Outdoor dining. 12 rooms. Closed 3 weeks in Feb., end Oct. to end Nov., Sun. evening and Wed. MF$

Pavillon Sévigné ⌦ ⌦ ▯▯
10, place Sévigné – 03200 **Vichy**
Tel. 70.32.16.22
37 rooms. Charming hotel. View. Former residence of Madame de Sévigné, with a French-style garden.

SOUTH-EAST

Savoie

Le Manoir ⌦ ⌦ ▯
37, rue George-Ier
73100 **Aix-les-Bains**
Tel. 79.61.44.00; tlx. 980793
73 rooms. Very quiet, comfortable hotel with attractive garden.

L'Abbaye ⌦ ⌦ ▯▯
15, chemin de l'Abbaye
74000 **Annecy**
Tel. 50.23.61.08; tlx. 385417
8 rooms, 3 suites. Quiet hotel in a 16th-century former abbey with tree-shaded terrace and garden. Outdoor dining. MF$

Auberge de l'Eridan ⌦▯▯▯
7, av. de Chavoires – 74000 **Annecy**
Tel. 50.66.22.04
Excellent cuisine. View. Outdoor dining. Garden. Closed 3 weeks Feb.—Mar., mid-Aug. to early Sep., Sun. evening and Wed.

Ombremont ⌦ ⌦ ▯▯
73370 **Le Bourget-du-Lac**
Tel. 79.25.00.23; tlx. 980832
18 rooms. Good cuisine. Quiet hotel in a park. View of lake and mountains. Outdoor swimming pool. Outdoor dining. Closed end Dec. to early Feb.

Roubatcheff ⌦▯▯
6, rue du Théâtre – 73000 **Chambéry**
Tel. 79.33.24.91
Good cuisine. Closed mid-June to mid-July, Sun. evening and Mon.

Auberge du Bois-Prin ⌦ ⌦ ▯▯
Les Moussoux – 74400 **Chamonix**
Tel. 50.53.33.51
11 rooms. Quiet chalet hotel. Superb view of Mont-Blanc range. Garden. Outdoor dining. Closed 4 weeks May—June, early Oct. to mid-Dec. and Wed. lunch.

Mont-Blanc ⌦ ⌦ ▯▯
Place de l'Eglise – 74400 **Chamonix**
Tel. 50.53.05.64; tlx. 385614
46 rooms. View, beautiful garden, outdoor swimming pool, tennis and sauna. Outdoor dining.

La Bergerie ⌦▯▯
73120 **Courchevel**
Tel. 79.08.24.70
Popular restaurant. Savoyard specialities. Closed from Easter to Dec. MF$

Hôtel Royal ⌦ ⌦ ▯▯▯
74500 **Evian-les-Bains**
Tel. 50.75.14.00; tlx. 385759
129 rooms. Quiet hotel with superb view of lake and mountains. Park, outdoor swimming pool, tennis. Outdoor dining. Closed mid-Dec. to mid-Feb.

Mont-Blanc ⌦ ⌦ ▯▯▯
Place de l'Eglise – 74120 **Megève**
Tel. 50.21.20.02; tlx. 385854
65 rooms. Charming hotel. Well-furnished rooms. Terrace, swimming pool, sauna. Closed mid-Apr. to early June.

Le Prieuré ⌦ ▯▯
68, Grande-Rue
74200 **Thonon-les-Bains**
Tel. 50.71.31.89
Good cuisine. 17th-century decor. Closed Sun. evening and Mon.

Auberge du Père Bise ⌦ ⌦ ▯▯▯
Talloires – 74290 **Veyrier-du-Lac**
Tel. 50.60.72.01; tlx. 385812
Excellent cuisine. 25 rooms. Lakeside hotel. View. Outdoor dining. Closed mid-Apr. to early May and mid-Dec. to mid-Feb., Tues., and Wed. lunch.

Dauphiné

Park Hotel ⌦ ⌦ ▯▯
10, pl. Paul-Mistral – 38000 **Grenoble**
Tel. 76.87.29.11; tlx. 320767
56 rooms. Attractive decor. Closed 3 weeks in Aug.

Poularde Bressane ⌦▯
12, place P.-Mistral – 38000 **Grenoble**
Tel. 76.87.08.90
Good cuisine. Closed Aug., end Dec., Sat. lunch and Sun.

Rhône Valley

Les Hospitaliers ⌦ ⌦ ▯▯
Poët-Laval
26160 **La Bégude-de-Mazenc**
(Dieulefit)
Tel. 75.46.22.32
20 rooms. Pleasant hotel in rebuilt 12th-century castle village. Swimming pool. Good cuisine. Outdoor dining. Open early Mar. to mid-Nov. MF$

Paul Bocuse ⌦▯▯▯
69600 **Collonges-au-Mont-d'Or**
(Lyon)
Tel. 78.22.01.40; tlx. 375382
Outstanding cuisine. Elegant restaurant.

Grand Hôtel Concorde 🛏️ 🍽️ ▯▯
11, rue Grôlée – 69002 **Lyon**
Tel. 78.42.56.21; tlx. 330244
140 rooms. Renovated hotel with sound-proofed and air-conditioned rooms. MF$

Cour des Loges 🛏️ 🍽️ ▯▯▯
6, rue du Boeuf – 69005 **Lyon**
Tel. 78.42.75.75; tlx. 330831
63 rooms. Excellent new hotel in old Lyon. Imaginative modern decor. Very comfortable rooms. Hanging garden.

Restaurant Henry 🍽️ ▯
27, rue de la Martinière
69001 **Lyon**
Tel. 78.28.26.08
Good cuisine. Elegant, modern decor. Frescoes. Closed Mon., and Sat. lunch. MF$

Léon de Lyon 🍽️ ▯▯
1, rue Pléney – 69001 **Lyon**
Tel. 78.28.11.33
Excellent cuisine. Closed 2 weeks Dec.—Jan., Sun., and Mon. lunch.

Pierre Orsi 🍽️ ▯▯
3, place Kléber – 69006 **Lyon**
Tel. 78.89.57.68; tlx. 305965
Excellent cuisine. Elegant, charming decor. Closed Sun. MF$

Phénix 🛏️▯
7, quai Bondy – 69005 **Lyon**
Tel. 78.28.30.40
36 rooms. In the old part of town.

La Tour Rose 🍽️ ▯▯
16, rue Boeuf – 69005 **Lyon**
Tel. 78.37.25.90
Good cuisine. 17th-century building in the old town. Closed Sun.

Alain Chapel 🍽️ 🛏️ ▯▯▯
01390 **Mionnay**
Tel. 78.91.82.02; tlx. 305605
Outstanding cuisine. Outdoor dining. 13 rooms. Garden. Closed Jan., Mon., and Tues. lunch.

Troisgros 🍽️ 🛏️ ▯▯▯
Place de la Gare
42300 **Roanne**
Tel. 77.71.66.97; tlx. 307507
Outstanding cuisine. 22 rooms. Closed Jan., Tues., and Wed. lunch.

Pierre Gagnaire 🍽️ ▯▯
3, rue Georges-Teissier
42000 **Saint-Etienne**
Tel. 77.37.57.93
Excellent cuisine. Closed Feb. school holidays, 3 weeks in Aug., end Dec., Sun. and Mon.

Michel Chabran 🍽️ 🛏️ ▯▯
Av. du 45ᵉ-Parallèle
Pont-de-L'Isère
26600 **Tain-l'Hermitage**
Tel. 75.84.60.09; tlx. 346333
Excellent cuisine. 12 modern rooms. Outdoor dining. Terrace, garden. Closed Sun. evening and Mon. (Oct. to end Mar.) MF$

Pic 🍽️ 🛏️ ▯▯
285, av. Victor-Hugo
26000 **Valence**
Tel. 75.44.15.32
Outstanding cuisine. Outdoor dining. Garden. 6 rooms. Closed one week in Feb., Aug., Sun. evening and Wed.

Georges Blanc 🍽️ 🛏️ ▯▯▯
01540 **Vonnas**
Tel. 74.50.00.10; tlx. 380776
Outstanding cuisine. 23 pleasant rooms. Outdoor swimming pool, garden, tennis. Closed early Jan. to mid-Feb., Wed., and Thurs. except in the evening in season.

Provence

Hostellerie des Remparts 🛏️ 🍽️ ▯
6, place d'Armes
30220 **Aigues-Mortes**
Tel. 66.53.82.77
19 rooms. Tastefully furnished hotel in 18th-century residence. Outdoor dining. Closed early Nov. to early Mar.

Hôtel des Augustins 🛏️▯▯
3, rue de la Masse
13100 **Aix-en-Provence**
Tel. 42.27.28.59
38 rooms. Restored former convent. Comfortable, small rooms.

Paul Cézanne 🛏️▯▯
40, av. Victor-Hugo
13100 **Aix-en-Provence**
Tel. 42.26.34.73; tlx. 403158
44 rooms. Attractively furnished hotel. Closed Jan.

Le Clos de la Violette 🍽️ ▯▯
10, av. de la Violette
13100 **Aix-en-Provence**
Tel. 42.23.30.71
Good cuisine. Pleasant restaurant. Outdoor dining. Garden. Closed 3 weeks in Jan., first 2 weeks in Nov., Sun., and Mon. lunch.

D'Artalan 🛏️▯
26, rue du Sauvage – 13200 **Arles**
Tel. 90.93.56.66
44 pleasant rooms furnished in Provençal style.15th-century building.

Jules César 🛏️ 🍽️ ▯▯
Bd des Lices
13631 **Arles**
Tel. 90.93.43.20
55 rooms. Former convent with cloister and enclosed garden, outdoor swimming pool. Lou Marquès restaurant. Good cuisine. Outdoor dining. Restaurant closed in Dec. MF$

Hôtel Mireille 🛏️ 🍽️ ▯
2, place Saint-Pierre
13200 **Arles**
Tel. 90.93.70.74; tlx. 440308
34 rooms. Situated in a residential area. Swimming pool. Outdoor dining. Closed mid-Nov. to Mar. MF$

Hôtel d'Europe 🛏️ 🍽️ ▯▯
12, place Crillon
84000 **Avignon**
Tel. 90.82.66.92; tlx. 431965
48 rooms. Beautiful 16th-century residence. Outdoor dining. Restaurant closed 3 weeks in Jan., 1 week in Aug., Sat. lunch and Sun.

L'Auberge de France 🍽️ ▯▯
28, place de l' Horloge
84000 **Avignon**
Tel. 90.82.58.86
Good cuisine. In the centre of Avignon, close to the Palais des Papes. Modern decor. Closed Jan., mid-June to early July, Wed. evening and Thurs. MF$

Hôtel de Garlande 🛏️▯
20, rue Galante
84000 **Avignon**
Tel. 90.85.08.85
12 rooms. Small, renovated hotel.

Hiély-Lucullus 🍽️ ▯
5, rue de la République
84000 **Avignon**
Tel. 90.86.17.07
Excellent cuisine. Closed first 2 weeks in Jan., 2 weeks in June—July, Mon. (except July) and Tues.

La Bonne Etape 🍽️ 🛏️ ▯▯
04160 **Château-Arnoux**
Tel. 92.64.00.09; tlx. 430605
Excellent cuisine. 11 rooms. Tasteful furnishings. Swimming pool. Closed early Jan. to mid-Feb., end Nov., Sun. evening and Mon. out of season.

Château des 🍽️ 🛏️▯
Fines Roches
84230 **Châteauneuf-du-Pape**
Tel. 90.83.70.23
Good cuisine. Amid the vines. View. 7 rooms. Closed Christmas to mid-Feb., and Mon.

Auberge La Régalido ⌁ ⌁▯▯▯
Rue Frédéric-Mistral
13990 **Fontvieille**
Tel. 90.97.60.22; tlx. 441150
14 rooms. Quiet, luxurious hotel with pretty garden. Outdoor dining. Closed end Nov. to early Feb. Restaurant also closed Mon. (except July—Sep.) and Tues. lunch. MF$

L'Oustau ⌁⌁▯▯▯
de Baumanière
Les Baux-de-Provence
13520 **Maussane-les-Alpilles**
Tel. 90.54.33.07; tlx. 420203
Outstanding cuisine. Elegant restaurant. Outdoor dining on flowered terrace. 13 rooms. Tennis, swimming pool. Closed mid-Jan. to early May, Wed. (out of season) and Thurs. lunch.

L'Enclos ⌁⌁▯▯
de la Fontaine
Quai de la Fontaine – 30000 **Nîmes**
Tel. 66.21.90.30; tlx. 490635
62 rooms. Quiet hotel with flowered garden. Outdoor dining. Restaurant closed Sat. lunch.

Le Vieux Castillon ⌁⌁▯▯▯
Castillon du Gard
30210 **Remoulins (Pont-du-Gard)**
Tel. 66.37.00.77; tlx. 490946
33 rooms. Quiet hotel at the heart of a medieval village. Good cuisine. Outdoor dining. Outdoor swimming pool. Closed mid-Jan. to mid-Mar.

Mas de la Fouque ⌁⌁▯▯▯
Route d'Aigues-Mortes
13460 **Saintes-Maries-de-la-Mer**
Tel. 90.47.81.02; tlx. 403155
13 rooms. Modern hotel in spectacular setting amid the marshes of the Camargue. Outdoor swimming pool, tennis. Closed early Nov. to mid-Mar. MF$

L'Abbaye de ⌁⌁▯▯
Sainte-Croix
Route de Val-de-Cuech
13300 **Salon-de-Provence**
Tel. 90.56.24.55; tlx. 401247
19 rooms. Former abbey in a park, with a spectacular view and rich history. Comfortable rooms. Outdoor swimming pool. Outdoor dining. Open Mar. to Nov. MF$

La Magnaneraie ⌁⌁▯▯
37, rue du Camp-de-Bataille
30400 **Villeneuve-lès-Avignon**
Tel. 90.25.11.11; tlx. 432640
21 rooms. Charming hotel with pretty garden for outdoor dining. Tennis, swimming pool. MF$

Côte d'Azur

La Bonne Auberge ⌁▯▯▯
at N7 – 06600 **Antibes**
Tel. 93.33.36.65; tlx. 4740989
Excellent cuisine. Terrace. Outdoor dining. Closed mid-Nov. to mid-Dec., and Mon. (except in the evening from early Apr. to end Sep.)

L'Ecurie Royale ⌁▯▯
33, rue Vauban – 06600 **Antibes**
Tel. 93.34.76.20
Good cuisine. Closed 2 weeks in Jan., Aug., Sun. evening, Mon., and Tues. lunch (Oct. to May).

Le Cagnard ⌁⌁▯▯
Rue du Pontis-Long (Haut-de-Cagnes)
06800 **Cagnes-sur-Mer**
Tel. 93.20.73.21; tlx. 462223
Good cuisine. 10 rooms. Charming hotel. View. Outdoor dining. Closed early Nov. to mid-Dec. and Thurs. lunch.

Beau Séjour ⌁⌁▯▯
5, rue des Fauvettes – **06400 Cannes**
Tel. 93.39.63.00; tlx. 470975
46 rooms. Modern rooms with terrace facing a garden and swimming pool.

Carlton Intercontinental ⌁⌁▯▯▯
58, La Croisette – 06400 **Cannes**
Tel. 93.68.91.68; tlx. 470720
295 rooms. Luxurious grand hotel. View, private beach. MF$

Le Festival ⌁▯
52, La Croisette – 06400 **Cannes**
Tel. 93.38.04.81
Outdoor dining. Closed end Nov. to end Dec.

Gray d'Albion ⌁⌁▯▯▯
38, rue des Serbes – 06400 **Cannes**
Tel. 93.68.54.54; tlx. 470744
173 rooms. Modern hotel with luxurious fittings. Private beach. Royal Gray restaurant with excellent cuisine and elegant modern decor. Restaurant closed in Feb., Sun. and Mon. MF$

Majestic ⌁⌁▯▯▯
14, La Croisette – 06400 **Cannes**
Tel. 93.68.91.00; tlx. 470787
262 rooms. Large, comfortable hotel. Outdoor dining. View, outdoor swimming pool, private beach. Closed mid-Nov. to mid-Dec. MF$

Martinez ⌁⌁▯▯▯
73, La Croisette – 06400 **Cannes**
Tel. 93.68.91.91; tlx. 479708
400 rooms. Renovated luxury hotel with view. Outdoor swimming pool,

private beach, tennis. La Palme d'Or restaurant with excellent cuisine. Closed end Nov. to end Jan. MF$

Palma ⌁▯
77, La Croisette – 06400 **Cannes**
Tel. 93.94.22.16; tlx. 470826
47 rooms. Rooms overlooking the sea.

Hôtel de Provence ⌁⌁▯
9, rue Molière – 06400 **Cannes**
Tel. 93.38.44.35
30 rooms. Comfortable, modern hotel. Provençal decor. Garden.

Château ⌁⌁▯▯▯
de la Chèvre d'Or
Rue du Barri – 06360 **Eze-Village**
Tel. 93.41.12.12; tlx. 970839
11 rooms. Quiet hotel overlooking the sea. Breathtaking view. Outdoor swimming pool. Good cuisine. Open early. Mar. to Dec. MF$

L'Hermitage ⌁⌁▯
du Col d'Eze
La Grande Corniche
06360 **Eze-Village**
Tel. 93.41.21.11
14 rooms. Small hotel with view. Swimming pool. Restaurant closed Wed. lunch and Mon. MF$

Panorama ⌁▯
2, place du Cours – 06130 **Grasse**
Tel. 93.36.80.80; tlx. 970908
36 rooms. Modern, welcoming hotel.

La Terrasse ⌁⌁▯▯▯
(Hôtel Juana)
Av. Georges-Gallice
06160 **Juan-les-Pins**
Tel. 93.61.08.37/70; tlx. 470778
Excellent cuisine. 45 rooms. Outdoor dining. Outdoor swimming pool. Open end Mar. to end Oct.

Grand Hôtel de Genève ⌁▯
3 bis, rue Reine-Elisabeth
13001 **Marseille**
Tel. 91.90.51.42; tlx. 440672
45 rooms. Near the old port.

Au Jambon de Parme ⌁▯▯
67, rue de la Palud – 13006 **Marseille**
Tel. 91.54.37.98
Good cuisine. Closed mid-July to mid-Aug. and Sun. evening.

Le Petit Nice ⌁⌁▯▯▯
Anse de Maldormé – 13007 **Marseille**
Tel. 91.52.14.39; tlx. 401565
Excellent cuisine. View of the sea. Outdoor dining. 14 rooms. Swimming pool (sea water). Hotel closed Jan. Restaurant also closed Mon.

Sofitel Vieux Port 🛏 🍴 ⬛
36, bd Charles-Livon
13007 **Marseille**
Tel. 91.52.90.19; tlx. 401270
127 rooms. Comfortable hotel. Panoramic restaurant with superb view of the old port. Outdoor swimming pool.

Beach Plaza 🛏 🍴 ⬛⬛⬛
22, av. Princesse-Grace
98000 **Monte-Carlo**
Tel. 93.30.98.80; tlx. 479617
313 rooms. A complete beach resort in itself. Modern hotel with balconied rooms. View, swimming pools and beach. Outdoor dining. MF$

Hermitage 🛏 🍴 ⬛⬛⬛
Square Beaumarchais
98000 **Monte-Carlo**
Tel. 93.50.67.31; tlx. 479432
230 rooms. Luxurious hotel with view. Belle Epoque restaurant. Outdoor dining. Indoor swimming pool. MF$

Le Louis XV 🍴 ⬛⬛⬛
Place du Casino – 98000 **Monte-Carlo**
Tel. 93.50.80.80; tlx. 469925
Excellent cuisine. Luxurious decor. Closed mid-Nov. to mid-Dec., Tues. and Wed. MF$

Polpetta 🍴 ⬛
2, rue Paradis – 98000 **Monte-Carlo**
Tel. 93.50.67.84
Italian cuisine. Informal atmosphere. Outdoor dining. Closed mid-Feb. to mid-Mar., last 2 weeks in Oct. and Tues. MF$

La Ferme de Mougins 🍴 ⬛⬛
10, av. Saint-Basile
06250 **Mougins**
Tel. 93.90.03.74; tlx. 970643
Good cuisine. Former farmhouse. Outdoor dining on pleasant terrace. Garden. Closed mid-Feb. to mid-Mar., Thurs., and Sat. lunch. MF$

Le Mas Candille 🛏 🍴 ⬛⬛
Boulevard Rebuffel
06250 **Mougins**
Tel. 93.90.00.85; tlx. 462131
22 rooms. Quiet, charming hotel with view, terraced gardens and outdoor swimming pool. Outdoor dining. Closed 2 weeks in Jan.

Le Moulin de Mougins 🍴 🛏 ⬛⬛⬛
06250 **Mougins**
Tel. 93.75.78.24; tlx. 970732
Outstanding cuisine. Outdoor dining. Garden. 5 rooms. Closed end Jan. to end Mar. Restaurant also closed Mon. (except evening from mid-July to end Aug.) and Thurs. lunch.

Grand Hôtel Aston 🛏 🍴 ⬛⬛
12, av. Félix-Faure – 06000 **Nice**
Tel. 93.80.62.52; tlx. 470290
157 rooms. Charming renovated hotel. Attractive roof-garden.

Beach Regency 🛏 🍴 ⬛⬛⬛
223, promenade des Anglais
06000 **Nice**
Tel. 93.83.91.51; tlx. 461635
322 rooms. Large, modern hotel with bright, cheerful rooms. Roof-top swimming pool. Restaurant with terrace bar. Fitness centre. MF$

Hôtel Brice 🛏 🍴 ⬛
44, rue du Mal-Joffre – 06000 **Nice**
Tel. 93.88.14.14; tlx. 470658
61 rooms. Comfortable hotel. Provençal furnishings. Winter garden.

Hôtel de Lausanne 🛏
36, rue Rossini – 06000 **Nice**
Tel. 93.88.85.94; tlx. 461269
40 rooms. Small hotel with character. Small, but attractively furnished rooms. MF$

Négresco 🛏 🍴 ⬛⬛⬛
37, promenade des Anglais
06000 **Nice**
Tel. 93.88.39.51; tlx. 460040
140 rooms. Luxurious, grand hotel. Period furnishings. View. Le Chantecler restaurant with excellent cuisine. MF$

L'Oasis 🛏
23, rue Gounod – 06000 **Nice**
Tel. 93.88.12.29; tlx. 462705
38 rooms. Quiet hotel. Central situation. Comfortable, simple rooms.

Pullman 🛏 ⬛
28, av. Notre-Dame – 06000 **Nice**
Tel. 93.80.30.24; tlx. 470662
192 rooms. Modern hotel with roof-top swimming pool. View. MF$

Ruffel 🍴 ⬛
10, bd Dubouchage – 06000 **Nice**
Tel. 93.62.05.45
Good cuisine. Outdoor dining. Closed Sep. and Sun.

Sofitel Splendid 🛏 🍴 ⬛⬛
50, bd Victor-Hugo – 06000 **Nice**
Tel. 93.88.69.54; tlx. 460938
116 rooms. Swimming pool on the 8th floor and superb view over the town. Outdoor dining.

Monte-Carlo
Beach Hôtel 🛏 🍴 ⬛⬛⬛
Avenue du Bord-de-Mer, Saint-Roman
06190 **Roquebrune-Cap-Martin**

Tel. 93.78.21.40
46 rooms. All rooms with terrace overlooking the sea. Tennis, swimming pool, private beach.

Le Roquebrune 🍴 ⬛⬛
100, av. J.-Jaurès
06190 **Roquebrune-Cap-Martin**
Tel. 93.35.00.16
Good cuisine. Closed Jan. and Nov., Wed., and Thurs. lunch (out of season) and lunch except weekends in summer.

Grand Hôtel 🛏 🍴 ⬛⬛⬛
du Cap-Ferrat
Bd du Gal-de-Gaulle
06230 **Saint-Jean-Cap-Ferrat**
Tel. 93.76.00.21; tlx. 470184
57 rooms. Recently renovated luxury hotel in park. View. Good cuisine. Outdoor dining. Tennis, outdoor swimming pool and private funicular to the beach. Open Apr. to Oct. MF$

Petit Trianon 🍴 ⬛⬛
Bd du Gal-de-Gaulle
06230 **Saint-Jean-Cap-Ferrat**
Tel. 93.76.05.06
Good cuisine. Outdoor dining. Pergola. Open Feb. to end Oct., closed Wed. evening and Thurs.

La Colombe d'Or 🛏 🍴 ⬛⬛
06570 **Saint-Paul**
Tel. 93.32.80.02; tlx. 970607
15 rooms. Old-Provence style. Modern paintings. Outdoor dining on pleasant terrace. Outdoor swimming pool and Roman garden. Closed mid-Nov. to end Dec.

La Bastide des Salins 🛏 ⬛⬛
Route des Salins – 83990 **Saint-Tropez**
Tel. 94.97.24.57
10 rooms. New, charming hotel in a park. Large, attractive rooms.

Byblos 🛏 🍴 ⬛⬛⬛
Av. Paul-Signac – 83990 **Saint-Tropez**
Tel. 94.97.00.04; tlx. 470235
82 rooms. Quiet, luxury hotel with view, outdoor swimming pool, garden. Outdoor dining.

Le Chabichou 🍴 ⬛⬛⬛
Av. Foch – 83990 **Saint-Tropez**
Tel. 94.54.80.00
Good cuisine. Elegant restaurant. Open mid-May to mid-Oct.

Le Mas de Chastelas 🛏 🍴 ⬛⬛⬛
Route de Gassin – 83990 **Saint-Tropez**
Tel. 94.56.09.11; tlx. 462393
21 rooms. Pleasant hotel among the vineyards. Outdoor dining. Swimming pool, tennis.

La Tartane ⊷ ═ ▯▯
Rte des Salins – 83990 **Saint-Tropez**
Tel. 94.97.21.23
12 rooms. Quiet, charming hotel. Terraces, swimming pool. Open mid-Mar. to early Nov.

Saint-Christophe ⊷ ═ ▯▯
47, av. de Miramar
06590 **Théoule-sur-Mer**
Tel. 93.75.41.36; tlx. 470878
40 rooms. Modern comfort in a relaxed atmosphere. Panoramic view. Outdoor swimming pool and private beach. Outdoor dining. Open mid-Mar. to mid-Oct. MF$

Altéa La Tour Blanche ⊷ ═ ▯▯
Bd Amiral-Vence
83000 **Toulon**
Tel. 94.24.41.57; tlx. 400347
92 rooms. Renovated hotel. Superb view of Toulon and the roadstead. Outdoor dining. Outdoor swimming pool.

La Bastide de Tourtour ⊷ ═ ▯▯
83690 **Tourtour**
Tel. 94.70.57.30; tlx. 970827
25 rooms. Quiet hotel with panoramic view. Good cuisine. Outdoor dining. Outdoor swimming pool and tennis. Open Mar. to Nov. MF$

Château Saint-Martin ⊷ ═ ▯▯▯
Rte de Coursegoules – 06140 **Vence**
Tel. 93.58.02.02; tlx. 470282
15 rooms. Quiet hotel in the mountains overlooking Vence. Good cuisine. Outdoor dining. Outdoor swimming pool, tennis. Open mid-Mar. to mid-Nov. MF$

Hôtel Welcome ⊷ ═ ▯▯
1, quai Courbet
06230 **Villefranche-sur-Mer**
Tel. 93.76.76.93; tlx. 470281
35 rooms. Charming hotel with comfortable rooms. View. Outdoor dining. Closed end Nov. to end Dec. MF$

SOUTH-WEST

Périgord

Moulin du Roc ═ ⊷ ▯▯
Brantôme
24530 **Champagnac de Bélair**
Tel. 53.54.80.36; tlx. 571555
Excellent cuisine. 14 rooms. Former oil press. View. Swimming pool, garden. Outdoor dining. Closed mid-Jan. to mid-Feb., mid-Nov. to mid-Dec., Tues., and Wed. lunch.

Le Centenaire ═ ⊷ ▯▯
24620 **Les Eyzies-de-Tayac**
Tel. 53.06.97.18; tlx. 541921
Excellent cuisine. 24 rooms. Outdoor dining. Swimming pool, garden. Open early Apr. to early Nov. Restaurant closed Tues. lunch.

Cro-Magnon ⊷ ═ ▯
24620 **Les Eyzies-de-Tayac**
Tel. 53.06.97.06; tlx. 570637
24 rooms. Transformed and enlarged 18th-century coaching station. Good cuisine. Outdoor dining. Flowered garden, shady terrace and outdoor swimming pool. Open end Apr. to mid-Oct. MF$

Beau Site ⊷ ═ ▯
46500 **Rocamadour**
Tel. 65.33.63.08; tlx. 520421
55 rooms. Situated in centre of Rocamadour. View. Attractive decor. Outdoor dining. Open end Mar. to end Oct. MF$

L'Aubergade ═ ▯▯
52, rue Royale – 47270 **Puymirol**
Tel. 53.95.31.46
Excellent cuisine. 13th-century building. Garden. Closed Mon. from Sep. to June.

Château de la Treyne ⊷ ═ ▯▯
Lacave – 46200 **Souillac**
Tel. 65.32.66.66; tlx. 531427
12 rooms. Restored château on cliff overlooking the Dordogne. Period furnishings. Large park. Swimming pool, tennis, sauna. Open early Apr. to mid-Nov. MF$

Atlantic Coast

Hôtel de France ═ ⊷ ▯▯
Place de la Libération – 32000 **Auch**
Tel. 62.05.00.44; tlx. 520474
Excellent cuisine. 29 rooms. Hotel with attractive decor. Pleasant bar/lounge. Closed Jan., Sun. evening and Mon. MF$

Le Chapon Fin ═ ▯▯
5, rue Montesquieu – 33000 **Bordeaux**
Tel. 56.79.10.10
Excellent cuisine. 1900s decor. Closed 2 weeks in Apr., 3 weeks in July, Sun. and Mon.

Hôtel Majestic ⊷ ▯
2, rue de Condé
33000 **Bordeaux**
50 rooms. Charming, comfortable hotel.

Le Rouzic ═ ▯▯
34, cours du Chapeau Rouge
33000 **Bordeaux**
Tel. 56.44.39.11
Good cuisine. Closed Sat. lunch and Sun.

Le Relais de Margaux ⊷ ═ ▯▯
33460 **Margaux**
Tel. 56.88.38.30; tlx. 572530
28 rooms. Attractive, quiet hotel. View, park, outdoor swimming pool, tennis. Outdoor dining. Open early Mar. to end Nov.

Les Brises ⊷ ▯
Chemin de la Digue-Richelieu
(av. P.-Vincent)
17000 **La Rochelle**
Tel. 46.43.89.37; tlx. 790821
50 rooms. Pleasant, quiet hotel. Attractive terrace. Memorable view of the islands.

Le Champlain ⊷ ▯
20, rue Rambaud
17000 **La Rochelle**
Tel. 46.41.23.99; tlx. 790717
33 rooms. Attractively furnished, comfortable rooms. Flowered garden. Open early Mar. to early Nov.

François Ier ⊷ ▯
13, rue Bazoges
17000 **La Rochelle**
Tel. 46.41.28.46
34 rooms. Situated in the old part of town. Large rooms.

Richard Coutanceau ═ ▯▯
Plage de la Concurrence
17000 **La Rochelle**
Tel. 46.41.48.19
Excellent cuisine. Pleasant restaurant. Closed Sun., and Mon. evening.

Hostellerie ⊷ ═ ▯▯
de Plaisance
Place du Clocher
33330 **Saint-Emilion**
Tel. 57.24.72.32
12 rooms. Former medieval cloister overlooking Saint-Emilion. Comfortable, attractive rooms. View, garden. Outdoor dining. Closed Jan. MF$

Relais du Bois ⊷ ═ ▯▯
Saint-Georges
Rue de Royan-Cours Genêt
17100 **Saintes**
Tel. 46.93.50.99; tlx. 790488
30 rooms. Quiet hotel next to an 11th-century castle keep. Blend of ancient and modern. View, park and indoor swimming pool. Outdoor dining. MF$

Pyrenees

La Réserve ⊠ ≡ 🍴
Rte de Cordes – 81000 **Albi**
Tel. 63.60.79.79; tlx. 520850
*22 rooms. Quiet hotel in a sprawling
hacienda, in a park on the banks of the
Tarn, with view, outdoor swimming
pool and tennis. Open Apr. to Nov.
MF$*

Hostellerie Saint-Antoine ⊠ ≡ 🍴
17, rue Saint-Antoine – 81000 **Albi**
Tel. 63.54.04.04; tlx. 520850
*56 rooms. Quiet hotel with antique
furniture and garden. Good cuisine.
MF$*

Château de Brindos ≡ ⊠ 🍴
Rte de l'Aviation
64600 **Anglet (Biarritz)**
Tel. 59.23.17.68; tlx. 541428
*Good cuisine. 13 rooms. Attractive in-
terior. Situated at lakeside. Park.
View. Outdoor swimming pool, tennis.*

Corneille ⊠ ≡ 🍴
5, av. A.-Dumas – Luchon
31110 **Bagnères-de-Luchon**
Tel. 61.79.36.22; tlx. 520347
*52 rooms. Quiet hotel in a park, with
tasteful decor. Open early Apr. to end
Oct.*

Eurotel ⊠ ≡ 🍴
19, av. de la Perspective
64200 **Biarritz**
Tel. 59.24.32.33; tlx. 570014
*60 rooms. Modern hotel near the
beach. View over the sea. Open Easter
to end Oct.*

Le Palais ⊠ ≡ 🍴
1, av. de l'Impératrice
64200 **Biarritz**
Tel. 59.24.09.40; tlx. 570000
*117 rooms. Pleasant, luxurious and
quiet hotel. View. Swimming pool,
garden, beach, sauna, fitness club.
Good cuisine. Open mid-Apr. to mid-
Nov. MF$*

Café de Paris ≡ 🍴
5, place Bellevue – 64200 **Biarritz**
Tel. 59.24.19.53
*Good cuisine. Elegant restaurant.
View. Open end Mar. to early Nov.
Closed Mon. out of season.*

Hôtel Argi-Eder ⊠ ≡ 🍴
Rte Notre-Dame-de-l'Aubépine
Ainhoa – 64250 **Cambo-les-Bains**
Tel. 59.29.91.04; tlx. 570067
*30 rooms. Quiet hotel with comfort-
able rooms. View, beautiful garden,
outdoor swimming pool and tennis.*

*Open early Apr. to mid-Nov. Closed
Wed. (except June–Sep.) MF$*

Le Grand Ecuyer ⊠ ≡ 🍴
Rue Voltaire – 81170 **Cordes**
Tel. 63.56.01.03
*15 rooms. Medieval building with at-
tractive interior. View of the valley.
Good cuisine. Open Easter to end
Oct. Restaurant closed Mon. (except
July–Aug.). MF$*

Hostellerie ⊠ ≡ 🍴
du Vieux Cordes
81170 Cordes
Tel. 63.56.00.12
*21 rooms. Quiet, charming hotel. Simple
rooms with fabulous view. Outdoor
dining. Terrace. Closed Feb. and Wed.
(except July -Aug.). MF$*

Michel Guérard ≡ ⊠ 🍴
et Les Prés d'Eugénie
Eugénie-les-Bains – 40320 **Geaune**
Tel. 58.51.19.01; tlx. 540470
*Outstanding cuisine. 28 tastefully
decorated rooms. Swimming pool,
tennis. Open early Mar. to end Nov.*

Le Grand Hôtel ⊠ ≡ 🍴
43, bd Thiers
64500 **Saint-Jean-de-Luz**
Tel. 59.26.12.32; tlx. 571487
*45 rooms. Belle Epoque building over-
looking the bay. Luxurious rooms. Good
cuisine. View, swimming pool, beach.
Outdoor dining. Closed Jan. and Feb.*

Les Pyrénées ≡ ⊠ 🍴
19, place Gal-de-Gaulle
64220 **Saint-Jean-Pied-de-Port**
Tel. 59.37.01.01
*Excellent cuisine. 25 rooms. Closed
last 3 weeks in Jan., 4 weeks in Nov.—
Dec., Mon. evening and Tues. out of
season.*

Hôtel des Beaux-Arts ⊠ 🍴
1, place du Pont-Neuf
31000 **Toulouse**
Tel. 61.23.40.50; tlx. 532451
20 rooms. Small renovated hotel. View.

Les Jardins de l'Opéra ≡ ⊠ 🍴
et Grand Hôtel de L'Opéra
1, place du Capitole –31000 **Toulouse**
Tel. 61.23.07.76; tlx. 521998
*Excellent cuisine. 46 rooms. Charm-
ing hotel in the centre. Tastefully decorated rooms. Garden. Swimming pool.
Closed 2 weeks in Aug. and Sun.*

Vanel ≡ 🍴
22, rue Maurice-Fontvieille
31000 **Toulouse**
Tel. 61.21.51.82

*Excellent cuisine. Closed Aug., Sun.,
and Mon. lunch.*

Francis Darroze ⊠ ≡ 🍴
40190 **Villeneuve-de-Marsan**
Tel. 58.45.20.07; tlx. 560164
*30 rooms. Outdoor swimming pool,
garden. Good cuisine. Closed Jan.
and Mon. (Oct. to June).*

Languedoc-Roussillon

Lou Mazuc ≡ ⊠ 🍴
12210 **Laguiole**
Tel. 65.44.33.24
*Outstanding cuisine. 13 rooms. Open
end Mar. to mid-Oct. Restaurant
closed Sun. lunch and Mon.*

International ⊠ ≡ 🍴
1, place de la Tine – 12100 **Millau**
Tel. 65.60.20.66; tlx. 520629
*110 rooms. 8-storey hotel. View. Roof-
top lounge. Good cuisine. Restaurant
closed Sun. evening. MF$*

La Musardière ⊠ ≡ 🍴
34, av. de la République
12100 **Millau**
Tel. 65.60.20.63
*12 rooms. Luxurious little hotel in a
park. Unique colour-coordinated
rooms. Good cuisine. Open early Apr.
to early Nov. Restaurant closed Mon.
(except in Aug.). MF$*

Le Chandelier ≡ 🍴
3, rue Leenhardt – 34000 **Montpellier**
Tel. 67.92.61.62
*Good cuisine. Closed Feb. school
holidays, 3 weeks in Aug., Sun., and
Mon. lunch.*

Grand Hôtel du Midi ⊠ 🍴
22, bd Victor-Hugo
34000 **Montpellier**
Tel. 67.92.69.61; tlx. 490752
*49 rooms. Charming, renovated hotel.
Large, spacious rooms.*

Belle Rive ⊠ ≡ 🍴
12270 **Najac**
Tel. 65.29.73.90
*42 rooms. Quiet hotel. Beautiful setting
on river bank. Simple rooms. Swimming pool, terrace, garden. Outdoor
dining. Open Apr. to Nov. MF$*

Réverbère ≡ 🍴
4, place Jacobins – 11000 **Narbonne**
Tel. 68.32.29.18
*Good cuisine. Closed Sun. evening and
Mon.*

All the Nuts and Bolts for a Successful Journey

ACCOMMODATION

See also CAMPING

France offers an immense variety of accommodation to suit every taste and pocket.

Hotels are classified in five categories, from one star to four-star luxury. Room rates, fixed according to amenities, size and the hotel's star rating, must by law be posted outside and inside the establishment.

For advance reservations, especially during holiday periods, you can obtain lists of officially approved hotels throughout France from the French tourist office in your country (see p. 361). Many *départements* have an official booking service called *Loisirs-Accueil,* where you can reserve a hotel room, a *gîte rural* (see below) or space for a tent on a campsite; a list of these centres is also available at the French tourist office. On the spot, local tourist offices *(office du tourisme* or *syndicat d'initiative)* can supply lists of hotels in the area. The *Accueil de France* offices located in tourist offices in the cities make room reser-

340

vations for personal callers at a small fee. In addition, major airports and railway stations have hotel reservation desks. In the arrivals hall of Paris's Roissy–Charles-de-Gaulle airport, there's an electronic machine with free telephone to a wide selection of hotels. If you make a reservation by telephone and don't specify your time of arrival, the establishment is only obliged to keep the room for you until 7 p.m.

Outside peak periods, many seaside hotels close from Sunday lunchtime till Monday morning, and some close for the entire winter season.

If there is a restaurant attached to your hotel, it is customary to have dinner there the first night. Some hotels offer a discount for this, and it's often worth eating there—reduction or not—to try the local specialities. *Pension complète* (full board—all meals) can usually be obtained for any stay of three or more days. *Demi-pension* (half board—breakfast and evening meal) terms are in general available outside the peak holiday periods. *Hôtel garni* means that only room and breakfast are offered. An establishment simply labelled "hôtel" may not have a restaurant, especially in big towns.

Reservation telephone numbers for some major hotel chains in France (numbers beginning "05" are toll free and can only be obtained within France):

Altea and Arcade hotels	05.28.88.00
Balladins, Les	05.35.55.75
Best Western	(1) 43.41.22.44
Campanile	(1) 47.57.11.11
Climat de France	05.11.22.11
Concorde	05.05.00.11
Confortel-Louisiane	(1) 49.11.01.01
Cottage Hotel	83.98.46.56
Etape Coqvert	(1) 34.17.00.02
Fimotel	05.07.27.27
Grilotel	(1) 39.70.60.71
Hilton International	05.31.80.40
Holiday Inn	(1) 43.55.39.03
Ibis-Urbis, Mercure, Novotel and Sofitel	(1) 60.77.27.27
Inter-Continental	05.90.85.55
Inter Hotel	(1) 43.20.85.97
Logis et Auberges de France	(1) 43.59.86.67
Minotels France-Accueil	(1) 45.83.04.22
Pullman International	05.28.88.00
Relais Bleus, Les	05.21.79.82
Relais et Châteaux	(1) 47.42.00.20
Relais du Silence	(16) 76.68.10.69

Some private **châteaux** also take in a limited number of guests. Write to any of the following:

Châteaux-Accueil
78100 Saint-Germain-en-Laye

Châteaux en Vacances
B.P. 4, 78220 Viroflay

Etapes François-Cœur
172, Grande Rue – 92380 Garches

Rural lodgings **(Gîtes ruraux)**, normally stand for self-catering accommodation in renovated buildings in the countryside. Your *gîte rural* could be a small cottage, a village house, an apartment in the owner's house or a mountain hut where sleeping arrangements may be in a dormitory. Apply to the Fédération nationale des gîtes ruraux:

35, rue Godot-de-Mauroy – 75009 Paris
Tel. (1) 47.42.20.20

Pensions are mostly small, reasonably priced hotels or boarding houses. They are usually family-owned and provide meals.

If you would like to stay on a **farm** in France, you should contact Agriculture et Tourisme:

9, avenue Georges V, 75008 Paris
Tel. (1) 47.23.55.40

And there are **holiday villages** *(village de vacances)*—apartments grouped together, with sports and leisure activities on the spot—as well as **"green" holiday centres** *(station verte de vacances)*, in relaxed settings. Write to La Maison du tourisme vert, at the same address as the Fédération nationale des gîtes ruraux above.

Local tourist offices can recommend agencies with complete lists of **villas** and **apartments** to let. You should reserve well ahead. The Fédération nationale des agents immobiliers (real estate agents) publishes the booklet *Allô-Vacances,* a guide to member rental agents throughout the country. Contact the French tourist office in your country or write directly to FNAIM:

6, rue de la Pépinière – 75008 Paris
Tel. (1) 42.93.04.42

There are about 200 **youth hostels** *(auberge de jeunesse),* well scattered over the country, with varying facilities. International membership cards are available from your national youth hostel association, as well as from the Fédération unie des auberges de jeunesse, the French Youth Hostels Federation:

27, rue Pajol – 75018 Paris
Tel. (1) 42.41.59.00

Or contact the Information and Documentation Centre for Young People—Centre d'information et documentation de la jeunesse (CIDJ):

101, quai Branly
75740 Paris Cedex 15
Tel. (1) 45.66.40.20

Young people will also find accommodation in "international meeting centres" *(centre de rencontres internationales),* which are more modern and comfortable, and therefore more expensive, than youth hostels. A free list of these centres is available from the French tourist office in your country.

Do you have any vacancies?	**Avez-vous des chambres disponibles?**
I'd like a single/ double room.	**Je voudrais une chambre pour une personne/deux personnes.**
with bath/shower/ private toilet	**avec bains/douche/ toilettes privées**
What's the rate per night/week?	**Quel est le prix par nuit/semaine?**
What's my room number?	**Quel est le numéro de ma chambre?**
I'd like to leave this in your safe.	**Je voudrais déposer ceci dans votre coffre-fort.**

AIRPORTS *(aéroport)*

Paris is the major gateway to France, but many international flights operate to other big cities (Lyon, Nice, etc.).

Paris is served by two international airports, *Roissy–Charles-de-Gaulle,* about 25 kilometres (15 miles) north-east of the city, and *Orly,* 16 km. (10 mi.) to the south. Most intercontinental flights use the ultra-modern Roissy.

The two airports are linked by coach and helicopter. In normal traffic conditions, the journey by coach takes about 50 minutes, while the helicopter takes approximately 25 minutes.

To get from Roissy–Charles-de-Gaulle to Paris, you can take the Air France coach to the Porte Maillot Air Terminal (at Palais des Congrès), a journey of at least 30 minutes, or the RATP (the Paris Transport Authority) bus No. 350 to Gare du Nord or Gare de l'Est, which takes about 50 minutes. Trains from Roissy to Gare du Nord (RER line B) leave the airport every 15–30 minutes and take 35 minutes.

From Orly, an Air France coach service runs to the Invalides Air Terminal in Paris and takes approximately 40 minutes in normal traffic conditions, while RATP buses ("Orly Bus") travel to Denfert Rochereau in about 30 minutes. The train from Orly ("Orly Rail") to the Invalides via Gare d'Austerlitz (RER line C) takes some 40 minutes. Trains run from early morning to late at night.

There is also a helicopter service between the airports and Paris. The trip from Roissy to Paris (Héliport de Paris) takes 15 minutes, from Orly to Paris, less than 10 minutes. The Héliport de Paris is situated at 4, avenue de la Porte de Sèvres in the south-west (*métro* Balard). For reservations, call Hélifrance, tel. (1) 45.54.95.11.

The taxi trip from the airports to the centre of Paris is expensive for single passengers, but worthwhile for three. (Many taxis will not take more than three passengers.)

Paris airports, flight arrivals and departures information:

Arrivals, tel. (1) 43.20.12.55
Departures, tel. (1) 43.20.13.55

Other flight information:
Roissy, tel. (1) 48.62.22.80
Orly, tel. (1) 48.84.32.10

Porter!	**Porteur!**
Can you help me with my luggage?	**Pouvez-vous m'aider à porter mes bagages?**
Please take these suitcases to the bus/taxi rank!	**Prenez ces valises à l'arrêt du bus/ la station de taxis, s'il vous plaît!**
How much is that?	**C'est combien?**
Where are the luggage trolleys (baggage carts)?	**Où sont les chariots à bagages?**
Where's the bus for... ?	**D'où part le bus pour... ?**

BICYCLE RENTAL
(location de vélos/bicyclettes)

Bicycle rental shops are plentiful even in small towns. In addition, SNCF, the French National Railways, operate a cycle rental service at railway stations (listed in the brochure *Guide du train et du vélo*). Bicycles may be hired at one station and returned to another. You will need your passport or identity card, and you'll have to pay a deposit, unless you hold a major credit card.

The Fédération française de cyclotourisme gives out detailed information on bicycle touring in France:

8, rue Jean-Marie Jégo – 75013 Paris
Tel. (1) 45.80.30.21

Many towns also have **mopeds** (called *vélomoteur, cyclomoteur* or *mobylette*) for hire. Wearing crash helmets is obligatory. Minimum age to ride a moped built not to exceed 45 kph (28 mph) is 14. These vehicles are not allowed on motorways (expressways).

I'd like to hire a bicycle for a day/a week.	**Je voudrais louer une bicyclette pour une journée/une semaine.**

CAMPING

There are close to 10,000 campsites to choose from in France—in categories from one to four stars. Most have some sports facilities on site or close by, and many rent out bicycles. During peak season you should make reservations well in advance, especially in popular tourist regions like the Côte d'Azur (Riviera). Lists of regional campsites are available from French tourist offices abroad.

The *International Camping Carnet,* a pass that gives modest discounts and insurance coverage throughout Europe, is required at some campsites in France. It can be obtained through your automobile association.

Camping outside official sites *(camping sauvage)* may be widespread in certain areas, but it is prohibited in all nature reserves and national parks, as well as in the Midi and on Corsica, and—to prevent forest fires—advised against throughout the country. However, you may put up a tent on private property if you have the owner's permission. The sign *"Camping Interdit"* means that no camping is allowed.

The Fédération française de camping-caravaning issues an official guide to camping in France. Address:

78, rue de Rivoli – 75004 Paris
Tel. (1) 42.72.84.08 – Telex 214 042

You can also camp on a farm in France. Contact the Fédération nationale des gîtes ruraux and ask for their booklet *Camping à la Ferme.* Address:

35, rue Godot-de-Mauroy – 75009 Paris
Tel. (1) 47.42.20.20

Or camp at a château. A special brochure on château camping can be obtained from:

Castel-Camping-Caravaning "Les Ormes"
35120 Epiniac
Tel. 99.48.11.96

For practical information on camping in France, consult the Association camping club de France:

218, boulevard Saint-Germain
75007 Paris
Tel. (1) 45.48.30.03

Or call *Inter-Loisirs,* tel. (1) 42.30.13.13, a service run by the radio station France-Inter, which can help you find a campsite.

Is there a campsite near here?	**Y a-t-il un camping près d'ici?**
Have you room for a tent/caravan (trailer)?	**Avez-vous de la place pour une tente/caravane?**
May we camp on your land?	**Pouvons-nous camper sur votre terrain?**

CAR RENTAL *(location de voitures)*

See also DRIVING IN FRANCE. All major rental agencies handle French and foreign makes. Local firms sometimes offer lower prices than the international companies. Weekend rates and weekly unlimited mileage rates are usually available, and it's worth inquiring about any seasonal deals. There are also some good bargains to be had if you book your car together with your plane or train ticket from your home country.

To hire a car you must show your driving licence (held for at least one year) and passport or identity card. The minimum age is from 18 to 25 depending on company and the car's engine size, or even 30 if a particularly expensive car is involved. A substantial deposit is usually required unless you hold a credit card recognized by the rental firm. Third-party insurance is always included; with an extra fee per day you can obtain full insurance coverage.

Chauffeur-driven cars can be hired at major rental companies. However, if you know your itinerary in advance, you should arrange for a package deal with your travel agent before leaving.

I'd like to hire a car.	Je voudrais louer une voiture.
for one day/ a week	pour une journée/ une semaine
unlimited mileage	kilométrage illimité
Are there any weekend arrangements?	Existe-t-il des forfaits de fin de semaine?
Do you have any special rates?	Proposez-vous des tarifs spéciaux?
I want full insurance.	Je voudrais une assurance tous risques.

CHILDREN

France has an abundance of leisure and amusement parks vying for children of all ages. The parks offer attractions like playgrounds, pools, water slides, go karting, donkey and pony riding, and many have zoos with domestic or wild animals. Ask at the French tourist office for their brochure Les Parcs de Loisirs, listing amusement parks all over France.

Even in the cities, the younger set will find a lot to do. In Paris, for example, there are the zoos in the Bois de Vincennes and in the Jardin des Plantes, the Botanical Gardens near Gare d'Austerlitz. The popular Jardin d'Acclimatation of the Bois de Boulogne is a very special games-and-zoo park, complete with pony rides, marionette shows and other diversions. And then there is the Eiffel Tower, the Georges Pompidou Centre and boat trips on the Seine.

As for baby-sitting, hotel receptionists can often arrange for a sitter, especially at resort hotels where there are clubs specializing in activities for young children during the day. Otherwise, baby-sitters sometimes advertise in supermarkets and in the local papers under "Garderie d'enfants" or "Crèche". In cities, reputable student and service organizations can provide baby-sitters. Ask at your hotel or the tourist office.

You should try to request a sitter at least a day ahead.

Can you get me/ us a baby-sitter for tonight/ tomorrow night?	Pouvez-vous me/ nous trouver une baby-sitter pour ce soir/demain soir?

CIGARETTES, CIGARS, TOBACCO

Tobacco is a state monopoly in France. Tobacconists (débit de tabac) are recognized by the sign "Bar-Tabac" (a bar licensed to sell tobacco) or "Tabac-Journaux" (a newsagent with similar rights) and a double red cone. They are often found at café cash desks, too.

A packet of.../ A box of matches, please.	Un paquet de.../ Une boîte d'allumettes, s'il vous plaît.
cigarettes with/ without filter	des cigarettes avec/ sans filtre
with dark/ light tobacco	des cigarettes brunes/blondes
cigars	des cigares
pipe tobacco	du tabac pour pipe

CLIMATE AND CLOTHING

The climate in France is varied, but mild. Obviously, the further south you go, the warmer it becomes. The northern and western areas (including Paris) enjoy a temperate climate. The region to the east has warmer summers and colder winters, while the Mediterranean coastal area is marked by hot, dry summers and mild, showery winters. With the exception of this coast, rainfall is sporadic all year round, with most precipitation between January and April and least in August and September.

The weather in Paris is usually good. In winter, the temperature is quite bearable—Paris under snow is a rare event, but very pretty—and once it gets started, the spring is unbeatable. Summer is often hot, but not scorching, and the autumn gently warm.

Except in winter, medium-weight attire is usually adequate. However, even in the southern summer, when light cotton clothes are all you need during the day, a sweater or a jacket comes in handy for an occasional chilly evening, and you are likely to need rain wear at any time of the year.

° Fahrenheit		Jan	Feb	Mar	Apr	May	Jun	Jul	Aug	Sep	Oct	Nov	Dec
Lyon	max.	41	45	55	61	68	75	81	79	73	61	50	43
	min.	30	32	37	43	48	55	59	57	54	45	39	32
Marseille	max.	50	54	59	64	72	79	84	82	77	68	59	52
	min.	36	36	41	46	52	59	63	63	59	50	43	37
Paris	max.	43	45	54	61	68	73	77	75	70	61	50	45
	min.	34	34	39	43	50	55	59	57	54	46	41	36
° Celsius		Jan	Feb	Mar	Apr	May	Jun	Jul	Aug	Sep	Oct	Nov	Dec
Lyon	max.	5	7	13	16	20	24	27	26	23	16	10	6
	min.	−1	0	3	6	9	13	15	14	12	7	4	0
Marseille	max.	10	12	15	18	22	26	29	28	25	20	15	11
	min.	2	2	5	8	11	15	17	17	15	10	6	3
Paris	max.	6	7	12	16	20	23	25	24	21	16	10	7
	min.	1	1	4	6	10	13	15	14	12	8	5	2

*Minimum temperatures are measured just before sunrise, maximum temperatures in the afternoon.

Casual—but tasteful—wear is the general rule, and few restaurants insist on a tie. Nevertheless, more formal dress is expected in theatres, casinos and at the opera. Topless bathing is accepted on most beaches in France. When visiting churches, sober clothing should be worn.

COMMUNICATIONS

Post offices *(bureau de poste)* display a sign with a stylized blue bird and/or the words "Postes et Télécommunications" (P & T or PTT). In addition to normal mail service, you can make local and long-distance telephone calls, send telegrams and receive and send money at any post office. In cities, the main post office is open from 8 a.m. to 7 p.m., Monday to Friday, and from 8 a.m. till noon on Saturdays. Smaller post offices usually have a lunch break between noon and 2 p.m. In Paris, the post office at 52, rue du Louvre is open 24 hours a day.

Mailboxes are painted yellow, and often set into a wall. You can also buy stamps *(timbre)* at a tobacconist *(débit de tabac),* from vending machines (also yellow) and, occasionally, at hotels and from postcard and souvenir vendors.

Poste Restante/General Delivery. — You can have your mail addressed to you in any town c/o *Poste Restante.* In municipalities with more than one post office, it will be sent to the main post office *(poste principale* or *poste centrale)* unless otherwise indicated. Make sure that the sender knows the postal (zip) code of the town or district

(see DISTRICTS OF PARIS) you'll be staying in. You'll have to show identification to retrieve mail, and pay a small fee for the service.

Telegrams *(télégramme).* — All post offices accept domestic and international telegrams. You can also dictate a telegram over the phone (dial 14). A telegram can be handed in at the post office up to ten days before you want it sent. Reply-paid *(réponse payée)* cables are accepted by post offices and, if you require, you can be notified of the time of arrival when sending a telegram.

Telephone *(téléphone/taxiphone).* — Long distance and international calls can be made from any phone box *(cabine téléphonique),* but if you need assistance in placing the call, go to the post office or get your hotel to do it (if you make a call from your hotel, you are likely to be charged extra). If you want to make a reverse-charge (collect) call, dial 10 and ask the operator for *"un appel en PCV"* (pay-say-vay) and state the number required. This service is not valid for telephone numbers within France.

There are two types of pay phones. One takes coins (50 centimes, 1 franc, 5 and sometimes 2 francs), the other is card operated. Phone cards *(télécarte)* are sold at post offices, railway ticket counters and shops recognized by a "Télécarte" sign, and are valid for 40 or 120 charge units. The *télécarte* system is gradually phasing out coin-operated phones, but the latter can still be found in post offices.

To make an international call, dial 19 and wait for a continuous burring tone before dialling the country's number, the area code and the subscriber's number. Some country codes:

Australia	(19)	61
Austria	(19)	43
Belgium	(19)	32
Canada	(19)	1
Denmark	(19)	45
Eire	(19)	353
Finland	(19)	358
India	(19)	91
Japan	(19)	81
Netherlands	(19)	31
New Zealand	(19)	64
Norway	(19)	47
Singapore	(19)	65
South Africa	(19)	27
Sweden	(19)	46
Switzerland	(19)	41
United Kingdom	(19)	44
United States	(19)	1
West Germany	(19)	49

If you want international inquiries, dial 33 between the 19 and the code of the country for which you need to know the number, e.g. 19 + 33 + 44 for U.K. inquiries. For inquiries concerning the U.S. or Canada, dial 11 instead of 1 (19 + 33 + 11).

For long-distance calls within France, there are no area codes (just dial the 8-digit number of the person you want to call), except when telephoning from Paris or the Paris region (Ile-de-France) to the provinces (dial 16 and wait for the dialling tone, then dial the 8-digit number of the subscriber) and from the provinces to Paris or the Ile-de-France (dial 16, wait for the dialling tone, then dial 1 followed by the 8-digit number). If all else fails, call the operator for help—12 in French, (1) 42.33.44.11 in other languages.

Where's the nearest post office?	Où se trouve le bureau de poste le plus proche?
A stamp for this letter/postcard, please.	Un timbre pour cette lettre/carte postale, s'il vous plaît.
What's the postage for a letter to...?	Quel est le tarif d'une lettre pour...?
air mail	par avion
express (special delivery)	par exprès
registered	en recommandé
Is there any mail for...?	Y a-t-il du courrier pour...?
I'd like to send a telegram/ telex/fax.	Je voudrais envoyer un télégramme/ télex/téléfax.
May I use your phone?	Puis-je utiliser votre téléphone?

COMPLAINTS

Take inadequacies with tolerance and tact. But if something goes seriously wrong, don't hesitate to complain. Do it on the spot and to the correct person. At a hotel or restaurant, this will be the manager (maître d'hôtel or directeur). In extreme cases, you can get help at a police station (commissariat de police), or, failing that, the regional administration office (préfecture or sous-préfecture). Ask for the "service du tourisme".

CRIME AND THEFT

As in most big cities, the entertainment districts of Paris, Nice and Marseille are places to be wary in; keep to well-lit streets at night. Watch your wallet and handbag—especially in crowds. Deposit items of value in your hotel safe and obtain a receipt for them. It is a good idea to leave any large amounts of money there as well, or to keep money and credit cards in a pouch inside your clothes.

Lock your car at all times and leave nothing valuable inside. The car parks at lookout points are classic targets for thieves.

Keep a photocopy of your plane ticket and other personal documents, with a note of the phone and telex numbers of your travel agent: it could come in useful in case of loss or theft.

Any loss or theft should be reported at once to the nearest commissariat de police.

I want to report a theft.	Je voudrais signaler un vol.
My ticket/wallet/ passport/handbag/ credit card has been stolen.	On m'a volé mon billet/portefeuille/ passeport/sac à main/ma carte de crédit.

CUSTOMS *(douane)*, ENTRY AND EXIT REGULATIONS

See also DRIVING IN FRANCE

Citizens of EEC countries, Switzerland, Liechtenstein, Andorra, Monaco and San Marino need only a valid identity card or passport to enter France. For citizens of the U.K., a "British Visitors Passport" (valid for one year) or a "British Excursion Document for Travel to France" (available at the post office for trips of up to 60 hours within a month) is acceptable. Nationals of other countries require a visa; apply to your nearest French consulate. Though European and North-American residents are not subject to any health requirements, visitors from further afield may require a smallpox vaccination. Check with your travel agent before departure.

The chart below shows some customs allowances for France. However, note that they are subject to change at short notice.

New goods for personal use originating outside the EEC: 300 F, originating in EEC countries: 2,400 F.

For what you can bring back home, ask before your departure for the customs notice setting out allowances.

Pets. — It is prohibited to bring dogs or cats under 3 months old into France. A maximum of three animals are allowed of which only one may be less than 6 months old, accompanied by rabies vaccination certificates issued from 30 up to 365 days before departure.

Currency restrictions. — There's no limit to the importation or exportation of local or foreign currencies or traveller's cheques, but cash amounts exceeding 50,000 F or its equivalent should be declared on arrival to facilitate re-export; ask for the form *Déclaration d'importation en France de billets de banque étrangers.*

Reimbursement of sales tax. — Foreign visitors returning home can have the VAT/sales tax (TVA—tay vay ah)—imposed on almost all goods in France—refunded on larger purchases (for visitors from non-EEC countries, 1,200 F regardless of the number of articles; for visitors from EEC countries, 2,400 F per article). Residents of non-EEC countries must fill out a form (three copies) and give two copies to the customs when leaving France for the refund to be sent to their home. Residents of EEC countries will have to get the form stamped by the customs or excise service of their country and personally mail the papers to the Bureau des douanes de Paris-La Chapelle:

61, rue de la Chapelle - 75018 Paris

For further customs regulations, contact the Bureau d'information des douanes:

182, rue Saint-Honoré - 75001 Paris
Tel. (1) 42.60.35.90

I've nothing to declare.	**Je n'ai rien à déclarer.**
It's for my personal use.	**C'est pour mon usage personnel.**

DISTRICTS OF PARIS

Paris is divided into 20 municipal districts *(arrondissement).* All postal (zip) codes start with the digits 750 and finish with the number of the *arrondissement* in question (e.g. 75001 is the first district). The different districts with a choice of sights, attractions, etc., are:

1er arrondissement (75001), Louvre: Palais du Louvre, Jardin des Tuileries, Orangerie, Palais-Royal, Comédie-Française, Palais de Justice, Sainte-Chapelle, Conciergerie, Forum des Halles, Place Vendôme.

2e arrondissement (75002), Bourse: Bourse (Stock Exchange), Bibliothèque Nationale, Rue de la Paix (goldsmiths and furriers).

	Cigarettes		Cigars		Tobacco	Spirits	Wine		Perfume		Toilet water
1)	400	or	100	or	500 g.	1 l.	2 l.		50 g.		1 l.
2)	300	or	75	or	400 g.	1½ l. and	5 l.		75 g.	and	⅜ l.
3)	200		50		250 g.	1 l.	2 l.		50 g.		¼ l.

1) Visitors arriving from countries outside Europe.
2) Visitors arriving from EEC countries with non-duty-free items (tax paid).
3) Visitors from EEC countries with duty-free items, or from other European countries.

3e arrondissement (75003), Temple: Le Marais, Musée Picasso.

4e arrondissement (75004), Hôtel de Ville: Hôtel de Ville (City Hall), Beaubourg (Centre Georges Pompidou), Notre-Dame de Paris, Ile Saint-Louis, Place des Vosges.

5e arrondissement (75005), Panthéon: Quartier Latin (Sorbonne, Panthéon), Musée de Cluny, Jardin des Plantes.

6e arrondissement (75006), Luxembourg: Jardin du Luxembourg, Place Saint-Germain-des-Prés, Ecole des Beaux-Arts, Institut de France.

7e arrondissement (75007), Palais Bourbon: Eiffel Tower, Champ-de-Mars, Ecole militaire, Hôtel des Invalides, Musée d'Orsay, Musée Rodin, Invalides Air Terminal.

8e arrondissement (75008), Elysée: Boulevard des Champs-Elysées, Place de la Concorde, Arc de Triomphe, Palais de l'Elysée, church of the Madeleine, Faubourg Saint-Honoré, Parc de Monceau, Gare Saint-Lazare.

9e arrondissement (75009), Opéra: Opéra, Musée Grévin, Folies-Bergère, "grands boulevards" (Boulevard des Capucines, Boulevard des Italiens).

10e arrondissement (75010), Enclos Saint-Laurent: Place de la République, Musée de l'Affiche, Gare du Nord, Gare de l'Est.

11e arrondissement (75011), Popincourt: Colonne de Juillet (Place de la Bastille), Place de la Nation.

12e arrondissement (75012), Reuilly: Palais omnisports de Paris-Bercy, Bois de Vincennes, Gare de Lyon, Gare de Paris-Bercy.

13e arrondissement (75013), Gobelins: Manufacture des Gobelins (tapestry museum), Gare d'Austerlitz.

14e arrondissement (75014), Observatoire: Montparnasse, Cimetière du Montparnasse, Parc Montsouris.

15e arrondissement (75015), Vaugirard: Parc des Expositions, Institut Pasteur, Tour Montparnasse, Gare Montparnasse.

16e arrondissement (75016), Passy: Bois de Boulogne, Jardin du Trocadéro, Musée de l'Homme, Musée du Cinéma, Musée Guimet, Musée Balzac.

17e arrondissement (75017), Batignolles: Palais des Congrès, Porte Maillot Air Terminal.

18e arrondissement (75018), Butte-Montmartre: Montmartre (Sacré-Cœur, Place du Tertre, Moulin Rouge).

19e arrondissement (75019), Buttes-Chaumont: Parc des Buttes-Chaumont, La Villette (Cité des sciences et de l'industrie, Géode, Zénith).

20e arrondissement (75020), Ménilmontant: Cimetière du Père-Lachaise.

DRIVING IN FRANCE

See also CUSTOMS, ENTRY AND EXIT FORMALITIES AND DISTANCE CHART p. 365.
To take a car into France, you will need:
- A valid driving licence.
- Car registration papers.
- Insurance coverage (the green card is no longer obligatory for vehicles registered in Western Europe, but comprehensive coverage is recommended; drivers of vehicles registered in other countries must show proof of insurance or buy an international insurance card at the French border)
- A red warning triangle and a complete set of spare bulbs

Drivers and front-seat passengers are required by law to wear seat belts. Children under 10 may not travel in the front (unless the car has no back seat). Driving on a foreign provisional licence is not permitted in France. Minimum age is 18. Motorcycle drivers and passengers must be covered by insurance and wear crash helmets. Dipped headlights must be used at all times.

Driving regulations. — Drive on the right, overtake (pass) on the left. (*Serrez à droite* means "keep to the right".) British drivers should be careful not to forget this rule momentarily; for example when they emerge from a one-way street, a refuelling stop, at a T-junction or when turning left at traffic lights. In built-up areas, give automatic priority to vehicles coming from the right. The priority will be taken in any case, so it's only wise to "offer" it first. But the *priorité* rule does not apply at roundabouts (traffic circles). Outside built-up areas—at junctions marked by signs with a cross or a yellow square on a white background—the more important of two roads has right of way. The use of car horns in built-up areas is allowed only as a warning. At night, lights should be used for this purpose. Fines for speeding or exceeding the drink-and-drive alcohol level (maximum 0.8 g.) are payable in cash on the spot.

Studded snow tyres (tires) can be used from November 15 to March 15.

Speed limits. — On dry roads: 130 kph (81 mph) on toll motorways (expressways); 110 kph (68 mph) on urban motorways and dual carriageways (divided highways); 90 kph (56 mph) on other roads (80 kph/ 50 mph on the Boulevards Périphériques surrounding Paris); and 45 or 60 kph (28 or 37 mph) in towns and built-up areas. When roads are wet, limits are reduced by 10 kph (6 mph), except for motorways, where maximum speed in fog, rain or snow is reduced by 20 kph (12 mph). For cars fitted with studded tyres, the maximum speed is 90 kph.

Motorcycles: 51–80 cc., 75 kph (46 mph); from 81 cc., as for cars.

The word *rappel* means a restriction is continued.

Road conditions. — The road information centre *Inter-Service-Route* operates 24 hours a day from Paris. Phone (1) 48.99.33.33. Most of the time, there is someone who speaks English. For the motorway network, there is a separate information service, the *Centre de renseignements des autoroutes,* tel. (1) 47.05.90.01.

Blue road signs lead to motorways *(A-autoroute),* white ones to other roads. Brown signs indicate touristic attractions and green ones stand for *itinéraires bis,* which propose alternative roads to avoid heavy traffic (a green arrow on a white background indicates north–south, while the opposite direction is shown by a white arrow on green background). During the summer months, you can get information on these alternative itineraries at the *Bison futé* ("wily buffalo") road centres. The letter *N* stands for *route nationale* (main road), *D,* for *route départementale* (secondary road, maintained by the département concerned), *V,* for *chemin vicinal* (local road).

The motorways are privately owned, with sizable tolls *(péage)* according to vehicle size and distance travelled. All amenities (restaurants, toilets, service stations) are available, plus orange emergency (S.O.S.) telephones every 2 km. (1.2 mi.). Service stations are located about every 25 km. (16 mi.) and are usually open round the clock.

Beware of traffic jams on the major roads and motorways at long weekends and in the school holiday weeks in February, at Easter, and during the summer holiday period (July and August).

Parking. — There's 24-hour parking at more than 200 railway stations throughout the country. In town centres, most street parking is metered. The blue zones *(zone bleue),* often signposted "Disque Obligatoire", require a parking disc *(disque de stationnement),* obtainable from petrol (gas) stations or stationers. Set it to show the time you arrived and it will indicate when you have to leave. Then display it in the car, visible through the windscreen (windshield). Don't leave your car in an area marked *"Zone Piétonne"* (pedestrian precinct), even less if the sign says *"Stationnement Gênant"* (parking obstructive) or *"Stationnement Interdit"* (parking prohibited).

Breakdowns *(panne).* — Dial 17, wherever you are in France, and the police can put you in touch with a garage that will come to your rescue. At a price, though, so it is wise to take out an international breakdown insurance before leaving home. Local garages usually provide towing facilities and spare parts for European cars. Always ask for an estimate before authorizing repairs, and expect to pay VAT sales tax (TVA) on top of the cost.

Fuel and oil *(essence; huile).* — Fuel is available in super (98 octane), normal (90 octane), unleaded (95 octane) and diesel. Unleaded petrol (gas) is still not easily found.

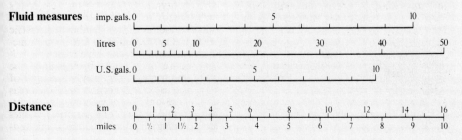

Fluid measures

imp. gals.	0		5		10
litres	0	5	10	20	30	40	50
U.S. gals.	0		5		10

Distance

| km | 0 | 1 | 2 | 3 | 4 | 5 | 6 | 8 | 10 | 12 | 14 | 16 |
| miles | 0 | ½ | 1 | 1½ | 2 | 3 | 4 | 5 | 6 | 7 | 8 | 9 | 10 |

All grades of motor oils are on sale. Service-station attendants expect to be tipped.

It is prohibited to carry spare cans with more than 5 litres of fuel in the car (10 litres if unleaded). No spare petrol is allowed on the ferry crossing to Corsica.

Road signs. — Most road signs are the standard pictographs used throughout Europe, but you may encounter these written signs as well:

Accotements non stabilisés	*Soft shoulders*
Allumez vos phares	*Switch on headlights*
Céder le passage	*Give way (Yield)*
Chaussée déformée	*Bad road surface*
Chutes de pierres	*Falling rocks*
Déviation	*Diversion (Detour)*
Gravillons	*Loose gravel*
Impasse	*Cul-de-sac (Dead end)*
Nids de poule	*Potholes*
Ralentir	*Slow down*
Serrez à droite/gauche	*Keep right/left*
Sortie de camions	*Lorry (Truck) exit*
Travaux	*Road works (Construction ahead)*
Véhicules lents	*Slow vehicles*
Verglas	*Icy road*
Virages	*Bends/Curves*
driving licence	**permis de conduire**
car registration papers	**carte grise**
Are we on the right road for...?	**Sommes-nous sur la route de...?**
Is there a carpark nearby?	**Y a-t-il un parking à proximité?**
Full tank, please.	**Le plein, s'il vous plaît.**
super (premium)/ regular/ unleaded/diesel	**super/normale/ sans plomb/gas-oil**
Check the oil/ tyres/battery, please.	**Veuillez contrôler l'huile/les pneus/la batterie.**
My car has broken down.	**Ma voiture est en panne.**
There's been an accident.	**Il y a eu un accident.**

ELECTRIC CURRENT

220-volt, 50-cycle is almost universal in France, though 110 volts may still be encountered. Sockets (outlets) take round, 2-pin (occasionally 3-pin) plugs, so you will probably need an international adaptor plug, available at many airports before departure.

What's the voltage? 110 220	**Quel est le voltage:** cent dix ou deux cent vingt?
an adaptor plug	**une prise multiple**
a voltage transformer	**un transformateur**
a battery	**une pile**

EMBASSIES AND CONSULATES
(ambassade; consulat)

Contact the embassy or consulate of your home country when in trouble (loss of passport, problems with the police, serious accidents). All embassies are in Paris. There are consulates in other major cities, listed in the telephone directory *(bottin* or *annuaire)* under "Consulats".

Australia. — 4, rue Jean-Rey, 75015 Paris; tel. (1) 40.59.33.00 (*métro* Bir-Hakeim).

Canada. — 35, avenue Montaigne, 75008 Paris; tel. (1) 47.23.0l.0l (*métro* Alma-Marceau).

Denmark. — 77, avenue Marceau, 75016 Paris; tel. (1) 47.20.32.66 (*métro* Alma-Marceau).

Eire. — 12, avenue Foch (enter from 4, rue Rude), 75016 Paris; tel. (1) 45.00.20.87/ 45.00.89.43 (*métro* Charles-de-Gaulle-Etoile).

Finland. — 39, quai d'Orsay, 75007 Paris; tel. (1) 47.05.35.45 (*métro* Invalides).

India. — 15, rue Alfred-Dehodencq, 75016 Paris; tel. (1) 45.20.39.30 (*métro* La Muette).

Japan. — 7, avenue Hoche, 75008 Paris; tel. (1) 47.66.02.22 (*métro* Charles-de-Gaulle-Etoile).

Netherlands. — 7, rue Eblé, 75007 Paris; tel. (1) 43.06.61.88 (*métro* Duroc).

New Zealand. — 7 ter., rue Léonard-de-Vinci, 75016 Paris; tel. (1) 45.00.24.11 (*métro* Victor-Hugo).

Norway. — 28, rue Bayard, 75008 Paris; tel. (1) 47.23.72.78 (*métro* Franklin D. Roosevelt).

South Africa. — 59, quai d'Orsay, 75007 Paris; tel. (1) 45.55.92.37 (*métro* Invalides).

Sweden. — 17, rue Barbet-de-Jouy, 75007 Paris; tel. (1) 45.55.92.15 (*métro* Saint-François-Xavier).

U.K. — 35, rue du Faubourg Saint-Honoré, 75008 Paris; tel. (1) 42.66.91.42 (*métro* Concorde).

U.S.A. — 2, avenue Gabriel, 75008 Paris; tel. (1) 42.96.12.02 (*métro* Concorde).

EMERGENCIES *(urgences)*

See also HEALTH AND MEDICAL CARE.
You can get assistance anywhere in France by dialling 17 for the police *(police secours)* or 18 for the fire brigade *(pompiers),* who also turn out for medical emergencies.

Please call the police.	**Appelez la police, s'il vous plaît.**
Call a doctor/ an ambulance quickly.	**Appelez d'urgence un médecin/une ambulance.**

FAIRS AND SPORTS EVENTS

For festivals, see p. 301.
Fairs and festivals are celebrated all year round. The listing below shows some of the major annual events. For further details, ask for the brochures *France en Fête* and *Festivals* for the current year at the French tourist office.

February. — Paris: cycle race at Bercy (6 days) and "Prêt à Porter", fashion show (4 days). Le Touquet: "Enduro", motorcycle race (1 day).

March. — Paris: agricultural show (8 days).

April. — Le Mans: 24-hour motorcycle race.

April–May. — Paris: "Foire (fair) de Paris" (13 days).

May. — Paris: marathon. Monaco: Formula 1 Grand Prix.

May–June. — Paris: French Open, international tennis championship (14 days).

June. — Le Mans: 24-hour car race.

July. Country-wide: "Tour de France", bicycle race with final sprint along Paris's Avenue des Champs-Elysées (20 days). Le Castellet: Formula 1 Grand Prix.

September. — Paris: "Prêt à Porter", fashion show (4 days). Le Castellet: "Bol d'Or", motorcycle race (2 days).

September–October. — Paris: international motor show (12 days).

October. — Paris: 6-hour motorboat race and "Grand Prix de l'Arc-de-Triomphe", horse-race at Longchamp.

November. — Beaune: wine auction (1 day).

December. — Paris: international boat show (11 days).

FOREST FIRES

Every summer, fires devastate forests in southern France. Do your part in preventing them—put out cigarettes carefully, do not light campfires, and be especially careful if using a grill or primus stove on a picnic.

GETTING TO FRANCE

See your travel agent or the French tourist office in your home country well before departure for help with timetables, budget and personal requirements. Try to avoid France's major school holiday periods (February, Easter and July–August).

By Air
Scheduled flights. — Paris can be reached by scheduled flights from most capitals of the world. Air France, the French national airline, connects Paris with more than 170 destinations in some 80 countries. A number of international flights also operate to Lyon, Nice and many other cities, including Ajaccio, Bastia and Calvi in Corsica. Therefore, to avoid having to travel miles from point of departure to point of arrival, look into regional possibilities.

Paris is served by two international airports, Roissy–Charles-de-Gaulle and Orly (see p. 342). The average journey time between Paris and London is 1 hour, New

York 7 hours (less than 4 hours by Concorde), Toronto 9 hours, Sydney 24 hours and Johannesburg 14 hours.

Charter flights and package tours. — Paris is the starting point for the majority of tours of France. Wine-tasting, gourmet and shopping tours, as well as tours of the château country and hotel-barge cruises through the vineyards are included in package deals leaving from European and major North-American cities. You can also hire a barge or cabin cruiser and sail it yourself (no permit is required) along some of France's 8,000-km. (5,000-mi.) network of navigable canals and rivers—in Burgundy, Brittany, the Midi. Among the inclusive holiday packages are special tours for visitors with a common interest such as cookery courses, painting courses, etc. You can also choose from fly-drive and fly-rail schemes and the Air France–SNCF (the French National Railways) fly-rail-and-drive savings.

By Road
There's free access to France from all its neighbouring countries, but note that citizens of most non-EEC countries need a visa (see CUSTOMS, ENTRY AND EXIT REGULATIONS). Motorways in Belgium, Luxembourg and West Germany are toll free, but in Spain, Italy and France, you have to pay tolls according to distance travelled. In Switzerland, you'll have to buy a sticker *(vignette)*—valid for the current year—at the border, to be displayed on the windscreen.

For travellers from the U.K. and Eire, cross-Channel operators offer plenty of special deals at competitive prices; a good travel agent will help you to find the ferry suitable for your destination in France.

Ferries also connect France with the islands of Guernsey and Jersey, with North-African cities (Sète–Tanger/Oran, Marseille–Alger/Benjafa/Skikda/Tunis), the Italian island of Sardinia and the Spanish islands of Ibiza and Majorca.

Regular **coach** services operate from major European cities, including London, to Paris, and numerous lines join Paris and regional cities such as Bordeaux, Lyon and Nice.

By Rail
SNCF offices will help tourists plan their trip.

Canada. — *French National Railroads,* 1500 rue Stanley, Montreal, Que. H3A 1R3, tel. (514) 288 825 55. *French National Railroads,* 55 University – Suite 600, Toronto, Ont. M5J 2C7, tel. (416) 368 86 39.

U.K. — French National Railways, 179 Piccadilly, London W1V 0BA, tel. (01) 493 9731.

U.S.A. — French National Railroads, 610 Fifth Avenue, Rockefeller Centre, 5th floor, New York, NY 10020, tel. (212) 582-2816/17.

Travellers from countries where SNCF is not represented should contact their national railways or a travel agent.

The European national railways networks offer a wide range of bargain tickets. Many of the railpasses mentioned below must be obtained before leaving home.

The *Eurailpass,* an individual ticket available for people residing outside Europe, the U.S.S.R., Turkey and North Africa (Tunisia, Algeria, Morocco), is valid for unlimited 1st-class rail travel in 16 European countries (Austria, Belgium, Denmark, Eire, Finland, France, West Germany, Greece, Italy, Luxembourg, the Netherlands, Norway, Portugal, Spain, Sweden and Switzerland), including travel on some private railways, buses and many ferryboats and steamers. The *Eurail Saverpass* is a special 1st-class ticket for three or more people travelling together (two or more between October 1 and March 31), while the *Eurail Flexipass,* for North Americans, Mexicans, Australians and New Zealanders (also for 1st class), offers more flexibility for nine days' travel within a 21-day period. The *Eurail Youthpass* for travellers under 26 years of age allows one month's or two months' unlimited 2nd-class rail journeys, but surcharges are required for travelling on fast trains like EuroCity (EC), Intercity (IC), TGV, Rapide, etc., and for certain ferry-crossings during high season.

For residents of European countries, there's the *Rail Europ S (RES)* ticket which entitles senior citizens to purchase train tickets at reduced prices. A family of at least three people can buy a *Rail Europ F* card; the holder pays full fare, the rest of the family obtain a 50% reduction. The whole family is also entitled to a 30% reduction on Sealink and Hoverspeed Channel crossings. Europeans under 26 years of age can purchase an *Inter-Rail* card which allows one month's unlimited 2nd-class travel.

Anyone permanently residing outside France can buy the *France-Vacances-Pass* called *France Railpass* overseas, which gives unlimited travel for any four days to be used within 15 days, or any nine or 16 days to be used within one month. It also provides free transfer by rail to and from Paris and its airports, unlimited travel on the Paris *métro* and bus system for one or two days and reduction on car rentals, sightseeing, entry to museums and a range of regional tourist attractions.

Other offers by SNCF include: *Carte Couple/Carte Famille,* issued to married couples and families and allowing a 50% reduction on all children's fares; *Carte Jeune,* a seasonal offer of half price for young people under 26, with a bonus of a free couchette; and *Carte Vermeil,* half-price rail travel for men aged 62 or over and for women of 60 or over. But be careful: these offers don't apply to peak travel days. Ask at the railway station for a *Calendrier Voyageurs,* which shows by colour coding when you can begin each stage of your journey. Anyone can start travelling during "blue" periods, families also where it's marked white. Red indicates peak times, when you'll have to pay the difference.

The journey from London to Paris takes from 6 to 11 hours by train. British Rail and SNCF offer London-to-Paris services with the possibility of overnight carriages from London. From Boulogne hoverport, there's a 2-hour, 20-minute turbotrain service to Paris (Gare du Nord). Shortest travel time between Brussels and Paris is 2½ hours, between Geneva and Paris 3½ hours.

GUIDES AND INTERPRETERS
(guide; interprète)

Syndicats d'initiative (see TOURIST INFORMATION OFFICES) can help you find qualified official guides and interpreters. Guides engaged all day should be offered lunch.

Bus companies offer many guided tours, and reputable travel agencies furnish guides and cars. It's customary to tip the guide.

We'd like an English-speaking guide.	Nous aimerions un guide parlant anglais.
I need an English interpreter.	J'ai besoin d'un interprète anglais.

HEALTH AND MEDICAL CARE

Make sure that your health-insurance policy covers illness and accidents abroad. If it does not, ask your insurance representative, automobile association or travel agent about special insurance plans. Visitors from EEC countries with corresponding health-insurance facilities are entitled to medical and hospital treatment under the French social-security system. Before leaving home, ensure that you are eligible and have the appropriate forms required to obtain this benefit in case of need.

Doctors who belong to the French social-security system *(médecins conventionnés)* charge the minimum. If you're taken ill or have a toothache, your hotel receptionist can probably recommend an English-speaking doctor or dentist; otherwise, ask at the local *syndicat d'initiative* or, in an emergency, the gendarmerie.

The stomach trouble that hits many travellers is generally not due to drinking tap water, which is safe in towns all over France. Fatigue, too much sun, change of diet and too much food and drink are the causes of most minor complaints. Serious gastro-intestinal problems lasting more than a day or two should be looked after by a doctor. Don't be surprised if a doctor prescribes suppositories; in France, they're considered the best and fastest way of getting drugs into the bloodstream.

In the Paris area, two private hospitals serve the Anglo-American community:

American Hospital of Paris
63, boulevard Victor-Hugo – 92202 Neuilly
Tel. (1) 47.47.53.00

Hôpital Franco-Britannique
48, rue de Villiers – Levallois-Perret
Tel. (1) 47.58.13.12

Throughout France, dial 18 (the fire brigade) for an ambulance. In Paris, you can get advice for other urgent medical problems by dialling SOS Médecins at (1) 47.07.77.77, or SAMU *(Service d'aide médical urgent)* at (1) 45.67.50.50.

Tap water is safe to drink except from taps marked "Eau Non Potable" (not drinking water). A wide variety of mineral water *(eau minérale),* fizzy (carbonated) and still (non-carbonated), is on sale everywhere. You pay a deposit *(consigne)* on glass bottles (refunded when you take the empties back).

Pharmacies display green crosses. Staff are generally helpful in dealing with minor ailments and can recommend a nurse *(infirmière)* if you need an injection or other special care. Pharmacies are open during shopping hours, and there is usually one per district that operates at night and at weekends. The opening schedule is displayed in the window of other pharmacies and published in the local papers. In Paris, the pharmacy at 84, avenue des Champs-Elysées, tel. (1) 45.62.02.41, is open 24 hours a day.

Bring along an adequate supply of any prescribed medication.

The campaign to prevent AIDS (in French: SIDA) is supported by the widespread availability of condoms *(préservatifs)* from machines in public entertainment places as well as over the counter in pharmacies.

Where's the nearest (all-night) pharmacy?	**Où se trouve la pharmacie (de garde) la plus proche?**
I need a doctor/ dentist.	**Il me faut un médecin/ dentiste.**
I've a...	**J'ai...**
headache/ stomach ache/ fever	**mal à la tête/ mal à l'estomac/ de la fièvre**

HITCH-HIKING *(auto-stop)*

This is permitted everywhere except on motorways (expressways). If you do hitch-hike, it's always wiser to go in pairs.

Can you give me/us a lift to...?	**Pouvez-vous m'/ nous emmener à...?**

HOURS OF OPENING
(heures d'ouverture)

Banks open from 9 a.m. to 4 p.m. on weekdays (many closing for lunch from noon till 2 p.m.) and close either on Saturdays (cities and main towns) or Mondays. All banks are closed on major national and regional holidays and most close early on the day preceding a public (legal) holiday.

Churches. — Generally from 7 a.m. to noon and from 2 to 7 p.m. Larger churches and cathedrals stay open during lunchtime in summer.

Department stores and supermarkets are generally open from 9/9.30 a.m. to 7/7.30 p.m., Tuesday to Saturday. Most close Monday morning or whole day, but many supermarkets open on Sunday mornings.

Groceries, bakeries, butchers. — 7/8/ 8.30 a.m. to noon and 2 to 6.30/7/7.30 p.m., Monday to Saturday. Many open on Sunday mornings.

Museums close on Easter Sunday and Monday, on Christmas Day and generally on national holidays. National museums are normally open from 9.30 a.m. to noon and from 2 to 5.30 p.m., Wednesday to Monday. During low season, many museums close or have reduced hours; check before going.

Post offices. — Main offices open from 8 a.m. to 7 p.m., branches from 8 a.m. to noon and from 2 to 7 p.m., Monday to Friday, from 8 a.m. to noon on Saturdays.

When does the... open/close?	**A quelle heure ouvre/ferme...?**
bank	**la banque**
church/cathedral	**l'église/la cathédrale**
museum	**le musée**
post office	**le bureau de poste**
shop	**le magasin**
department store	**le grand magasin**
supermarket	**le supermarché**

LANGUAGE

The clearest, purest French spoken in France is that of the Loire Valley around Touraine. In Paris, you'll also hear well-enunciated French—but spoken quite quickly—as well as innumerable accents since many of the capital's inhabitants come from the provinces or further afield. Despite opposition from purists, many Anglicisms have crept into French.

Minor regional languages are spoken in Brittany (Breton—an ancient Celtic tongue resembling Welsh), at the western end of the Pyrenees (Basque) and in French Catalonia at the eastern end of the Pyrenees (Catalan). In Alsace and parts of Lorraine, many people still speak the old German dialect, and some people around Dunkirk *(Dunkerque),* near the Belgian border, speak Flemish (almost identical to Dutch). The people of Provence and the Côte d'Azur have a charming, droll accent, drawing out their syllables. Here in the south-east, you'll also hear all sorts of rolling Italianate dialects, especially Niçois, Monegasque and Corsican.

Although a certain number of Frenchmen speak some English, they much prefer a tourist making an effort to speak French, even if it's only the odd word. The Berlitz phrase book *French for Travellers* covers almost all the situations you're likely to encounter in your travels in France. If further help is required, the Berlitz French-English/English-French pocket dictionary contains the basic vocabulary a tourist will need, plus a menu-reader supplement.

Good morning/ Good afternoon.	Bonjour.
Good afternoon/ Good evening.	Bonsoir.
Good night.	Bonne nuit.
Goodbye.	Au revoir.
Do you speak English?	Parlez-vous anglais?
I don't speak (much) French.	Je ne parle pas (bien) français.
Could you speak more slowly?	Pourriez-vous parler plus lentement?
I didn't understand.	Je n'ai pas compris.

LOST PROPERTY

Restaurant and café personnel are quite honest about keeping forgotten or lost objects until the owner reclaims them. In general, if you lose a personal object, you should go to the nearest *gendarmerie* or *commissariat de police*. Loss of passport or identity papers should be reported to your embassy or consulate. For lost credit cards, call (Paris):

American Express	(1) 47.08.31.21
Diners Club	(1) 47.62.75.00
Eurocard/MasterCard	(1) 43.23.46.46
Visa/Carte Bleue	(1) 42.77.11.90

In Paris, lost objects usually end up at the Bureau des objets trouvés at 36, rue des Morillons, 75015 Paris, tel: (01) 48.28.32.36.

I've lost my wallet/ handbag/ passport.	J'ai perdu mon portefeuille/sac à main/passeport.

MAPS

Small street maps are given away at tourist offices, banks and hotels. Detailed country maps—like the IGN *(Institut géographique national)* No. 901 and the Michelin No. 915 (1/1,000,000) and No 400 (motorways/expressways)—and regional maps are sold in bookshops and at newsagents. The Comité national des sentiers de grande randonnée publishes a series of detailed maps—*Topoguide*—for hiking throughout France.

The maps in this book were prepared by Hallwag A.G., Bern.

Do you have a map of the city/ of the region?	Avez-vous un plan de la ville/une carte de la région?

MONEY MATTERS

Currency. — The French franc (abbreviated F, FF or Fr.) is divided into 100 centimes (ct.).

Coins: 5, 10, 20, 50 ct.; 1, 2, 5, 10 F.
Banknotes: 20, 50, 100, 200, 500 F.

For currency restrictions, see CUSTOMS, ENTRY AND EXIT REGULATIONS.

Banks and currency exchange. — Hours may vary, but most banks are open Monday to Friday from 9 a.m. to 4 p.m. (from 9 a.m. to noon and 2 to 4 p.m. in smaller towns). Some currency-exchange offices are open on Saturdays. Your hotel may also come to the rescue, though you'll get a less favourable rate of exchange. The same applies to foreign currency or traveller's cheques changed in stores, boutiques or restaurants. Take your identity card or passport along when you go to cash traveller's cheques.

Credit cards can be used in a number of hotels, restaurants, department stores and at many petrol (gas) stations, but less commonly in supermarkets and rarely in smaller shops like bakeries and groceries.

Traveller's cheques and **Eurocheques** are accepted in cities and larger tourist resorts. Outside the towns, it's best to have some ready cash handy.

Note: A sales tax (TVA) is imposed on almost all goods and services in France. In hotels and restaurants, this is accompanied by a service charge. Tourists from abroad can have the TVA refunded on larger purchases.

Where's the nearest bank/currency-exchange office?	**Où se trouve la banque/le bureau de change la/le plus proche?**
I'd like to change some pounds/dollars.	**Je voudrais changer des livres sterling/des dollars.**
What's the exchange rate?	**Quel est le cours du change?**
Could you give me some change?	**Pouvez-vous me donner de la monnaie?**
Do you accept traveller's cheques?	**Acceptez-vous les chèques de voyage?**
Can I pay with this credit card?	**Puis-je payer avec cette carte de crédit?**

NATIONAL AND REGIONAL PARKS

France is dotted with nature parks, created to preserve the natural environment, the flora and the fauna of the different regions. They cover an astonishing variety of landscapes, from the plains of the north to the mountains of the south and the east. Aside from walking, hiking, bicycling and riding paths, many offer accommodation in rural lodgings or on campsites, and leisure activities like wind-surfing, delta flying, fishing, canoeing, etc. For information on the parks, write to the Fédération des parcs naturels de France:

4, rue de Stockholm – 75008 Paris
tel. (01) 42.94.90.84

NEWSPAPERS AND MAGAZINES
(journal; magazine)

The Paris-based *International Herald Tribune* and other major English-language newspapers and magazines are available at main newsagents in resorts and larger towns. For the best information on what's on in Paris, buy the weekly magazine *Pariscope* or *L'Officiel du Spectacle*. In the provinces, the *syndicats d'initiative* often publish a similar, smaller periodical.

Have you any English-language newspapers?	**Avez-vous des journaux en anglais?**

POLICE

In cities and larger towns, you'll see the blue-uniformed *police municipale;* they are the local force who direct traffic, keep order and investigate crime. In smaller towns and villages, the *gendarmes* have this responsibility; they wear blue trousers and black jackets with white belts. The *garde mobile,* also called *motards* or *police de la route,* patrol the roads on powerful motorcycles.

Throughout France, in case of need, dial 17 for police assistance.

Where's the nearest police station?	**Où est le poste de police le plus proche?**

PUBLIC (LEGAL) HOLIDAYS
(fête légale)

January 1	Jour de l'An	New Year's Day
May 1	Fête du Travail	Labour Day
May 8	Armistice 1945	Victory Day
July 14	Fête Nationale	Bastille Day
August 15	Assomption	Assumption
November 1	Toussaint	All Saints' Day
November 11	Armistice 1918	Armistice Day
December 25	Noël	Christmas Day
Movable dates:	Lundi de Pâques	Easter Monday
	Ascension	Ascension
	Lundi de Pentecôte	Whit Monday

The following are France's national holidays. If one of them falls on a Tuesday or Thursday, many French people take the Monday or Friday off as well to make a long weekend (but this rarely affects shops or businesses).

Are you open tomorrow?	**Est-ce que vous ouvrez demain?**

RADIO AND TV *(radio; télévision)*

In summer, the French radio France-Inter broadcasts news and traffic information in English, usually at 8 a.m., 1 p.m. and 7 p.m. You can easily tune in to BBC programmes on short or medium-wave radios.

The TV channels are TF1, Antenne 2, FR3, La Cinq and M6. (Canal Plus [4] is subscriber-only.) All programmes, except for a few late-night foreign films (normally on Fridays and/or Sundays) are in French.

356

RELIGIOUS SERVICES
(offices religieux)

France is predominantly Roman Catholic. Times of mass are posted at church entrances and on green roadside signboards at the entrance to towns and villages. Other major religious denominations have congregations in the cities, many with services in English. Ask at the hotel reception or the local tourist office.

For information on places and times of worship in Paris and its surrounding area, contact the Centre d'information et de documentation religieuse, which also provides details of other religious activities in the capital:

8, rue Massillon - 75004 Paris
Tel. (1) 46.33.01.01

The centre is open from 9 a.m. to noon and from 2 to 6 p.m., Monday to Friday.

Is there a ... near here?	Y a-t-il près d'ici... ?
Catholic church	**une église (catholique)**
Protestant church	**un temple**
mosque	**une mosquée**
synagogue	**une synagogue**
At what time is mass/the service?	**A quelle heure commence la messe/ le culte?**

RESTAURANTS

See also p. 315.

Restaurants in France are classified by travel agencies, automobile associations and gastronomic guilds with a variety of codes—stars, knives and forks, chef's hats, and so on. Look at the numberplate (license plate) on the cars in the restaurant's parking area—if they're mostly local, there's a good chance that it's a good establishment. Other eating places include **cafés**, which serve snacks, tea, coffee, soft drinks, beer, wine and spirits. Many also sell sandwiches— substantial affairs made from half a *baguette*—and some prepare complete meals. In the morning, there is usually a basket of croissants on the table; you help yourself and tell how many you've taken when you pay. A **bistrot** is a small café-restaurant offering simple meals like omelettes, steak and chips (fries) and "dishes of the day"

(plat du jour) or other house specialities, while a **brasserie** is a larger café-restaurant serving copious local dishes. **Rôtisseries** specialize in grilled meat; they may be quite expensive. In the country, you will find **auberges, hostelleries** and **relais de campagne;** they serve full meals, and the food can be superb. **Restoroutes** are large restaurants linked to service-stations on the motorways (expressways) with table and/or self service. Also in the countryside, if you hit on the right **relais routier**—roughly equivalent to a roadside diner—the food can be excellent.

All restaurants are obliged by law to display their prices, including service, outside. Tipping is not obligatory, but if the service has been especially good, an extra 5 to 10% is appropriate. However, it is customary to round off the overall bill.

Lunch *(déjeuner)* is usually served from noon to 2 p.m., while dinner *(dîner)* starts at about 7.30 p.m.; in Paris, restaurants tend to fill up around 8 or 9 p.m. If you want to eat out on a Sunday afternoon— French families' big day out for lunch—it is best to book a table in advance.

To help you order

Waiter!/Waitress!	Garçon!/Mademoiselle!
May I have the menu, please?	**Puis-je avoir la carte?**
Do you have a set menu?	**Avez-vous un menu du jour?**
I'd like to pay.	**L'addition, s'il vous plaît!**
I'd like a/an/some...	**Je voudrais...**
bread	**du pain**
butter	**du beurre**
coffee black/with milk/ with cream	**un café noir/au lait/crème**
dessert	**un dessert**
fish	**du poisson**
fruit	**des fruits**
ice cream	**une glace**
meat	**de la viande**
milk	**du lait**
pepper	**du poivre**
potatoes	**des pommes de terre**

salad	une salade
salt	du sel
soup	une soupe
sugar	du sucre
tea	un thé
(mineral) water	de l'eau (minérale)
wine	du vin

...and read the menu

agneau	lamb
ail	garlic
anguille	eel
bœuf	beef
canard	duck
champignons	mushrooms
chou	cabbage
chou-fleur	cauliflower
côte, côtelette	chop, cutlet
crevettes	shrimps, prawns
cuisses de grenouille	frog's legs
dinde	turkey
épinards	spinach
escargots	snails
foie	liver
fraises	strawberries
framboises	raspberries
frites	chips (French fries)
fruits de mer	seafood
gigot (d'agneau)	leg (of lamb)
homard	lobster
huîtres	oysters
jambon	ham
langouste	spiny lobster
langue	tongue
lapin	rabbit
lard	bacon
moules	mussels
nouilles	noodles
oie	goose
oignons	onions
petits pois	peas

poire	pear
pomme	apple
poulet	chicken
raisins	grapes
riz	rice
rognons	kidneys
saucisse/saucisson	sausage
saumon	salmon
truite	trout
thon	tunny (tuna)
veau	veal
volaille	poultry
à l'alsacienne	with sauerkraut and pork
à l'ancienne	with wine sauce, carrots, onions and mushrooms
à l'anglaise	boiled
à la bordelaise	with wine sauce, shallots, mushrooms and marrow
à la bourguignonne	with mushrooms, pearl onions and red-wine sauce
à la broche	spit-roasted
en croûte	in a pastry crust
en daube	casseroled
à la dieppoise	with white wine sauce, mussels and shrimps
à la flamande	cooked in beer
à la forestière	with mushrooms, potatoes and bacon
à la lorraine	braised in red wine with red cabbage
à la lyonnaise	with onions
à la nage	simmered in white wine
à la niçoise	with garlic, anchovies, olives, onions and tomatoes
à la normande	with butter and fresh cream or apples and cider
Parmentier	with potatoes
printanière	with spring vegetables
à la provençale	with garlic, onions, herbs, olives, oil and tomatoes
à la vapeur	steamed

SIGHTSEEING

Local tourist offices can help you find qualified guides and give you a list of guided tours.

Paris-based sightseeing companies offer excursions by coach, boat, train or plane. Apart from tours of Paris itself, like panoramic cruises on the Seine (see p. 74), art-highlights and Paris-by-night coach tours, you can choose among day trips to Versailles, Fontainebleau, Chartres, Chantilly, the abbey of Mont-Saint-Michel, Normandy and the D-Day landing beaches, Champagne, etc., two- and three-day tours of the châteaux of the Loire Valley and 3- to 12-day tours of Provence and the Côte d'Azur.

In Paris, a simple and excellent way to sightsee is to hop on or off, as many times and wherever you like, one of the coaches of the Inter-Transport—all on the same ticket. The route followed in a 2½-hour tour (departure every hour) takes in the most interesting highspots of a Paris visit (Madeleine, Eiffel Tower, Louvre, Montmartre, etc.). Tickets are available at bus stops and from Les coches parisiens, 9, place de la Madeleine.

For detailed information on Paris's historic monuments, contact the Caisse nationale des monuments historiques:

62, rue Saint-Antoine – 75004 Paris
Tel. (1) 42.74.22.22–28

| Can you recommend a sightseeing tour/an excursion? | **Pourriez-vous me conseiller une visite guidée/une excursion?** |

SPAS

Thermal centres all over France specialize in treatment of neurological, dermatological, respiratory, gynaecological, digestive and other disorders, as well as relaxation, revitalization, beauty, health and slimming cures. Some are old-established institutions—like Aix-les-Bains, Divonne-les-Bains, Evian-les-Bains, Thonon-les-Bains in or near the Alps—but new centres, often linked to a hotel, are set up every year.

Thalassotherapy, the treatment of various ailments like anaemia, cellulitis, poor circulation, obesity and rheumatism using processes involving sea water and algae cures are found in coastal centres in Picardy (Le Touquet), Normandy (Trouville, Deauville, Granville, etc.), Brittany (Quiberon,

Perros-Guirec, Roscoff, Carnac, etc.), further down the Atlantic coast (Ile de Ré, Biarritz), along the Mediterranean coast (Port-Barcarès, Cap d'Agde, Cannes, Nice) and in Corsica (Porticcio).

For detailed information, write either to the local *syndicat d'initiative* or to the regional tourist office (see TOURIST INFORMATION OFFICES). Or contact the Union Nationale des Etablissements Thermaux (UNET):

16, rue de l'Estrapade – 75005 Paris

SPORTS ORGANIZATIONS

For information on specific sports activities in France, write to the following organizations:

Bicycle tours (see also BICYCLE RENTAL). — Bicy Club de France, 8, place de la Porte-Champerret, 75017 Paris; (01) 47.66.55.92.

Canoeing, kayaking, rafting. — Fédération française de canoë-kayak, 17, route de Vienne, 69007 Lyon; tel. 78.61.32.74.

Fishing. — Conseil supérieur de la pêche, 134, av. de Malakoff, 75016 Paris; tel. (01) 45.01.20.20.

Golf. — Fédération française de golf, 69, avenue Victor-Hugo, 75016 Paris; tel. (01) 45.02.13.55.

Hiking. — Fédération française de randonnées pédestres, 9, avenue George-V, 75008 Paris; tel. (01) 47.23.62.32.

Hunting. — Office national de la chasse, 85 bis, avenue de Wagram, 75017 Paris; tel. (01) 42.27.81.75.

Mountaineering. — Club alpin français, 9, rue La Boëtie, 75008 Paris; tel. (01) 47.42.38.46.

Parachuting. — Fédération française de parachutisme, 35, rue Saint-Georges, 75009 Paris; tel. (01) 48.78.45.00.

Riding tours. — Fédération des randonneurs équestres de France, 16, rue des Apennins, 75017 Paris; (01) 42.26.23.23.

Sailing, water sports. — Fédération française de voile, 55, avenue Kléber, 75016 Paris; tel. (01) 45.53.15.45

Open-air sports centres. — Union nationale des centres sportifs de plein air, 62, rue de la Glacière, 75013 Paris; tel. (1) 43.36.05.20.

Skiing, winter sports. — Association des maires des stations françaises de sports d'hiver, 61, boulevard Haussmann, 75008 Paris; tel. (1) 47.42.23.32.

THEATRE TICKETS

In Paris, theatre tickets can be bought in advance at the following agencies:

Cédartour
16, avenue de l'Opéra - 75001 Paris
Tel. (1) 42.96.14.33/42.96.46.47

Chèque-Théâtres
33, rue Le Peletier - 75009 Paris
Tel. (1) 42.46.72.40

Daisy
78, avenue des Champs-Elysées
75008 Paris
Tel. (1) 43.59.24.60/43.59.80.39

Gefco
69, avenue de la Grande-Armée
75016 Paris - Tel. (1) 45.02.13.90

Marivaux
7, rue Marivaux - 75002 Paris
Tel. (1) 42.97.46.70

Night and Day
81, boulevard Gouvion Saint-Cyr
75017 Paris - Tel. (1) 47.57.25.09

Opéra-Théâtres
1, rue Auber - 75009 Paris
Tel. (1) 47.42.85.84

Pérossier
6, place de la Madeleine - 75008 Paris
Tel. (1) 42.60.58.31/42.60.57.70

S.O.S. Théâtres
73, av. des Champs-Elysées - 75008 Paris
Tel. (1) 42.25.67.07/42.25.03.18

A theatre-kiosk in the Place de la Madeleine sells "last minute" tickets at a reduced price.

Tickets for the Paris Opera can be booked, up to 13 days before the performance, by writing to, or phoning (from noon to 6 p.m., Monday to Saturday), the Théâtre de l'Opéra, Service location par correspondance:

8, rue Scribe - 75009 Paris
Tel. (1) 47.42.53.71

For information on dates and performances:
tel. (1) 47.42.57.50.

TIME DIFFERENCES

France follows Central European Time (GMT + 1), and from the last Sunday in March to the last Sunday in September, clocks are put one hour ahead (GMT + 2).

What time is it? **Quelle heure est-il?**

Summer time chart:

Los Angeles	3 a.m.
New York	6 a.m.
London	11 a.m.
Paris	**noon**
Johannesburg	noon
Sydney	8 p.m.
Auckland	10 p.m.

TIPPING *(pourboire)*

Hotel porter, per bag	5 F
Hotel maid, per week	50–100 F
Lavatory attendant	2 F
Waiter	5–10% (optional)
Taxi driver	10–15%
Hairdresser/Barber	10%
Tour guide	10%

A 15% service charge is generally included automatically in hotel and restaurant bills. Rounding off the overall bill by a few francs helps cement an entente cordiale with waiters. It is considered normal to hand bellboys, doormen, cinema and theatre ushers, service-station attendants, etc., a coin or two for their services. The chart below will give you some guidelines.

Thank you, this is for you.	**Merci. Voici pour vous.**
Keep the change.	**Gardez la monnaie.**

TOILETS *(toilettes)*

Public conveniences in France range from the fly-infested squalid "footpad and hole-in-the-ground" to luxury three-star facilities, which you can usually predict by the general cleanliness of the establishment. It's best to use the toilets in cafés, which are generally free. A saucer with small change on it means that a tip is expected. In some out-of-the-way places, you may be given a big iron key or even a detachable door handle, to open the door. If you insist on luxury, look for a major hotel and glide past the reception desk as if you owned the place.

If there is no light-switch, the light will usually go on when you lock the door. Women's toilets are marked *Dames,* and men's either *Messieurs* or *Hommes.*

A recent innovation is the *Sanisette:* a cream-painted, cylindrical metal contraption, looking something like a telephone booth. You insert a 1-franc piece in the slot to open the door. When you come out, the whole thing is swilled, scrubbed and polished, ready for the next person. Don't let young children go in there alone, they might not be able to open the lock to get out.

Where are the toilets, please?	**Où sont les toilettes, s'il vous plaît?**

TOURIST INFORMATION OFFICES

French tourist offices abroad can help tourists plan their holiday. They do not, however, book tours or hotel rooms.

Australia. — French Tourist Bureau, Kindersley House, 33 Bligh Street, Sydney, NSW 2000; tel. (2) 231-5244.

Canada. — Services Officiels Français du Tourisme, 1981 Avenue McGill College, Tour Esso, Suite 490, Montréal, Que. H3A 2W9; tel. (514) 288-4264.

French Government Tourist Office, 1 Dundas Street W., Suite 2405, P.O. Box 8, Toronto, Ont. M5G 1Z3; tel. (416) 593-4717.

Denmark. — Det Franske Turistbureau, Frederiksberggade 28, 1459 København K; tel. (01) 11 49 12.

India. — French Government Tourist Office, c/o Air France, Ashoka Hotel, 50 B Chanakyapuri, New Delhi 110021; tel. (11) 60 47 75.

Japan. — French Government Tourist Office, Landic No 2 Akasaka Carlton Centre, 10.9. Akasaka 2 Chome, Minato Ku, Tokyo 107; tel. (03) 35.82.69.65.

Netherlands. — National Frans Verkeersbureau, Prinsengracht 670, 1017 KX Amsterdam; tel. (020) 20 31 41.

Norway. — c/o Fransk-Norsk Handelskammer, Dronningens gt., 8B, 0152 Oslo 1; tel. (02) 20 37 21/29.

South Africa. — French Tourist Office, Carlton Centre, 10th Floor, Commissioner Street, Johannesburg 2001; tel. (11) 331-9252. Postal address: P.O. Box 10819, Johannesburg 2000.

Sweden and Finland. — Franska Turistbyrån, Norrmalmstorg 1 Av, 11146 Stockholm; tel. (08) 24 39 75.

U.K. and Eire. — French Government Tourist Office, 178 Piccadilly, London W1V 0AL; tel. (01) 493-6594.

U.S.A. — French Government Tourist Office, 610 Fifth Avenue, Suite 222, New York, NY 10020-2452; tel. (212) 757-1125

French Government Tourist Office, 645 North Michigan Avenue, Suite 6, Chicago, IL 60611; tel. (312) 337-6301.

French Government Tourist Office, World Trade Center, N 103, 2050 Stemmons Freeway, P.O. Box 58610, Dallas, TX 75258; tel. (214) 742-7011/12.

French Government Tourist Office, 9401 Wilshire Boulevard, Room 840, Beverly Hills, Los Angeles, CA 90212-2967; tel. (213) 272-2661.

French Government Tourist Office, 1 Hallidie Plaza, Suite 250, San Francisco, CA 94102-2818; tel. (415) 986-4174.

In France, each region has its own tourist office *(comité régional du tourisme* or *agence régionale du tourisme):*

Alsace. — Hôtel du Département, 68006 Colmar Cedex; tel. 89.23.21.11.

9, rue du Dôme, B.P. 53, 67061 Strasbourg Cedex; tel. 88.22.01.02.

Aquitaine. — 24, allée de Tourny, 33000 Bordeaux; tel. 56.48.55.50.

Auvergne. — 43, avenue Julien, B.P. 395, 63011 Clermont-Ferrand Cedex; tel. 73.93.04.03.

Brittany. — 3, rue d'Espagne, B.P. 4175, 35041 Rennes Cedex; tel. 99.50.11.15.

Burgundy. — Conseil Régional, B.P. 1602, 21035 Dijon Cedex (for correspondence).

1, rue Nicolas-Berthot, 21000 Dijon; tel. 80.55.24.10.

Centre-Val de Loire. — 9, rue Saint-Pierre Lentin, 45041 Orléans Cedex; tel. 38.54.95.42/43.

Champagne-Ardennes. — 5, rue de Géricault, 51000 Châlons-sur-Marne; tel. 26.64.35.92.

Corsica. — 22, cours Grandval, B.P. 19, 20176 Ajaccio Cedex; tel. 95.51.00.22.

Dauphiné. — Maison du Tourisme, 14, rue de la République, B.P. 227, 38019 Grenoble Cedex; tel. 76.54.34.36.

Franche-Comté. — 32, rue Charles-Nodier, 25000 Besançon; tel. 81.83.50.47.

Ile-de-France. — 73, rue Cambronne, 75015 Paris; tel. (1) 47.83.73.96.

Languedoc-Roussillon. — 12, rue Foch, 34000 Montpellier; tel. 67.60.55.42.

Limousin. — 8, cours Bugeaud, 87039 Limoges Cedex; tel. 55.79.57.12.

Lorraine. — 1, place Saint-Clément, B.P. 1004, 57036 Metz Cedex 1; tel. 87.33.60.00.

Midi-Pyrénées. — 12, rue Salambo, 31022 Toulouse; tel. 61.47.11.12.

Nord-Pas-de-Calais. — 26, place Rihour, 59000 Lille; tel. 20.60.60.60.

Normandy. — 46, avenue Foch, 27000 Evreux; tel. 32.31.05.89.

Pays-de-Loire. — Maison du Tourisme, Place du Commerce, 44000 Nantes; tel. 40.48.15.45.

Picardy. — 11, mail Albert-1er, B.P. 2616, 80026 Amiens Cedex; tel. 22.97.37.37.

Poitou-Charente. — 2, rue Sainte-Opportune, B.P. 56, 86002 Poitiers Cedex; tel. 49.88.38.94.

Provence-Alpes-Côte d'Azur. — 4 La Canebière, 2 rue Beauvau, 13001 Marseille; tel. 91.54.35.36.

Riviera-Côte d'Azur. — 55, promenade des Anglais, 06000 Nice; tel. 93.44.50.59.

Vallée du Rhône. — 5, place de la Baleine, 69005 Lyon; tel. 78.42.50.04.

Savoie-Mont Blanc. — 9, boulevard Wilson, 73100 Aix-les-Bains; 73.88.23.41.

In addition, each town of any importance—and many small places, as well, with specific sights of interest—have a local tourist office (*syndicat d'initiative* [S.I.] or *office du* [or *de*] *tourisme*), mostly found near the centre of town. Tourist-office staff are usually helpful with up-to-date information on local transport, restaurants, entertainment, etc., as well as with advice on what places to visit and how and when to go. Hours vary, but in the summer most open every day except Sundays from 9 or 9.30 a.m. to noon or 1 p.m. and from 1 or 2 to 6 or 6.30 p.m. Out of season, many are closed or work on greatly reduced hours. Most have at least one person who speaks English.

Paris's main tourist office is located at 127, avenue des Champs-Elysées, 75008 Paris; tel. (1) 47.23.61.72. Branches operate at the major railway stations, the airports and terminals. For a selection of the princi-pal events in the capital, in English, French or German, call 47.20.88.98/47.20.94.94/47.20.57.58, respectively.

Where's the tourist office?	**Où est l'office du tourisme?**

TRAVELLING IN FRANCE

See also BICYCLE RENTAL, CAR RENTAL and DRIVING IN FRANCE.

By city transport. — Cities and larger towns have urban bus *(autobus)* services *(service urbain)*—a particularly good way to get around and sightsee as you go.

Paris's **underground/subway** *(métro),* the world's second oldest, is also one of the world's most efficient. Trains have both 1st- and 2nd-class carriages, but 1st-class carriages are open to all ticket holders be-fore 9 a.m. and after 5 p.m. There are two networks, the urban *métro* for Paris and the inner suburbs and the faster regional RER *(Réseau Express Régional)* lines. The *métro* is linked to the suburban SNCF system.

Buy a book of 10 tickets *(carnet)* if you plan to take the *métro* several times, or an orange identity card *(carte orange),* valid for a week or a month on buses and the *métro*. *Paris Sésame* is a special tourist ticket allowing unlimited travel on buses and 1st-class *métro* for two, four or seven days. Maps (see also p. 73) posted at every station make the system easy to use. The service starts daily at 5.30 a.m. and ends at 1.15 a.m.

RATP *(Régie autonome des transports parisiens),* the Paris Transport Authority, has information offices at 53 bis, quai des Grands-Augustins (75006 Paris) and at Place de la Madeleine (75008 Paris). You can call there at 43.46.14.14 round the clock for information on public transport in Paris.

Taxis may be hailed in the street—look for one with its "Taxi" sign fully lit up—or picked up at a taxi rank *(station de taxi)*. In towns of any size, there are stands at the railway stations as well as in the centre. To obtain a cab by phone, look under "Taxis" in the local telephone directory. Rates are usually higher in small towns where runs are shorter, and there's always a supplement for luggage. If you have a good distance to go, ask the fare beforehand. When dining on a rainy night, ask your restaurant to phone for a taxi at the end of the meal. But remember, taxis ordered by telephone pick you up with meter already running.

Many taxis do not take more than three passengers for insurance reasons. They are metered (except in the deepest countryside where it is advisable to ask the rate first). It is customary to tip in the region of 10 per cent.

By inter-city bus. — Regular long-distance bus *(car/autocar)* services *(service interurbain)* are efficient, comfortable, relatively inexpensive and fairly frequent. Details about schedules and reduced rates are available at the bus terminal *(gare routière)*, which is often situated at, or close to, the town's railway station. For general information on inter-city bus services, contact the Fédération nationale des transports routiers—the National Road Transport Federation:

6, rue Paul-Valéry – 75116 Paris
Tel. (1) 45.53.92.88

Several bus transport companies also organize special sightseeing tours, as do the French National Railways.

By train. — SNCF *(Société nationale des chemins de fer français),* the French National Railways, run an extensive rail service covering nearly 6,000 destinations throughout the country. Trains are backed up by a network of SNCF-operated bus and coach services.

All the main lines converge on Paris. There is an excellent network of ultra-rapid express trains, TGVs *(Train à Grande Vitesse*—1st and 2nd class, advance booking compulsory, certain trains with supplement). The Paris–Lyon stretch takes 2 hours, Paris–Besançon 2½ hours, Lille–Lyon 4½–5 hours, Paris–Marseille 4½–5 hours, Paris–Nice 7½–8 hours. Auto-train (train-auto-couchette) services are also available from all major towns; advance reservation is compulsory.

Remember to validate any train ticket bought in France by inserting it in one of the orange upright machines (called a *machine à composter* or *composteur)* at the stations. If it is not clipped and dated, the train conductor *(contrôleur)* is entitled to fine you.

Children under the age of 4 travel free (unless individual accommodation is required); aged 4 to 11 inclusive, they pay half fare (but full sleeping charges). The SNCF offer a wide range of cut-price fares

—see GETTING TO FRANCE, p. 351. For rates, timetables, reservations, etc., call SNCF's Central Information Service: (1) 45.82.50.50 or (1) 42.61.50.50.

By boat. — (See also the box "Paris by Boat", p. 74.) For Corsica, there are regular ferry connections from Marseille to Ajaccio, Bastia and Propriano, from Toulon to Ajaccio, Bastia and Calvi and from Nice to Ajaccio, Bastia, Calvi and L'Ile Rousse. Information is available at railway stations and from SNCM *(Société nationale maritime Corse Méditerranée):*

12, rue Godot-de-Mauroy – 75009 Paris
Tel. (1) 42.66.60.19

Motor-launch *(vedette)* services, often part of the SNCF, operate between the islands of Brittany (Belle-Ile, Bréhat, Ile aux Moines, etc.) and the mainland all year round (but with considerably reduced service outside the peak holiday season). Schedules are posted at embarkation points, but you can always obtain your own from the local *syndicat d'initiative.* Times often depend on tides and other weather conditions.

In summer, boat trips on the Seine as it winds its way through eastern Normandy are a relaxing way of enjoying the surrounding greenery. There are day cruises from Le Havre to Rouen, as well as shorter trips, with food on board. Harbour boat trips are another possibility, particularly a tour of the forts around Cherbourg's port basin. Alternatively, there are day trips to the Channel Islands—known as *les îles Anglo-Normandes*—from Granville, Carteret and Cherbourg. Many lakes, too, have boat services.

By plane. — Air Inter, France's principal domestic airline, and other short-haul carriers fly between Paris and regional airports such as Bordeaux, Lyon, Marseille, Montpellier, Mulhouse, Nantes, Nice, Strasbourg and Toulouse, and link provincial cities directly with each other. The number of flights is increased in the summer. Inquire about special reductions for domestic routes according to day and time of flight (up to 60%), for groups, youths, students, couples and senior citizens. There are also regular air-taxi services between a number of provincial towns.

Air Inter – tel. (1) 45.39.25.25

When's the next bus/ train/ boat/plane for... ?	Quand part le prochain bus/train/ bateau/avion pour... ?

I'd like a ticket to...	**Je voudrais un billet pour...**
What's the fare to...?	**Quel est le prix du billet pour...?**
single (one-way)/ return (roundtrip)	**aller simple/ aller-retour**
first/second class	**première/seconde classe**
I'd like to make seat reservations.	**Je voudrais réserver des places.**
sleeping car/ couchette	**wagon-lit/couchette**
dining car	**wagon-restaurant**
Where can I get a taxi?	**Où puis-je trouver un taxi?**
Please get me a taxi.	**Appelez-moi un taxi, s'il vous plaît.**

USEFUL EXPRESSIONS

yes/no	**oui/non**
please/thank you	**s'il vous plaît/merci**
excuse me/you're welcome	**excusez-moi/je vous en prie**
where/when/how	**où/quand/comment**
how long/how far	**combien de temps/ à quelle distance**
what/why/who	**quoi/pourquoi/qui**
yesterday/today/ tomorrow	**hier/aujourd'hui/ demain**
day/week/month/ year	**jour/semaine/mois/ année**
(to the) right/ left/straight ahead	**(à) droite/ gauche/tout droit**
near/far	**près/loin**

up/down	**en haut/en bas**
good/bad	**bon/mauvais**
big/small	**grand/petit**
more/less	**plus/moins**
full/empty	**plein/vide**
cheap/expensive	**bon marché/cher**
hot/cold	**chaud/froid**
open/closed	**ouvert/fermé**
free (vacant)/occupied	**libre/occupé**
old/new	**vieux/neuf**
here/there	**ici/là**
early/late	**tôt/tard**
easy/difficult	**facile/difficile**
right/wrong	**juste/faux**
I don't understand.	**Je ne comprends pas.**
Does anyone here speak English?	**Y a-t-il quelqu'un ici qui parle anglais?**
Can you tell me...?	**Pouvez-vous me dire...?**
Can you help me?	**Pouvez-vous m'aider?**
Where is/are...?	**Où est/sont...?**
I'd like...	**Je voudrais...**
How much does this cost?	**Combien coûte ceci?**
Monday	**lundi**
Tuesday	**mardi**
Wednesday	**mercredi**
Thursday	**jeudi**
Friday	**vendredi**
Saturday	**samedi**
Sunday	**dimanche**

WEIGHTS AND MEASURES

Temperature
°C
°F
−30 −25 −20 −15 −10 −5 0 5 10 15 20 25 30 35 40 45
−20 −10 0 10 20 30 40 50 60 70 80 90 100 110

Length
cm   0   5   10   15   20   25   30
inches   0   2   4   6   8   10   12
metres   0   1 m   2 m
ft./yd.   0   1 ft.   1 yd.   2 yd.

Weight
grams   0   100   200   300   400   500   600   700   800   900   1 kg
ounces   0   4   8   12   1 lb.   20   24   28   2 lb.

Distance Chart

	Toulouse	Strasbourg	Rennes	Perpignan	Paris	Orléans	Nice	Nantes	Mulhouse	Marseille	Lyon	Lille	Le Havre	Dijon	Clermont-Ferrand	Cherbourg	Calais	Brest	Bordeaux	Biarritz
Biarritz	291	1260	634	446	780	658	850	527	1024	690	825	997	851	833	561	843	1075	823	190	
Bordeaux	253	1040	436	457	583	460	813	329	825	653	577	799	653	682	369	645	877	625		190
Brest	891	1076	244	1095	597	545	1495	296	1098	1339	1024	813	482	874	799	405	710		625	823
Calais	1001	637	415	1204	297	414	1229	672	728	1073	758	112	283	608	685	457		710	877	1075
Cherbourg	911	845	209	1115	361	393	1289	316	892	1133	818	470	228	668	745		457	405	645	843
Clermont-Ferrand	392	583	514	461	390	307	640	453	482	484	208	607	589	288		745	685	799	369	561
Dijon	727	335	625	639	313	295	664	594	229	453	192	530	512		288	668	608	874	682	833
Le Havre	919	689	286	1108	205	304	1133	393	736	977	662	297		512	589	228	283	482	653	851
Lille	929	524	565	1126	219	336	1151	594	617	995	680		297	530	607	470	112	813	799	997
Lyon	534	488	775	446	463	444	471	626	382	315		680	662	192	208	818	758	1024	577	825
Marseille	399	803	1090	311	778	760	188	995	698		315	995	977	453	484	1133	1073	1339	653	690
Mulhouse	917	118	849	829	537	519	680	818		698	382	617	736	229	482	892	728	1098	825	1024
Nantes	595	856	107	799	377	299	1154		818	995	626	594	393	594	453	316	672	296	329	527
Nice	559	959	1246	471	934	916		1154	680	188	471	1151	1133	664	640	1289	1229	1495	813	850
Orléans	578	598	296	891	119		916	299	519	760	444	336	304	295	307	393	414	545	460	658
Paris	709	486	348	909		119	934	377	537	778	463	219	205	313	390	361	297	597	583	780
Perpignan	204	934	906		909	891	471	799	829	311	446	1126	1108	639	461	1115	1204	1095	457	446
Rennes	702	827		906	348	296	1246	107	849	1090	775	565	286	625	514	209	415	244	436	634
Strasbourg	1022		827	934	486	598	959	856	118	803	488	524	689	335	583	845	637	1076	1040	1260
Toulouse		1022	702	204	709	578	559	595	917	399	534	929	919	727	392	911	1001	891	253	291

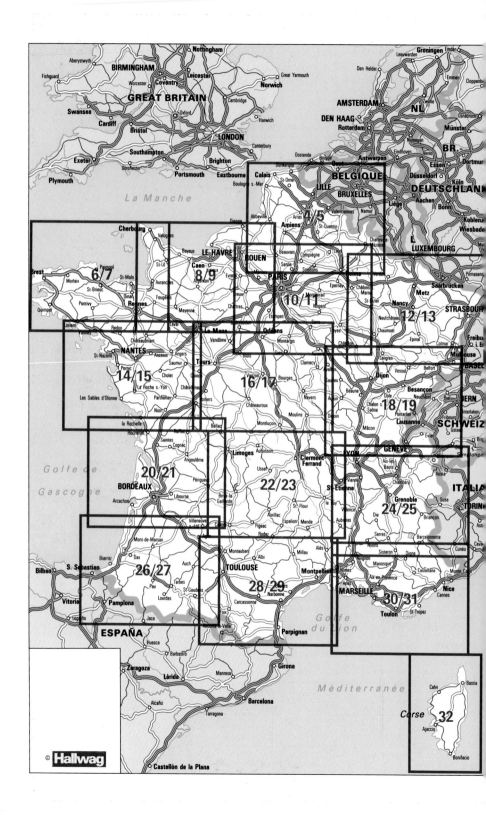

FRANKREICH
FRANCE

FRANCIA
FRANCE

Autobahn mit Anschlussstelle Tankstelle, Restaurant, Motel Autoroute avec échangeur Station-service, restaurant, motel	Autostrada con svincolo Stazione di servizio, ristorante, motel Motorway with interchange Filling station, restaurant, motel
Autobahn im Bau mit Eröffnungsdatum Autoroute en construction avec date de mise en service	Autostrada in construzione con data d'apertura Motorway under construction with opening date
Autostrasse (international, régional) Route rapide à chaussées séparées (internationale, régionale)	Superstrada a carreggiate separate (internazionale/regionale) Dual carriageway (international, regional)
Grosse internationale Durchgangsstrasse Route de grand transit internationale	Strada di gran transito internazionale Major international throughroute
Sonstige internationale Fernverkehrsstrasse Autre route de transit internationale	Altra strada di transito internazionale Other international throughroute
Überregionale Fernverkehrsstrasse Route de transit interrégionale	Strada di transito interregionale Interregional throughroute
Regionale Verbindungsstrasse Route de liaison régionale	Strada di collegamento regionale Regional connecting road
Lokale Verbindungsstrasse Route de liaison locale	Strada di collegamento locale Local road
Strassen im Bau Routes en construction	Strade in construzione Roads under construction
Entfernungen in km Distances en km	Distanze in km Distances in km
Strassennummern: Europastrasse, Autobahn, Nationalstrasse Numéros des routes: route européenne, autoroute, route nationale	Numerazione stradale: strada europea, autostrada, strada nazionale Road classification: European road, motorway, national road
Pass, Berg, Ort mit Höhenangabe (m) Col, sommet, localité avec altitude (m)	Valico, vetta, località con altitudine (m) Pass, summit, locality with altitude (m)
Eisenbahn, Berg-/Luftseilbahn Voie ferrée; téléphérique/funiculaire	Ferrovia, funivia/funicolare Railway, mountain/cable railway
Autoverlad: per Eisenbahn Transport des autos: par voie ferrée per Fähre par bac	Trasporto automobili: per ferrovia Car transport: by rail su chiatta by ferry
Flughafen Aéroport	Aeroporto Airport
Schloss/Burg, Kirche/Kloster, Ruine Château/fort, église/couvent, ruine	Castello/fortezza, chiesa/convento, rudero Castle, church/monastery, ruin
Antike Stätte, Höhle, Leuchtturm Vestige antique, grotte, phare	Antichità, grotta, faro Site of antiquity, cave, lighthouse
Campingplatz, bemerkenswerter Ort Camping, localité intéressante	Campeggio, località interessante Camping site, place of interest
Staatsgrenze Frontière d'Etat	Confine di Stato National boundary

©1988 ©1988
I - VI   VII - XII

10
3 3 3 4 2 5
5 2 3
10

E 7   A 9   60

1528   Elm
2967   648

2 h

1 : 1 000 000

0	10	20		40		60		80 km

0		10		20		30		40		50 miles

C A D E 1

Alderney
St. Anne
C. de la Hague
Auderville
901
2
8
Urville
Fermanville
St-Pierre-Eglise
Pte de Barfleur
Barfleur
Beaumont-Hague
19
CHERBOURG
Tourlaville
13
10
Réville
hannel
Octeville
20
Quettehou
St-Vaast-la-Hougue
904
Vasteville
E3
10
Delasse
Aumeville
St. Sampson
St. Peter Port
Siouville
15
Valognes
745
Quinéville
Is. St-Marcouf
les Pieux
9 7
Guernsey
Quettetot
Bricquebec
Montebourg
13
Ravenoville
Sark
Colomby
Utah Beach
Ment Comm.
la Marc-du-Parc
Ste-Mère-Eglise
16
2
Grandcamp
Barneville-Carteret
St-Sauveur-le-Vic.
Blosville
4
Ste-Marie
la Cambe
Islands
Portbail
Neufmesnil
10
Carentan
Isigny
Formign
la Camb
13
(G. B.)
8
3
la Haye-du-Puits
75
St-Jores
Saintenay
174
Trevières
la Fotelate
Jersey
Lessay
9
St-Jean-de-D.
12
Créances
le Hommet
Périers
Pont-Hebert
St. Aubin
Gorey
Montsurvent
St-Sauveur-Lend.
St-Lô
Bér
St. Helier
Gouville
St-Sauveur-Lend.
972
St-Samson
Vj/douville
174
Coutainville
Coutances
Marigny
Tórign
(48)
le Mesnil-Herm.
Hyenville
Villebaudon
Tessy s-V
Cam
Montmartin-s-M.
Hauteville-s-M.
N
Hambye
Percy
8
O
Quettreville
971
Gavray
Is. Chausey
Bréhal
Etouvy
Granville
924
Beauchamps
103
Villedieu
Pte du Grouin
St-Pair
175
Côte d' Emeraude
Rothéneuf
Jullouville
la Haye-Pesnel
l'Epine
St-Sever-Calvados
Cap Fréhel
Carolles
973
Sartilly
14
175
St-Pois
Sables d'Or les Pins
St-Jean-le-Th.
77
Genêts
Brécey
Erquy-Plages
St-Lunaire
St-Malo
Paramé
Cancale
Avranches
Chérence
Sou
le-Val-André
St-Cast
Dinard
St-Servan
Mont-St-Michel
44
Juvigny
Mort
Matignon
St-Briac
le Vivier
Pontaubault
Montigny
977
Pléneuf
Hénanbihen
Ploubalay
Pleslin
Châteauneuf
22
Ducey
807
16
St-Hilaire-du-Harc.
32
St-Denoual
Plancoët
137
Dol
19
St-James
le Teille
St-René
Bourseul
176
le Vieux Bourg
la Boussac
12
Louvigné
808
Lamballe
DINAN
26
Trans
St-Ouen
798
Landivy
Noyal
82
12
Vildé
St-Pierre-de-P.
Bazouges
Antrain
Tricheae
177
Langouhèdre
176
Jugon
le Hinglé
Cuguen
11
155
St-Brice
Landéan
Dé
Plénée-Jug
Evran
Tremblay
la Tannière
Collinée
65
Broons
St-Domineuc
Combourg
Bain-s-R.
Romagné
FOUGÈRES
St-Dé
Eréac
E50
Caulnes
Tinténiac
E3
12
la Pellerine
269
St-Vran
St-Jouan-de-l'I.
Bécherel
Hédé
175
St-Aubin-d'Aub.
St-Aubin-du-C.
178
Dompierre
69
Ernée
Plémet
164
Trémorel
Médréac
Iroudoer
137
St-Christophe
Tailhs
Juvigné
Merdrignac
52
St-Meen
Montauban
33
Gevezé
cvaigne
Liffré
Val-d'Izé
la Croixille
la Baco
Ménéac
G
Montgerval
St-Gilles
Dé
Mohon
Mauron
St-Péran
Boisgervilly
Montfort
RENNES
Vitré
le Bourgneu
30
St-Ouen-des-J.
Lou
Gael
Paimpont
Mordelles
157
50
Châteaugiron
E50
Guilhers
St-Malo
766
Néant-s-Y.
24
34
Pont Réan
Vern
Argentré-du-Plessis
la Gravelle
19
osselin
60
Beignon
N
Plélan-le-Grd.
Baulon
Guichen
le Ballon
Moulins
Montjean
LAV
Ploërmel
166
Augan
Guer
Guignen
137
Janzé
la Guerche
St-Poix
Cossé-le
la Chapelle
le Roc-André
Maure-de-B.
177
Lohéac
Poligné
Retiers
Laubrières
Quelaines
Malestroit
Monteneuf
Pipriac
le Sel
163
Roe
Ballots
171
Craon
St-Congard
Carentoir
Messac
Thourie
178
15
Chelun
St-Aignan-s-R.
Martigné

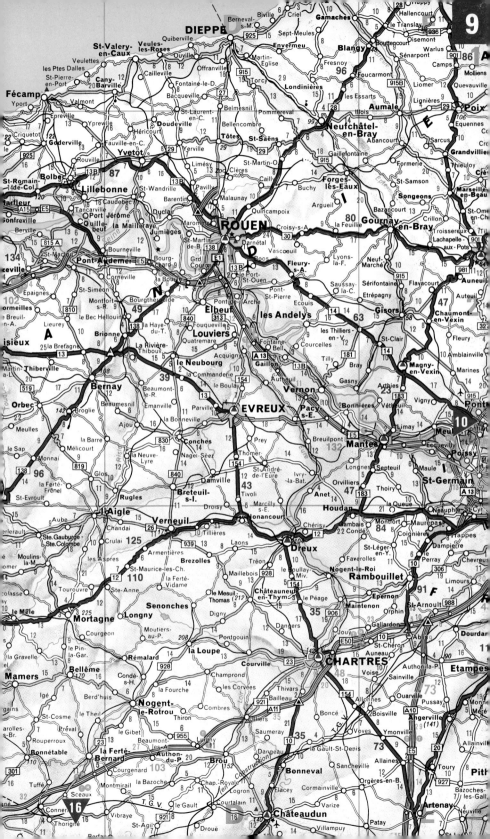

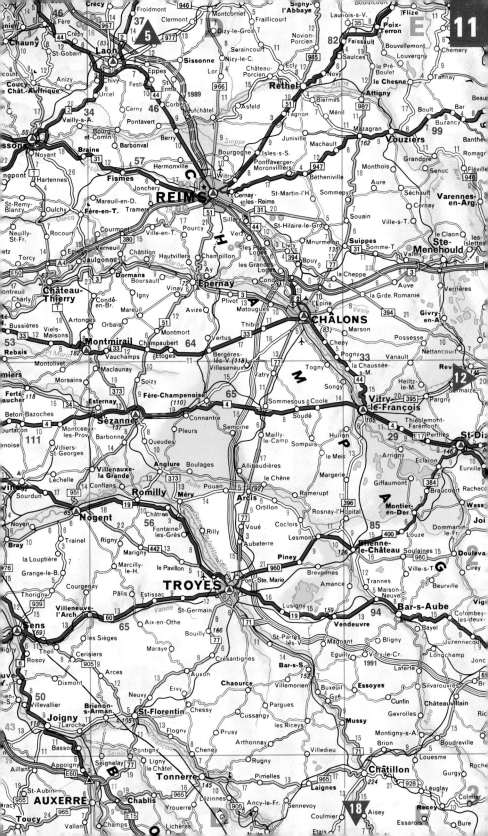

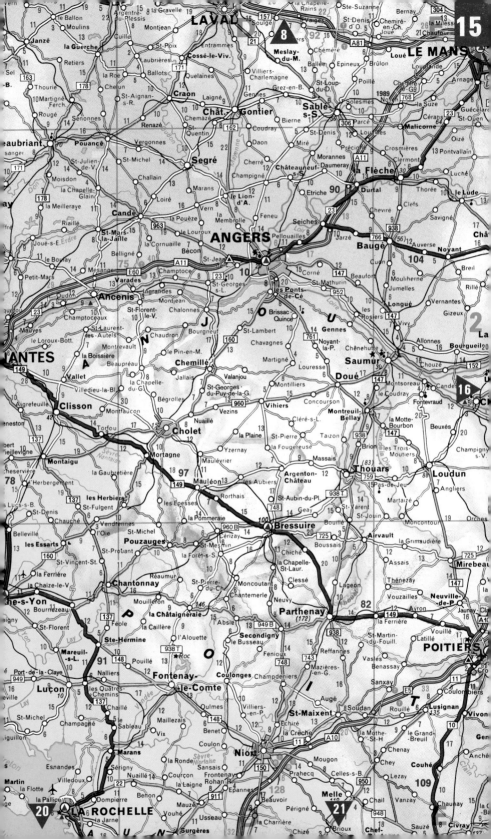

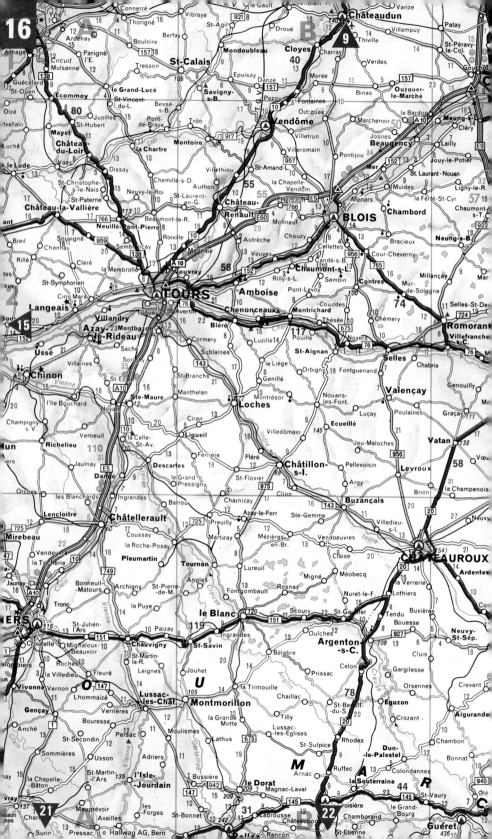

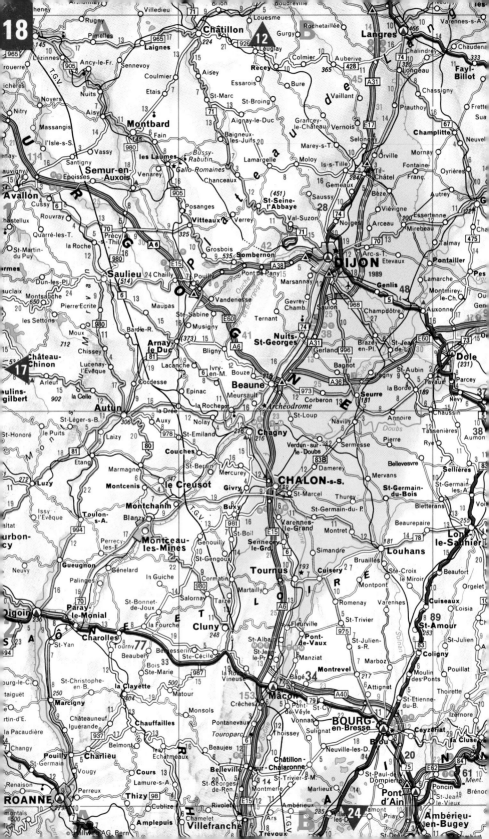

14

l'Aiguillon

Phare des Baleines · les Portes
Villedoux
Sérigny
Ars · la Couarde · St-Martin · la Flotte
22
Ile de Ré · le Bois-Plage
la Pallice · Dompierre
LA ROCHE
la Jarne
Châtelaillon-Plage · Puydroudr
16
21
Phare de Chassiron · St-Denis
137 69
Breuil
Chéray · Boyardville
St-Pierre d'O · Fouras
la Cotinière · Port-des-Barques
Ile d'Oléron · Dolus · le Château · Rochefort
Ors · Martrou
St-Agnant
le Chapus · Beurl
St-Trojan · Marennes
Ronce-les-Bains · St-Jea d'Ang
la Tremblade · 733
Etaules · Cadeui
Phare de la Coubre · Mornac
la Palmyre · l'Eguille
St-Palais-s-M. · Saujo
Royan · St-Georges-de-D
Pointe de Grave · Meschers
Soulac · le Verdon · Talmont
Talais
Grayan · St-Vivien
Montalivet-les-B. · Vensac · Valeyrac
Vendays-Montalivet · 215
St-Christoly
Lesparre-Médoc
Hourtin-Plage · St-Gaux · St Es
Hourtin · Pau
Lac d'Hourtin-Carcans · St. Laurent-et-Benon
Carcans-Plage · Carcans · Listrac
Maubuisson · Brach
Lacanau-Océan · Castelnau-de-M.
Men Fre Longarisse · Lacanau · Ste-Hé
de Lacanau · Salaunes
le Temple · St. Médard
le Porge
Lège · BOR
Arès · Blagon · Pierroto
Piquey-Plage · Andernos · 250
Bassin Arcachon · Taussat · Audenge · Marchepri
Cap Ferret · Arcachon · Gujan · Facture
Pyla · Mestras · Mios
Pilat-Plage · la Teste · Caudos · Salles
652
Etang de Cazau · Sanguinet
Biscarrosse-Plage
26 · le Muret
Biscarrosse · Parentis-en-Born

Hallwag AG, Bern

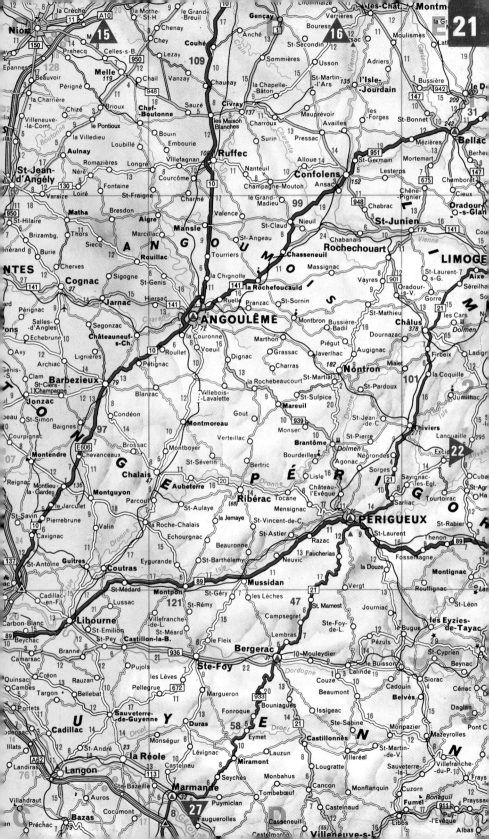

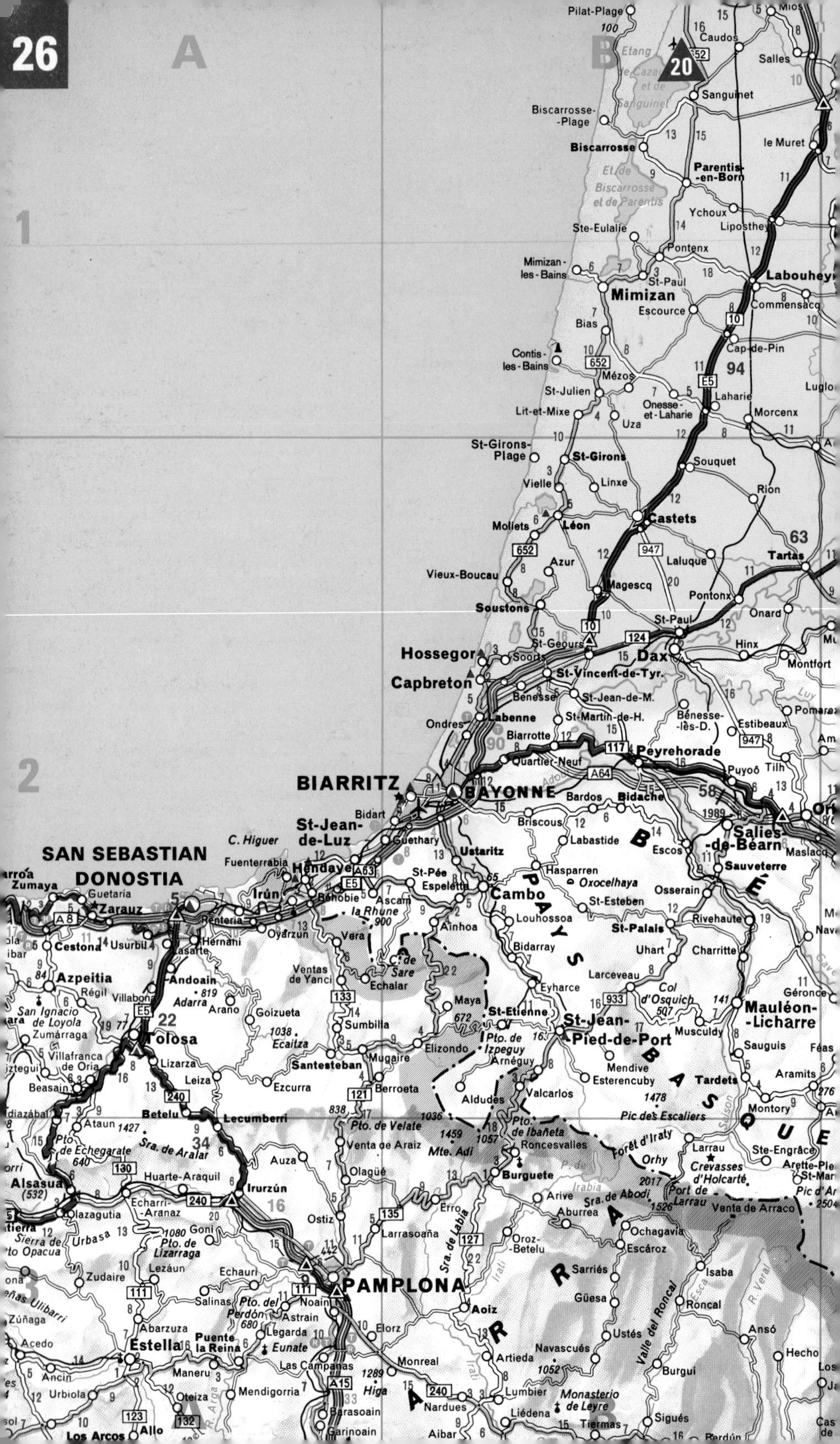

Pilat-Plage
100
Caudos
Mios
20
E52
Salles
Biscarrosse-Plage
Sanguinet
Biscarrosse
Et de
Biscarrosse
et de Parentis
le Muret
Parentis-en-Born
Ste-Eulalie
Ychoux
Liposthey
Labouheyi
Pontenx
Commensacq
Mimizan-les-Bains
St-Paul
Mimizan
Escource
10
Bias
Cap-de-Pin
Contis-les-Bains
652
Mézos
E5
94
St-Julien
Laharie
Lit-et-Mixe
Onesse-et-Laharie
Uza
Morcenx
St-Girons-Plage
St-Girons
Souquet
Vielle
Linxe
Rion
Castets
Moliets
Léon
652
Laluque
Azur
947
Tartas
63
Vieux-Boucau
Magescq
Pontonx
Onard
Soustons
St-Paul
Hinx
10
124
Dax
Montfort
Hossegor
St-Geours
Soorts
15
St-Vincent-de-Tyr.
Capbreton
St-Jean-de-M.
Bénesse
Bénesse-lès-D.
Estibeaux
Ondres
Labenne
St-Martin-de-H.
947
Pomarez
Biarrotte
90
Biarritz
117
Peyrehorade
Puyoô
Tilh
Quartier-Neuf
A64
58
BIARRITZ
Bidart
BAYONNE
Bardos
Bidache
1989
Salies-de-Béarn
St-Jean-de-Luz
Briscous
Labastide
Escos
Sauveterre
C. Higuer
Guéthary
Ustaritz
SAN SEBASTIAN
Fuenterrabia
St-Pée
Hasparren
Oxocelhaya
Osserain
Rivehaute
DONOSTIA
Hendaye
A63
Cambo
St-Esteben
St-Palais
Zumaya
Guétaria
Irún
Bobobie
Espelette
65
Uhart
Charritte
Zarauz
A8
Renteria
Ascain
la Rhune
900
Ainhoa
Louhossoa
Larceveau
Nav
Cestona
Usurbil
Hernani
Oyarzun
Vera
Bidarray
Eyharce
Col d'Osquich
507
141
Mauléon-Licharre
Azpeitia
Villabon
Adarra
Arano
Goizueta
Maya
672
St-Etienne
933
Musculdy
Sauguis
Féas
Zumárraga
E5
Adarra
Sumbilla
Pto. de Izpeguy
St-Jean-Pied-de-Port
Aramits
22
Tolosa
133
Mendive
Tardets
Larrasoaña
Lizarra
Santesteban
Mugaire
Elizondo
Arnéguy
Esterencuby
Montory
276
Beasain
Leiza
Ezcurra
121
Berroeta
Valcarlos
1478
Villafranca de Oria
240
Betelu
Lecumberri
838
Aldudes
Pic des Escaliers
240
Ataun
1427
Pto. de Velate
1459
Pto. de Ibañeta
Orhy
Larrau
Ste-Engrâce
Sra. de Aralar
1036
2017
Crevasses d'Holcarté
Alsasua
130
Huarte-Araquil
Venta de Araiz
Mte. Adi
Roncevalles
Port de Larrau
Venta de Arraco
Echarri-Aranaz
240
Irurzún
Olagüe
Erro
Burguete
Sra. de Abodi
1526
Olazagutia
16
Ostiz
135
Larrasoaña
127
Oroz-Betelu
Escároz
Isaba
1080
Goñi
Pto. de Lizarraga
Lezáun
Echauri
Sarriés
Roncal
Zudaire
Salinas
Pto. del Perdón
Noain
Aoiz
Güesa
Estella
111
Puente la Reina
Eunate
Astrain
Elorz
Artieda
Ansó
Hecho
Abarzuza
Legarda
Monreal
Navascués
Ustés de Leyre
Burgui
Mendigorría
A15
1289
Higa
240
Lumbier
1052
Liédena
Sigüés
Los Arcos
123
132
Allo
Garinoain
Aibar
Tiermas

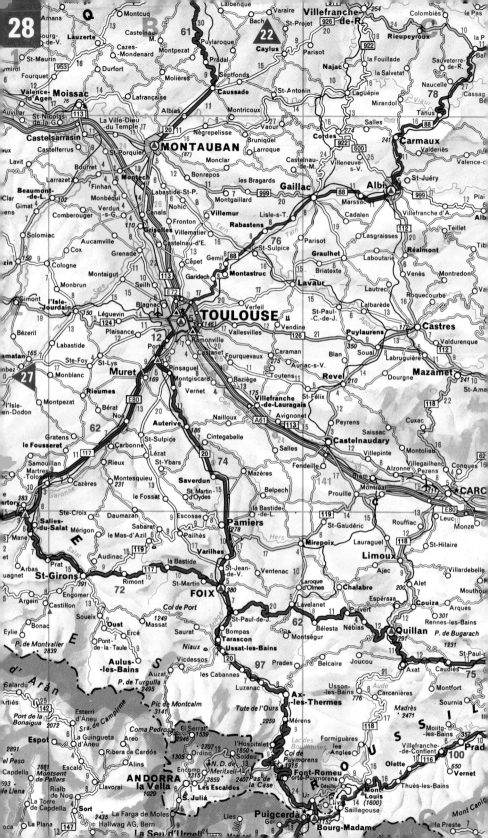

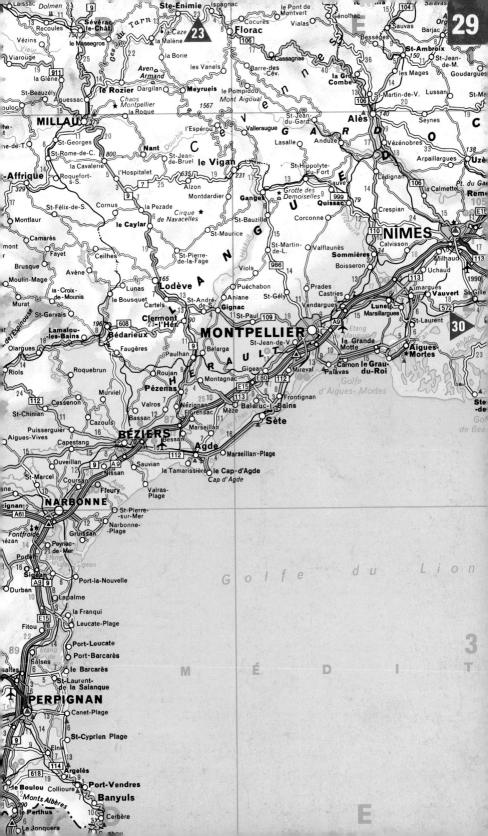

INDEX

Page numbers in **bold face** refer to the main entry.